CHESS

MADE SIMPLE

CHESS
MADE SIMPLE

BY

MILTON L. HANAUER, M.S., J.D.
Director of N.Y.C. Interscholastic Chess League
Former N.Y. State Champion
Member, U.S. International Team

MADE SIMPLE BOOKS
DOUBLEDAY & COMPANY, INC.
GARDEN CITY, NEW YORK

Printed in the United States of America

TABLE OF CONTENTS

CHAPTER V

CHAPTER VI

CHAPTER VII

CHAPTER VIII

CHAPTER IX

CHAPTER X

CHAPTER XI

CHAPTER XII

CHAPTER XIII

CHAPTER XIV

CHAPTER XV

CHAPTER XVI

CHAPTER XVII

CHESS

MADE SIMPLE

INTRODUCTION

Night after night every one of the 1,500 seats was taken; hundreds milled around the entrance and in the anteroom—so great was the interest when the United States chess team played a series of matches with visiting Soviet players. Men, women and children watched the moves with rapt attention, as they were recorded on the huge wall boards which formed the background for the sixteen players who occupied the stage.

And the players? The youngest were in their early twenties; the oldest in their forties: giants of chess, the best in their countries, the leading chess countries in the world.

The winners? There were many winners. The U.S.S.R. won the match 20-12. Our youngsters (LARRY EVANS, ARTHUR BISGUIER and the BYRNE brothers, Robert and Donald) held their own against their four famous opponents (TAIMANOV, PETROSIAN, AVERBAKH, and KOTOV, respectively), scoring 8-8 against players who made a better than even showing in the recent World's Candidates' Tournament. Our four times' Champion SAMUEL RESHEVSKY made an even score against VASSILY SMYSLOV, who had just tied with the World's Champion, MIKHAIL BOTVINNIK, in a match for the championship. But the real winners were the people of both countries—those of the U.S.A., who conferred a warm welcome and displayed excellent sportsmanship, and those of the U.S.S.R., who acknowledged the American sportsmanship and warmth in a series of articles in *Pravda*, the official Soviet newspaper.

Why did the U.S.S.R. win? If the U.S.A. has such fine players, why couldn't they win?

Chess is the national game of the U.S.S.R. Their players are numbered in the tens of millions; their children learn the game at the age when ours learn to play with blocks, or to roll a ball.

And why not? Give a child a chess set, and he will be delighted at the sight of the fascinating pieces. Teach him their names, and he will be filled with pride at his accomplishment. Then place them on a chessboard, and teach him the moves, and you will open a world of magic which will become more and more wonderful as he progresses into it.

Youngsters have played chess for years. In the town of Strobeck, Germany, chess was made part of the school curriculum as long ago as the year 1011 A.D.—two hundred years before Robin Hood drew his first bow.

In Milwaukee ten thousand school children each year participate in a municipal chess project, climaxed by a tournament.

And they play chess well! REUBEN FINE, ALBERT C. SIMONSON and LARRY EVANS were members of the United States international team while they were still in their teens. GEORGE KRAMER and WILLIAM LOMBARDY won the New York State Championship at the age of 16—the latter is the present champion—in a tournament of recognized "masters," a title given only to those who have proved themselves in national and international competition. That the author won the New York State title at the age of 18, and played on the U.S. International Team two years later, makes him one of the graybeards with whom chess is commonly (and mistakenly) associated.

This book is for you and your children. It is written to remove some of the mystery with which chess is surrounded. Its purpose is to introduce to you, in simple and logical steps: the pieces, their values, their powers, and their combined strength; the three phases of the game—opening, middle game and end game; and the excitement, as well as the wit and humor, in situations where two persons are battling each other with unusual forces at their command—peacefully, over a chessboard.

A BRIEF CHESS HISTORY

The beginnings of chess are shrouded in the mystery of unrecorded history—but one thing is certain. The game was first played in India, where its name was "Chaturanga," the "war game." The board upon which it was played, the *astāpada,* had been used for other (dice) games for hundreds of years, with the result that many claims have been made for the antiquity of the game. But Greek and Roman writers never mentioned chess. The first time mention of it appears is in Sanskrit, the classical language of India, in the early 7th Century A.D.

From India, chess spread to Persia (now Iran). Then the Moslems conquered Persia and South India, numbering chess among their captives. Through the Arabs (Moslems) it spread to other parts of Asia, to Africa, and to Europe.

The chess pieces were named first after the components of an Indian Army: a King (or shah) a Counselor, two Elephants, two Horses, two Chariots and eight Foot-soldiers. As the game moved from country to country, the pieces changed: in different places the King was a prince, a lord or a general; the Counselor (the present Queen) was a lord, a tiger, a dog, a general or a minister; the Elephant (now a Bishop) became a camel, a nobleman or a counselor; the Chariot became a boat; the Footsoldier (Pawn) a shell or a child. Only the Horse (now called Knight) remained the same.

At first, the moves of the Counselor were limited: he could jump one square diagonally or straight ahead. At the beginning of the 16th Century there suddenly appeared a new version of chess: *scacchi alla rabiosa* (Italy) or *echecs de la dame enragée* (France)—that is, "chess of the mad queen." In this kind of chess, the queen can move any number of squares in a straight line or on a diagonal, backward or forward. The "new" chess caught on quickly and soon the displaced or "old" chess disappeared. It remained only for "castling" to be introduced for us to have the game we now play.

When you look at a beautifully carved chess set, you may try to determine what country it came from. Is the third piece an elephant? Then the set might come from India, or Burma, or Mongolia. Is the piece next to the King a tiger? That set is from Tibet. Is the piece on the corner square a boat? The set is from Java or Siam.

Or you may wonder who was the original owner of an ancient set. Was it an Indian prince? Do those elaborate carvings mean that a Malayan played with them? Are the pieces of rubies and emeralds? They are part of the marvelous treasure of Khusraw II Parwiz of Persia. Is this ancient camel set practically new? Perhaps it is the set of Sa'id b. Jubair, the famous Negro Persian, who excelled in blindfold play.

Is it a set of Sèvres China? Perhaps it belonged to Napoleon I, who loved to play chess. Or is it a simple set, of French boxwood, which might have belonged to Benjamin Franklin, who paused in his political activities and scientific investigations long enough to write "The Morals of Chess." A more elaborate set, the pieces of which hold musical instruments? Perhaps it belonged to the great Philidor, master musician and chess player.

Or perhaps you might see a miscellaneous collection of buttons and coins, broken pieces and headless horses—those are the sets of the boy who plays on the front steps with his friend, transported to a world of adventure and make-believe.

CHAPTER I

THE PIECES AND THE BOARD

THE PIECES

First, let us meet the **King.** ♚ ♔ He is the man with the cross on his crown, one of the two largest chess pieces.

He is your most important piece, because **if you lose the King, you lose the game.**

In the early days of chess, he was known as the "Shah," the Persian King. When the Shah was captured, the players said: "Shah mat!" (the King is dead!). We still say **"Checkmate"** when the King is captured.

To help protect him, your King is defended by many pieces. First and foremost is the **Queen.** ♛ ♕ She is the other large piece, the one with a coronet around her head. Like all women behind the throne, she is the **most powerful** person in the kingdom. On the chessboard, she stands next to the King, in the center of the board.

In some old chess sets, you will see another figure in place of the Queen. In Persia it was the "Farzin," the Counselor. In other countries, the piece was represented by a lord, a tiger, a dog, a general or a minister.

Next, let us look at the **Bishop.** ♝ ♗ He is the piece with the split cap—the Bishop's mitre—although at one time he was an elephant, and the two points on his hat represented the elephant's tusks. In French sets, he's a jester—*le fou.* Perhaps you can make out his nose in the air, and his mouth in a grin. Or perhaps his top is the puff on a jester's cap, and the piece below his head the ruff on his costume.

And now, the **Rook.** ♜ ♖ Once a chariot, a boat, he became an elephant when, in India, the counselor replaced the elephant at the side of the King. In some old sets he is a warrior, in others, a group of warriors on horseback. He first appeared as a tower or "castle" in a book published in the early sixteenth century. It is called *tour* (tower) in French, and *turm* in German, but we still use the word rook, which meant elephant!

Then, the **Knight.** ♞ ♘ It is not hard to tell which piece he is, for his horse's head sets him apart. In some sets he is a horseman, a knight in shining armor. But in any game, he is the brave charger who hurdles other pieces as he steps from white square to black, and then back to white again.

Finally, the **Pawn.** ♟ ♙ He is the foot soldier, the infantryman, who clears the way for the other pieces. Like an infantryman, he can kill.

And who knows—he may be a prince in disguise! For if this common soldier reaches the end of the board, he becomes any piece you want—Queen, Rook, Bishop or Knight! He becomes this even if you still have your original pieces on the board!

Now you know what the pieces look like. Let us next look at the field of battle.

THE BOARD: THE FIELD OF BATTLE

Chess is a war game. It is a struggle between two opposing armies, which begin with exactly

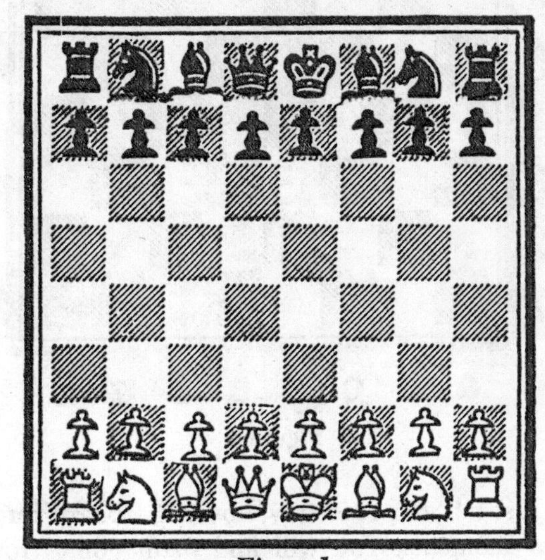

Figure 1

the same forces. These forces are placed so that similar pieces are opposite one another.

The game is played on a board eight squares long and eight squares wide—64 squares in all. It is exactly the same as a checkerboard, except that in chess *all* the squares are used.

In the center stand the King and Queen. The Queen is on the square of her color—White Queen on white square; Black Queen on black square. The White Queen is at the left of the White King. If you look at the board from the Black side, however, you will find that the Black Queen is at the Black King's right.

Next to the King and the Queen are the Bishops; then, the Knights. In the corner squares stand the Rooks.

The eight Pawns on each side are arranged in front of the pieces.

Set up your pieces on your board without looking at the diagram. Time yourself.

Did you remember:

1. Queen opposite Queen; King opposite King?

2. Queen on the space of its color?

Try it again.

Now let's look at the board alone:

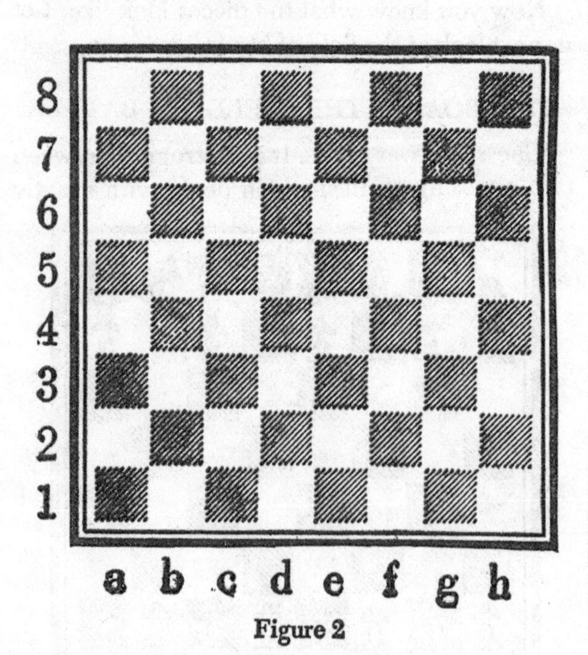

Figure 2

Just let your eyes travel over the board for a few moments. You will find them going from left to right, or up and down; or perhaps along the white squares, or the black ones.

Now look at the letters and the numbers at the edges of the board. They are placed there so that each square has an identity, a name represented by a letter and a number, at the place where they meet.

The square in the lower left hand corner is a1; the square above it a2; then a3, a4, etc., all the way to a8.

To the right of a1 is b1; then c1 etc., to h1.

The lettered lines are called **files:** the "a" file, "b" file, "c" file, etc.

The numbered lines are **ranks:** the 1st rank, 2nd rank, to the 8th rank.

The lines of succession of white or black squares are called **diagonals.** The long black diagonal starts at a1, and continues b2, c3, d4, e5, f6, g7 and h8. The long white diagonal starts at h1, and moves through g2, f3, e4, d5, c6 and b7 to a8.

Exercise No. 1

1. On what rank are the White Pawns?
2. On what rank are the Black Pieces?
3. Name all the squares on the black diagonals starting at a3.
4. What are the names of the four center squares?
5. Name the original squares of the White Rooks; the Black Rooks.
6. Name the original squares of the White Knights; the Black Bishops.
7. On what squares do the Kings and Queens stand?
8. Which diagonals cross the center squares?
9. Name the squares occupied by all the pieces in the following diagram:

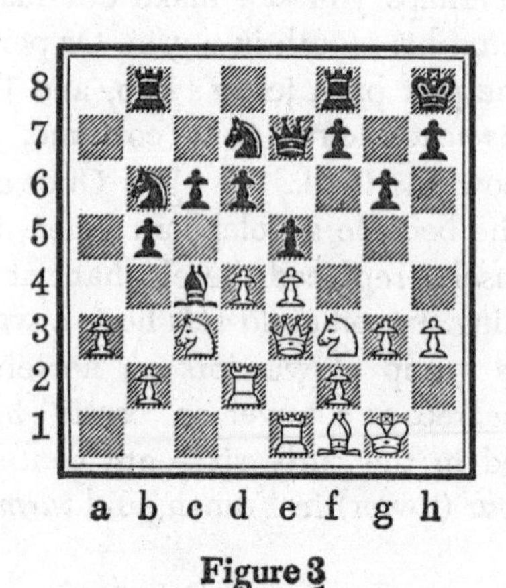

Figure 3

CHAPTER II

THE POWERS OF THE PIECES

1. The King

Now that we know what the pieces look like, and *where* they move; let us see *how* they move. First, again, the King:

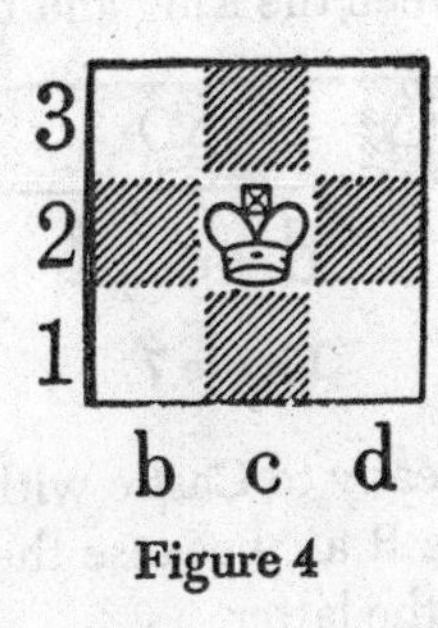

Figure 4

The King moves one square in any direction. From c2, as shown above, he can go to b1, b2, b3, c1, c3, d1, d2, or d3. He has eight moves in all. Put him on a 1, however, and he has only three moves; from b1, c1, etc. or a2, a3, etc., he has only five. This brings us to notice—

The power of a piece increases as it approaches the center of the board.

The King does not have a very long move. However, the King is the most valuable piece, because **if you lose the King, you lose the game.**

The King can not move into a square where an enemy piece can capture him. Let us extend our diagram:

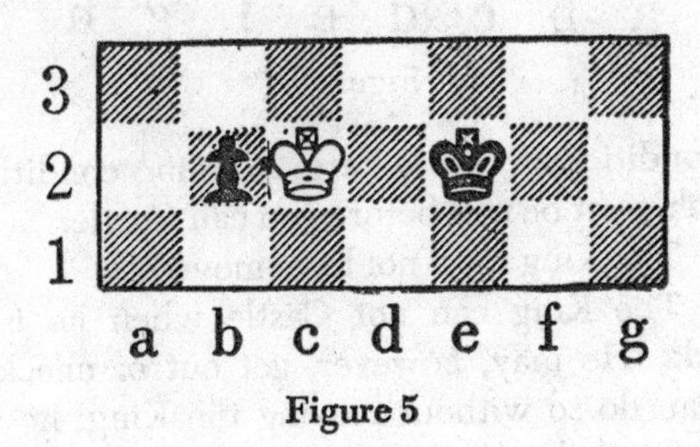

Figure 5

The White King can *not* go to d1, d2, or d3, because the Black King can capture him on those squares. If it were Black's move, he could not go to d1, d2, or d3, either.

How do we write a move?

We name: (1) The piece.

(2) The square it comes from.

(3) The square it goes to.

White can move:

K c2 – b1 (The – means "to").

K c2 – b3 (K is the abbreviation for King).

K c2 – c3

He can also **capture** the Black Pawn on b2. When you capture a piece in chess, you move your piece onto the square occupied by an enemy piece, and take the enemy piece off the board. "Captures" or "takes" is written "x." The White King can, therefore, move:

K c2 x P b2

The Pawn comes off, and the White King lands on b2.

When a King is attacked, we warn our opponent by saying "Check." A King which is attacked is "in check." The White King above could not capture a Pawn on d2, because he would be moving into check (i.e., the Black King could capture him).

If a King is "in check," a player must attend to him. If the King can not move out of check, it is **checkmate.** The King is dead, and the game is lost. We will explain how to checkmate a King later.

2. The Rook

In the corners of the board stand the **Rooks**—White Rooks on a1 and h1; Black Rooks on a8 and h8. The Rook is a very powerful piece: he is worth five Pawns—more than any other piece except the Queen.

The Rook moves **forward and back, left or right on a straight line.** He moves on a rank or a file, as many squares as he chooses. He **can *not*** jump, so his own man on a rank or file will block him. He captures like the King—which is to say, moves on to the square occupied by an enemy piece, and takes the captured piece off the board.

What moves can be made by the Rooks in the following diagram?

Figure 6

The White Rook on d5 can move along the file to d6, d4 or d3; he can capture the Black Rook on d7 or the Black Knight on d2. He can move along the rank to c5, e5 or f5; or capture the Bishop on g5. He can *not*, however, move to d1, d8 or h5 (because he can not jump over a piece); nor can he move to b5 (because his own Pawn is there to block him) nor to a5.

The White Rook on a1 can move to a2, b1, c1, d1, e1, f1, g1 and h1. The last move would be written R a1 – h1 ch because on h1 the Rook would **check** the Black King, on h8.

The Black Rook on d7 can move on the **rank** to a7, capturing the White Queen; to b7, c7, e7, f7 and g7, where he would capture the White Knight. He can move on the **file** to d8, d6 or d5, where he can capture the White Rook.

The Black Rook on f8 can move along the 8th rank to any square except h8; or along the f file to any square. He would **check** the White King on f3.

Exercise No. 2

Write all the captures and checks in short notation.

If you place a Rook any place on an empty board you will find that he has fourteen moves —no more, no less. The only thing that can limit the Rook is a blockade by his own pieces, or by an enemy piece. At the beginning of the game, the Rook has no moves at all, because he is blocked by his own Pawn and Knight.

The best way to get a Rook into action is through an open file. The files opened soonest are the center files: d, e, c or f; therefore, you must be ready to move the Rook to one of those files as soon as it is open.

At the same time, your King should not be in a place where lines are open, because the enemy pieces are able to attack him there.

In order to accomplish both these aims, a player is allowed a special privilege known as:

3. Castling

Once during the game, a player is allowed to **Castle.** This is possible when there is no piece remaining between the King and the Rook:

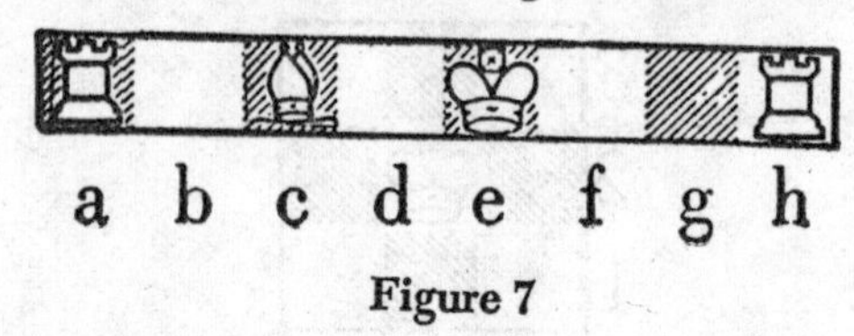

Figure 7

The King is ready to Castle with the Rook h1, but not with the R a1, because the Bishop on c1 is in the way of the latter.

How do you Castle? Move the King two squares toward the Rook, and place the Rook on the *other* side of the King.

Examples:

Before Castling:

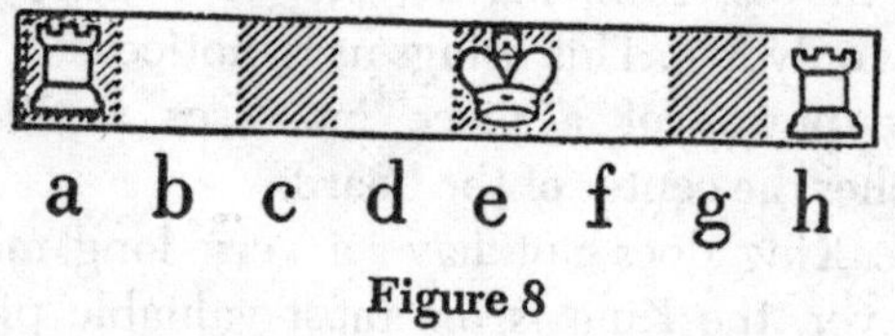

Figure 8

After Castling:

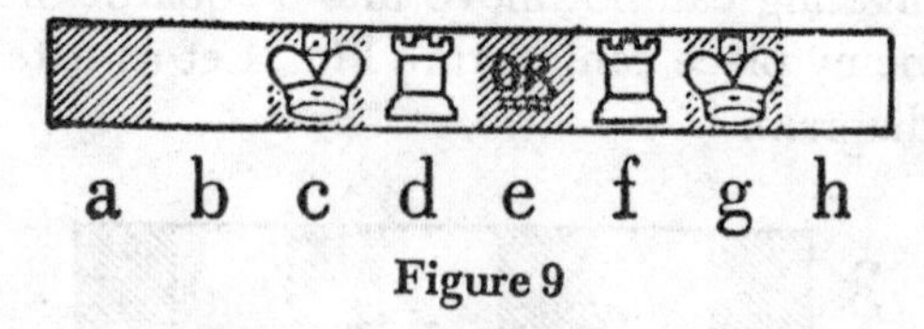

Figure 9

Conditions: There are certain conditions which must be met before you can Castle:

1. The King must not have moved.
2. The King can not Castle when he is in check. (He may, however, get out of check, if he can do so without moving the King; he can then Castle later.)
3. The King can not move **through** check or **into** check.
4. The King can not Castle on the side of a Rook which has moved; he may, however, Castle with the other Rook.

In the following diagram, neither King can Castle. Why?

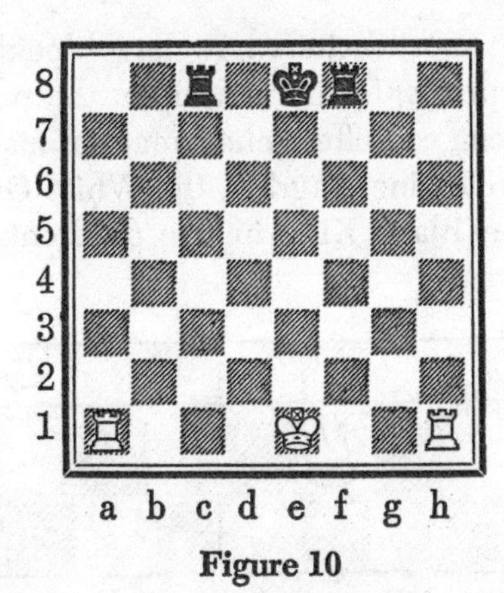

Figure 10

The Black King can no longer Castle because both Black Rooks have moved.

The White King has not yet lost his privilege. However, he can not Castle with the Rook a1 because when he lands on c1, he will be in check (by the R c8). He can not Castle with the Rook on h1 because when he goes from e1 to g1, he will pass through check at f1 (by the R f8).

We shall return to Castling later.

4. The Bishop

The Bishop moves on a diagonal—back and forth, as many squares as you like. He is limited only by the edge of the board or by a blockade of his own pieces.

Since a Bishop moves **only** on a diagonal, he can never change the color of the squares he moves on. Each player has two Bishops, one starting on a white square, the other on a black.

The value of a Bishop is three (pawns). A Rook is worth two pawns more than a Bishop. However, two Bishops have considerably more value than two times one Bishop. A glance at the following diagrams will show the power of two Bishops:

Figure 11

Two centralized Bishops dominate the board.

Figure 12

These Bishops dominate the center.

In the second diagram, the Bishops have been developed in a manner known as a **fianchetto**, or wing development. (The word is Italian and the *ch* is pronounced "k.") The b and g Pawns must be pushed forward one square, to give the Bishops room.

Players talk of a "good" Bishop and a "bad" Bishop. This refers to the relation of the Pawns to the Bishop: a "good" Bishop is one whose Pawns are on the opposite color; a "bad" Bishop is limited by the placement of his own Pawns on the same color. For example:

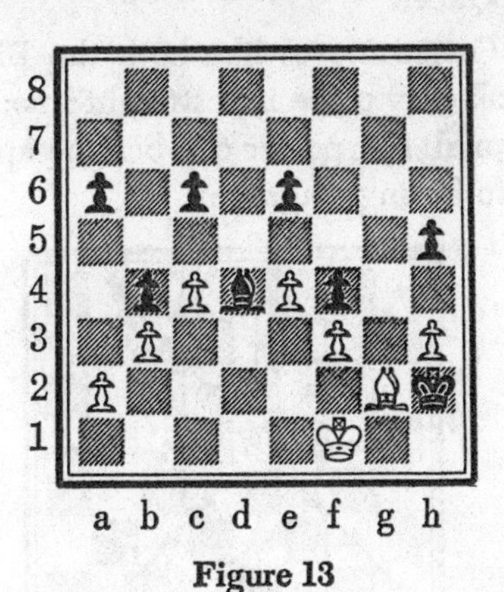

Figure 13

White has a "bad" Bishop. All his Pawns are on white squares—squares of the same color as his Bishop's. Black has a "good" Bishop: he has many black squares to move on, because his Pawns (as well as White's) are on white squares.

As a matter of fact, all that Black has to do is move his Bishop along the diagonal a7 – g1 (but not to f2, where he can be captured) and eventually the White King will have to move away from his Bishop, and allow it to be captured.

You will find more about the power of the Bishop in later sections of the book.

Another weakness of a Bishop is the fact that a King and Bishop together can not checkmate an enemy King:

Figure 14

The Black King is cornered, he can not move; **but he is not in check.** There is, therefore, no checkmate.

It is, instead, a **stalemate,** and, according to the rules, the game is a draw. Try several positions—Bishop and King can never checkmate a King.

A Rook and King, on the other hand, can checkmate a King. This is another reason for the greater value of a Rook.

5. The Queen

The Queen moves like both the Bishop and the Rook—any place in a straight line: rank, file or diagonal. Her power can best be appreciated by the following diagram:

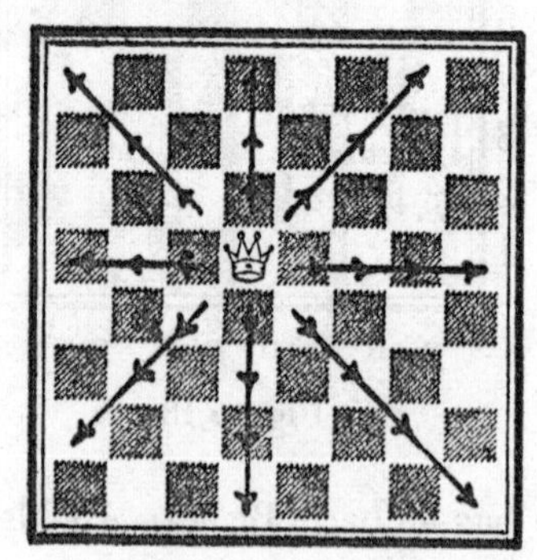

Figure 15

The value of a Queen is greater than the combined value of a Rook and a Bishop. It is worth two Rooks (or about 10) or three minor pieces (Bishops or Knights) which would make 9. For years, writers have disagreed about this value, although most writers now have decided on 9. It all depends, in the end, upon the position.

A Queen can effect **checkmate** in many ways. In the following diagram, the White Queen can **mate** the Black King in five different ways in one move:

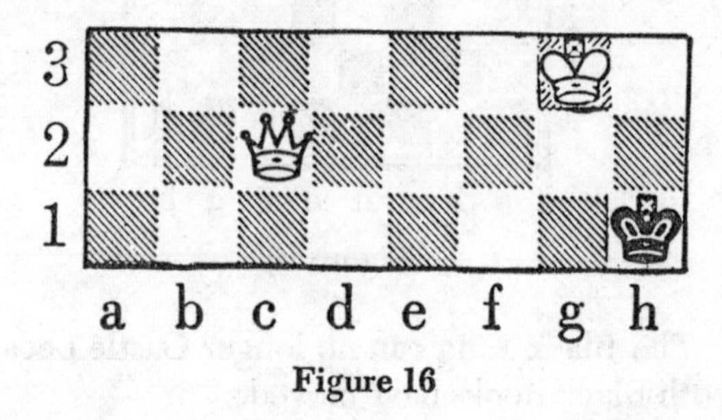

Figure 16

On b1, c1, d1, g2 and h2, the Queen can check and mate the Black King. A Rook on c2 could checkmate on c1; a Bishop could not mate at all.

A Queen captures like every other piece: she places herself on the square occupied by an enemy piece and removes the piece from the board. Find the captures which the White Queen can make on the following diagram:

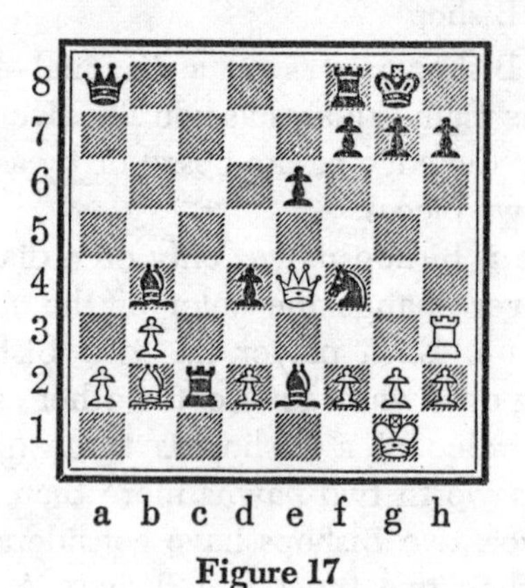

Figure 17

The White Queen can capture the Black Queen at a8; the R c2, the B e2, the Knight on f4, the Pawn at d4 or the Pawn at e6.

Best of all, however, would be Q x P h7 checkmate. The Black King cannot recapture the White Queen, because she is defended by the R h3. The K can not move to f8, f7 or g7, because he is blocked by his own pieces. It is, therefore, **checkmate.**

6. The Fork

The **fork** is not a chess piece. It is a weapon employed by pieces in order to win material.

Because of their long range actions, the Rook, Bishop and Queen can often attack two enemy pieces at one time. This is called a fork. If one of the enemy pieces is a King, the fork becomes a powerful weapon, because the opponent must guard his King, allowing the other piece to shift for himself.

Examples of forks follow:

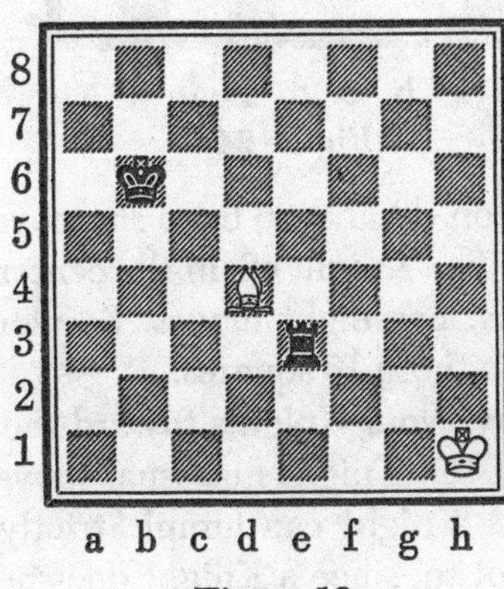

Figure 18

The White Bishop d4 attacks the Black King b6 (saying "check") and the Rook on e3. The King must move; whereupon the Bishop captures the Rook.

Figure 19

It is White's move. His Bishop can capture the Pawn on c6, thereby forking the King (with "check") the Rook a8 and the Kt e4. The King must move, after which White has his choice of capturing Rook or Knight.

White, to move, has a choice of forks: R e6 – g6 ch attacks King and Bishop. R e6 – e8 ch attacks King and the Knight. (Fig. 20)

Rook and Bishop forks are easy to see. Forks with the Queen, however, are more difficult, be-

Figure 20

cause there are so many of them. Examine this position, and look for the forks:

Figure 21

Q – b3 ch attacks King, Bishop and Knight.
Q – c6 ch attacks K and R a8, as well as P b5.
Q – g6 ch attacks K and R h5.
Q – e4 ch attacks K, B b4, R a8 and Kt e3.

Other checks would not be good because the Queen could be captured (i.e., on a2, c4, c8 and f5.)

A fork without a check could be Q c2 – e2. There is another on c5, but the Queen could be captured by the B or R. On c3 the B could capture the Queen; on a4, the R or P.

We have named, however, twelve possible forks by the Queen!

The Knight, too, is dangerous:

7. The Knight

The Knight (abbreviation: Kt) is the only piece which does not move in a straight line. His move is two squares in one direction and one at right angles: (Fig. 22)

From c3, the Knight can capture any one of the Black Pawns, on a2, a4, b1, b5, d1, d5, e2

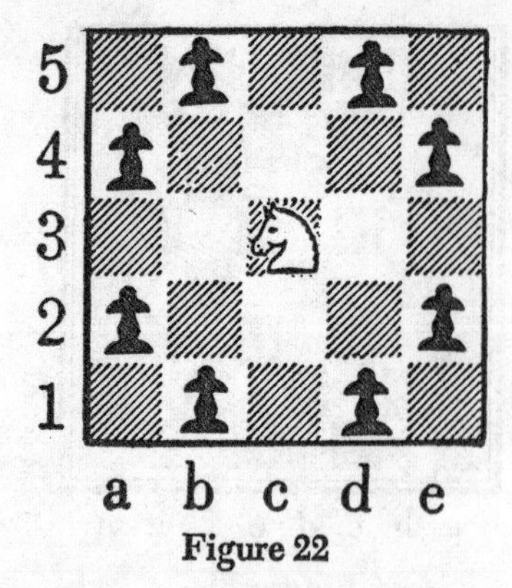

Figure 22

and e4. Notice that the Knight is on a black square, and moves from Black to White. On its next move, the Knight would move back to a Black square.

It is obvious that the range of a Knight is limited: it takes four moves from the *a* to the *h* file, or from the first to the eighth rank. On the other hand, he can get to any square on the board, whereas the Bishop moves on only half the squares.

The value of a Knight is about the same as that of the Bishop: **3 Pawns.** Another reason for this is that the Knight with a King can not checkmate an enemy King; the best he can do is stalemate, which is a draw.

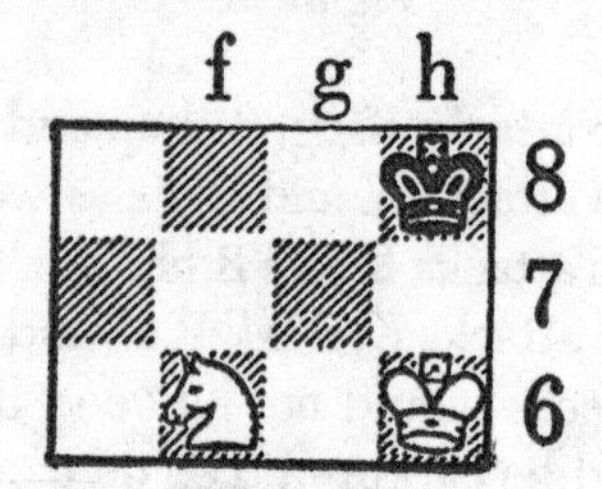

Figure 23

Black has no move, but **he is not in check.** It is a stalemate. (Fig. 23)

As a matter of fact, two Kts can not *force* a checkmate, unless the enemy King walks into it. **For that reason, many players prefer Bishops to Knights, since two Bishops can force a mate.**

Like other pieces, the Knight becomes more powerful as he approaches the center of the board: (Fig. 24)

The Knight a1 has only two moves; so would any Knight have from a corner square. Kt h7, one step nearer the center, has three moves—to f8, f6 and g5. The Knight g2, one square nearer the center, has four moves (e1, e3, f4 and h4). Knights on d2 and g6 have six moves each. (Find them!) The Knight c6, in the center square of 16 squares, has eight moves. So would any Knight within those 16 squares.

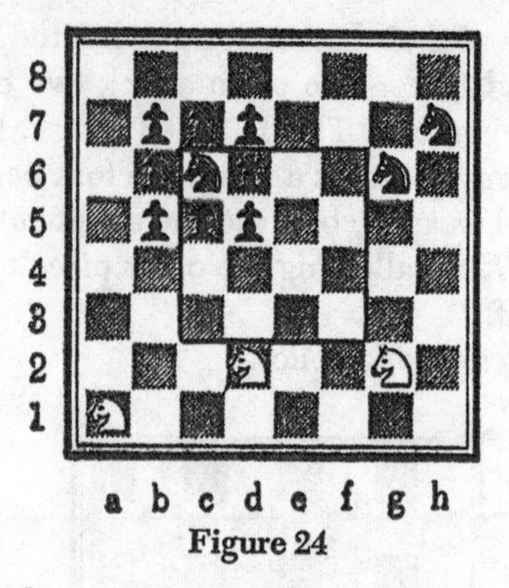

Figure 24

Motto: Move your Knights toward the center!

Because of the Knight's unusual move, many people say: **A Knight can jump!** Strictly speaking, that is not so, since a Knight does not move in a straight line. The only thing which can prevent a Knight from moving on to a certain square is for one of the Knight's own men to be on that square.

In the diagram above, the Knight on c6 can move to any one of its squares (a5, a7, b8, b4, d8, d4, e7, e5) even though it seems to be surrounded by its own Pawns.

At the beginning of a game, the Knights are placed next to the Rooks—on b1, g1, b8 and g8. One move by each will bring them to the squares c3, f3, c6 and f6—from which they train their lances on the center:

Figure 25

Since the moves of the Knights are limited at the beginning of the game, **it is advisable to move them before the other pieces.** In fact, EMANUEL LASKER, World Chess Champion for 27 years (1894-1921) stated in his *Common Sense in Chess:* **"Develop your Knights before your Bishops!"**

Knights are demons for forks:

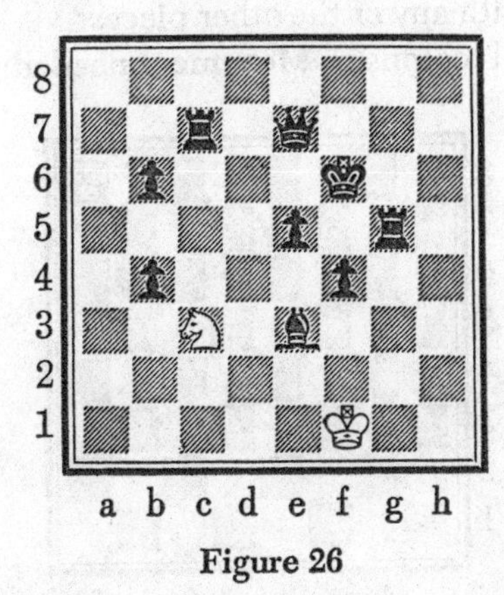

Figure 26

The Knight can give a "family check" at d5, attacking seven Black pieces including the King. He can also fork K and R from e4.

Because of his limited move, however, the Knight can be "bullied" by the other pieces:

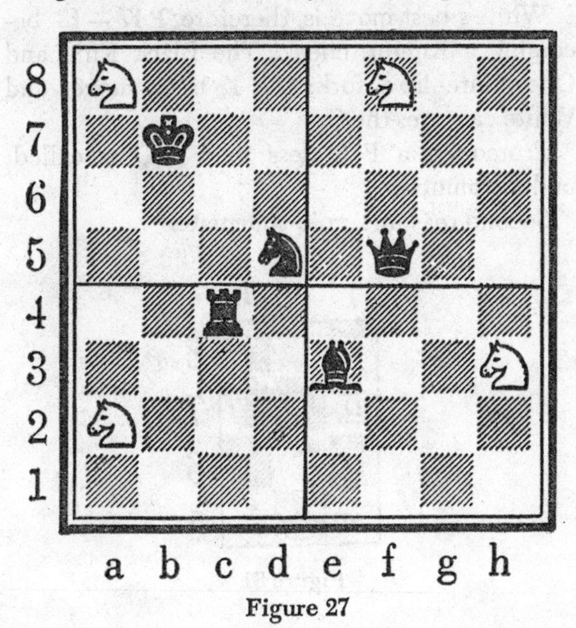

Figure 27

The Knight a2 is guarded by the R c4, which can capture it wherever it moves (to b4, c3 or cl).

Knight a8 has two moves, both guarded by the Kt d5. The King b7 attacks the Knight, and guards its escape squares.

Kt h3 is under guard of the B e3, which can capture it wherever it moves: to f2, f4, gl or g5.

The Q f5 is all ready to capture the Kt on f8, not only attacking it, but guarding its escape squares d7, e6, g6 and h7.

Moral: Keep your Knights in or near the center, where they have more moves.

8. The Pawn

The Pawn is the infantryman of chess. Eight of them on each side range on the second and seventh ranks, where they protect the more important pieces.

The Pawn **moves forward only,** and very slowly: **one square at a time,** except for the first time each Pawn moves, when he can, **if he wishes, move two squares.**

Remember: **Every Pawn can move forward two squares on his first move.**

Also: A Pawn does not capture in the same manner in which he moves. **He captures diagonally forward, one square to the left or right.** Example:

Figure 28

White can move P b2 – b3 or b4; P d4 – d5; P f2 – f3 or f4. He can **capture** P e4 x P f5 or P d4 x P e5.

Black can move P c4 – c3. He can capture P e5 x P d4 or P f5 x P e4. He can also move P f5 – f4.

A voice from the gallery is objecting: "That isn't quite fair."

What isn't fair?

"That Pawn on b2."

What do you mean?

"If the Pawn on b2 moves to b4, he deprives the c Pawn of the right to capture him. That isn't fair."

It isn't. But he doesn't.

"What do you mean?"

Let's look the situation over carefully:

Figure 29

White moves P b2 – b4. **On the very next move only,** Black can treat this move as though it were P b2 – b3, and capture P c4 x P b3.

This is called Pawn takes Pawn *en passant*, which means **while passing.**

If Black does not exercise his privilege on the first opportunity (his next move) he loses it, and the move stands.

Suppose that White had played P e3 – e4. Black could **not** take this Pawn **en passant.** He lost no privilege when the White Pawn moved.

Suppose that it was Black's move, and he played P c4 – c3. White then played P b2 – b4. Could Black capture this pawn? No. He could not take it if White played (after P c4 – c3) P b2 – b3. Since he has lost no right by the move, he can not claim injustice.

P x P en passant can be played only (1) when a Pawn moves two squares (2) when it could have been captured if it had moved only one; **and (3) on the next move only!**

The Pawn, for a common foot soldier, is capable of surprises. But here is the biggest surprise of all:

When a Pawn reaches the eighth rank (for Black; the first) he can become—any piece you want to make him: Queen, Rook, Bishop or Knight—even if you still have all the pieces you started with.

You mean you can have more than one Queen?

Yes—nine, if you can make eight new ones.

But if you can take a Queen, why should you bother with any of the other pieces?

Several reasons: 1. **Movement needed:**

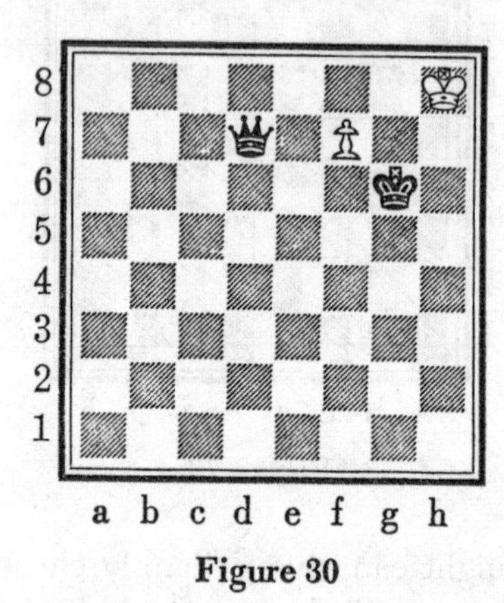

Figure 30

White can play P f7 – f8, becoming a Queen. If he does, however, Black will answer Q d7 – h7 checkmate!

White's best move is, therefore, P f7 – f8, becoming a Knight, check! The Black King and Queen are in a fork; the K must move, and White captures the Q.

Promoting a P to less than a Q is called: **underpromotion.**

Second reason: **Avoid stalemate.**

Figure 31

White can play P f7 – f8 (Q) but then Black would have no moves. Since he would not be in check, the position would be a stalemate (a draw).

White could avoid the stalemate by P f7 –

f8 (B) or (Kt) but then he would not be left with enough material to win.

The correct move is P f7 – f8 (Rook). After . . . K h7 – g7, checkmate can be effected in (at most) four moves: (1) R f8 – f5, K g7 – h7; (2) K g5 – f6, K h7 – g8; (3) R f5 – h5, K g8 – f8; (4) R h5 – h8 mate.

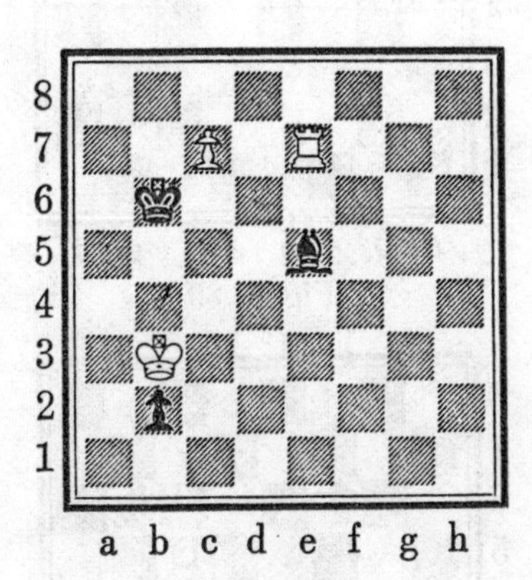

Figure 32

White would like to play P c7 – c8 (Q). If he does, however, Black answers P b2 – b1 (Q) *check*, and gets the jump on him. If White stops the Black Pawn by K b3 – c2 (or a2), Black captures the WP c7 with his Bishop, and the game will be a draw.

The correct move is P c7 – c8 (Kt) **check.** The BK can not approach the Kt, since the WR guards the 7th rank. After the BK moves, white has time for K b3 – c2. Later, he will capture the Pawn on b2 with his Knight. The **underpromotion** has given White time to carry out his plan.

There are other reasons for underpromotion, which will appear later.

The Pawn can fork two pieces. Often he will need the support of another Pawn:

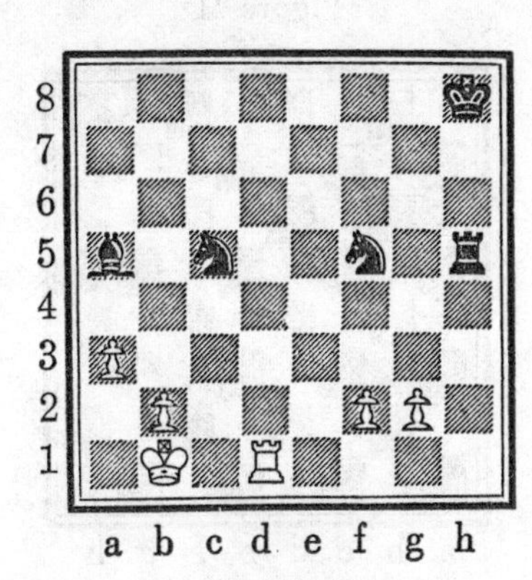

Figure 33

P g2 – g4 forks Kt and R.

P b2 – b4 forks B and Kt. Luckily, this Pawn is supported by the Pawn a3, since the B can capture on b4.

9. The King: Reprise

Back to the King again; does he have the power to attack?

Of course he has; as an attacking piece, he is only a little weaker than a Knight or Bishop! His value, therefore, although priceless so far as the life of the game is concerned, is, as a fighting unit, 2½.

For instance, here are some King forks:

Figure 34

The White King is in check. Nevertheless, he has three moves which will win material because of the ensuing forks:

K d6 – c5 wins one of the Pawns on b4 and c4.

K d6 – c7 wins the Kt b8 or the B c8.

K d6 – e7 wins the Kt f8 or the R f6.

Now for a summary:

Piece	Abbreviation	Value
King	K	? (2½)
Queen	Q	9-10
Rook	R	5
Bishop	B	3
Knight	Kt	3
Pawn	P	1

Exercise No. 3

In figures 35, 36, 37, 38, White moves first. What is his best move?

Sometimes a player has a choice of forks he can give. **The one he selects depends on (1) the value of the pieces he can win, (2) protection of the attacked pieces, (3) possible protection after**

the check, (4) counter-attack after he wins material.

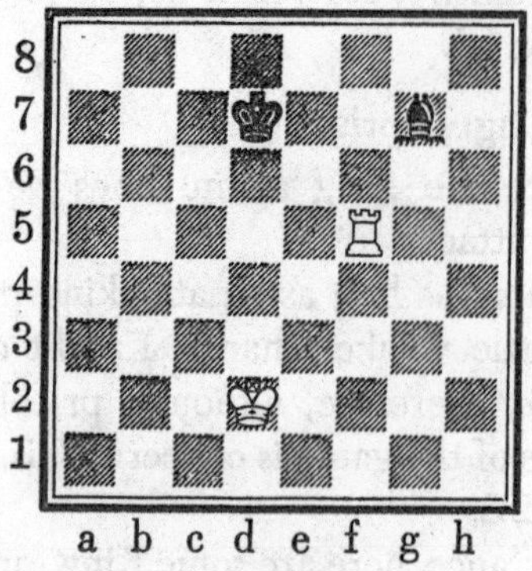

In the following diagrams, one or more of those points must be considered.

Figure 35

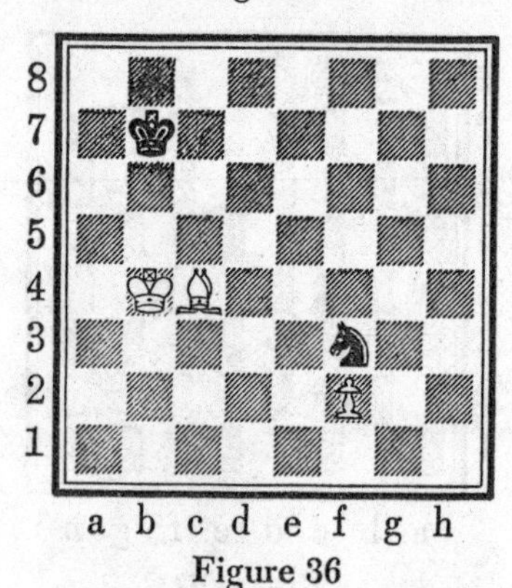

Figure 36

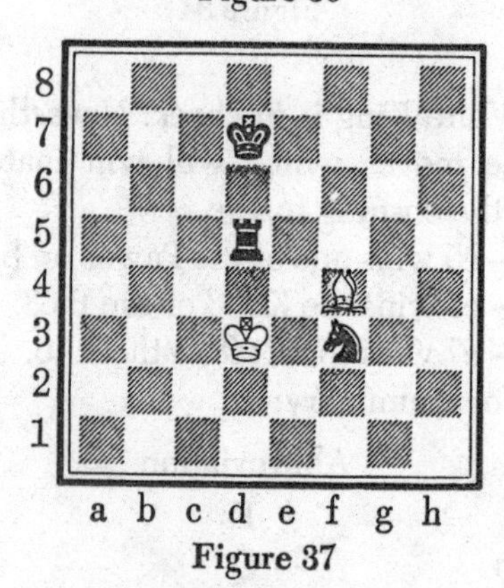

Figure 37

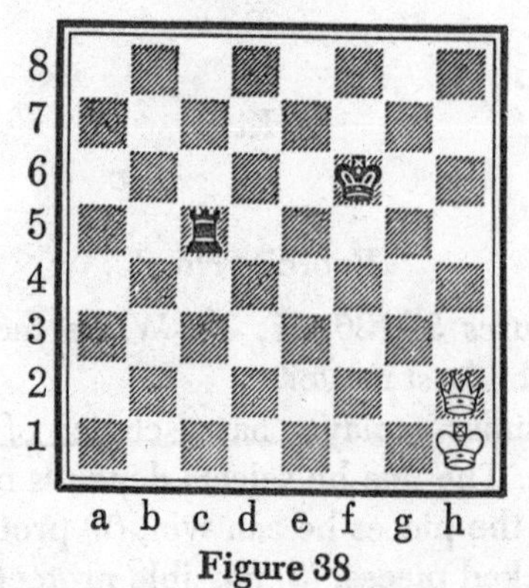

Figure 38

Figure 39

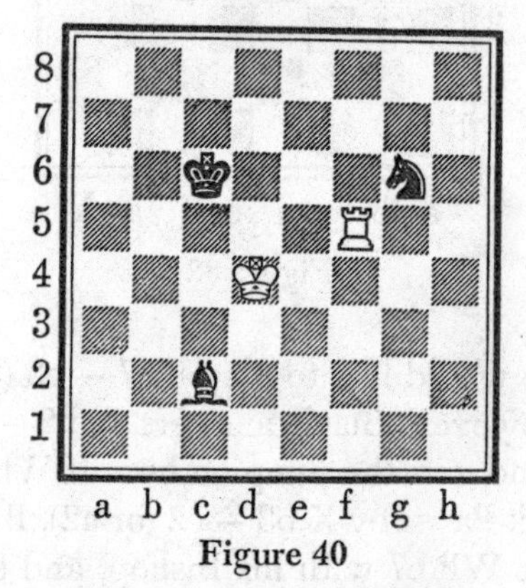

Figure 40

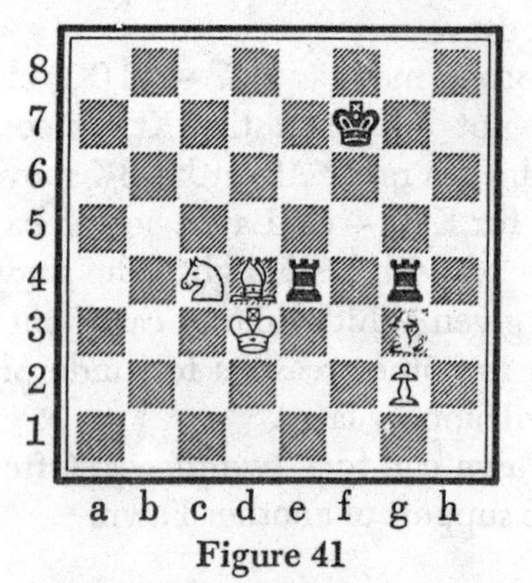

Figure 41

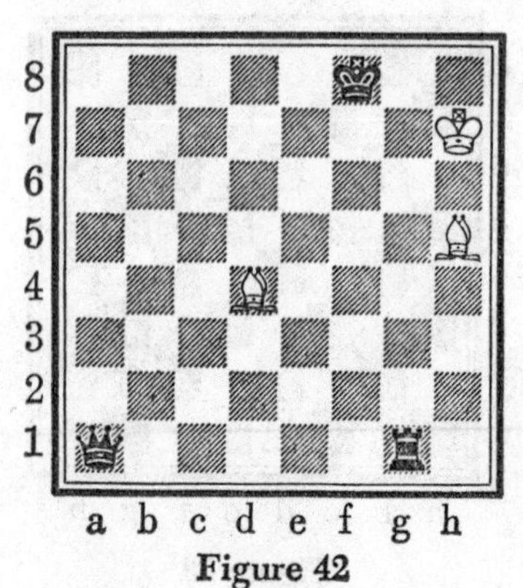

Figure 42

CHAPTER III

GOOD MOVES FOR THE PIECES

In chess, you can't always attack the opponent's King, nor even his other pieces. In the next chapter you are going to learn how to make the first moves in a game ("the opening") but first you should learn more about how to give your pieces their maximum power.

You have already learned several things. You know that **the power of each piece increases as it approaches the center of the board.** You know that certain pieces can paralyze other pieces because of their special movement. You know that pieces can be restricted by other pieces which are in their way, especially pieces on the same "side."

A great deal, then, depends upon the position of the pieces (this includes Pawns, of course) on the board. Let us emphasize the word **Board.** The pieces are limited by their own movement and the limits of the board.

1. GOOD MOVES FOR THE ROOK

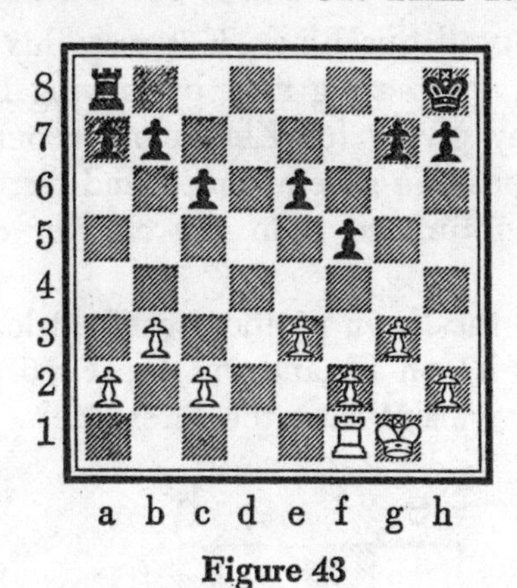

Figure 43

It is White's move. There does not seem to be too great a difference in the positions, and yet, if White makes the correct move, he will get an advantage which should enable him to win the game. The reasoning is simple:

A Rook moves in straight lines on ranks and files. Now he can move on a rank, but the f file is closed. The d file is open. On d1, the Rook increases his power by seven squares. Therefore: R f1 – d1.

If it had been Black's move, what would he have played? R a8 – d8, naturally. Therefore, White's move R f1 – d1 not only increases the power of *his* Rook, but prevents Black from doing the same.

What next? Threat: R d1 – d7. Reasons? (1) to capture the Black Pawns, (2) to keep the Black King and Rook on defensive squares on the first rank. **This is usually the strongest position for a Rook.** It is worth more than a Pawn, because it is a keystone for a winning plan: namely, **the advance of the King to the center and among the Black Pawns.**

Another example:

Figure 44

The move which (1) increases the power of the White Rook, (2) restricts the Black Rook and King (3) prevents a counterattack by Black is: R b1 – b6.

What would have happened if White had not played this move?

Black would play P b7 – b5 at the first opportunity. This would increase the power of his Rook by two squares, and decrease White's by two. It would start the Black Pawns toward their queening squares b1 and a1. It would increase the range of the Black King by denying White entry into his 6th rank. That's a great deal for one move to do!

Another example: (Fig. 45)

White would like to get in amongst the Black

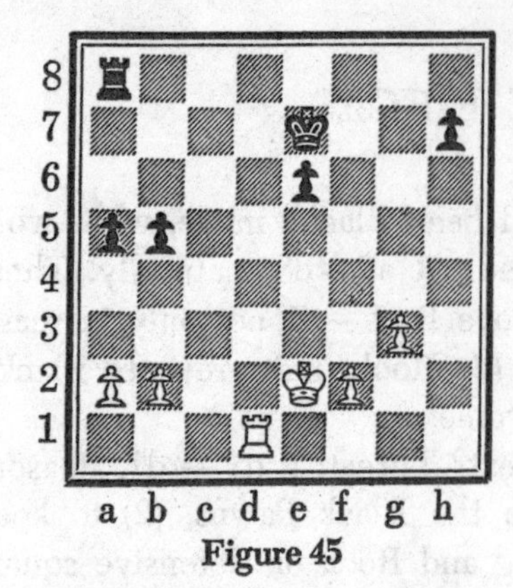

Figure 45

Pawns with his Rook. If he plays R d1 – c1, however, the Black King can defend by K – d6; or the Rook can go to b8.

The correct move is R d1 – h1. To avoid losing his Pawn on h7, Black must play R a8 – h8, thus cutting down the power of his Rook. Then White plays R h1 – h5, and wins the Pawn on a5 or b5, unless Black gives up the one on h7. White here changed one good square (d1) for another (h5) because he could attack enemy pieces from two directions on the latter square.

It is becoming obvious that the difference in positions depends a great deal upon the position of the Pawns. If the Pawn h7 were on f7, for example, White would not have had such an easy target. Before talking further about the major pieces, let us take some time to examine what is meant by a good Pawn position.

2. THE PAWN'S GOOD MOVES

"Pawn play is the soul of chess." Yet this soul has substance. Let us see:

Figure 46

White is a Pawn behind—but if it is his move, he has a won game. Why?

(1) The White Pawns on files **a**, **b**, and **c** can defend one another. The Black Pawns on files **a**, **c** and **e** are all **isolated**. They have to be defended by the King. If White places his King on c5, Black must play his King to b7. Then White would make Pawn moves until the Black King must move; whereupon he would capture the Pawn on c6. More Pawn moves, and he could penetrate via d7 (to win the P e6) or b7 (for the a Pawn).

(2) The two White Pawns on the g and h files hold the three Black Pawns—**if White holds tight** and lets Black exchange (P h7 – h5 x g4). In effect the single WP g4 holds the BP's g6 and g7.

(3) The Pawn e5 is in an aggressive position; Black P e6 is defending. Result: White King has more space to move in, more power to move. The Black King is restricted by his own Pawns, as well as the WP e5.

(4) Because of the absence of Black's Pawn on the **b** file, White can force through a Pawn on the a file.

Knowing all this Black, if it were his move, could put up a strong fight by moving P c6 – c5, thereby giving his King more room. Play over this position several times, and test it out. We shall return to it in the chapter on the Endgame.

Change the Pawn position just a little: place the Pawn h7 on f7, and put the P g6 on g7. Black now wins! What is the difference?

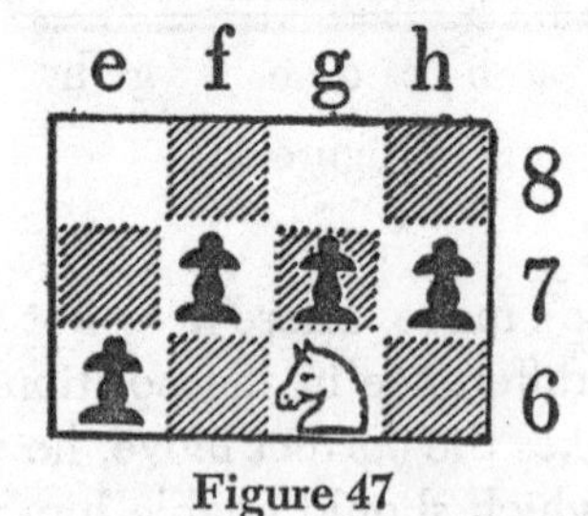

Figure 47

At some stage of the game, Black had to capture a piece (say, a Knight, as above) on g6. He should have played P h7 x Kt g6.

Rule: When capturing with a Pawn, capture toward the center.

Reasons: (1) to control more center squares;
(2) to keep the Pawns connected.

Exceptions to this rule: See the chapter on "The End Game (p. 88)." Again:

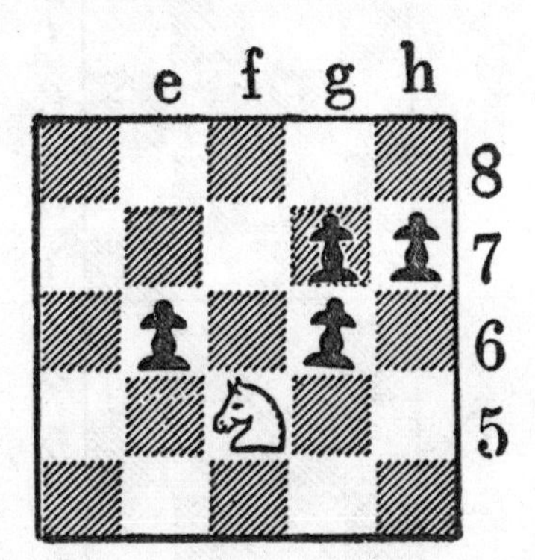

Figure 48

How should Black capture the Knight? P g6 x Kt f5. Reasons: (1) Undouble the Pawns (2) Capture toward the center.

Suppose the P g7 were on e7?

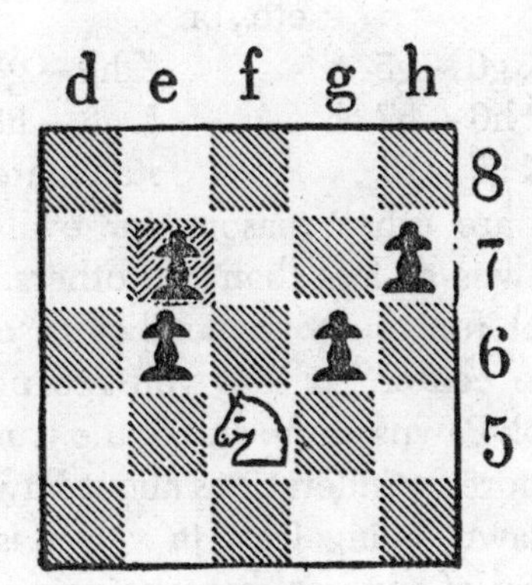

Figure 49

P e6 x Kt f5. Undouble the Pawns, all things being equal.

(In special cases, where the g file must be opened, or immediate control kept of d5, P g6 x Kt f5 might be preferred.)

Rule: Keep your Pawn structure fluid. Usually, that means one Pawn on each file. It also means: keep your Pawns abreast:

This position:

Figure 50

or this:

Figure 51

is better than:

Figure 52

(unless that pawn can push forward quickly!)

and certainly better than:

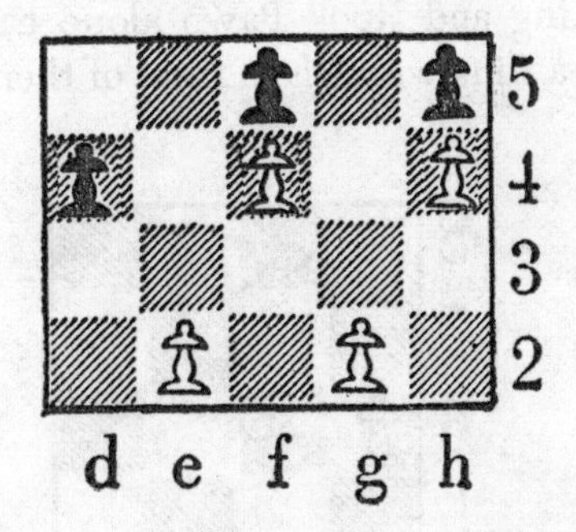

Figure 53

The Pawns on e2 and g2 are "backward"—i.e., they have no adjoining Pawns to protect them.

Pawns, however, must be considered in relationship with the other pieces. Especially is this true with respect to Bishops, which move on one color only. The same Pawn position can be

good

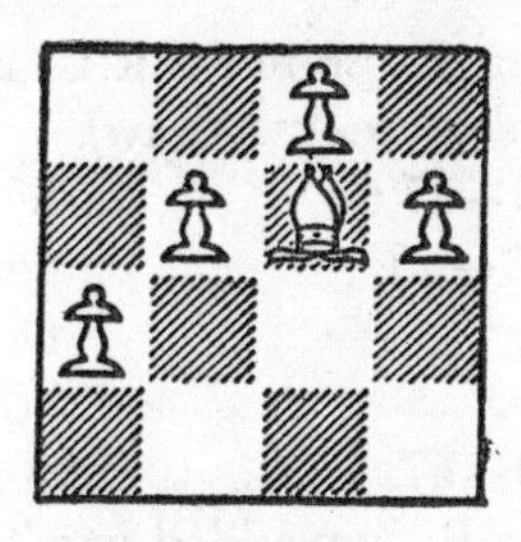

Figure 54

In this case, it supplements the power of the Bishop by guarding squares the B could not guard.

and bad

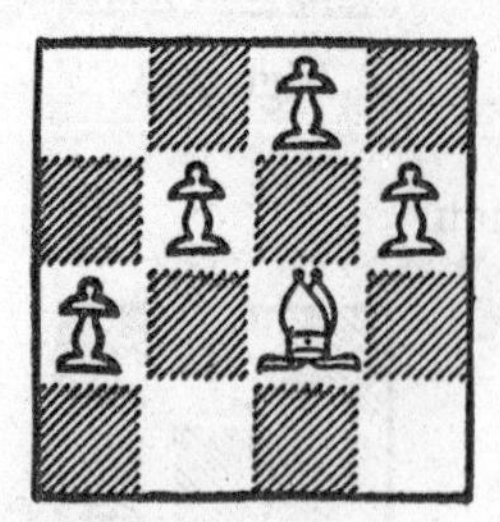

Figure 55

In this case it duplicates the power of the Bishop by guarding the same squares. It also shuts in the Bishop.

Rook Pawns have their peculiar weaknesses:

(1) King and Rook Pawn alone can not win against a King which is in front of them:

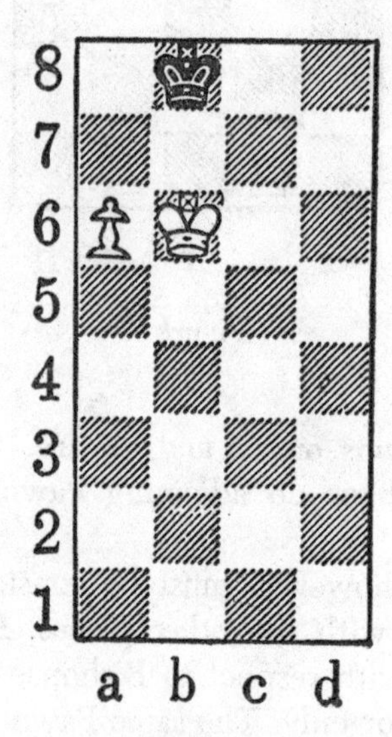

Figure 56

No matter whose move it is, the best White can do is stalemate (= a draw).

1. P a6 – a7 ch	K b8 – a8
2. K b6 – a6	stalemate, there being no check.
1. . . .	K b8 – a8
2. P a6 – a7	stalemate

(2) Even a Bishop added won't help, unless it controls the queening square:

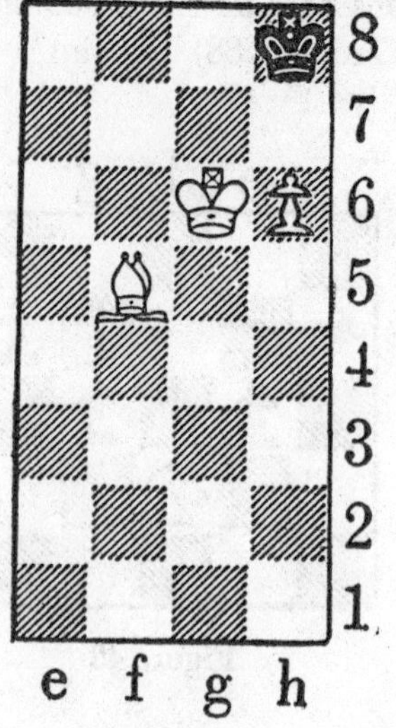

Figure 57

1. K g6 – f6	K h8 – g8
2. B f5 – e6 ch	K g8 – h7
3. K f6 – g5	K h7 – h8,
etc., or	
1. K g6 – g5	K h8 – g8
P h6 – h7 ch	K g8 – h8
K g5 – f6	stalemate

There are other reasons for evaluating the Rook Pawns as less than the others. Now it is important for you to remember to **capture toward the center**, so that you are not saddled with Rook Pawns at the end of the game.

Two more considerations about Pawns:

The Pawn, being least in value, is strongest for **control** of squares, because no enemy piece (except a Pawn) would dare let itself be exchanged for something of so little value.

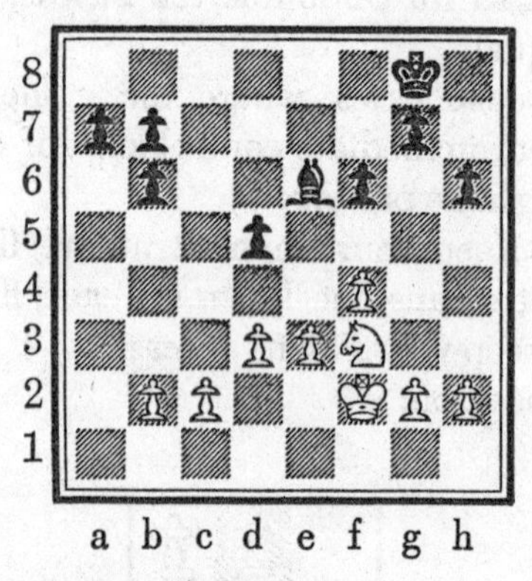

Figure 58

In the above position, the White Pawns guard or can guard all the squares in front of them.

Black, however, has an isolated Pawn on the d file. If White plays his Kt f3 to d4, no Black piece can drive it away.

(1) The weakness of an is ... is the square in front of it.

The Knight can eventual ... the King can cover that ... position, and a White Pa ... protect the Kt on d6 fron ... The Pawns on files c a ... though we know that ... sary to develop the pie ...

(2) every Pawn m ... because it gives up ... passes or joins. Paw ... to regain control of ...

You will find c ... chapter on the E ...

3. GOOD M ...

Good square ...

(1) in the c ...
(2) in fron ...
(3) on a s ...
(4) in a " ...
(5) in f ... lock-ader."

h

White's co ... f1 — e3, heading for the "holes" at d5 or ...

If Black plays . . . K g8 — f8, then Kt e3 — f5 wins the Pawn h6. If . . . B e7 — d8, Kt e3 — f5 wins the Pawn h6 or d6.

If Black replies . . . B e7 — f8, then White leaves the Knight on e3 while he forces an entry with his King:

1. Kt f1 — e3 B e7 — f8
2. K c2 — b3 P f7 — f6

(This is the only way for the Black King to get into play. It puts another Pawn on a black square, however, thereby limiting the Black Bishop further.)

... a2 — a4 K g8 — f7
... a4 x P b5 P a6 x P b5
... Kt e3 — d5!

... to f5, since the Bishop holds four of the ...'s squares from that spot.)

... . . . B f8 — e7

...7. Kt d5 — c7, winning the Pawn b5 and ...ntually the game.

...The square at d5 or f5 is called an "outpost."

Figure 60

Even if the White Knight could get to d5 or f5 in this position, he could be captured by the Bishop. Here he takes up the position of blockader by Kt e1 — d3. This move:

(1) blockades the Pawn d4.

(2) attacks the Pawns c5 (which is defended at the moment) and e5. The attack on c5 holds the Black Pawn on b6.

(3) prepared for an advance by P f2 — f4.

The Pawn on d4 is a "Passed Pawn" because no White Pawn stands between it and the Queening square d1. It is a peculiar feature of a Knight that from the square in front of a Passed Pawn, it attacks the Pawns which might defend the Passed Pawn. White, in the position above, can decide whether to advance by P f2 — f4 or P a2 — a3 and P b3 — b4.

4. GOOD SQUARES FOR THE BISHOP

The Bishop, too, stands well:

(1) in the center

(2) on an outpost

It can act:

(3) as a blockader.

Because of its special type of move, it stands best (4) on open diagonals.

There are, however, two types of moves frequently indulged in by a Bishop. One is (5) **The Pin.**

Figure 61

A glance at the position will show that the Black King and Knight are on the same diagonal—the color of the square of the White Bishop.

White has no time to threaten a fork, because the Black pieces can move away. But he can play B c2 – b3. This is a **pin.**

What can Black do? He can not move the Knight, for his King will be in check. The Knight is paralyzed; on the next move, the Bishop can take it off.

A Rook also can pin—on a rank or file; a Queen on a rank, file or diagonal. How many pins can you find for White in the following diagram?

Figure 62

First look for the Black King. Let your eyes roam along the diagonals starting at his square; then the file he stands on:

B el – a5—Pin on the Queen

B el – h4—Pin on the Knight

Q a4 – a5—Pin on the Queen

Q a4 – h4—Pin on the Knight

R al – dl—Pin on the Bishop

Q a4 – dl or d4—Pin on the Bishop

The pins above are all **real** pins. The pinned piece is paralyzed. Only the Queen could do anything—capture a Bishop or Queen on a5, because she has the same power of movement as the pinning piece. In a later chapter we shall consider what to do when you have a pin, and how to defend against it.

Some pins are **assumed** rather than **real,** because the pinned piece can move away, at a loss of material. The pins above, being against a piece screening a King, are real: **it is illegal to move the piece pinned, because the King will be exposed to check.**

Some assumed pins follow:

Figure 63

The Knight on d5 is doubly pinned: by the Q b3 on the Q e6 and by the B f3 on the R b7.

Yet the Knight *can* move. Black will lose material, but it is possible for the Knight to move —the pin is only an assumed pin.

If it were White's move in the diagram, he should play R a1 – d1, pinning the Kt a third time—against the R d8. Black can protect himself by R b7 – d7, getting out of two pins at one time by moving one piece and protecting the other. Now the Knight is pinned only on the Q; and on the next move—if White tries to double up his Rooks, for example, Black can move the Kt to c7, protecting the Q; or just move the Queen to a spot (say e7) where there will be no pin.

After (1) R a1 – d1, R b7 – d7;
White plays (2) R d1 x Kt d5! R d7 x R d5
(3) R f1 – d1!

Now the Rook is double pinned and thrice attacked. If 3 . . . R x R d1, 4. Q x Q e6, and White has won material. If Black tries to defend his Queen by 3. R d5 – d6, then White plays 4. Q x Q e6, R x Q e6; 5. R x R d8 ch, remaining a Bishop ahead.

(See Chapter V for more about pins.)

One more strong type of move for a Bishop is a **hurdle!** In this a Bishop attacks a piece; the piece must move, and the Bishop then captures a piece in back of the piece which has moved. An example:

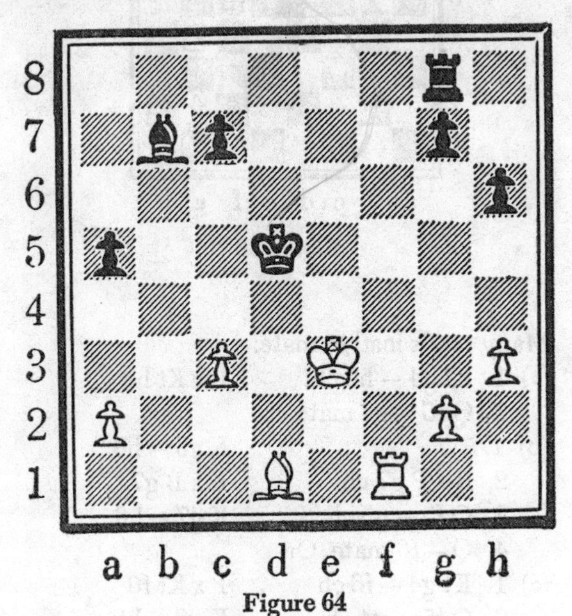

Figure 64

White, to move, looks at the Black King on d4. His eyes follow the diagonals **from that** square and he finds the Rook g8 on one diagonal, and the Bishop b7 on another. He looks at his own Bishop on d1 and he finds it can move.

B d1 – b3 check! The King must move; whereupon B b3 x R g8. Or, B d1 – f3 check! Again, the King must move, and then B f3 x B g7.

The Rook can have fun, too; R f1 – f5 check! The King must move, whereon R x P a5.

Do not depend too much upon the word "must." In the above diagram must *is* must: There is no other way of getting out of any of the three checks. (But see Chapter V for defenses to **hurdles.**)

Hurdles can be used against pieces other than the King. The idea is simple: a piece is attacked. To avoid capture, it must move out of the line of the attacking piece—which then continues past the square vacated to capture something else.

Figure 65

The Queen is an inviting target. R f1 – e1, R h4 – e4, B d2 – f4 are all moves which lead to hurdles. R h4 – h5 is not so effective because of the defense P f6 – f5. Which is the best?

Answer: R h4 – e4, which forces the win of the Queen for a Rook (10 – 5 = 5). Compare this with: B d2 – f4, which wins the B c7 (= 3). R f1 – e1, which gives time for Q e4 x R e1 **check**; B d2 x Q e1, R e8 x B e1 **check again**; K g1 – g2, Kt a5 – c6. (Gain = 10 for 8 = 2).

5. GOOD MOVES FOR THE QUEEN

Since the Queen moves like both Bishop and Rook, the same good moves for those pieces can be made by Her Ladyship. In addition, her strong forking powers make her more than a "triple threat."

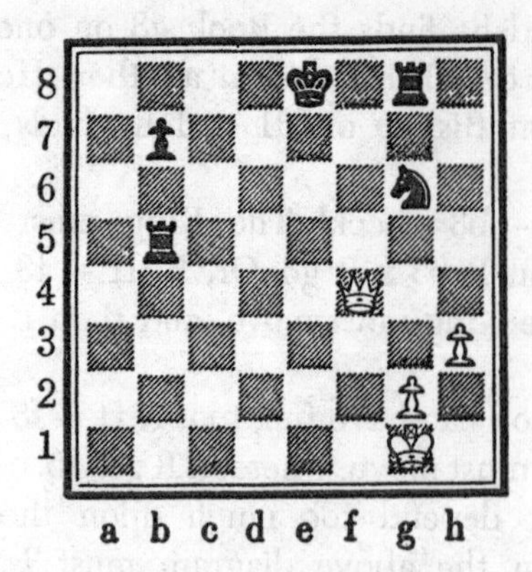

Figure 66

White has some inviting moves: a fork (Q – e4 ch); a hurdle (Q – b8 ch). The only good move, however, is the deadly pin: Q – a4. Black can not save his Rook. The fork Q – c4 is met by R b5 – b1 ch. After the pin, however, R b5 can not move.

The Queen is a strong mating force, particularly when one of the other pieces helps her:

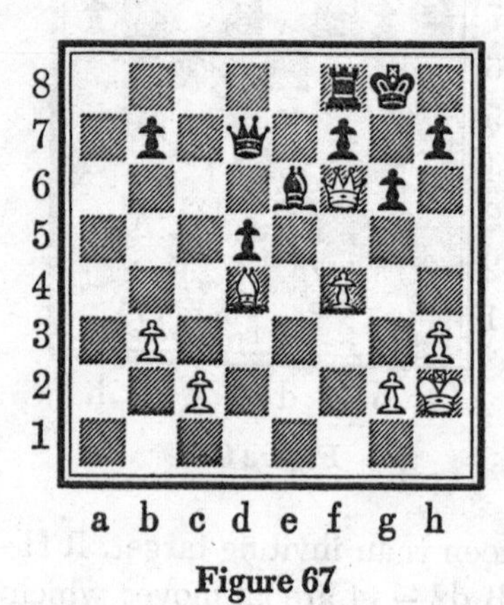

Figure 67

Nothing can stop Q f6 – g7 mate or Q h8 mate.

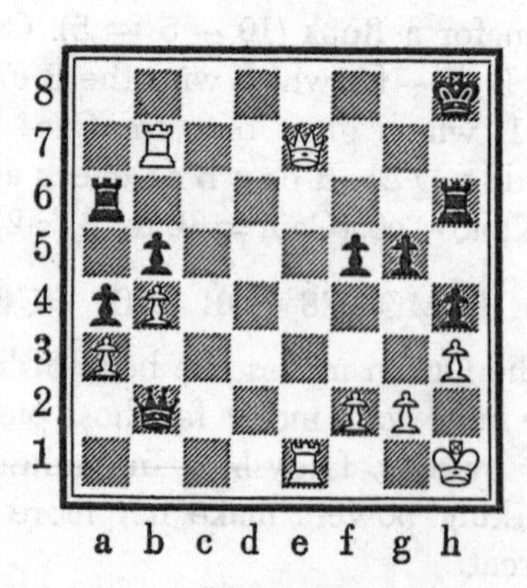

Figure 68

White doesn't threaten much: merely checkmate on six different squares! The mates on h7 and g7 are covered by the Rook h6 and Q b2. The mates on the 8th rank (b8, d8, e8 and f8) can be covered by R a6 – a8. But then follow: Q e7 – e8 ch, R a8 x Q e8; R e1 x R e8 checkmate.

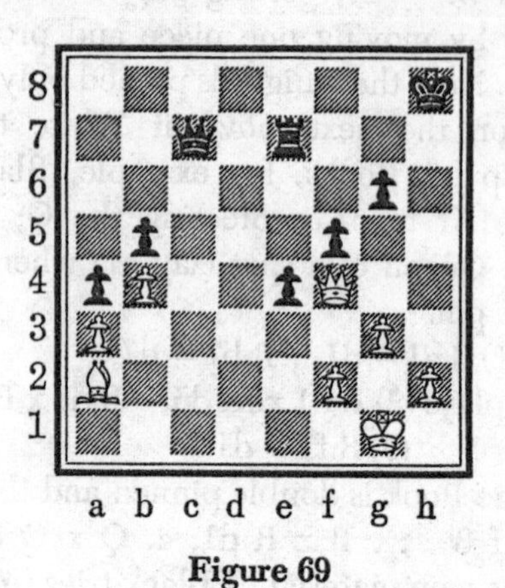

Figure 69

Q f4 – h6 ch, R e7 – h7 (The Bishop a2 guards g8) Q h6 – f8 mate.

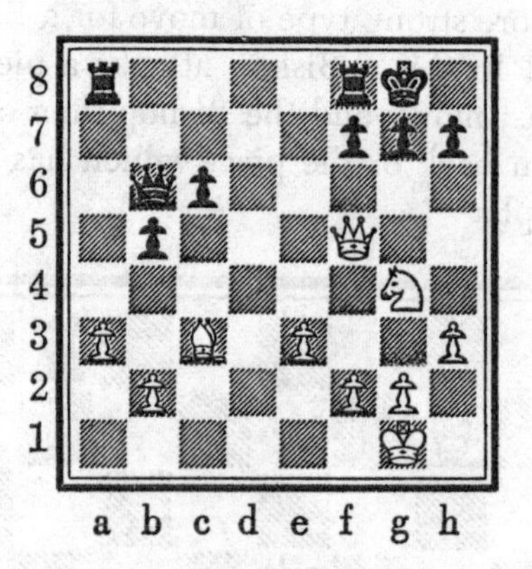

Figure 70

Many roads lead to mate:

(a)	1. Kt g4 – h6 ch!	P x Kt h6
	2. Q f5 – g4 mate or	
(b)	1. . . .	K g8 – h8
	2. B x P g7 ch	K x B g7
	3. Q f5 – g5 ch	K g7 – h8
	4. Q – f6 mate. Or	
(c)	1. Kt g4 – f6 ch	P x Kt f6
	2. Q f5 – g4 ch	K g8 – h8
	3. B x P f6 mate. Or	
(d)	1. Kt g4 – f6 ch	P x Kt f6
	2. Q f6 x P and mate at g7 or h8. Or	

(e) 1. Kt g4 – h6 ch K g8 – h8
2. Q f5 – f6 P x Q f6
3. B x P f6 mate. Or

(f) 1. Kt g4 – h6 ch K g8 – h8
2. Q f5 – f6 R f8 – g8
3. Kt x P f7 mate. This is a "smothered mate."

(g) 1. Kt g4 – f6 ch K g8 – h8
2. Q f5 x P h7 mate

6. GOOD MOVES FOR THE KING

It must have occurred to you that the King should be concerned first with his own safety.

Many pins and forks are possible when the King is out in the open, where he can be attacked easily. At the beginning of the game, therefore, the King should seek shelter behind a solid phalanx of Pawns. He should have some room to move, to avoid a smothered mate. He should castle, in order to allow coordination of the Rooks, in most positions. *Where* he should castle depends upon the strategy of the game and upon the Pawn position. In some positions, where the Pawns are ripped up on both sides of the board, he may be safer in the center.

But safety does not mean cowardice. In certain positions the King, even at the beginning of the game, is the only piece which can hold a certain square. In that case he must move to hold it:

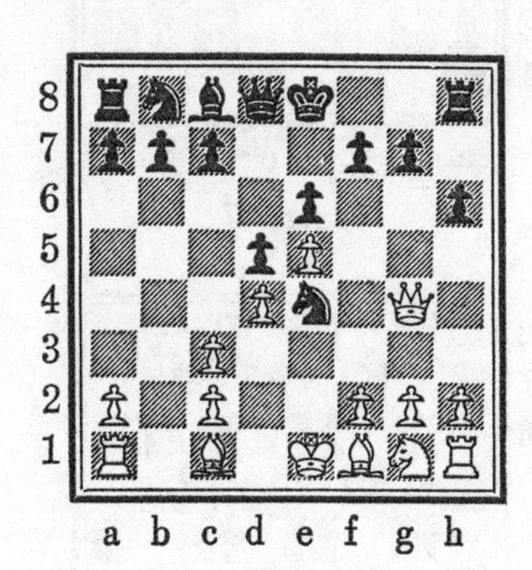

Figure 71

Black's move. His g7 is under attack. R h8 – g8 won't do, because of B f1 – d3 and later to h7. P g7 – g6 would invite an attack by P h2 – h4 – h5. Castling would lose because of B x P h6 (the g pawn is pinned). The only move is K e8 – f8, and Black must make it.

However, it is at the end of the game that the King comes into his most powerful role. He can attack Pawns, or blockade them:

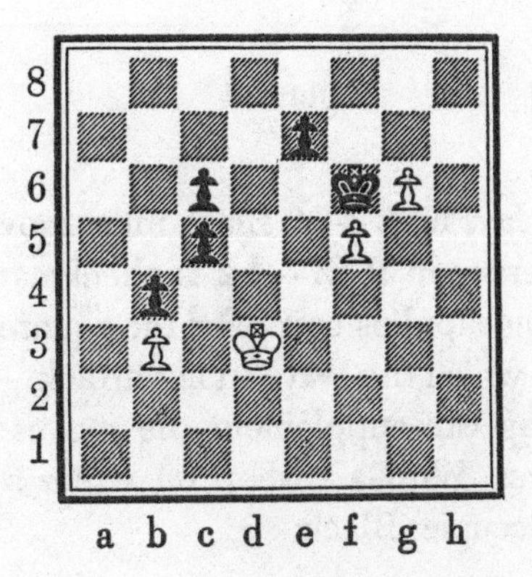

Figure 72

The Black King f6 is blockading the White Pawns f5 and g6. He can not capture the P f5 because P g6 would go to g8 and become a Queen. But he can dissolve the Pawn connection by P e7 – e6. Then, after P x P e6, K x P e6; he can capture the Pawn on g6 as well.

The White King d3 can move to c4, from which he can capture the P c5 and then P c6 or b4, as he decides.

A King can be used to support a Pawn to its queening square:

Figure 73

White, to move, should play K a6 – b7. Nothing can stop the Pawn c6 from going to c7 – c8, and making a Queen. The King can help attack the enemy King:

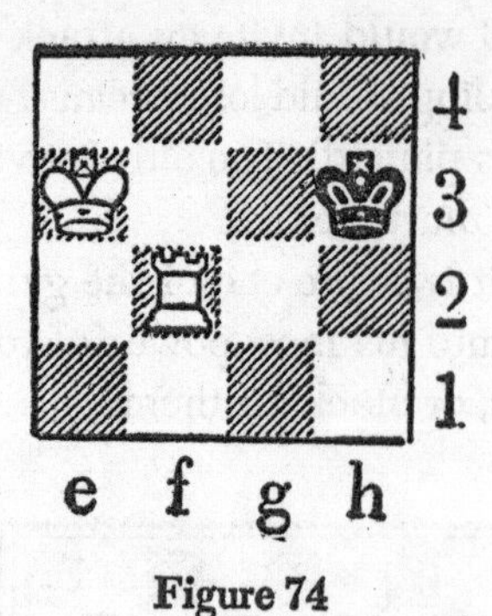

Figure 74

White plays K e3 – f4. Black must move K h3 – h4, whereupon R f2 – h2 is checkmate. The White King supplies cover for the squares (here g3, g4, g5) which the WR can not attack.

The King can supplement the moves of the other pieces. With a Bishop on white squares, the King occupies Black:

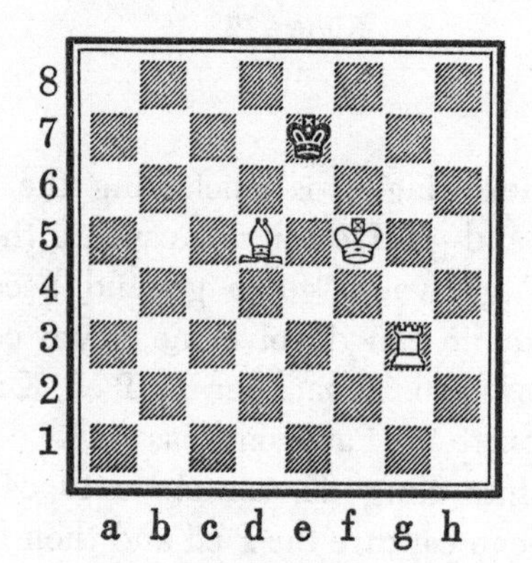

Figure 75

White should play K f5 – e5, covering the black squares while the Bishop covers the white ones.

In the following diagram, White is trying to checkmate Black. The White King cannot check, but he can prevent the Black King from escaping. The question is: where? The Bishop must deliver the final check, with the King in the corner. That means that the Knight must check the Black K on the white square g8—which he must do from a black square without interfering with the Bishop. On f6 he would be in the Bishop's way; so would the White King. The Knight must, therefore, check on h6—which the King must leave clear.

Now the jigsaw pieces fall neatly into place:

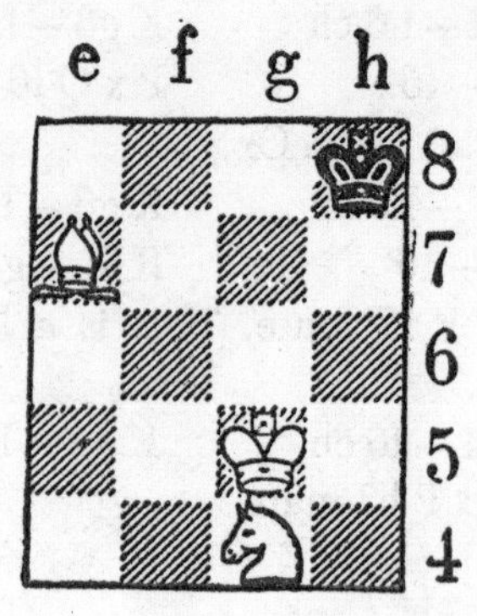

Figure 76

1. K g5 – g6 K h8 – g8
2. Kt g4 – h6 ch K g8 – h8
3. B e7 – f6 checkmate!

At this point, you know enough about the movements and powers of the pieces to be able to play a game with all the pieces on both sides. The next chapter will show you what to do at the beginning of a game. Before you proceed, however, review what you have learned by finding the best moves in the following positions.

White is to move in all cases.

Exercise No. 4

I.

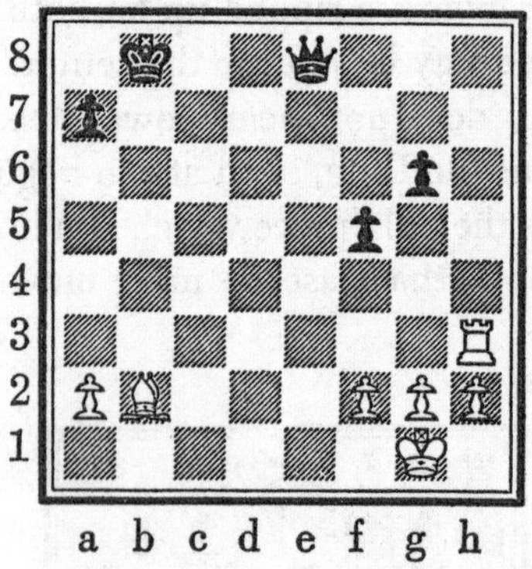

Figure 77

II.

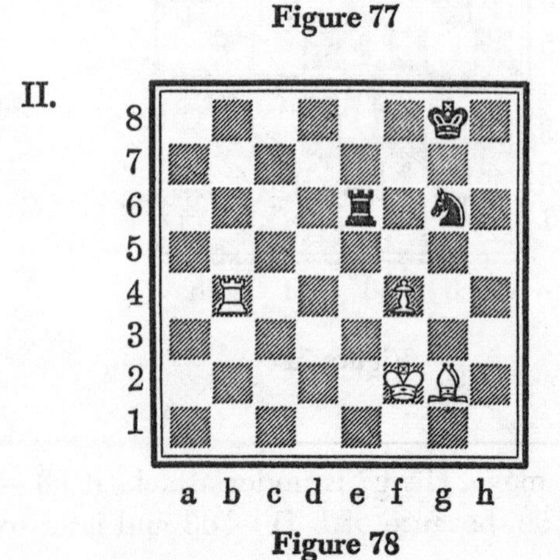

Figure 78

III.

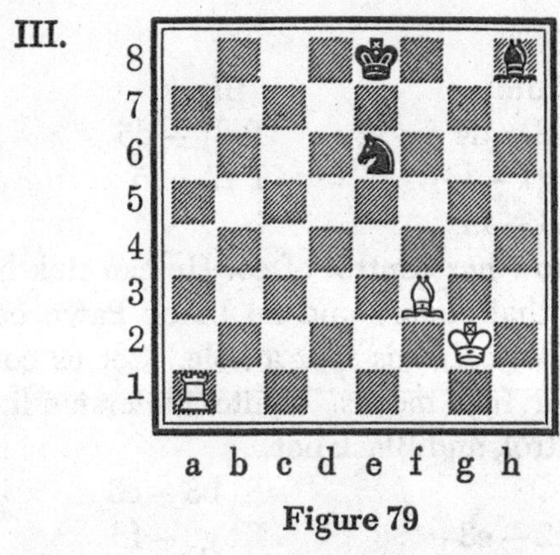

Figure 79

IV.

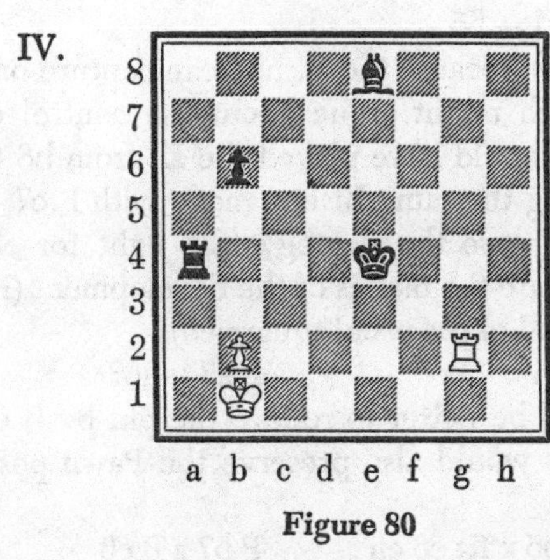

Figure 80

V.

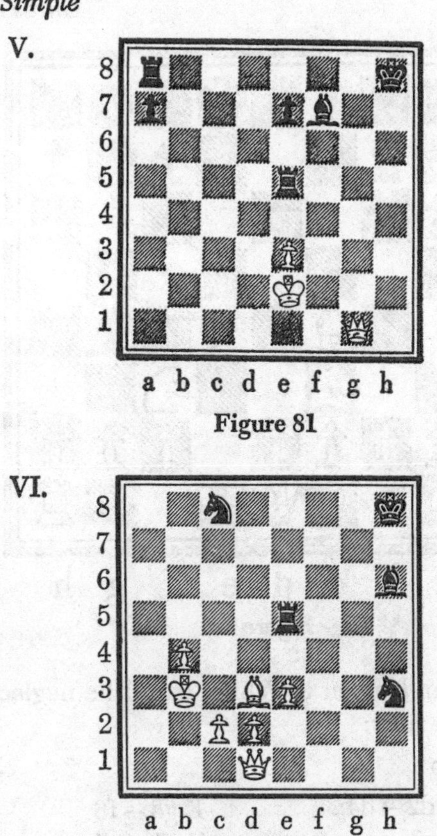

Figure 81

VI.

Figure 82

CHAPTER IV

THE OPENING

Now that you know the pieces, how they move and some of the things they can do, you might ask: How do I start a game? I set up the pieces—and then what?

The first few moves in a game are called "the opening." Here are some of the things you should do:

1. Move out all your pieces. We call this: "Develop your pieces."

2. On each new move, put a new piece into play. This is known as "development."

3. Pawns are not pieces. Move only those pawns which you must move in order to develop the pieces properly.

Remember: Pawns do not move backwards. You can not guard a square with a pawn that has pushed past it.

Let us see what happens when one player follows these rules, and the other does not:

Game #1

	White	Black
1.	P e2 – e4	P e7 – e5
2.	Kt g1 – f3	P d7 – d6
3.	B f1 – c4	B c8 – g4
4.	Kt b1 – c3	P a7 – a6

White has a **good position.** He has moved out three pieces and only one pawn—the one necessary to make room for the Bishop he has developed. He has moved the pieces toward the center, so that they have maximum power. (Fig. 83)

Black has a **bad position.** He has moved three pawns, and only one piece. This piece seems to pin the White Knight on f3, for, if the knight moves, Black can capture the White Queen. But:

5.	Kt x P e5	B g4 x Q d1
6.	B c4 x P f7 ch	K e8 – e7
7.	Kt c3 – d5	checkmate!

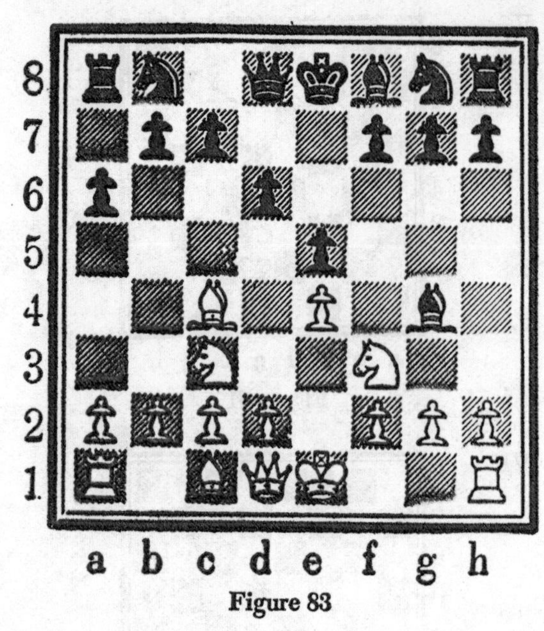

Figure 83

This can happen to White, too, if he neglects the above rules:

Game #2

1. P d2 – d4	K g8 – f6
2. P c2 – c4	P e7 – e5
3. P d4 – d5	B f8 – c5
4. B c1 – g5	Kt f6 – e4
5. B g5 x Q d8	B c5 x P f2
	Checkmate!

Foolish play by White? You will find this game in the U. S. Open Championship at Philadelphia, 1936. It was won by the author.

. . . Which brings us to Rule Number Four:

4. If you can move two pieces, move first the piece whose moves are most limited.

This means Knights before Bishops usually; and minor pieces before Queens.

5. Move your pieces toward the center of the board.

We have seen that the power of a piece increases as it comes closer to the center of the board. A Knight on c3 or f3 has eight moves; on d2 or e2, six moves, and on a3 or h3, only four.

On c3 and f3, the two Knights guard the vital center squares d4, d5, e4 and e5. So would the two Black Knights on c6 and f6.

6. Try to control a line in the center of the board.

7. Try to control a square on that line.

What do we mean by **control?** A simple example:

Game #3

White	Black
1. P d2 – d4	P d7 – d5
2. Kt g1 – f3	P f7 – f5
3. B c1 – f4	

White now has control of e5. He can sink his Knight in that square and no Black Pawn can chase it. (We call this spot a **hole.**) Let us continue for a few moves, White understanding center control, and Black not.

3. . . .	Kt b8 – c6
4. P e2 – e3	Kt g8 – f6
5. B f1 – b5	

Why b5? Because the Bishop can capture one piece which might argue about the control of e5. Black should have played the Kt from b8 to d7, meeting the same Bishop move with P c7 – c6. In this case the **strategy** (the fight for e5) would dictate the **tactics** of the development (Kt – d7 instead of the usual square c6).

5. . . .	P a7 – a6?

It would be better to relieve the pin by B c8 – d7. This would also preserve the Pawn position.

6. B b5 x Kt c6 ch	P b7 x B c6
7. Kt f3 – e5	

White violates Rule 2 by moving this piece a second time, before his other pieces are developed. However, again strategy demands this, for if White waited one more move, Black could play P e7 – e6 and then P c6 – c5, straightening out his pawns again. Now he must defend the Pawn on c6: if he moved it, he would lose it.

7. . . .	B c8 – d7
8. Kt b1 – d2. The Knight heads for f3.	
8. . . .	P e7 – e6
9. O – O (Castles)	

Rule 8. Castle in order to (a) connect your Rooks; (b) bring the King into safety; (c) get the Rooks into play via the center files, which are usually opened up.

Rule 9. Castle when you want to, or when you have to—but not just to make a move.

In the game, White wants to open up the files in front of the Black King.

Black can not go to e4 with his Knight, because of

10. Kt d2 x Kt e4	P f5 x Kt e4
11. Q d1 – h5 check	K e8 – e7
12. Q h5 – f7 check	K e7 – d6

13. Kt e5 – c4 double check and mate.

Black could avoid being mated in this variation by 11. . . . P g7 – g6, but after 12 Kt e5 x P g6, he would lose his Queen. Work this out!

Back to the game:

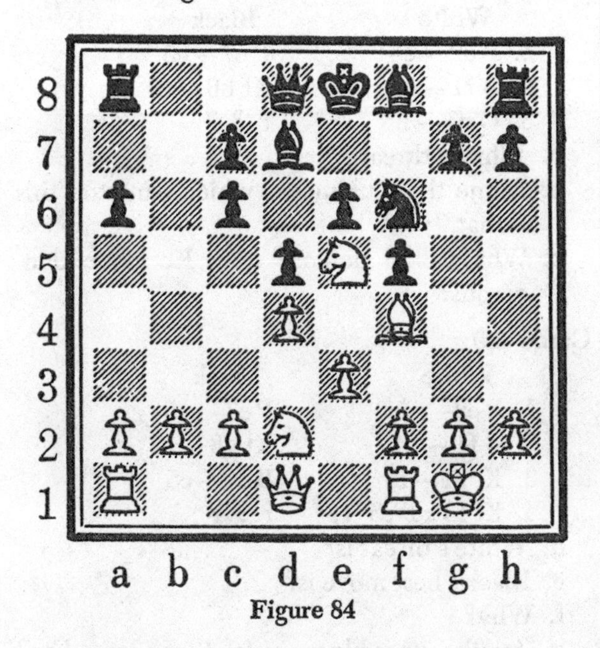

Figure 84

9. . . .	B f8 – b4
10. P c2 – c3	B b4 – a5?

Remember: Black does not understand the importance of fighting for the center; otherwise, he would play this Bishop to d6.

11. P f2 – f3	R a8 – b8?
12. P b2 – b4	B a5 – b6

Here, the Bishop is well bottled up. However, White does not take anything for granted (see move 21).

13. P e3 – e4	P f5 x P e4
14. P f3 x P e4	P d5 x P e4
15. B f4 – g5	

A murderous pin!

15. . . .	0 – 0 (Castles)
16. Kt d2 x P e4	B d7 – e8

After White's next move, there is no way for Black to avoid a great loss of material. But let us look closely at the diagram, to see what White's control of the center has done: (Fig. 85)

—It has allowed White to develop all his pieces toward a certain goal (attack on the Knight).

—It will lead to the gain of material.

—It will also lead to an attack against the Black King.

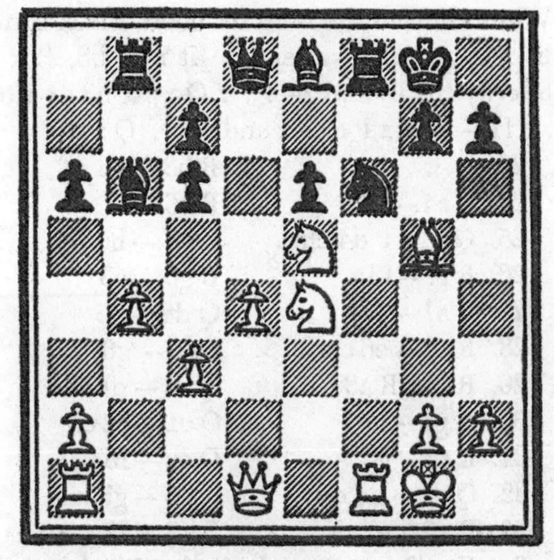

Figure 85

—It has split Black's forces, so that he cannot bring them together.

—It has limited Black's moves, so that he cannot escape from the pin.

—If Black tries to keep forces equal, he will expose his King. He will then be checkmated.

And yet—

There is an "and yet!"

If White moves his Queen, in order to attack the Kt f6 again (Q – f3) he will let loose the imprisoned Bishop on b6: . . . B x P d4 ch; P c3 x B d4, Q d8 x P d4 ch; K g1 – h1, Q d4 x Kt e4 —and the whole good position disintegrates!

Go back to the diagram. The correct move is:

17. Kt e5 – g4

The idea is: to attack the pinned piece with a piece of as little value as possible. Neither Knight can be captured, for then B g5 x Q d8.

Now suppose Black tries:

17. . . .	B e8 – g6

(This connects his Rooks, prevents a check on the g file, and forces White to act quickly.)

18. Kt e4 x Kt f6 ch	P g7 x Kt f6
19. B x P f6	R f8 x B f6

White threatened Kt g4 – h6 checkmate!

20. Kt g4 x R f6 ch	K g8 – g7
21. Q d1 – g4	P e6 – e5

This Pawn can not be taken by the P d4, which is pinned by the B b6.

22. Kt f6 – d7

A threefold fork—R, B and P.

22. . . .	P e5 x P d4
23. P c3 – c4!	

White shuts in the B b6 for good. Black could still put up a fight after 23. Kt x R b8, P x P check (by the B) and 24 . . . Q x Kt b8 or after 23, R f1 – f8, P x P check and . . . Q x R.

23. . . .	R b8 – a8
24. P c4 – c5	B b6 – a7
25. Q g4 x P d4 ch	K g7 – h6
26. R f1 – f8	B g6 – e8
27. R a1 – e1	Q d8 – g5
28. R e1 – e6 ch	B e8 – g6
29. R f8 x R a8	Q g5 – c1 ch
30. K g1 – f2	Q c1 – c2 ch
31. K f2 – g3	Q c2 – f5
32. Q d4 – h4 ch	K h6 – g7
33. R e6 – e7 ch	B g6 – f7

34. Kt d7 – e5—and all the Black pieces are lost, with checkmate to follow.

Notice how control of the center allowed White to

a. Split the enemy forces;
b. develop all his pieces on open lines;
c. attack first one objective (the Kt f6)
d. and then the King;
e. win material
f. and more material;
g. and, finally, the game.

Before we speak further of opening theory, here are some speedy games to try on your chess board. Which rule does each one violate?

Game #4 — The Scholar's Mate

White	Black
1. P f2 – f3	P e7 – e5
2. P g2 – g4	Q d8 – h4 checkmate.

Game #5

1. P e2 – e3	P f7 – f5
2. P d2 – d4	P g7 – g5
3. Q d1 – h5 checkmate	

Game #6 — Smothered Mate

1. P e2 – e3	Kt b8 – c6
2. P g2 – g3	Kt c6 – e5
3. Kt g1 – e2	Kt e5 – f3 checkmate

Game #7 — The Fool's Mate

1. P e2 – e4	P e7 – e5
2. B f1 – c4	Kt b8 – c6
3. Q d1 – f3	B f8 – c5?
4. Q f3 x P f7 checkmate	

This last game is very tempting to try against a beginner; but if he moves 3. . . . Kt g8 – f6, the mate is covered, and the White Queen is out where it can be chased, with the gain of time for Black's development.

Exercise No. 5

Game #8

White	Black
1. P e2 – e4	P e7 – e5
2. B f1 – c4	Kt b8 – c6
3. Q d1 – h5	? ? ?

a. White's threat is?
b. Name the four moves which can stop this threat.
c. Why is the defense of a Kt move dangerous?

Game #9

White	Black
1. P e2– e4	P e7 – e5
2. B f1 – c4	Kt g8 – f6
3. Kt g1 – f3	B f8 – c5
4. Kt f3 x P e5 (?)	? ? ?

d. White's threat is?
e. Black's best move is?
f. Why?
g. Another possible move for Black would be?
h. Why?
i. Why is the first move better?
j. Why is White's fourth move (Kt f3 x P e5) bad?
k. It wins a Pawn, doesn't it?

4. . . .	0 – 0 (Castles)
5. P d2 – d3	P d7 – d5
6. P e4 x P d5	R f8 – e8
7. P f2 – f4	B c8 – g4
8. Q d1 – d2	? ? ?

l. What is Black's best move now?

8. . . .	B c5 – d4
9. P c2 – c3	B d4 x Kt e5
10. P f4 x B e5	R e8 x P e5 ch
11. K e1 – f1	

m. How should Black continue? Many moves come to mind, considering:
1. The exposed White King.
2. The blockade by White's Queen of his own pieces.
3. The need for Black to develop his remaining pieces: the Kt b8, R a8 and Q d8.
4. The fact that the White Queen can not go to f2 or f4 because of the pin by R e5 – f5.

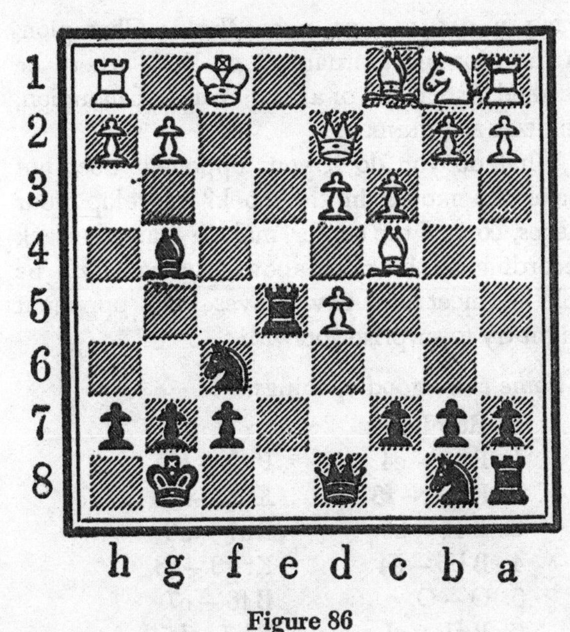

Figure 86

Any move made by Black must be part of a general plan or strategy.

The plan must be one of attack against the exposed White King. It should take place along the open e and f files.

For an attack to succeed, the attacking side must have all its heavy guns ready. Therefore, the plan of attack must include the development of the pieces still on the 8th rank.

The plan must also consider White's plan of defense. That plan will surely include:

1. the move P d3 – d4, so that the B c4 can defend the spot e2;
2. A Queen move, so that the B c1 can go to d2, to defend e1;
3. the sequence P h2 – h3; K f1 – g1 – h2 and R h1 – f1.
4. A Knight move (–a3) and the development of the R a1.

The most important piece in this defensive plan is the B c4, which will guard e2 and f1. Black should try to eliminate this Bishop at once. Therefore (to repeat):

m. How should Black continue?
  1. Simply?
  2. With a sacrifice?

12. . . .   Kt x P d5
13. B x Kt d5

n. Why does White exchange his Bishop?

13. . . .   R x B d5
14. P d3 – d4

o. Black can now pile up on this Pawn. How?
p. Should he?

14. . . .   Kt b8 – c6!

q. Why not Q – f6 ch?
r. Why not R – f5 ch?

15. P h2 – h3   Q d8 – h4
16. K f1 – g1   R a8 – e8
17. K g1 – h2

s. (1) Why not Q d2 – f2, since it can not be pinned? (2) Why not P h3 x B g4?
t. Both players have completed their plans. Black feels that now he should be able to win quickly. How should he proceed? Plan? Move?

17. . . .   Kt c6 – e5!
18. R h1 – f1

Figure 87

18. . . .   Kt e5 – f3 ch!!
19. R x Kt f3

u. After you finish the game in the book, figure out how Black wins after 19, P g2 x Kt f3.

19. . . .   B x R f3
20. P x B f3   R d5 – h5
21. Q d2 – g2

v. Has White escaped?

21. . . .   R e8 – e2!!
22. Q x R e2   Q x P h3 ch
23. K h2 – g1

w. Are you worried about the mate on e8?
x. Which is the best Queen check?

23. . . .   Q h3 – g3 ch
24. Q e2 – g2   Q g3 – e1 ch
25. Q g2 – f1   ? ?

y. Now what?

25. . . .   R h5 – h1 ch

26. K x R h1	Q e1 x Q f1 ch
27. K h1 – h2	Q f1 x B c1

There is no way for White to save his Rook. All the undeveloped pieces fall to the raiding Queen, except the Knight, which manages to escape.

Since White sees no way of saving the game, he gives up.

White resigns.

SOME GOOD OPENINGS

Playing over the moves of the games above must have convinced you that you need more knowledge of the tricks of the trade: the moves to take advantage of the powers of the pieces, the *tactics* of the game. In the meantime you will want to know about some good openings, so that you will be able to start a game on equal terms with your opponent. Here they are:

1. *Giuoco Piano* (The Go-Easy Game)

1. P e2 – e4	P e7 – e5
2. Kt g1 – f3	Kt b8 – c6
3. B f1 – c4	B f8 – c5
4. P d2 – d3	Kt g8 – f6
5. Kt b1 – c3	P d7 – d6
6. B c1 – g5	P h7 – h6
7. B x Kt f6	Q x B f6
8. Kt c3 – d5	Q f6 – d8
9. P c2 – c3	Kt c6 – e7
10. Kt d5 – e3	

Figure 88

Can you be sure the moves are good? White was J. R. CAPABLANCA, once World's Champion, in the Moscow tournament of 1936, where he finished first, ahead of a later World's Champion, MIKHAIL BOTVINNIK.

What do you do if your opponent does not make the moves in the book? Develop your pieces, control the center, make a plan of attack according to the rules above—and you will be able to meet any new moves your opponent might try to surprise you with.

Some more good openings:

2. Ruy Lopez

1. P e2 – e4	P e7 – e5
2. Kt g1 – f3	Kt b8 – c6
3. **B f1 – b5**	P a7 – a6
4. B b5 – a4	Kt g8 – f6
5. O – O	B f8 – e7
6. R f1 – e1	P b7 – b5
7. B a4 – b3	P d7 – d6
8. P c2 – c3	O – O
9. P h2 – h3	Kt c6 – a5
10. B b3 – c2	P c7 – c5
11. P d2 – d4	Q d8 – c7

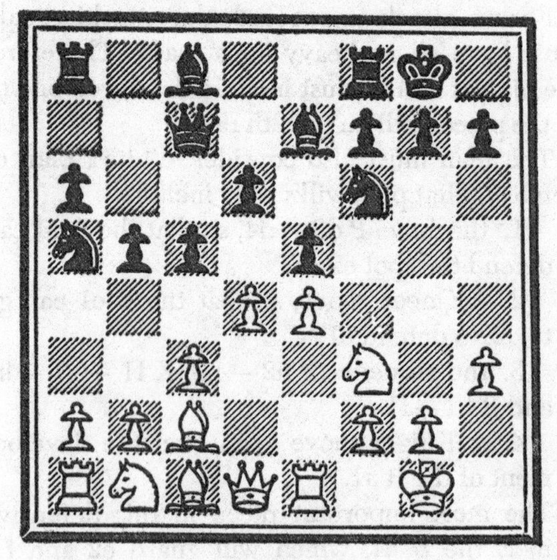

Figure 89

3. Scotch Game

1. P e2 – e4	P e7 – e5
2. K g1 – f3	Kt b8 – c6
3. **P d2 – d4**	P e5 x P d4
4. Kt f3 x P d4	Kt g8 – f6
5. Kt b1 – c3	B f8 – b4
6. Kt d4 x Kt c6	P b7 x Kt c6
7. B f1 – d3	P d7 – d5!

8. P e4 x P d5	P c6 x P d5
9. O – O	O – O
10. B c1 – g5	P c7 – c6
11. Q d1 – f3	B b4 – e7

Figure 90

4. **Sicilian Defense**

1. P e2 – e4	P c7 – c5
2. Kt g1 – f3	P d7 – d6
3. P d2 – d4	P c5 x P d4
4. Kt f3 x P d4	Kt g8 – f6
5. Kt b1 – c3	P a7 – a6
6. B f1 – e2	P e7 – e5
7. Kt d4 – b3	B f8 – e7
8. O – O	O – O
9. B c1 – e3	B c8 – e6
10. P f2 – f4	Q d8 – c7

Figure 91

CHAPTER V

MORE GOOD MOVES

We have learned some ways of gaining material in chess—by the strategems known as the **fork, the pin** and the **hurdle.** In this chapter, we shall examine more attacking weapons. First, let us meet the:

1. **Discovered Check**

Figure 92

It is White's move. Black is not in check, but any move of the Kt e5 will unleash the power of the R e1 – check to the K e8. The Knight, therefore, can go to any square without worrying (except to f7, where the Black King can capture him and get out of check at the same time).

What are some good squares for the Knight? On g6 he will attack the R h8; on c4 or d7 he can attack the Q b6. In every case the Black King must worry about the check from the R e1. The most attractive check is on d7, for if the K goes to d8, he walks into another discovered check, this time from the Q d1.

2. **Double Check**

Most powerful of all "discovered checks" is a **double check**—check by the piece moving *and* the piece unscreened.

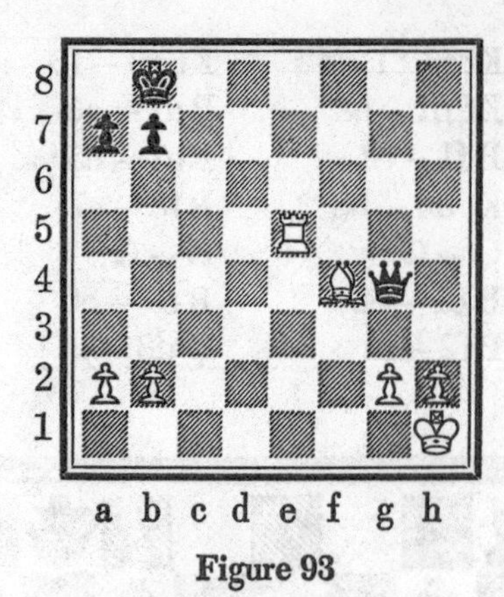

Figure 93

Black is not worried about a mere discovered check, for he can capture the Bishop if the Rook attacks his Queen. However, R e5 – e8 double check—and mate!

In the following diagram, White can double check or he can win Black's Queen, but it is more valuable to win a rank.

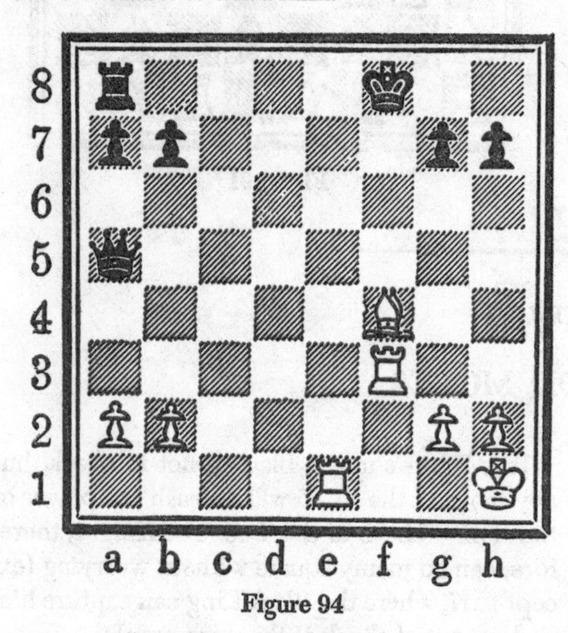

Figure 94

White can win the Queen by B – d2 ch or c7 ch (both checks are discovered by the R f3). He can also double check on d6—to no purpose, since the King can move to g8. On g8 the King could be checked on e8—were it not for that Rook on a8. The discovered check can win that eighth rank!

1. B f4 – b8 discovered check! K f8 – g8
2. R e1 – e8 checkmate!

Exercise No. 6

Try these for discovered checks: (Figs. 95-100)

I.

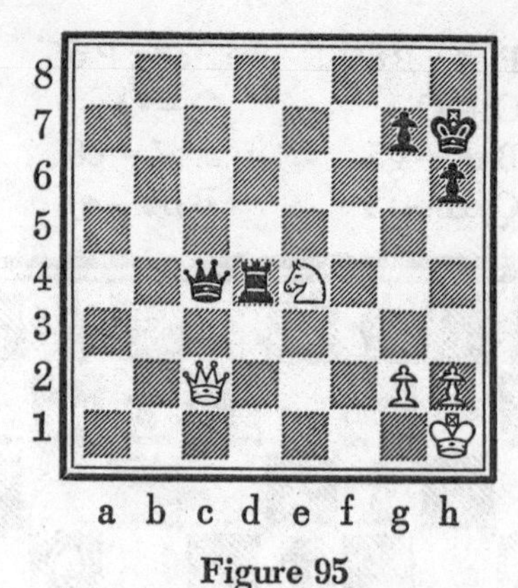

Figure 95

II.

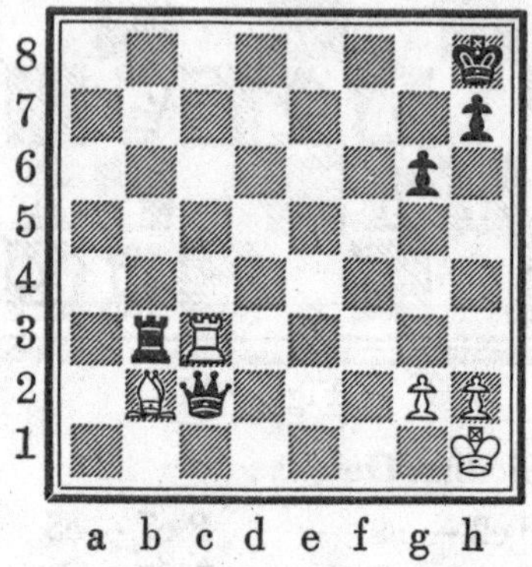

Figure 96

III.

Figure 97

IV.

Figure 98

V.

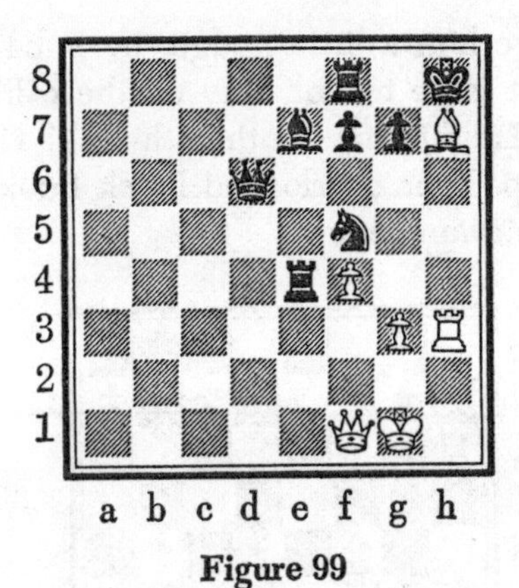

Figure 99

VI.

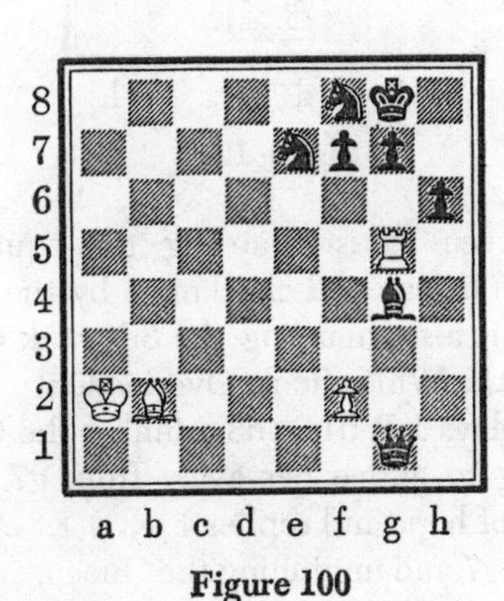

Figure 100

3. Desperado

Examine the following situation: (Fig. 101)

The White Knight *and* the White Bishop are attacked. There is no way in which *both* can be saved, since one can not protect the other. Both pieces, therefore, are desperadoes: since one or the other has to lose his life, he takes what he can get for it:

1. B x P e6	K x B e6
2. K g1 – f2	or
1. Kt x P f5 ch	P e6 x Kt f5
2. B b3 – c2.	

In each case, the reduced material gives White good chances for a draw.

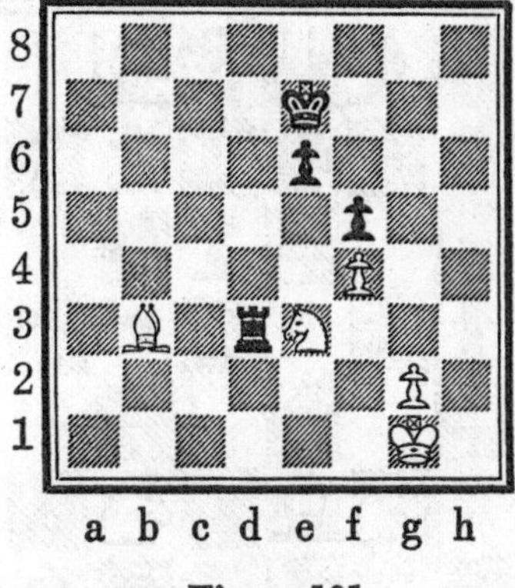

Figure 101

Another example:

Figure 102

White has attacked Black's Queen, and Black, instead of moving her, has attacked White's Queen in turn. Now the White Queen is a desperado, so she plays:

1. Q e4 x R e8! This makes the Black Queen a desperado, so Black replies: . . . Q d6 x R d1.

White still has a life to lose:

2. Q e8 x R f8 check! K x Q f8
3. R f1 x Q d1, with a Rook ahead.

A desperado situation can arise early in the game, as witness the following position at the end of White's tenth move, in a game for the World's Championship (1948) between the World Champion (M. Botvinnik) and the former champion (MAX EUWE):

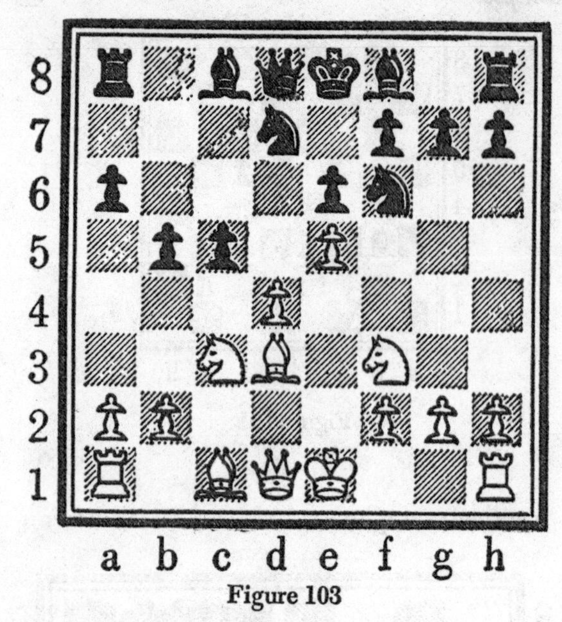

Figure 103

Black, to move, instead of moving his Kt f6, which is attacked by the P e5, played P c5 x P d4. This makes the W Kt at c3 a desperado. White played Kt c3 x P b5, not worrying about losing his Kt to the P a6, because he can capture the Kt f6.

But now Black's Knight is a desperado—either Kt, since he can win a Kt in return. He can play Kt d7 x P e5 and after Kt f3 x Kt e5, P a6 x Kt b5. (The game mentioned continued 11 . . . P x Kt b5. 12 P x Kt f6, Q d8 – b6.)

This series of moves is a regular opening, named the **Meran Defense to the Queen's Gambit** (see next chapter). It is frequently played in tournament games between great players.

4. Overloaded Piece

The **overloaded piece** is thoroughly occupied:

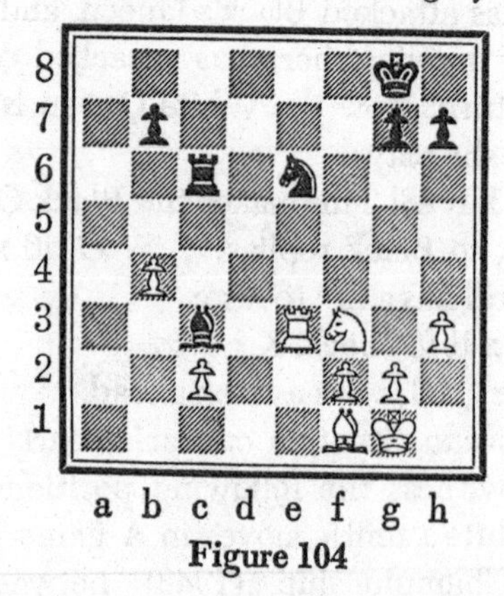

Figure 104

The Rook c6 is defending the Knight e6 and the Bishop c3, both attacked by the WR e3.

Just give him a little nudge—by P b4 – b5. Now what is he to do? Stay on the c file? He loses the Knight. Stay on the 6th rank? He loses the Bishop. Poor overloaded Black Rook!

Another example:

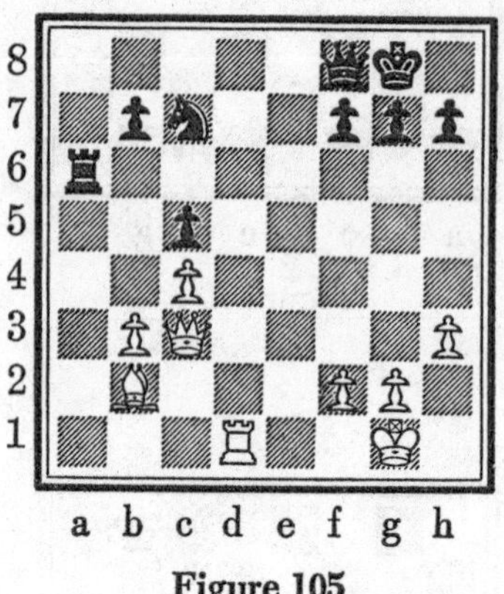

Figure 105

The Queen f8 is guarding the square g7 against the threatened checkmate by the White Queen. It is also guarding the 8th rank against a mate by the White Rook. Overloaded!

White plays 1 R d1 – d8, pinning the Queen, and trying to entice her away from g7. Black sees a ray of hope and replies 1 . . . Kt c7 – e8, defending g7 and unpinning the Queen.

But now the Knight is overloaded! 2 R d8 x Kt e8! Once more the overloaded Queen is attacked —and lost.

One more example, played by the author on the U. S. International Chess Team at the Hague, 1928 (Black was P. FRYDMANN of Poland):

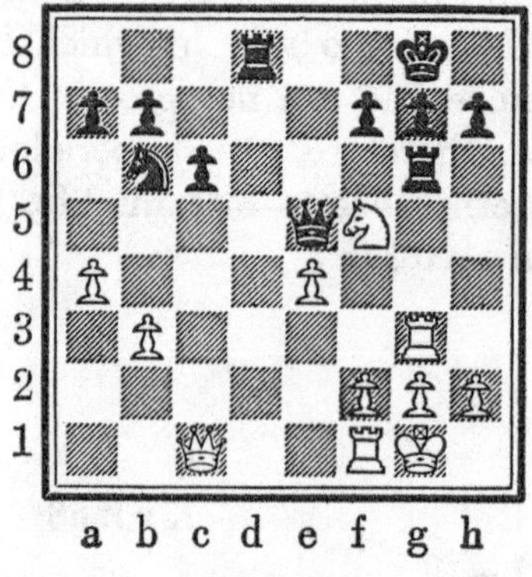

Figure 106

The position looks harmless for Black. His pieces are all developed; he has possession of the only open file, and his Queen is centralized.

Nevertheless, White creates an overloaded situation by **25. Q c1 – c3!** Suddenly the Black Queen finds itself embarrassed, having to protect e7 against a Kt check and also g7. For example, if 25 . . . Q e5 x Q c3, 26. Kt f5 – e7 ch, K g8 – f8; 27. Kt e7 x R g6 check, P h7 x Kt g6; 28. R g3 x Q c3. If Black plays 25 . . . Q – c7, then 26. Kt f5 x P g7. If he tries 25 . . . R g6 – e6, then 26. R g3 x P g7 ch.

Black must, therefore, protect the Q e5 and the square e7 at the same time. The only piece that can do that is the R d8: **25. R d8 – e8.** White moved 26. Q c3 x Q e5, R e8 x Q e5, **27. R f1 – d1!** This wins the Queen file, and produces another overloaded situation by the threat of R d1 – d8 mate: if R e5 retreats to e8, the Kt checks at e7 anyhow, and the R e8 can not capture it. 27 . . . K g8 – f8 won't do, because of 28. R d1 – d8 ch, R e5 – e8; 29. R d8 x R e8 ch, K x R e8; 30. R x R g6, P h7 x R g6; 31. Kt f5 – d6 ch and 32. Kt x P b7. On move 27 . . . P f7 – f6 cuts off the R g6 from the scene of battle, which will shift to the **d** file and the Queen's side of the board.

Black was forced to move **27 . . . P h7 – h6**, to get a loophole for his King. White then played simply **28. R g3 x R g6, P f7 x R g6; 29. Kt f5 – g3.** He now had a passed pawn on e4, which won the game quickly, added as it was to the possession of the Queen file and the threat to win the Knight by P – a5 (once the Black Rook went off the 5th rank).

The conclusion of the game was as follows:

(after 29. Kt f5 – g3) . . .	R e5 – c5
30. P h2 – h4!	P a7 – a5
31. R d1 – d8 ch	K g8 – h7
32. R d8 – b8	R c5 – c3
33. R b8 x P b7	R c3 x P b3
34. P e4 – e5	P c6 – c5
35. P e5 – e6	P c5 – c4
36. P e6 – e7	Resigns

Even at the end there is an overloaded situation: The Black Rook must stop the Pawn *and* guard the Knight; he can not do both. The poor Black King can not get into the game; for if 30 . . . P g6 – g5, 31. P h4 – h5.

Here is a refresher on **desperadoes** and **overloaded pieces:** (White to move in each case).

Exercise No. 6A

I.

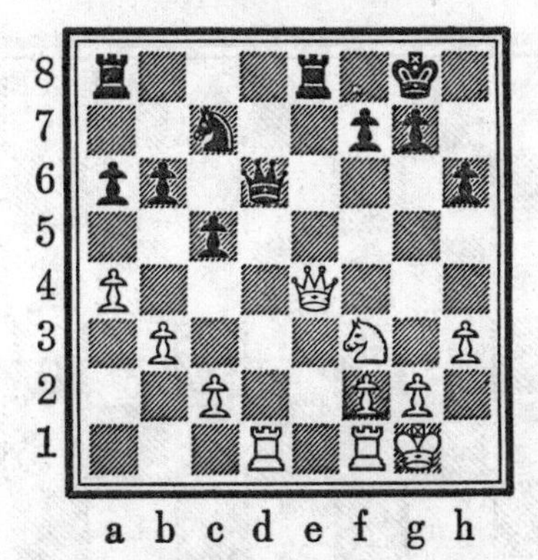

Figure 107

II.

Figure 108

III.

Figure 109

IV.

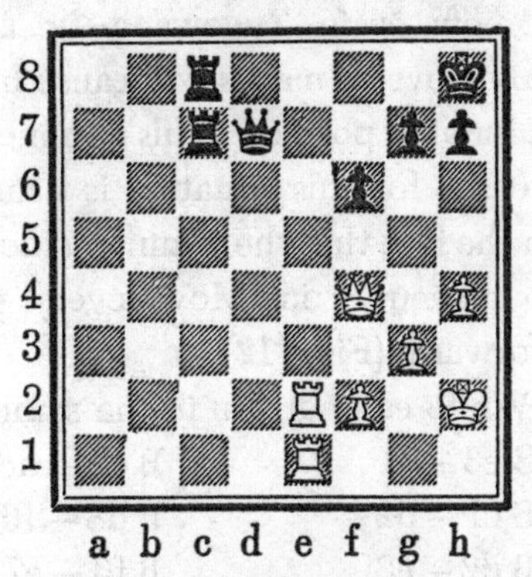

Figure 110

5. Zugzwang and 6. Tempo

Figure 111

It is White's move. He would be very happy if it were *not,* for any move made by Black would allow White to capture a Pawn or make an entry with his King leading to a Pawn capture: e.g.,

1 . . . B e8 – f7;	2 B x P c6
1 . . . B e8 – d7;	2 B x P g6
1 . . . K e7 – d7;	2 K e5 – f6
1 . . . K e7 – f7;	2 K e5 – d6

White, therefore maneuvers so as to get the same position with Black to move:

1. B e4 – c2	B e8 – f7
2. B c2 – d3	B f7 – e8
3. B d3 – e4	There you are!

The move White has gained (or lost, if you wish) is called **a tempo, a time move.**

Black now is in **Zugzwang—in a position where any move he makes will cause him to lose some material or position to his opponent.**

The reason for this situation is usually to be found in the fact that the winning side has more room to maneuver in. Move every piece one square forward: (Fig. 112)

Now White can not win in the same manner:

1. B e3 – c1	B e7 – d8
2. B c1 – d2	B d8 – f6
3. B d2 – e3	B f6 – e7

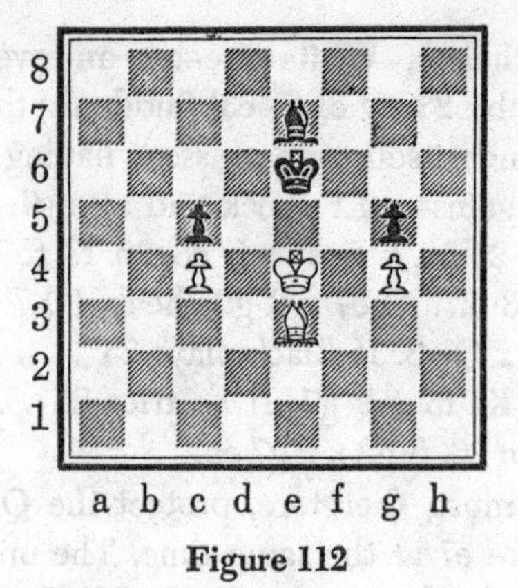

Figure 112

He looks further, and sees that the Bl B must also be on e7 when the WB is on e1:

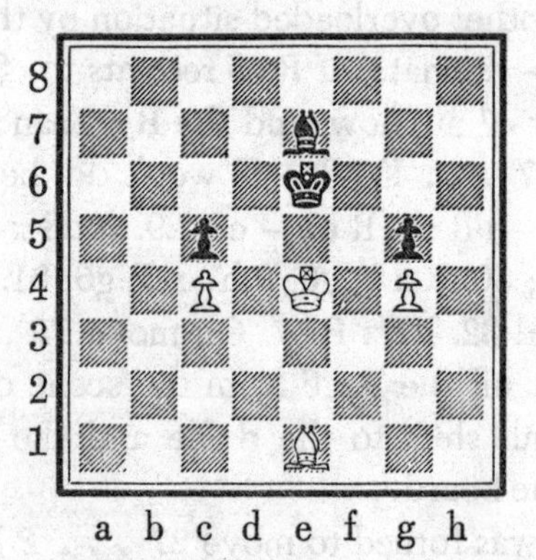

Figure 113

Black, to move, would lose:

1. . . .	B – d8 (or f6)
2. B – f2	B – e7

3. B – e3—and we have the first position where Black is in Zugzwang. Or try:

1. . . .	B – f8 (or d6)
2. B – d2	B – e7
3. B – e3	(Same position)

White, to move, can force this:

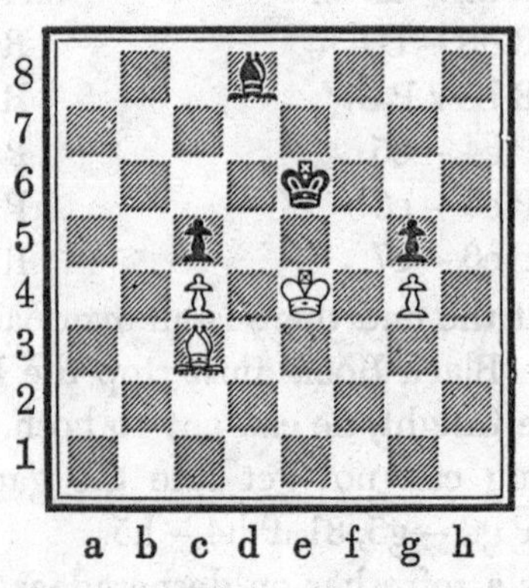

Figure 114

Looking ahead on the B's diagonal he sees two squares to **tempo** on, a5 and d2.

1. B c3 – d2 B d8 – f6
2. B d2 – a5 B f6 – e7
3. B g3 – e1 and wins, as above.

Another situation:

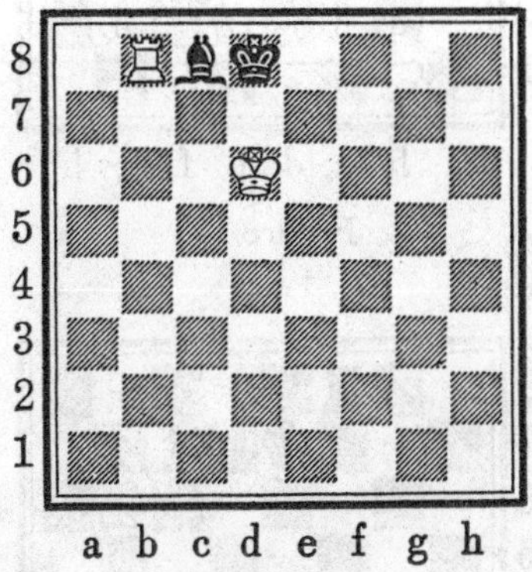

Figure 115

Black's only legal move is K d8 – e8, which would lose the Bishop.

White, to move, makes a **tempo**: R b8 – a8, forcing Black to move K d8 – e8, whereupon R a8 x B c8 ch, etc.

Another example:

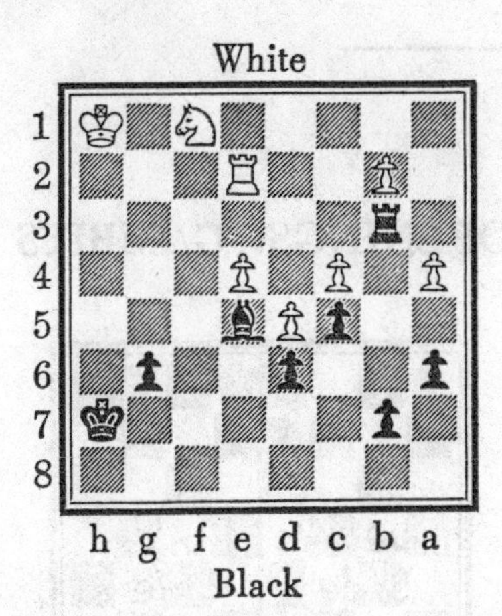

Figure 116

This is from a game played in the Hastings International Tournament of 1954-1955. The Dutch Champion, J. H. DONNER, with Black, could have won a Pawn from his opponent, W. A. FAIRHURST, the Champion of Scotland, by playing either R b3 x P b2 or B e5 x P b2.

He preferred, however, to set up a mild type of Zugzwang position by B e5 – f4. Why? White's one threat was to get his Knight via e3 to g4; then push his P e4 to e5, obtaining a passed pawn on the **d** file. The B move prevents the Knight from moving to e3. On h2, it can be exchanged. In the meantime, Black's King comes over from h7, to occupy the vacated square on e5.

It is interesting to note how much more value one great player places on restricting his opponent's pieces than on winning material!

7. Zwischenzug

Another German term—due, doubtless, to the fact that for years most of the tournaments were played in Germany and reported in books written in that language—this one means **"in-between move."** The idea is simple: You want to make a certain move. If you do, you will get an unpleasant response. Therefore, you first make a move which will make that reply impossible:

Figure 117

White would like to capture the P e5 with his R h5. If he does, however, Black replies R a8 – a4 ch. The WK is forced to d5 to protect his R; whereupon, R a4 – a5 ch wins the R.

But first the **zwischenzug** 1. R h5 – f5 check. Now if . . . K f6 – e6, 2 R f5 x P e5 ch, K e6 – f6; 3 R e5 – f5 ch, K f6 – e6; 4 R x P f4.

On move 1, if . . . K f6 – g6, we can stop for another **zwischenzug** 2. P h4 – h5 ch, forcing K g6 – h7, where it is out of play, and then capture on e5.

Another example: (Fig. 118)

White would like to capture the Rook on a5. If he does, however, he will be checkmated (by Q f6 x P b2). A **zwischenzug** will help: 1. B d2 – c3. The Queen f6 must move off the diagonal, and the WB can then capture the Bl R.

Solve this one yourself, before looking at the solution: (Fig. 119)

White would like to make a Queen by pushing his P f7 to f8. If he does, however, Black follows suit, by playing P c2 – c1 (Q) check—and mate! If White tries first 1. R e2 x P c2, then the recapture . . . R c8 x R c2 threatens mate. If then 2. K a1 – b1, R c2 – b2 check (zwischenzug) 3. K b1 – c1, B e8 – d7, and wins the game. 1. R e2 – d2 check is met by . . . K d7 – e6, attacking the Pawn, with all the same threats.

The correct move is (**zwischenzug**) 1. P f7 – f8 (Kt) **check**. The King can not move on to the **c** line, or he will lose the P c2 with check. Therefore: 1 . . . K d7 – d6. Now comes (zwischenzug) 2 R e2 – d2 check! The Knights now block off the **e** file, and the King is forced to cut off his Rook: 2 . . . K d6 – c6; 3. R x P c2 ch, K c6 – b7; 4 R x R c8, and White wins eventually by queening one of his Pawns.

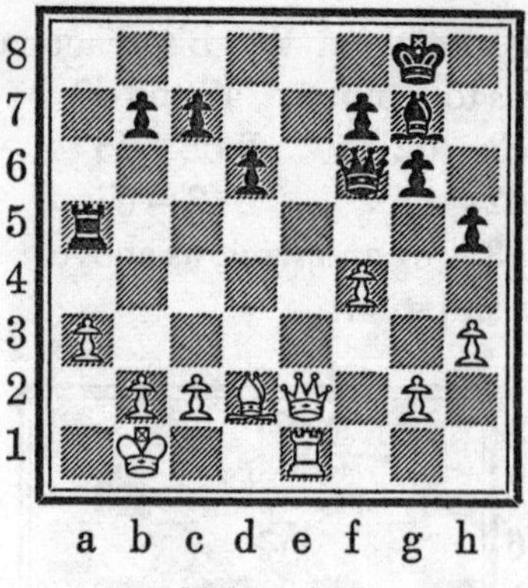

Figure 118

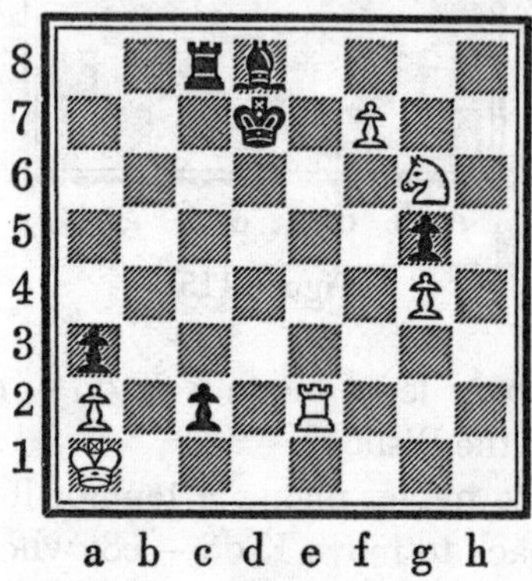

Figure 119

CHAPTER VI

DESCRIPTIVE NOTATION: MORE OPENINGS: GAMBITS

You may have noticed that when you see a game in the newspaper (American and British only), it is written differently.

Tradition accounts for this. We former colonists of Britain still cling to the notation which originated two hundred years ago. In the early books you might see something like this:

"King's Knight to his Bishop's third square."

More briefly, that would be written nowadays: **KKt – B3** or **Kt – KB3.** And this is how we arrive at the system: Let us reexamine the board: (Fig. 120)

When we first set up the pieces, the Kings are opposite each other. So are the Queens. If we draw a line down the middle of the board, we divide it into two halves: the King's side and the Queen's side.

Figure 120

The King is on the square called King One (K1); the Queen is on Q1. The Pawns in front of them are on K2 and Q2; squares in front of the Pawns are K3 and Q3; K4 and Q4, and so on up to K8 and Q8.

The major difference between the notation systems is that in this **descriptive notation,** the squares are numbered from both sides of the board. Thus, the Pawn in front of the Black King is on White's K7, but on Black's K2. The White Queen is on White's Q1, but on Black's Q8.

The moves: 1. **P – K4 P – K4** mean that each player moves the Pawn in front of his King two squares.

Each player has two Bishops, two Knights and two Rooks. These now become the King Bishop and Queen Bishop (KB and QB) King Knight and Queen Knight (KKt and QKt) and King Rook and Queen Rook (KR and QR). The Pawns in front of these pieces become the King Bishop Pawn (KBP) King Knight Pawn, etc., until our chess board looks like this:

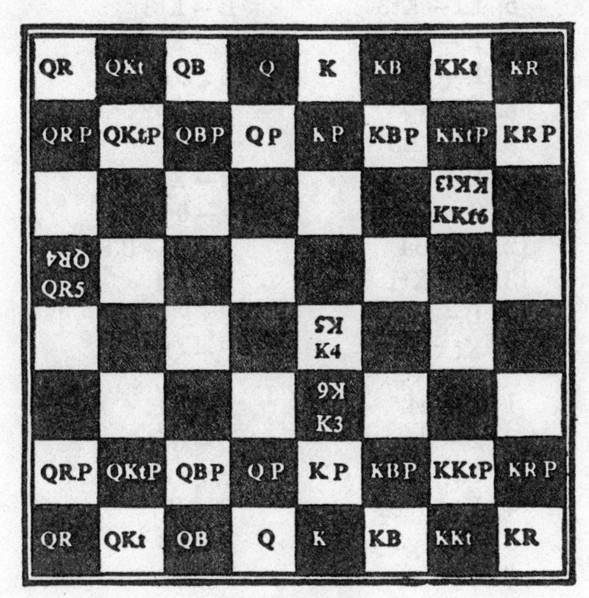

Figure 121

The pieces are placed on the 1 (*one*) file: Q1, QB1, QKt1 and QR1; K1, KB1, KKt1 and KR1. The Pawns are on the 2 (*two*) file: Q2, QB2, etc. The other squares are numbered 3 to 8: e.g., QB3, QB4, . . . to QB8; KKt3, KKt4 . . . to KKt8.

Since we measure from *both* sides of the board, White's QR5, is Black's QR4; White's KKt6 is Black's KKt3.

In noting games, unnecessary terms are left out. Thus, if we move our KP two squares, we write **P – K4,** since only that Pawn standing on K2 can go to K4.

However, if there are two Knights which can go to B3, we must specify which B3: **Kt – KB3** or **Kt – QB3.** (In the system we first learned, we should say simply **Kt – c3 or Kt – f3.**)

If two pieces of the same value can go to the same square, we must specify rank or file of origin. For example, after the moves 1. P – Q4 P – Q4 2 Kt – Q2 Kt – Q2, White, if he wants to move his Kt on KKt 1 to KB3 must write down **Kt (1) – B3,** since the other Knight can also go there. If he wants to move the Kt on Q2 to KB3, he must write: **Kt (2) – B3.** He could also write **Kt (Q) – B3** or **QKt – B3** for the same move.

In the following diagram White, to move, wants to capture the Pawn on his QB7 with a Rook. He must write: **R (Kt) x P** or **R (Q) x P.** He need not specify R (Q) x **QBP,** because if he took the KKtP, it would be a **check.**

Figure 122

After a Rook captures the Pawn, one of the Black Knights can recapture the Rook. This is written **Kt (3) x R or Kt (1) x R.**

If it were Black's move in the diagram, he could capture either White Rook with his Bishop. He writes B x R (Kt2) or B x R (Q2).

Place a Black Pawn on QKt5, and you would have to specify further: R (Kt7) x BP.

Exercise No. 7

1. In figure 123, page 52, name the squares of the White pieces from White's point of view, and the Black pieces from Black's point of view:

2. Where are the Black pieces, from White's point of view?

Now for some more openings; two in **both** notations:

Figure 123

French Defense: (Fig. 124)

1. P – K4	**P – K3**
2. P – Q4	**P – Q4**
3. Kt – QB3	B – Kt5
4. P – K5	P – QB4
5. P – QR3	B x Kt ch
6. P x B	Kt – K2
7. Q – Kt4	P x P
8. Q x Kt P	R – Kt1
9. Q x P	Q – B2
10. Kt – K2	QKt – B3
11. P – KB4	

1. P – e4	P – e6
2. P – d4	P – d5
3. Kt – c3	B – b4
4. P – e5	P – c5
5. P – a3	B x Kt c3 ch
6. P x B c3	Kt – e7
7. Q – g4	P c5 x P d4
8. Q x P g7	R h8 – g8
9. Q x P h7	Q – c7
10. Kt – e2	Kt b8 – c6
11. P – f4	

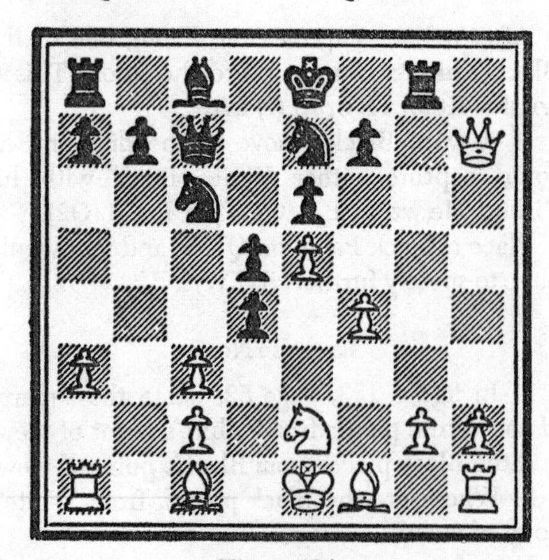

Figure 124

Note: On move 8, White must specify Q x **KtP**, since he can also take the QP or the KP. On move 9, however, he need not specify Q x **RP**, since Q x **BP** is **check.** Move 10 must specify the Knight. It could also be written Kt (1) – B3 or Kt (Kt) – B3.

The algebraic notation (second columns) can be simplified considerably. Move 7 for Black can be written c x d4; in some books you might find only cd: (the : meaning takes).

Caro-Kann Defense: (Fig. 125)

1. P – K4	**P – QB3**
2. P – Q4	**P – Q4**
3. Kt – QB3	P x P
4. Kt x P	B – B4
5. Kt – Kt3	B – Kt3
6. P – KR4	P – KR3
7. B – Q3	B x B
8. Q x B	Kt – Q2
9. Kt – B3	Q – B2
10. B – Q2	P – K3
11. 0 – 0 – 0	0 – 0 – 0
12. P – B4	Kt (1) – B3
13. K – Kt1	P – B4
14. B – B3	P x P
15. Kt x P	P – QR3

1. P – e4	P – c6
2. P – d4	P – d5
3. Kt – c3	P x P e4
4. Kt x P e4	B – f5
5. Kt – g3	B – g6
6. P – h4	P – h6
7. B – d3	B x B d3
8. Q x B d3	Kt – d7
9. Kt – f3	Q – c7
10. B – d2	P – e6
11. 0 – 0 – 0	0 – 0 – 0
12. P – c4	Kt (g8) – f6
13. K – b1	P – c5
14. B – c3	P x P d4
15. Kt x P d4	P – a6

You now have a wide choice of openings in case the first move is P – K4 (P – e4). Each of these openings has many variations, of which only one has been given. Entire books have been devoted to each of these openings.

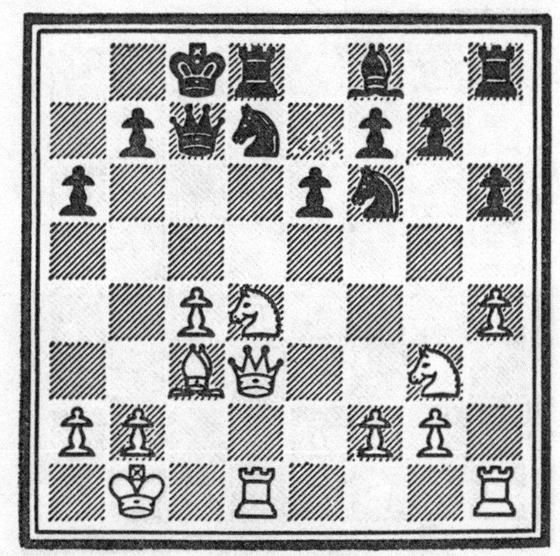

Figure 125

Each opening has its characteristics: e.g., in the **Ruy Lopez,** White tries to grip the center while he builds up a King's side attack; Black, on the other hand, attacks on the Queen's side. In the **Sicilian Defense** the situation is somewhat the same. In the **French Defense,** Black allows his King's side to be broken up, in order to have time to destroy White's center. The **Caro-Kann** is a solid defense, now not so popular as in the 1920's, when the World Champion, José Raul Capablanca, played it with great success, scoring some of his most famous victories with it. At the moment, the Sicilian is the most popular defense; the French second.

Why a "defense" at all? Why not let White play his Ruy Lopez or his Scotch game? Because lurking in the dark recesses of your opponent's mind might be a surprise opening with the dreaded name of "gambit." And woe betide him who knows naught of gambits!

Gambits

A gambit is a sacrifice. A player gives up a Pawn (usually a Bishop Pawn) for the following hoped-for advantages:

1. He lures a center Pawn (KP or QP) away from the center.
2. He gets a wide-open position for his pieces.
3. He develops his pieces quickly and naturally, while
4. His opponent spends time protecting his gambit Pawn; and
5. His opponent cramps his pieces' actions by defending the Pawn.

The most exciting gambit is the **King's Gambit.**

1. P – K4 P – K4
2. P – KB4 P x P (The gambit is accepted.)
3. Kt – KB3

Now what is Black to do? He can protect his Pawn painfully by 3 . . . P – KKt4, 4 . . . P – KR3, etc. But then White plays B – B4; Castles; P – Q4, etc., getting a strong attack against the Black King, which must remain in the wide-open center, while his pieces try to protect his gambit Pawn. Only a great deal of study and experience will enable you to get away with it. (See the next game for some of the troubles you will have.)

Modern players defend by (a) developing (b) countering.

The logical move for accomplishing these goals is:

3. . . . Kt – KB3

Now, if 4. P – K5, Kt – R4; and the Knight protects the gambit Pawn from a safe place, while the advanced White KP becomes an object of attack by . . . P – Q3. His exchange for that Pawn would bring the Black Bishop to Q3, from where it would protect the P on KB5 (f4).

4. Kt – B3 P – Q4

This freeing move should be made, whenever possible, in nearly all King's Gambits.

5. P x P Kt x P
6. Kt x Kt Q x Kt

The exchange, developing Black's Queen, is usually not good; but White hopes to drive her away with the gain of time.

7. P – Q4 B – K2

Strangely enough, this move of the B protects the Pawn on KB5 better than B – Q3—which White would meet by 8. P – QB4, Q – K5 ch; 9. K – B2, with threats of P – B5, B – Q3 and R – K1.

8. P – B4 Q – K5 ch
9. K – B2 B – KKt5
10. B – Q3 B – R5 ch

Attack by the defending Bishop! If 11. Kt x B? Q x QP ch and 12 . . . B x Q.

11. K – B1 Q – K2
12. B x BP Kt – B3
13. P – KR3 B x Kt
14. Q x B Kt x P
15. Q x P 0 – 0

16. Q – K4

If 16. Q x BP, Q – Kt5; 17. R – Q Kt1, Kt – K3; 18. Q – Q6, Q – R5, threatening Q x RP and R – Q1, with great advantage to Black.

16. . . .	Q x Q
17. B x Q	R (R) – K1
18. B – Q3	R – K2

Figure 126

The foregoing moves were from a game between E. CANAL, of Peru, and NORCIA, of Italy, in an International Masters Tournament in Venice, 1953. The winner of the tournament, Canal, played White. In the Position in the diagram, Black has control of the K file; he can double his Rooks, and has two well-placed minor pieces. White, on the other hand, has regained his gambit Pawn and has two Bishops. The bad position of the White King is a chronic symptom of the King's Gambit.

Some more exciting Gambits:

Muzio Gambit

1. P – K4	P – K4
2. P – KB4	P x P
3. Kt – KB3	P – K Kt4
4. B – B4	P – Kt5
5. O – O! (Fig. 127)	

White gives up a whole Knight! Why?

a. Black has no pieces developed.

b. Black has shattered his own King's side by (1) protecting his gambit Pawn (2) chasing the Knight.

c. The square f7 (KB7) is under attack by the B, and will be more so once the f file (KB file) is opened.

Still, Black must capture. . . .

5. . . .	P x Kt
6. Q x P	Q – B3

Figure 127

a. —defends the Pawn

b. —protects the vital diagonal a1 – h8

c. —threatens Q – Q5 ch and Q x B.

7. P – Q3	B – R3
8. Kt – B3	Kt – K2
9. B x P	B x B
10. Q x B	Q x Q
11. R x Q	P – KB4
12. P x P	P – B3
13. R – K1	K – Q1
14. B – B7	P – Q4
15. P – B6	Kt – Kt3
16. B x Kt	P x B
17. R – K7	Kt – Q2
18. R – Kt7	Kt – B1

This is analysis by one of the greatest players of his day (CHIGORIN). Black can wiggle out by . . . B – Q2 and K – B2 – Q3; or, if White moves 19. P – B7, K – K2.

8. Evans Gambit

1. P – K4	P – K4
2. Kt – KB3	Kt – Q B3
3. B – B4	B – B4
4. P – Q Kt4	B x P
5. P – B3	B – R4
6. P – Q4	P – Q3
7. O – O	B – Kt3

Black's seventh move (together with his sixth) is the feature of the defense (to the Evans Gambit) which was invented by DR. EMANUEL LASKER, World Chess Champion from 1894 to 1921.

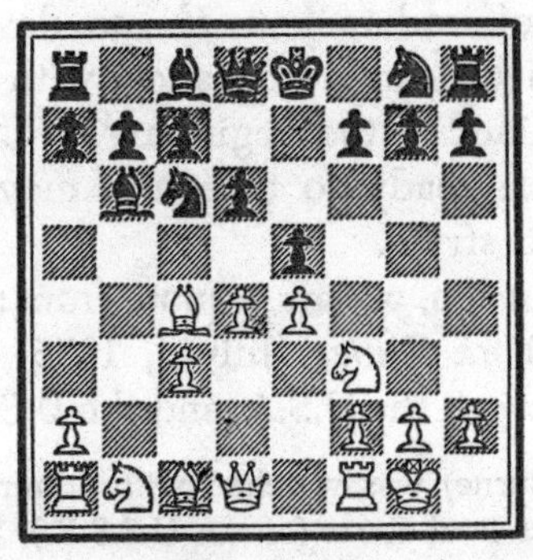

Figure 128

Black turns down the offer of a second Pawn; solidifies his center (move 6) and then attacks the White center (P on Q4). He does not exchange Pawns at this moment, because the WP on B3 prevents the Kt from coming to his natural square.

A game from an All-Gambit Tournament (Baden 1914) continued:

8. B – R3	P x P

Now he exchanges because he wants

a. to avoid the opening of the line a3 – f8

b. to attack quickly the point d4.

9. P x P	B – Kt5

This pin removes all protection from d4. Pushing the QP would block White's B on B4 and give Black a fine square on e5. White, therefore, counterpins.

10. B – Kt5	B x Kt
11. B x Kt ch	

Forced, since if 11 P x Kt, Q – Kt4 ch wins the B.

11. . . .	P x B
12. P x B	Kt – K2
13. K – R1	Kt – Kt3
14. R – Kt1	O – O

Black is a Pawn ahead, and has the better position because of White's exposed King. The Gambit has been repulsed.

Another famous gambit is the

Danish Gambit

1. P – K4	P – K4
2. P – Q4	P x P
3. P – Q B3	P x P
4. B – Q B4	P x P
5. B x KtP	

The Bishops look terrifying, but now comes our saving counter move:

5. . . .	P – Q4!
6. B x QP	Kt – K B3

Figure 128A

7. B x P ch!	K x B
8. Q x Q	Black has lost his Q!?
8. . . .	B – Kt5 ch!

Now it's White's turn!

9. Q – Q2 (else R x Q)	B x Q ch
10. Kt x B	

Let's count: All forces even; Bishops of opposite colors. The rest depends on the speedier plan of action and execution.

Gambits can be found in all openings—some good, and some bad. The American champion (until 1936) FRANK J. MARSHALL had great success with the

Wing Gambit

1. P – K4 P – Q B4 (**Sicilian Defense**)

2. P – Q Kt4! P x P

3. P – Q R3! and even after the spoilsports answered this with 3. . . .

P – Q4! he was still studying the variation at the time of his death:

4. P x P	Kt – K B3
5. Kt – K B3	B – Kt5
6. B – K2	Q x P
7. O – O	

In the **French Defense** there is a blockading gambit:

Blockading Gambit

1. P – K4	P – K3
2. P – Q4	P – Q4
3. P – K5	P – Q B4
4. Kt – K B3	P x P
5. B – Q3	

White strengthens the point e5 at all costs, while the presence of the Black Pawn on d4 prevents Black from gaining a similar square. The natural developing moves for Black make P –

B3 necessary. White can then exchange, and gain the square e5, or continue to blockade. This variation provided ARON NIMZOVICH, one of the world's greatest players, with some fine victories. You will find complete games in his books: *My System* and *Chess Praxis*.

In every opening, gambits can be found. They are fun to play in off-hand games. In match games, the player offering the gambit has the advantage of surprise on his side. In tournament games, where moves are timed, the advantage is doubled by the fact that the player to whom the gambit is offered has to decide, **before making even one move,** whether to accept it or not. The minutes ticking away in his ear often influence a hasty decision!

But you, as a player, should not worry about a gambit offered to you. If you develop your pieces quickly, in accordance with the principles outlined at the beginning of Chapter IV, you will be ready to take any move of your opponent in stride.

In conclusion, we must quote from a report in the *New York Times* (July 4, 1955) about the match between the U.S.A. and the U.S.S.R.:

> Robert (Byrne) was watched with admiration in his game against Paul Keres (of the U.S.S.R.). Byrne made a daring move: he opened with the King's Gambit.
>
> That gambit was once classic in chess but went out of fashion with the experts several decades ago. Keres wrote a book about the King's Gambit and revived it. Byrne dared to use it against Keres today.
>
> The story would be better if Byrne had scored a great success, but he didn't. When the game was adjourned, he was two Pawns behind.

CHAPTER VII

FURTHER POWERS OF THE PIECES: ATTACK, DEFENSE, COMBINATIONS, COUNTERATTACKS

ATTACK

The first rule of attack is:

a. **Attack what is nailed down.**

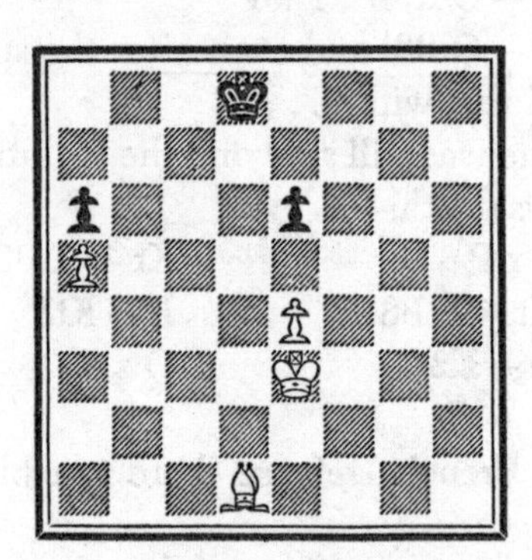

Figure 129

The Bishop can attack both Black Pawns. Pe6, however, can move to e5; whereas the Pa6 can not move. White's correct move is, therefore, B – e2 (B – K2).

Suppose, however, White's Pawn were at a4 instead of a5. If White played B – e2, Black could move Pa6 – a5. If then White moved Be2 – c4, attacking the Pe6, Black could answer Pe6 – e5. The Bishop could no longer attack the Black Ps, which would be on different colored squares.

The correct move (with the WP on a4, in the diagram above) would be Pa4 – a5:

b. **Nail it down!**

Now the Black King could defend the Pawn: 1 . . . Kd8 – c7; 2 Bd1 – e2 Kc7 – b7. But then 3 Pe4 – e5! nailing down the other Pawn, which the Bishop can capture when he is ready.

A third rule is obvious, yet must be stated:

c. **Attack what can not escape!**

Figure 130

The Black Knight appears to be all alone on the side of the board, and it seems logical to play **1 R – Kt4,** attacking him. However, Black replies 1 . . . P – Kt4, and after 2 R x P ch, K – B2 3 R – R5, Kt – Kt3.

A second look will reveal that it is the Black Bishop which can not escape. The correct move is, therefore, **R – Q Kt1,** preparing R – Kt8 and R x B.

d. Make use of the attack weapons: Fork, Pin, Hurdle.

A double (sometimes triple) attack is a means of nailing down an objective, since only one of the opponent's pieces can usually escape. If the King is one of the pieces, so much the better.

In some cases, however, it is necessary to combine several moves in order to gain material:

The White Rook pins the Black Bishop on the Rook. A glance at the Black King, however, shows that it is on the same diagonal as his Bishop. White, by sacrificing his Rook, **changes the power** of the Black piece into one which can be pinned against the King: (Fig. 131)

1. R x B! R x R
2. B – B4

Now the Rook is pinned, and can not be defended. White has given up a Rook (value = 5) and wins a Rook (5) and Bishop (3). Total gain = 3.

Other moves seem possible. For example White could play 1 B – B4 at once. Then if 1 . . . B x B, 2 R x R White gains 5 for 3, or 2. Not as good as the first case.

On B – B4, Black could try B – K3, seeming to protect his Rook. But White plays B x B check, and wins B and R.

If White moved first 1 B – B3, he would not win anything! Black could play 1 . . . B – K3 or even B – B3, defending his Rook and attacking White's Rook.

Another means of attack for White would be 1 B – Kt4, attacking the Rook. If Black replies 1 . . . R – Q1 or 1 . . . R – Q3, hanging on to his Bishop, White can play 2 R x B, R x R 3 B – K6 check, winning the Rook by a forking check.

What a variety of possibilities! Translated into basic terms we have:

1. Attack the pinned piece.
2. Change the power of a piece into one which you can pin (or fork).
3. Drive the defending piece onto a square where it can not be defended.

And for the defense: Move the pinned piece to defend the piece on which it is pinned.

Exercise No. 8.

Figure 131

I. To figure 131 add a White Pawn at QB2 (c2) and a Black Pawn at K2 (e7), and figure out the **one line of play** which will win material.

II. How would you win material in Figure 132?

Figure 132

Use of the **hurdle** as part of a combination must not be neglected. In the following diagram, the Black King and Queen are on a white diagonal—the color of the WB, which is attacked by the Black Q. If the B retreats to K2 or B1, in order to threaten a hurdle check, the Black K simply moves to Q3—and the threat is over. We notice that the WQ can check at KR1; but the Black K can move to Q3, protecting the Q.

Figure 133

However: 1 B – Kt7! pinning the Q, and luring it away from the protection of the King.

1. . . . Q x B
2. Q – R1 check, winning Q and game.

Here is a combination with the roles reversed:

Figure 134

1. R – QB4 (fork) or 1. R – QB1 (Pin) is met by . . . B – B4, protecting the Knight. But first:

1. R – R8 ch K – Q2
2. R x B! K x R
3. R – B1 pinning and winning the Kt. (White wins B and Kt for a R : 6 for 5)

Let us look a little deeper:

1. R – QB1 B – B4
2. P – Kt4 (attacking the protecting piece)
2. . . . Kt – Q5! with two forking threats—on e2 and f3.
3. R – R8 ch K – Q2! (Care is essential; if K – K2, 4 R – B7 ch and 5 P x B.) Now Black is safe, since the fork threat forces a R or K move by White, and the Bl K can escape via KB3 (f6).

For the attack: **a hurdle plus pin combination.**

For the defense: **Move the attacked piece with a counterthreat.**

Let's start again: 1 R – Q B4, B – B4; 2 P – Kt4? (attacking the defender). 2 . . . B – Q6! Another counterthreat: **a fork.** 3 R – B8 ch, K – Q2. Now Black will gain material—a R for a B or Kt.

Another example starts innocently enough:

Figure 135

White sees that the Bl B can retreat to f8 or e7, stopping many checks. He therefore exchanges it.

1. B x B R x B
2. R x R P x R

Now it comes:

3. Q x R! P x Q (If P – B5 ch, K – B
4. R – R8 ch K – Q2
5. R – R7 ch K – K3
6. R x Q, with a Rook ahead.

Let us go back to move 1:

1. . . . P x B
2. R – KB1 P – B5 ch
3. K – R1 Q – Q2 (If Q – K2, R(3) – KB3)
4. Q – R8 ch K – K2 The hurdle is set up.
5. R x P ch! K x R
6. R – R7 ch K – K3
7. R x Q K x R
8. Q – R7 ch K – K3
9. Q x R ch

White is far ahead in material, but he looks further:

10. Q – Kt5 ch K – K3?
11. Q – Q8!! Attack what can't escape!

Now wherever the R moves, he is lost.

11. . . . K – Kt4; 12 Q – K8 ch
11. . . . R – B4 or R2; 12 Q – Kt6 ch
11. . . . R – R3; 12 Q – QB8 ch.

Black should have gone to K5 on move 10. White would then win with his K side Pawns.

For the attack: **A hurdle can be prepared by a forcing check.**

A sacrifice can set up the hurdle.

For the defense: Examine carefully every move. Don't make a move just because it "looks" safe.

Exchange pieces which will be out of play.

Sometimes a piece can not be directly attacked, even if it is "nailed down." You must then prepare to attack it, preferably with a piece of little value.

Figure 136

The Black Knight is pinned. Strangely enough, the most direct method of attacking it is not the best one: 1 P – Kt4? P – Kt4; 2 P – R4, K – Kt3! 3 P – R5 ch Kt x P–and White does not have material enough for a win. As soon as White realizes that Black's only way of freeing himself is by the sequence of moves shown above (P – Kt4 and K – Kt3) the correct move becomes apparent.

1. P – R4!! Now, if . . . P – Kt4; 2 P x P and the Knight is attacked and lost. Any Black K move abandons the Kt.

Another example, to show how understanding of your opponent's plan of defense will show you the correct move:

Figure 137

The Black B is pinned. White wants to double his Rs on the QB file (R – B4 and R(2) – B2). If he does so immediately, however, the Black King comes over to defend: 1. R – B4? K – K2; 2. R(2) – B2, K – Q2. First, White must cut off the King:

1. R – K2!	P – R5!

Should White exchange? If he does, he opens the KKt file so that Black can escape with his Rook by checking on KKt1; then move his Bishop.

Should he let Black exchange? If so, he opens a Black diagonal for the Bishop to check on. (2R – B4? P x P; 3 P x P, B – Kt3 ch!)

The WK must move–and to a White square. Not to R1, because the R file can be opened (for a Black R escape check) nor to B1, because the advance of the RP will force open the R file. Therefore:

2. K – Kt2!	P – R6 ch
3. K – R1!	Now the plan proceeds:
3. . . .	P – Kt5
4. R – B4	P – B4
5. R(2) – B2	R – QR1
6. R x B ch	K – Kt3
7. P – B4! (threatens mate in 2)	P x Pe.p. (g4 x f3)
8. K – R2, and soon wins.	

The preparation was long: White made his plan, looked for defenses, avoided the defenses, and then proceeded.

If the attacking weapons are so strong, how can one defend against them? Following are methods of

DEFENSE

Defenses to the Pin

1. **Capture**–no loss.
2. **Capture**–to lose less.
3. **Interpose**
   (a) a piece of same power as the pinning piece.
   (b) a piece of lesser or equal value.
   (c) one piece, then another.
4. **Attack the pinning piece.**
5. **Protect the pinned piece.**
6. **Counter Pin.**
7. **Move** the sheltered piece with a threat.

Examples follow:

Figure 138

1. The Knight is well placed at Q5, but the threat of the loss of R for B dictates the move 1. Kt x B. Black replies Kt x Kt. The exchange of minor pieces has avoided loss for White.

Figure 139

2. The White Bishop is hopelessly lost. If White captures the pinning piece, however, he can limit his loss: 1. Q x R ch, K x Q, 2. B x B. White gains 5 + 3 for his 10 (loss = 2 instead of 3).

Aside from the smaller loss, White retains chances to win the game, with a B for 2 Ps. If he simply gave up the B, the winning chances, if any, would be with Black.

Figure 140

3. In order to save his pinned Bishop, White can **interpose** R – Q5 or R – Q2 (**a piece of the same power**) as the winning piece. Kt – Q5 would not do in *this* position, because it could be driven away by . . . P – B3. After 1. R – Q5, P – B3; 2. R x R, R x R; 3. R – Q2.

Figure 141

3(b). Here the Knight not only is pinned by the B, but is attacked by the Pawn. It seems completely lost. However,

1. P – B5!	B x P
2. P – K4!	This second interposition relieves the pin.

4. Attacking the pinning piece is a stratagem often used in the opening. For instance, in a French Defense, **McCutcheon variation,** after the moves:

1. P – K4	P – K3
2. P – Q4	P – Q4
3. Kt – QB3	Kt – KB3
4. B – Kt5	B – Kt5
5. P – K5	the pinned Knight is attacked.

Figure 142

Black counters 5 . . . P – KR3, attacking the pinning piece (the B). The seemingly dangerous

6. P x Kt	P x B
7. P x P	R – Kt1
8. Q – R5	Q – B3

9. Kt – K2 Q x KtP

is not bad for Black, who has two Bishops and an extra center Pawn. He will castle on the Q side. The usual line is:

6. B – Q2	B x Kt
7. P x B	Kt – K5
8. Q – Kt4	K – B
9. B – Q3	Kt x B
10. K x Kt	P – B4

Another opening, made popular for Black by World Champion Mikhail Botvinnik, is the following gambit in the **Semi-Slav Defense:**

1. P – Q4	P – Q4
2. P – QB4	P – K3
3. Kt – QB3	Kt – KB3
4. B – Kt5	P – B3
5. Kt – B3	P x P (the gambit accepted)
6. P – K4	P – QKt4 (to hold the Pawn)
7. P – K5	P – KR3
8. B – R4	P – Kt4 (attacking the pinning piece)

9. Kt x P (a sacrifice to maintain the pin.)

9. . . .	P x Kt
10. B x P	QKt – Q2

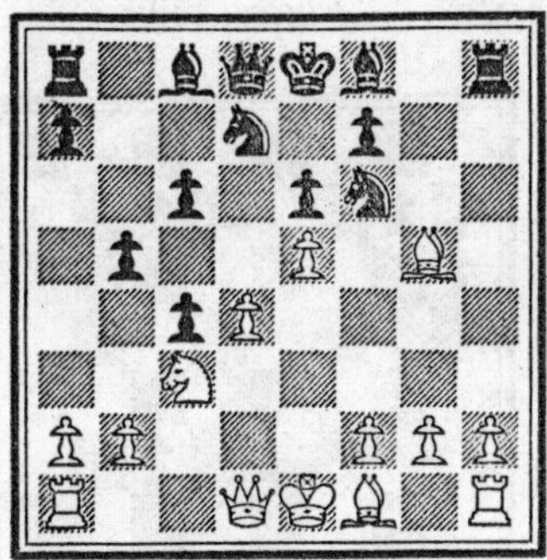

Figure 143

5. One of the simplest means of getting out of a pin is to protect the pinned piece:

Figure 144

White should play K – B3 or K – Q3, protecting the Knight and moving out of the line of the Rook. K – K3 or P – B3 would also protect the Knight, but it would remain pinned, and Black could win it by . . . P – B4.

Another example:

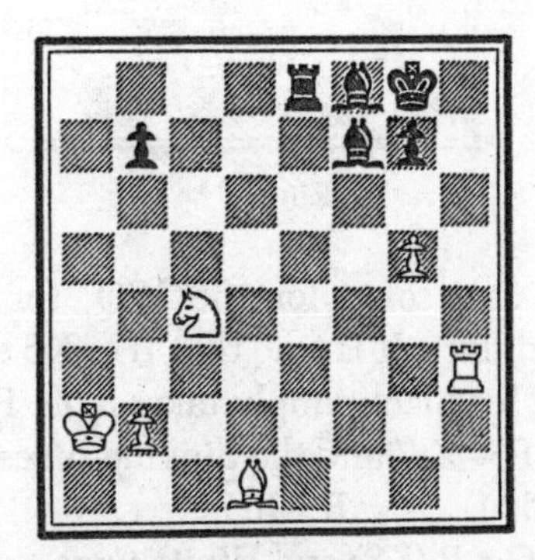

Figure 145

White should move 1. P – Kt3 or 1. B – Kt3, both of which would protect the Knight and also relieve the pin.

Not good would be 1. K – Kt3? or 1. R – B3? or 1. R – R4? because the Knight, altho protected, is still pinned, and would be lost after 1. . . . P – QKt4.

6. One of the prettiest defenses against a pin is by a **counter pin:**

Figure 146

The WQ is pinned, and seemingly lost, for no interposition is possible. White sees, however, that the Black K and B are on one diagonal. Thus—1. B – Kt3! and the Q is saved, since the Black B is now pinned.

Another example:

Figure 147

Don't feel sorry for the WQ, for she has a thousand lives. It is true that R – K6 does White no good, for Black simply takes it off. But:

1. R – Kt7 and the pinning piece is pinned.
   If 1. . . . R x R
2. Q x R (K8) and White wins.

7. Another defense is to move a piece with a counterthreat:

Figure 148

1. K – B2 relieves the pin and attacks a Black piece. If 1. . . . R x B, 2. K x Kt.

If the pin is not against the King, either piece can move with a counterthreat:

Figure 149

The White Knight is pinned and doubly attacked. To defend him by P – B3 would invite . . . P – B4. However, White has three defenses:

(a) 1. Q – QB3 (threatening checkmate on KKt7) . . . P – B4; 2. Kt – Kt3.

(b) 1. Kt – B5 (counterattack against a piece of equal value.) . . . R x Q; 2. Kt x Q.

(c) 1. Q – Q2, Q x Q; 2. Kt x Q.

Either piece was able to move with a counter threat.

In figure 137 we saw that one of the ways of relieving a pin was to move one of the pinned pieces away with a check. That, of course, is an immediate counterthreat.

Exercise No. 9: Defenses to Pins.

I.

Figure 150

II.

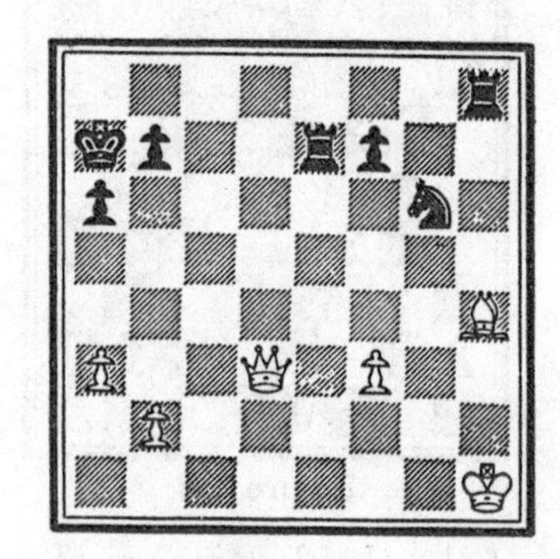

Figure 151

III.

Figure 152

IV.

Figure 153

V.

Figure 154

VI.

Figure 155

DEFENSES TO A FORK

These can be listed briefly:

1. **Capture with (a) no loss, (b) limited loss.**
2. **Interpose piece of equal power.**

Figure 156

3. **Move one forked piece to protect the other.**
4. **Move with a counterthreat: check, pin, fork, hurdle.**
5. **Move an unrelated piece with a threat.**

Two White pieces are forked, and he can not protect both. However, he can exchange Rooks:

1. R – R7 ch	K – Kt1
2. R x R	B x R

The fork has disappeared with the Rook.

Figure 157

White is in check, and may lose a full Rook at B6. However, he can limit his loss to the "exchange" by

1. R x B	R x R

Figure 158

King and Knight are forked. White can interpose three pieces at K4. But the only correct one is:

1. B – K4 (a piece of the same power). Now the Knight is protected as well as the King.

1. . . .	Kt – B4! Taking advantage of the Pin with a fork threat.
2. B x B	Kt x KP ch

3. K – R3 (Not K – Kt1, R – B8 mate!)
3. . . . Kt x B
4. R – K4 (limiting the Kt) P – Kt4
5. K – Kt2 P – Kt5
6. Kt – K4, and White is safe, with a draw in view.

Black avoids the fork threat with 6. . . . K – Kt3 (7 R – K6 ch, R – B3).

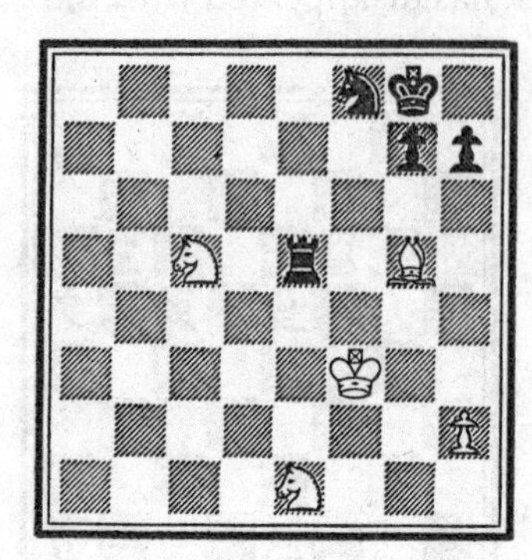

Figure 159

Black has just captured a Pawn on e5 and is happily contemplating his three way fork. However: 1. B – K3 or 1. Kt – K4 protects everything, defending one forked piece with the other, and blocking the Rook from the third.

Figure 160

Two pieces forked, and the Bishop pinned, White seemingly has cause for concern. But he can play:

1. B x P check, winning R and P for B; or, more spectacularly,

1. B – B4, pinning the Rook. After 1. . . . P x B, 2. R x R gains the "exchange" and will soon win the Pawn now on the B file.

The paralyzing power of the Pin can not better be illustrated.

Figure 161

Again two pieces are forked, this time with no possibility of mutual assistance. White looks for other threats:

1. R – R8 (threatening R x Kt mate).
1. . . . P – Kt3 (If K – Kt, 2. B – Kt3 pins the Rook)
2. B – Kt3 R x Kt
3. R x Kt ch K – Kt2
4. R – Kt8 checkmate!

We must be coming to the conclusion that any **tactical** threat such as we have been discussing in this chapter must be bound up with the general strategy and plan of the entire game. More about strategy in a later chapter. Now let us consider defenses to a **hurdle.** They will sound familiar:

DEFENSES TO A HURDLE

1. **Capture** with (a) no loss, (b) limited loss.
2. **Interpose.**
3. **Move with protection.**
4. **Move with counterthreat:** fork, pin, hurdle, check, mate.
5. **Counterthreat** after hurdle is completed.

Figure 162

The Black King *could* move to Q2, but after R x R, Q x Kt is impossible because of Kt – K5 ch. Better is:

1. . . . Q x R
2. Kt x Q O – O – O! forking B and Kt.

White can not save the pinned B, for if 3 P – B4, Kt x P.

Mathematically, Black loses Q (10) for R and B (8) instead of a clear R (5).

Figure 163

Check! and Black can not defend his Rook. If he gives up the Knight, however, he clears the square b7 for the King:

1. . . . Kt – Q1
2. R x Kt ch K – Kt2

(Black loses 3 instead of 5)

Figure 164

A double-barreled hurdle threat—and yet Black has not one but a variety of interesting defenses. Best is 1. . . . B – Kt5! getting the threatened piece away from the firing line, and taking advantage of the fact that 2 P – B3 is impossible, because the P is pinned. If 2 R x Q, B x Q, and both Rooks are attacked, White should move his Q: 2. Q – K1; then after . . . Q x QKtP; 3. P – B3, B – B4; 4. R – Kt3.

Other defenses, from the diagram, are:

1. . . . Q – KKt5
2. P – B3 Q – K3
3. R – K3 Q–QB3

This defense takes advantage of an unprotected piece—the Q. A third defense:

1. . . . Q – KR5

The threat is Q x RP ch and Q – R8 mate.

2. P – KKt3 B – Kt5
3. P – B3 B x KtP
4. P x B (Kt4)!

A fourth defense:

1. . . . Q – KB5, also threatening mate.

After

2. P – KKt3 B – Kt5
3. P – B3 B x BP
4. R x B, White has gained B for P.

A fifth defense:

1. . . . Q – K4, with a mate threat, is met by
2. Q x Q B x Q
3. R x B B x KtP
4. R x RP. White has won a clear B. The variety of defenses is amazing!

Exercises No. 10: Defense to Fork and Hurdle

I (White to Move)

Figure 165

II (Black to Move)

Figure 166

CHAPTER VIII

CHECKMATE AND STALEMATE

CHECKMATE

The ultimate goal of all chess games is to checkmate the opposing King. Checkmate occurs when (1) the King is attacked and (2) he **can not escape** from that attack **nor go to a square free from attack** by enemy forces.

The King can "escape" from attack by capturing his attacker, placing a piece between the attacker and himself (interposing) or moving. He can not interpose when attacked by a Knight. He must move out of a "double check," if he is able to do so.

It is not legal for one King to approach the other so that the latter can take him off. It does you no good to attack the other King when your King is attacked (unless the move allows your King to get out of attack).

When you attack a King, **the rules require you to warn your opponent by saying "check."** There is no penalty if you do not say "check," but you can not then capture his King on the next move. If he makes some move, not seeing that his King is attacked, he must replace the pieces as they were, and attend to getting his King out of "check." This is the only time that a move may be taken back in chess, for the rules clearly state:

1. **If you touch one of your men, you must move him. This is called "touch-move."**

2. **If you touch one of your opponent's men, you must capture him,** if it is legally possible.

3. **If you want to fix or adjust a piece** on a square, you may *first* say: ***"J'adoube"*** ("I adjust" in French) and then adjust the piece.

Back to the King: If, when your King is attacked, you make a move attacking your opponent's King (leaving yours attacked) you must retract the move and defend your King. It does no good to claim (as some beginners do): "If you take my King, I'll take yours. We both lose." The test is: **the one who loses his King first, loses the game.**

Now, to recognize a checkmate:

Figure 167

Black has just moved . . . P – B4 ch and it is White's job to get out of check, if he can.

Can he move his King? Not to KB3, K3 or Q5, for they are occupied by his own pieces. On Q3 he will be attacked by the Black Pawn on QB5; on K5 he will be attacked by the P on Q3, and on KB4 the Black King could capture him. On Q4 he could be captured by the Black B on QR2.

There remains only to see if White can capture the Pawn on KB5 attacking the King. The Rook (Q5) can not move, because he is pinned by the B on QKt2; the Kt on K3 is pinned by the R; the Q on B3 is pinned by the Q on KR8 and the B on Kt4 is pinned by the R on R5. **Not one of these pieces can move,** because if he leaves his square another Black piece can capture the White King.

The King himself can not capture the Pawn, because he will be moving onto a square where the Black King can capture him.

All hope is gone: The White King is checkmated.

What is the smallest amount you can have, and still be able to checkmate a King?

With some of your opponent's pieces blocking escape squares, you may checkmate with as little as a Knight alone, or a Bishop alone, or a King and a Pawn, as in the following diagrams:

Figure 168

In each case, the Black King is checkmated. 168 (b) is the famous **"smothered mate,"** which we will meet again as the final blow in "Philidor's legacy."

But these are unusual cases. Generally the equivalent of a Rook ahead is essential to effect a checkmate—**plus** the cooperation of your King.

Some common checkmates can be seen in the following diagrams:

(Rook & other pieces)

Figure 169

In mating positions with the **Rook** it is necessary usually to drive the King to one side of the board. Other pieces (best of all the King!) must assist.

(Mates with the Queen & other pieces)

Figure 170

The Queen, too, can not checkmate alone. Of course, with her increased power, she can effect more mates than the Rook.

Substitute the Q for the R in the previous set of diagrams. You will have four more typical mates. But substitute R for Q in these diagrams —and there are no mates.

Now for some mates with the minor pieces:

Figure 171

In most of these mates, the King must be driven not only to the side of the board, but to a corner square.

In the mate with B and Kt, (Fig. 171d) the King must be driven to the corner of the color of the square of the Bishop.

Full stories of how to bring about some of these mates will appear later in this chapter.

Before leaving this chapter, however, we will present the above mentioned **"Philidor's legacy."**

Figure 172

White has just played Q – B4 ch. Black can not move K – B1 because of Q – B7 mate. Therefore:

1. . . .	K – R1
2. Kt – B7 ch	K – Kt1
3. Kt – R6 double check	K – R1
4. Q – Kt8 ch!	R x Q
5. Kt – B7 mate!	

STALEMATE

Stalemate occurs when a King is not attacked, but his side has no legal move. The game is a draw.

In each of the following diagrams, Black is stalemated. He has no move, yet the King is not attacked. The game in each case is drawn.

Figure 173

The weakness of the B or Kt (in comparison with a R) can again be seen: even with a RP, a B can not win against a King, if the B is not on the same color as the Queening square. The best a lone B or Kt (with a K) can do against a K is to make a stalemate.

The threat of stalemate often helps a weaker side obtain a draw. For example:

Figure 174

Ordinarily Black should expect to win an ending where he is materially a R ahead (1Q = 2R's). However, where is he to move? He can not go on the B file, for then R – B2 pins and wins the Q. If he stays on the R and Kt files, the Rook keeps checking, gaining a draw by perpetual check. The only winning try is to play the K to Kt6 (g3). The game continues:

1. . . .	K – R6
2. R – R2 ch	K – Kt6
3. R – R3 ch!	K x R

Stalemate! The game is a draw.

Another example:

Figure 175

White would like to capture the Pawn on e5, for then he could draw the game. However, if he played 1. R x P, he would lose his R by . . . R – Kt5 and . . . R – Kt4 ch.

Looking at his King, he sees that he has only one move (to Q5). Remembering figure 173d he sees the way of getting rid of his last piece and plugging up the escape route:

1. R – K6 ch K x R

Stalemate! Of course, if the K doesn't take the R, then White can capture the Pawn, and be able to draw the ending.

Even our greatest players are helpless against stalemate on occasion. SAMUEL RESHEVSKY, many times U. S. Champion, was enjoying the Black position against CARL PILNICK, in the U. S. Championship of 1942, when the latter moved:

Figure 176

1. Q – B2!! and after Q x Q the game was drawn because of the stalemate.

The lesson was brought home to the author back in his college days. Playing for his team against KARL DRUCKLIEB, of the Staten Island Chess Club, he reached the following position (as Black):

Figure 177

Unconscious of what was going on (and feeling proud of those three extra Pawns), he played:

1. . . . P – Q5?

To his surprise, the reply was:

2. R x P!!—for if R x R, stalemate!

Black played 2. . . . **R – K Kt3,** for if 3 R – Kt4, R x R, the WK has a move: namely, K x R. White played:

3. R – K B4 threatening 4 R x P ch K x R stalemate again! Black answered:

3. . . . **R – K B3**

If 4. R x R, K x R;

5. K can take the P on R6. Then Black's QBP would go on to make a Queen. The game continued:

4. R – Q B4 P – B3
5. R – K B4! R – Q3
6. R – Q4 R – Q4 check!! and the stalemate threat being over, White resigned.

Exercise No. 11

I.

Figure 178

II.

Figure 179

III.

Figure 180

IV.

Figure 181

CHECKMATES WITH MINIMAL MATERIAL

Once you have won enough material to win a game, you should always win the game. This section will show you how to win scientifically, and with least effort.

1. King and Queen vs. King.

This is a win. The one danger is giving a stalemate to your opponent, but you can easily avoid this. Three important considerations are:

a. Use your Queen to **limit** the moves of the opposing King. A cut-off move is more important than a check.

b. Use your King. The King must help the Queen in the final mate.

c. Make sure your opponent has two moves at all times with his King, thereby avoiding stalemate.

White moves 1. Q – B4. This limits the Black K to the field cut off by the arrows. Now when the K moves, the Q can follow him to the side of the board, where, as we saw in Chapter X, it is necessary to effect the checkmate. (Fig. 182)

1. . . .	K – B3
2. Q – Q5	K – Q2
3. Q – B6	K – B1

Figure 182

4. Q – Q7	Stage one is completed.

Now the King moves over to confront his adversary.

4. . . .	K – Kt1
5. K – B6	K – R1
6. K – Q6	K – Kt1
7. K – K6	K – R1
8. K – B6	K – Kt1
9. Q – Kt 7 checkmate.	

Note how the Black King was allowed to wriggle. White resisted the temptation of playing 6 Q – KB7 stalemate!

2. King and Rook vs. King: a win.

The Rook needs the support of the King at all times. Substitute a Rook for the Queen in figure 182 and proceed:

1. K – Kt3

It would do no good to play 1. R – B4 because of 1. . . . K – Q5, chasing it.

1. . . .	K – Q4
2. R – B5 ch	K – Q5
3. K – Kt5	K – K5
4. K – B4	K – B5
5. K – Q4	K – B6
6. R – B5 ch	K – K7

Figure 183

We now meet a finesse which is important in all minor piece endings: the tempo. White likes his position, for if Black moves K – Q7, R – B2 ch forces him on to the first rank, where he can be mated. But White must move. He therefore makes a move to preserve the position, and force Black to move; namely,

7. R – B4!	K – Q7
8. R – B2 ch	K – B8
9. K – Q3	K – Kt8
10. K – B3	K – R8
11. K – Kt3	K – Kt8
12. R – B1 mate.	

3. K and two Bishops vs. K.

This is a win, as seen in Fig. 171c. The objective is to drive the opposing K into a corner; but first to the side of the board.

Figure 184

1. K – Q4 Use of the King is essential!

1. . . .	K – Q3
2. B – Kt3	K – B3
3. B – KB4	K – Kt4
4. B – B4 ch	K – Kt3
5. K – Q5	K – Kt2
6. K – Q6	K – Kt3
7. B – Q2	K – Kt2
8. B – K3	K – B1

The first phase is over; the King is on the side of the board.

9. B – Q5	K – Q1
10. B – B6	K – B1
11. B – Kt6	K – Kt1

12. B – Kt5 Room for the King, which must be at Kt6 or B7.

12. . . .	K – Kt2
13. B – R5	K – R2
14. K – B7	K – R1

15. B – B3 Remember: the Black King must have two moves. B – Kt6? is stalemate.

15. . . .	K – R2
16. B – Q4 ch	K – R1
17. B – B6 mate	

4. K, B and Kt vs. King.

This is a win, but a difficult one. The rules of chess say that a game is a draw if no Pawn has been moved or piece taken (this includes Pawns) for fifty moves. However, when an ending is known to be a win (as this is) a player is allowed twice the number of moves it should take him with best play. In this case, White should win in 34 moves from any position. That gives him 68.

Figure 185

These are the tactics White must employ:

1. The Black K must be driven to a Black corner (because the B is on a Black square)—either a1 or h8.

2. The B can guard only Black squares; therefore, Kt and K must guard the White squares.

3. The K must be used freely.

1. K – Q3, K – B3; 2. K – K4, K – Q3; 3. Kt – B4 ch, K – B3; 4. Kt – Q5 ch, K – Q3; 5. B – Q4, K – K3; 6. Kt – B4, K – K2, 7. K – Q5, K – Q2 (the Bl K heads for the "wrong corner,"); 8. B – K5, K – Q1; 9. B – Q6, K – B1; 10. Kt – Kt6 ch, K – Kt2; 11. K – B5, K – R3; 12. K – B6, K – R2; 13. B – B7.

The work of driving the King from the "wrong" to the "right" corner begins. (The position now is: White: K on c6; B on c7; Kt on b6; Black K on a7.)

13. . . . K – R3; 14. B – Kt8, K – R4; 15. Kt – Q5, K – R5; 16. K – B5, K – Kt6; 17. Kt – Kt4, K – Kt7; 18. B – B4, K – B6; 19. B – B1, K – Kt6; 20. B – Q2, K – R5; 21. Kt – B2, K – Kt6; 22. Kt – Q4 ch, K – R5. (The pieces, all on

Black squares, form an impenetrable barrier.) 23. K – B4, K – R6; 24. K – Kt5, K – Kt7; 25. K – Kt4, K – R7; 26. B – B1, K –Kt8; 27. B – R3, K – R7; 28. Kt – K2, K – Kt8; 29. K – Kt3, K – R8; 30. B – Kt2 ch, K – Kt8; 31. Kt – B3 mate.

Even at the end, White had to be careful: 30. Kt – B3?? Stalemate. The last two moves must be checks. The final position could start with the Bl K at Kt8; then the Kt would check first. In all final positions the WK (as in the 2B ending) must be on Kt3 or B2 (or Kt6 or B7); the B check at Kt2 (Kt7) and the Knight at B3 (B6).

The four crucial positions in this ending are shown on the following diagrams:

Figure 186

The Black King is in the "wrong corner." The White pieces prepare to drive him out.

Figure 187

The White pieces form an impenetrable barrier on the Q file. The Black King can not get to Q1 to escape.

Figure 188

The minor pieces bar the way to the B file. The King will now force the Black King into the corner.

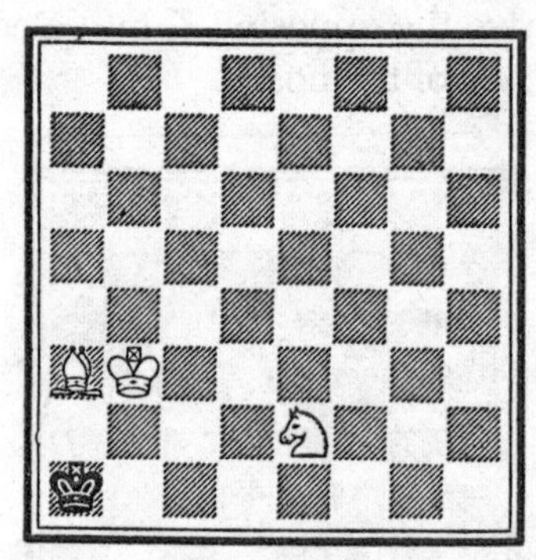

Figure 189

The mating set-up: WK at Kt3; WB at R3; WKt ready to go to B3 (but only with a check). The WK could be at B2 and the B at B1 as well.

This concludes our study of elementary endings.

Memorize these positions!!

Exercise No. 12

Set up the following positions and checkmate the Black King;

1. White: Ke1 Qd1
   Black: Ke8
2. White: Ke1 Rh1
   Black: Ke8
3. White Ke1 Bs c1 f1
   Black: Ke8
4. White: Ke1 Bc1 Ktg1
   Black: Ke8

CHAPTER IX

CHECKMATE COMBINATIONS AND OTHER SACRIFICES

During the game, certain weak spots develop because of the position of the pieces. A player who has made good moves occasionally finds himself with a preponderance of force in the vicinity of those weak spots. If he seizes his opportunity, he can not only gain material, but even win the game outright by checkmating the opposing King.

In the chapter on the Opening, we saw how White hit one of those weak spots (f7) before Black castled. (See Ch. IV.) Chapter VIII, Figure No. 180 demonstrated a weakness on g7 after Black had castled. In this chapter, we shall examine more weak spots, and what to do about them.

1. h7. After Black has castled, one weak point is h7 (White's QR7). In the course of normal development, the square is protected by a Knight on f6. But when that Knight is lured away. . . .

Figure 190

Black has just moved . . . Kt – B5, attacking the WQ. Temporarily, his K is not properly guarded, so:

1. B x P ch!	K x B
2. Q – R5 ch	K – Kt1

3. Kt – Kt5 . . . and nothing can stop the mate at R7.

What if Black had refused the sacrifice?

1. . . .	K – R1

2. Q – R5 threatening B – Kt6 dis. ch. and Q – R7 mate.

2. . . .	P – Kt3

3. Q – R6. Now nothing can stop the threat of B x P dis. ch. and Q – R7 mate.

2. g7. A second weak spot after Black has castled is g7 (Black's KKt2). One of the means of exploiting it is shown in the following diagram:

Figure 191

1. P – B6	P – KKt3
2. Q – R6 and	
3. Q – Kt7 mate.	

A vast difference one move can make! If it were Black's move in the diagram, he could play 1. . . . P – B3, stopping the threat and defending the second rank with his Queen.

A black-squared Bishop often assists the Queen in the attack on g7.

3. g7 and h7. Sometimes one of these weaknesses can be defended—at the cost of creating a weakness on the other square.

Figure 192

1. P – B6	P – Kt3

2. Q – Kt5 White wants to play the combination we have just seen. However, Black sees it, too, and figures that he has time to cover g7 with his Rook.

2. . . .	K – R1
3. Q – R6	R – KKt1

So far, so good. But a new weakness has developed—on h7.

4. Q x P ch!!	K x Q
5. R – R3 checkmate	

3b. g2 and h2

These are the same weaknesses as g7 and h7—after White has castled, in this case. In the following diagram Black, who had weaknesses in his Queen side, sacrificed a Knight in order to "open up" the White King. White's Queen came to the defense, and he seems safe. But the weaknesses are there! Black's move:

Figure 193

1. . . .	B – Kt2 (the lure)
2. Q x B	Q x KtP ch
3. K – R2	Q – R5 ch
4. K – Kt2	R – Q3
5. Q – B3	R – Kt3 ch
6. Q – Kt3	R – K7!
7. Q x R	RP x Q
8. B – B1	Q – Kt5 ch
9. K – R1	R – K4!
10. B – B4	R – R4 ch
11. B – R2	Q – B6 ch
12. K – Kt1	Q – R6 Threatening mate on R7 and R8. The B can not move.
13. R(1) – QR1	Q x B ch
14. K – B1	R – K4!
15. P – B3 (else Q – R8 mate)	R – K7
and	Q – B7 or Kt7 mate

The following points should be studied:

a. The original sacrifice, luring the key figure away from the defense.

b. The selection of the file for the Rook to check on.

c. The selection of the Rook for the check (leaving the K file guarded by the other Rook).

d. Taking advantage of the Pin of the Queen to create another pin: after 6. . . . R – K7, the P can not recapture on KKt3.

e. Making use of the 4th rank after the 3rd rank is blocked by the P on KKt3.

f. Prevention of the escape of the K by R – K4.

g. For geometry lovers, the maneuver R – K7 – K4 – R4 – K4 – K7.

h. Ignoring the B, which might have been captured on move 10, in order to continue the attack.

i. Placing now R before Q, then Q before R, now both on a rank, then on a file.

In the match U.S.A. vs. U.S.S.R. (Moscow, 1955) DONALD BYRNE, playing Black against E. GELLER, the 1955 Soviet Champion, reached the following position:

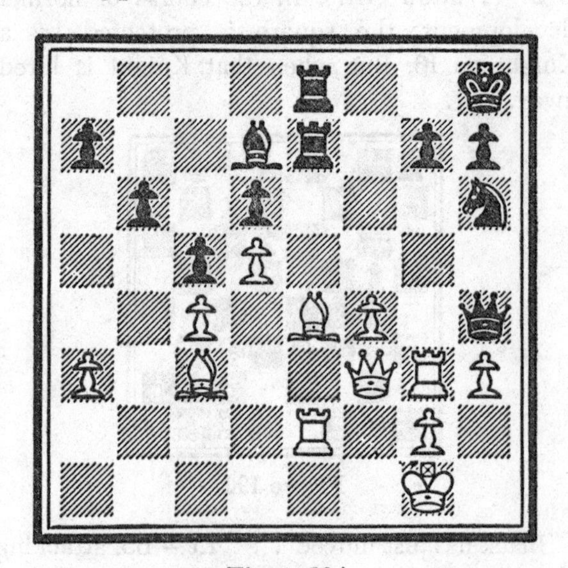

Figure 194

Byrne had been defending valiantly, and had been striving for . . . B – B4, exchanging White Bishops and finding a good defensive square for his Knight on B4, where it would defend his weak spot g7.

However, he now noticed that g7 was too weak!— If 1. . . . B – B4; 2. R x P!! R x R; 3. B x B, R x R; 4. Q x R, Kt x B; 5. Q – K8 mate!

He should have played 1. . . . K – Kt1, getting out of the eventual Bishop Pin; and after 2. P– B5, K – B1, getting out of the possible Rook Pin as well. (Not, however, 2. . . . R x B? 3.

R x P ch, K – B1; 4. P – Kt3! winning.) Now if the WB retreats from K4 (after all, it is now attacked without the possibility of R x P ch) Black can play Kt – Kt1 and – B3, with blockade of the strong B on QB3.

Unfortunately, he played:

30. . . . R – B2, and his opponent could answer

31. P – B5! without worrying about the B on K4, now defended as much as attacked.

31. . . . Kt – Kt1
32. R – Kt4 Q – Q1

Better is 32. . . . Q – R3; 33. B – Q2, Q – R4; 34. B – B3, Q – R3, etc.

33. R – B4 Kt – B3
34. B – Q3 R x R
35. Q x R Q – K2
36. Q – B3 P – QR3

Black, safe for the moment, advances where he has the majority of Pawns; but a moment is a short time!

37. P – Kt4!!

The rear of the battering ram.

37. . . . Kt – Kt1
38. P – B6! P x P

If . . . Kt x P, the Kt is pinned after P – Kt5.

39. P – Kt5!! Now the P is pinned—and on the King.

39. . . . P – Q Kt4
40. P x KBP Q – B1
41. Q – R5 Resigns

—The weakness at g7. If . . . Kt x P, 42. Q – R4, winning, the Knight, with more to follow. Otherwise, White plays 42. B x RP (the weakness at h7) . . . R x B; 43. P – B7 dis. ch., Q – Kt2 ch; 44. B x Q ch, K x B; 45. Q – Kt5 ch, K – B1; 46. Q x Kt ch and 47. P – B8 (Q) mate. If 41. . . . Q – R3; 42. Q x R, Q x R; 43. Q – Kt7 mate.

Finally, if 41. . . . Kt – R3, 42. R – R4! Kt – Kt1; 43. Q x RP ch!! R x Q; 44. R x R mate.

4. The Eighth Rank

Among the mating situations you must recognize is one where the opposing King is on the eighth (or first) rank. First look at chapter VIII, figures 169, 170; then try to apply it to the following figures:

White

Black

Figure 195

Black, to move, can capture the WKt; then check with his Q on KR8. The WK would be able to escape to the protection of his own pieces.

Visualizing the mate situation, however, Black plays:

1. . . . Q – R8 ch!
2. K x Q R x Kt checkmate.

Figure 196

The Black King is in a mating situation, with his 1st (White's 8th) rank uncovered. White does not allow him time for . . . P – R3 or . . . P – Kt3:

1. R x P! R x R
2. Q x R Q – B1

(not . . . Q x Q? 3 R – K8 ch, Q – B1; 4 R x Q mate)

(nor . . . R – Q5; 3 Q x Q, R x Q; 4 R – K8 mate).

3. R – KB1. Besides the threat of mate in two, R – B8 ch threatens to win the Q. A Pawn move (. . . P– R3 or Kt3) is not feasible.

3. . . . K – Kt1
4. Q – Q5 ch K – R1
5. Q – Q7 (Not 5 Q x BP? Q x Q, defending the square where the R can check.)

5. . . .	Q – K Kt1
6. Q – K7	(Not 6 R – K1? R – Q5! and 7 . . . R – Q1)

Now the Black Queen is lost, with a check, so that any counter by the White Rook is useless: e.g., 6 . . . R – Q5; 7 R – B8, R – Q2 or K5; 8 R x Q check!

White used the mate threat (1) to win the P on Q6; (2) to maneuver his Q off the Q file, where the Black R could counterattack it and gain time for defense; 3) to win the opposing Queen.

Figure 197

Black has just defended the threat against his KKtP by . . . B – B1. "Where is the pin?" you might ask. Look at the Black King, the Bl KBP and the White B on QB4. The KBP is pinned. That means no protection for the square KKt3 (g6), since the KRP has moved.

1. Kt x P ch	P x Kt
2. Q – Kt6 ch	B – Kt2
3. Q x B checkmate	

Figure 198

The Black Bishop is pinned—which means that the square h6 (Black's KR3) is unprotected.

1. Q – R6 ch	K – Kt1
2. Q x B mate!	

Recognition of these situations (or of similar ones) will help you figure out combinations many moves deep. But a weakness does not consist usually of only one square. In fact, the last example might illustrate the weakness of

6. The Long Diagonal

Figure 199

The open long diagonal a1 – h8 invites mating combinations.

1. R x Kt! Now, if . . . R x Q, 2 R – R8 mate.

1. . . .	K x R

The threat is removed; but now the Pawn on g6 is pinned.

2. Q – R5 ch	K – Kt1
3. Q – R8 mate.	

In the author's first game in the New York State Tournament, 1926, he met the redoubtable HERMANN HELMS, chess reporter for the *New York Times*, editor of the *American Chess Bulletin* and State champion of 1925.

The following position occurred:

Figure 200

Black is well protected, with all his weak spots covered. If anything it is White's King side that has weaknesses, the WB which might have filled up the "holes" at g2, f3 and h3 having been exchanged.

Nevertheless, White saw an opportunity of opening the Black long diagonal, and played:

1. **R x Kt**	**R x R**
2. **Kt x KP**	**R(3) – B1**
3. **Kt – Kt4**	

The diagonal is open, and White threatens to clear it by B x B and Q – Kt2, plus a check at KB6 with a Knight.

3. . . .	**P – KR4**
4. **Kt (Kt4) – B6 ch**	**K – R1**
5. **Q – K3**	

White sees the possibility of a check on h6, when the B on g7 is pinned.

5. . . .	**R – B7**

The Rook hits the big threat, the pinning piece.

Figure 201

6. **Kt x RP!!**

Threat: (7) Q – R6 ch, K – Kt (the B is pinned!); (8) B x B, Kt x B; (9) Q x Kt mate—or (8) . . . P x Kt, (9) Q – R8 mate.

The situation is amusing, what with the WB attacked twice and the Kt once. What can Black do? If: 6. . . . R x B?? (7) Kt x B, K x Kt; (8) Q – B3 ch and (9) Q x R, with two Pawns plus.

(6) . . . R x B, (7) Kt x B, Kt x Kt; (8) Kt – B6 threatening mate by Q – R6, (8) . . . Kt – B4; (9) P x Kt, K – Kt2; (10) Q – K5 (attacking the R and threatening discovered check along that wide-open long diagonal). (10) . . . R x RP, (11) Kt – K8 double check, K – R3; (12) Q – R8 ch, K – Kt4; (13) Q – R4 ch, K x P; (14) Q – B4 checkmate!

My opponent, however, had a little surprise up his sleeve:

6. . . .	**R x Kt**
7. **B x B ch**	**K – Kt1**

Now, if White rushes to play Q – R6, R x Kt —and bye, bye, baby!

8. **P x R**	**Kt x B**

(If 8 . . . P x Kt, (9) P x Kt, K x B, (10) P – K7, and the Pawn Queens.)

9. **Kt – B6 ch**	**Black resigns**

If (9) . . . K – B1, (10) Q – R6, threatening (11) R – K8 mate (the Knight is pinned!) or (11) Q – R8 mate.

7. The Seventh Absolute

In many of the elementary mates we saw that the King had to be driven to the edge of the board. In cases where Rooks and Queens gave the mates, those pieces usually controlled the rank or file in front of the King: thus if the K were on the 8th (or 1st) rank, the R or Q stood on the 7th (or 2nd); if the K were on the a or h file, the R or Q stood on the **b** or **g** respectively.

When there are no Pawns to hinder the Rs or Q, we say that they control the "seventh absolute." For example in:

Figure 202

White controls the "absolute" 7th rank. He threatens mate by Q x RP, Q – Kt7, Q – B8, K8 or Q8 and R – Q8: six ways in all! That's too great a burden for one man to defend. Still, if you place a Bl P on g7 and the Bl R on g8, all the mate threats would be defended. The reason is: the 7th rank is no longer "absolute," the Pawns guard the King, and the pieces can cover the Pawns.

The following diagram shows a position reached by the author (Black) against JOHN

FOSTER (White) in a game in the Marshall Chess Club Championship (1950).

Figure 203

As prescribed, the WK is on the edge of the board—two edges, since he is in the corner. The Q Kt file is "absolute."

A mate had been threatened on Q Kt2, which White covered by his B by moving it to QB1. The B, however, blocks the WRs from the square Q Kt1. A Rook to back up the Q would be ideal. Black moved:

1. . . . R – Q Kt1

and White resigned, for if:

2. Kt x R R x Kt
3. Q – K4 (defending Q Kt 1) B x B
4. R – K2 (defending Q Kt2; if R x B? Q – R6 is mate).
4. . . . Q – B6 ch
5. K – R2 Q – R6 mate.

In another game, Black used the "seventh absolute" to get a draw:

Figure 204

White played (1) B – B1! with great expectations of gaining material, because of the hurdle. Black, however, answered (1) . . . R x BP and after:

2. B x B R – Kt7 ch

3. K – B1 R x RP

mate was threatened on **h1** (W KR1). White could do nothing better than

4. K – Kt1 R (R) – Kt7 ch
5. K – B1 R – KR7
6. K – Kt1 R (R) – Kt7 ch

—and the game was a draw by repetition of moves.

Exercise No. 13

Find White's best moves in the following diagrams. Write several moves for each diagram before referring to the solution.

I.

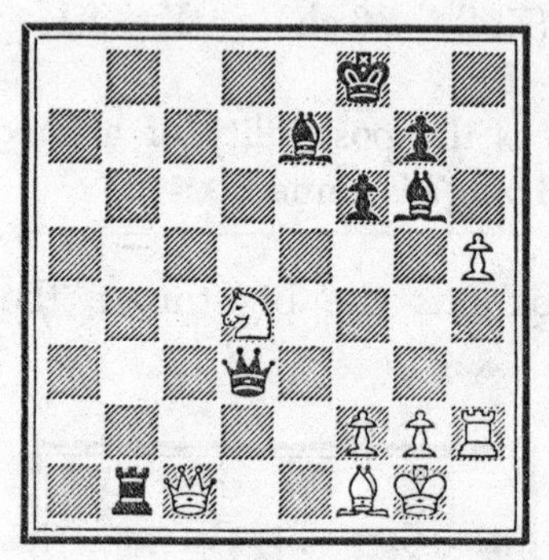

Figure 205

II.

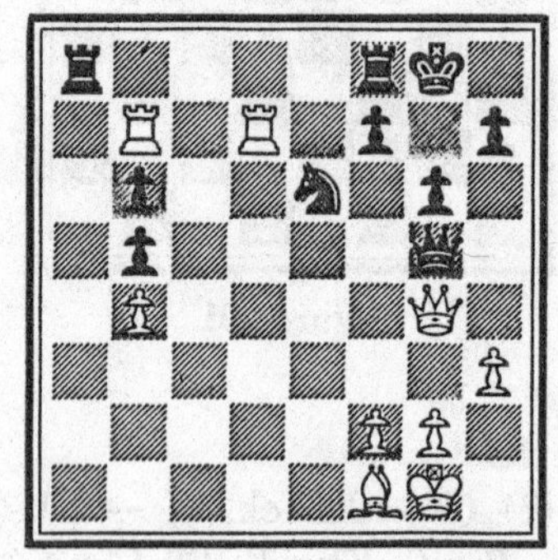

Figure 206

III.

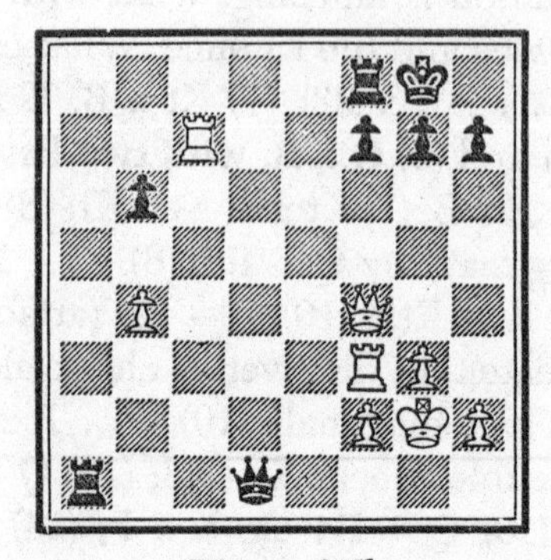

Figure 207

IV.

Figure 208

OTHER SACRIFICES

We have already seen how players sacrifice material in order to gain more material or to effect checkmate. There are other reasons for sacrifices, which are just as important as those for material gain. The most important of these reasons is:

1. To Improve the Position of a Piece

Figure 209

It is obvious that once Black plays . . . P – Q Kt4 the White Bishop will never get into action unless White marches over with his King, captures the P on b3, then moves K – c2, P – b3 —and, finally, the Bishop.

In the meantime, Black will gobble up the WPs on the f and g files, and queen his g Pawn. White *must*, therefore, play:

1. P – Kt5, even at the cost of this Pawn, in order to extricate the Bishop. After (1) . . . P x P, (2) P – Kt4 (advancing where he has more material), (2) . . . K – K3, (3) B – B8 K – Q4, (4) B – Kt7 Kt – K5, (5) P – B5, Black will have something to worry about in turn. The freedom of the Bishop will insure a draw for White.

2. To Gain a Specific Square

Figure 210

Kings and Knights depend upon squares rather than lines (ranks, files, diagonals) for their power. White can turn the diagrammed position to his favor by:

1. P – Q5! gaining Q4 for both King and Knight. Black should not capture (If . . . P x P; (2) Kt – Q4, B – K1; (3) P – B5, etc.) but play:

1. . . .	P – K4!
2. P x P	B x P!

and, although White would keep his advantage, the Bishop's scope on the open board might hold matters for Black. The game might continue:

3. P x P ch	K x P
4. Kt – Q4	K – K4

4. . . . B – B3 would lose: (5) Kt x B, K x Kt; (6) K – K4 (The Opposition: see the later chapter on the endings) K – Q3; (7) K – Q4 and Black must yield ground.

Black's plan is to capture W's gP for his bP, thereby freeing his own gP for a possible queening.

5. Kt x P	K – B4
6. Kt – Q6 ch	

White's plan is to win the Bishop by advancing his QKtP to the 7th (where the B must capture it to prevent its becoming a Queen). His King will hold Black's KKtP.

6. . . .	K x P
7. P – Kt5	K – R5

It is too late to retreat: (7) . . . K – B3; (8) P – Kt6, K – K3; (9) P – Kt7, B x P forced;

8. P – Kt6	

White must not be distracted by Black's threat, on the one hand; nor by the inviting QBP on the other. He must carry out his plan.

8. . . .	K – R6
9. P – Kt7	B x P

10. **Kt x B**	**P – Kt4**
11. **Kt – Q6**	**P – Kt5**
12. **Kt x P**	**P – Kt6**
13. **Kt – Q2**	**P – Kt7**
14. **K – B2**	**K – R7**
15. **Kt – B3 ch**	**K – R8**
16. **P – Kt4**	

There is no stalemate, since Black *can* play P – Kt8 (Q), whereupon the Kt can take it off. The WP goes on to queen. Black resigns.

We have played this ending out in order to show how moves at all stages of the game are governed by a definite plan. Alternate plans are possible at different stages of the game, and sometimes it is wise to change a plan.

In the diagrammed position, if it had been Black's move, he would have played (1) . . . P – Q4, in order to spoil White's plan. He would have had no chance to win the game; but, then, neither would White, since the position would have been blocked.

On move 8 White might have tried one of the alternate plans suggested: namely, to move his King back to K Kt1, a Black square from which no Black piece could chase him. Let us see what would have happened:

Figure 211

(8) K – B2, K – R6; (9) K – Kt 1, K – Kt 6. The Black King is now free to attack the QBP. If he can remove both WPs, the game is a draw. (10) P – Kt 6, K – B6; (11) Kt x P, K – K5! (Not . . . K – K7???) (12) Kt – R5, B – R1; (13) K – B2, (Hoping to defend the QBP with his K) (13) . . . K – Q6! (14) P – B4, K – Q5; (15) K – K2, K – B4; (16) P – Kt7, B x P; (17) Kt x B ch, K x P draw.

3. To Contain Enemy Forces

The above example showed also the weakness of a Bishop: like a leopard, he cannot change his spots. As a result, the WK could not be bridged from the square K Kt1. In the following diagram, the players have Bishops "of opposite color," they are standing on different colored squares. White, with one Pawn ahead, however, has two connected Pawns in the center **on the squares of the opposing Bishop.** This restrains that piece, and gives his own B free rein: (Black to move)

Figure 212

Black (EDWARD LASKER) played (36) . . . K – B2? and his opponent BOGOLJUBOW (New York Tournament 1924) answered (37) R x R ch, K x R; (38) B – Q2, winning quickly. The WB held the two Black Q side Pawns.

The last move gives us a cue to what should have happened:

36. . . .	**R x R**
37. **B x R**	**P – Kt5!!**
38. **P x P**	**B – R3**

The freed Bishop forces the WPs to black squares, where they block their own B, and allow the Bl B free range.

39. **P – Q4**	**B – Q6**
40. **P – K5**	**B – B5**
41. **K – B2**	**P – QR3**
42. **K – K3**	**B – Q4**
43. **P – Kt3**	**K – B2**
44. **K – B4**	**P – R3**
45. **B – Q6**	**K – K3**
46. **B – B8**	**P – KR4**
47. **K – Kt5**	**B – K5**

There is no way for White to control the White squares. The game would be a draw.

4. To Advance a Strategic Plan

5. To Forestall Enemy Plans

These objectives go together so often that an example for one must include the other.

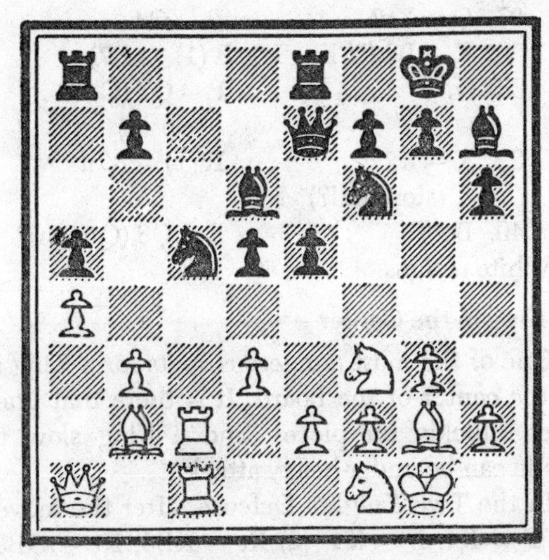

Figure 213

This complicated position existed in a game between RICHARD RETI (White) and Dr. EMANUEL LASKER in the famous New York 1924 Tournament. Reti had defeated Capablanca, then the World Champion; now he was meeting the former World Champion and tournament leader. In addition, he was playing his own opening, the **Reti Opening**, holding back his center Pawns on **e2** and **d3**, and controlling center squares with pieces. Even the Queen is taking a back seat on **a1**.

Black (Lasker) has developed simply, and his last move (Kt – B4) has attacked a Pawn defensible only by W's Q. But to move his Q to R2 would mean that White has to give up his strategic plan. Also, Q – R2 is not palatable because of . . . Kt – R3, threatening . . . Kt – Q Kt5, forking Q and R—and forcing another Q move plus a R move away from the strategic squares. White was, therefore forced to sacrifice:

17. R x Kt — B x R
18. Kt x P

For the R, he has a B and P—not quite enough. But the Black center is half gone, the diagonal a1 – h8 well controlled, and his pieces remain well placed.

18. . . . — Q R – B
19. Kt – K3 — Q – K3

Not . . . B x Kt, which would give White the square d4 for his B.

20. P – R3 — B – Q3

To say that a World Champion made a mistake would be presumptuous, were it not for the fact that the future World Champion, ALEXANDER ALEKHINE, who annotated the game for the tournament book, made the suggestion: (20) . . . P – QKt3, holding the B where it could drill on the square **d4**, now weakened by the absence of the Bl KP, was better.

21. R x R — R x R

Now Kt (K5) – Kt4! would have won the QP by removing a defending piece: the Kt on **f6.** Then the sacrifice on move 17 would have been heard around the world! Alas, he played (22) Kt – B3, and eventually lost. (For the rest of the game, see the tournament book.)

6. To Queen a Pawn

Figure 214

Materially, White is behind, for B + Kt are worth two Pawns more than a Rook. However, his threatening Pawns allow:

1. R x P (Kt7) — Kt x R
2. P – R6

This exposes a weakness of the Knight, which *can not* stop the R Pawn in this position.

2. . . . — B x P

Hoping for P x Kt, B – Q3

3. P – R7! and the Pawn queens.

A more stringent example:

Figure 215

The Black Pawns are menacing enough, both being close to queening. It is the sacrifice that gives the extra push. Black (RETI, again, vs. JANOWSKI, New York, 1924) played:

32. . . .	R x Kt!
33. R x R	Q x R!!
34. Q x Q	P – R7
35. K – R2	P – R8 (Q)

and, with a piece ahead, won quickly.

7. To Launch a King-Side Attack

An attack without an immediate checkmate in view can be started and continued by a sacrifice, which unleashes all one's forces. For example:

Figure 216

White, being satisfied that he had the Black pieces bottled up on the Q's side, decided to start an attack on the K's wing by chasing the Queen:

29. R – R3

He was more than mildly surprised:

29. . . .	**Q x R!!**
30. **P x Q**	**Kt – B6**

Now, if (31) Q x Kt, P – Q5 ch wins the Q.

31. **K – Kt2?**

White is willing to give up R for Kt, and moves his K to escape the resultant pin of his B on the first rank. A better defense would be (31) R – K and (32) Q – Q2. Now his K is still under the B's fire.

31. . . .	**R – R7**

The pin is on the second rank.

32. R – QB1	Kt – K7 (Fork!)
33. Q – Q2	P – Q5 ch (Release!)
34. K – B1	Kt x R
35. Q x Kt	R – R8 (Pin!)
36. B – Kt1 (Defense to Pin by Interposition)	
36. . . .	P – Q6 (*En avant!*)
37. Q – Kt2	B – Q4
38. K – B2 (If K – K1, R (1) – R7)	
38. . . .	P – Q7 (Getting closer)
39. K – K2 (stopped!?)	R (1) – R7!!
40. B x R	P – Q8 (Queen)!

White resigns.

8. King in the Center

One of the most dangerous spots for a King is in the center of the board. It is there that lines open quickly for pieces; and a King slow to castle can be under heavy attack.

In the Two Knights Defense, after the moves (1) P – K4, P – K4; (2) Kt – KB3, Kt – QB3; (3) B – B4, Kt – B3; (4) Kt – Kt5, P – Q4; (5) P x P, Kt x P(?) we arrive at:

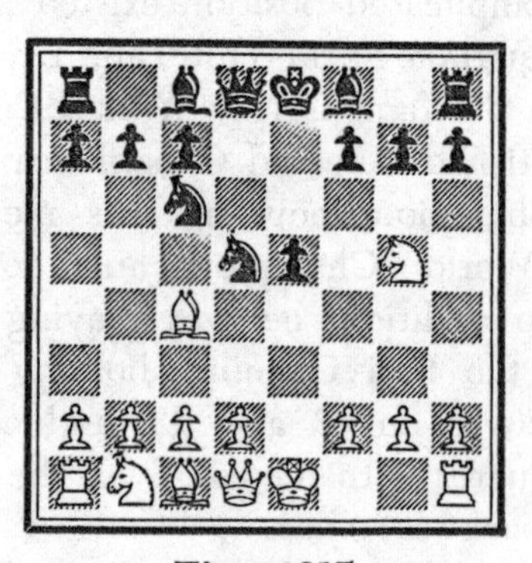

Figure 217

White now plays (**Fegatello Attack**):

6. **Kt x P** giving up a piece in order to keep the Black King under fire in the center. Continue:

6. . . .	K x Kt
7. Q – B3 ch	K – K3 (protecting the Kt, now twice attacked.)
8. Kt – B3	Kt – Kt5 (of course, only the Kt on QB3 can move.)
9. Q – K4 (defending QB2)	P – B3
10. P – QR3	Kt – R3
11. P – Q4	Kt – B2
12. B – B4	K – B2
13. B x P	B – K3

White has two Pawns for his Kt and is well developed; Black's King is in the center. Play several games with your friends and see who wins.

Now let us see what happens if Black, instead

of recapturing the Pawn on move 5, sacrifices it.

(1) P – K4, P – K4; (2) Kt – KB3, Kt – QB3; (3) B – B4, Kt – B3; (4) Kt – Kt5; P – Q4; (5) P x P, **Kt – QR4.**

6. P – Q3. An alternative is (6) B – Kt5, P – B3! (7) P x P, P x P; (8) B – K2.

6.	. . .	**P – KR3**
7.	**Kt – KB3**	**P – K5**
8.	**Q – K2**	**Kt x B**
9.	**P x Kt**	**B – QB4**
10.	**Kt (3) – Q2**	**O – O**
11.	**Kt – Kt3**	**B – Kt5!**
12.	**Q – B1**	

Figure 218

Now it is White's King in the center; his Queen blocking him from castling. All Black's pieces are developed, only one of White's. Try playing *this* position also.

To sum up: there are many reasons for sacrifices. In previous chapters we mentioned **speedy development** and **direct mating attacks,** as well as **material gain or avoidance of greater loss.** In this chapter we spoke more of **positional considerations** (gaining a line or a square; containing enemy forces); of **strategic considerations** (furthering your plan or holding back that of your opponent); or of **long-range plans** (attack against a King, or holding the King in the center). There are many other reasons for sacrifices, but they would fall under one of the categories mentioned. RUDOLPH SPIELMANN, a great attacking player, wrote a book called **The Art of Sacrifice,** which we suggest you read. The greatest teacher, however, is experience. Your successes and failures (for there will be both) will awaken in you the judgment as to when you should go ahead, and when you should resist what might be almost irresistible.

Exercise No. 14

Here are three problems which the author had to decide in tournament games:

I.

Figure 219

White: M. Hanauer

Black: Jeremiah F. Donovan

Tournament: Ventnor City Masters, 1941.

White "feels" that a sacrifice is in the air. The general reasons are: better development of the White pieces; better general development possible (i.e., the Black Knight has only one move, to a spot where it will block the B, which in turn blocks the Kt); more space. Specific reasons are:

The Black Rooks are not connected; the Bl R on Q1 is defended only by the B on B3, which is overloaded, since it must also defend K Kt2. If, for example, the W Kt on Q4 moves, Black can not capture first the R and then the B, because of R – Q8 mate. If the Kt moves to B2 or B3, Black can play R x R ch; R x R, B – K2. But if White plays **Kt – B5**, the Black B can not move from B3 because the KKtP would be lost, and his King opened up.

After 1. **Kt – B5** **R x R ch**

2. **R x R** **P x Kt**

(the sacrifice)

3. **B x B** **P x B**

4. **R – Q8 ch** **K – Kt2**

5. **Q – B3** Black is in a mating net, one threat being (6) Q – Kt3 ch; (7) R – Kt8, (8) Q – R3 or 4 mate; the other being (6) Q – Kt4, (7) Q – B8 ch, etc.

Now White and Black actually made moves 1 – 5 above, from the diagram. Was White correct in his sacrifice?

II. About ten years later, against the same opponent, in the Marshall C. C. Championship of 1951, the following position arose:

Figure 220

White has a strong position, with the pin of the Bishop. If he moves Q – Kt6, for example, Black must play R(1) – K1, and wait for White to make known his plans.

But on this move, White can make a Queen sacrifice in two ways:

(A) 1. R x B — R x Q
2. R x R ch — K – B
3. R x Kt P followed by
4. R(1) – K7, which can not be stopped: if Q – Q, (5) R x RP, etc.

(B) 1. Q x R ch — K x Q
2. R x B ch — K – B
3. R x P ch — K – Kt1
4. R – Kt6 or 4R – K7, with similar threats of doubling on the 7th rank.

Should he sacrifice?

III. VS. A. ZIMMERMAN (Black) in an interclub match 1950.

Figure 221

What is White's correct move?

CHAPTER X

SECURING A DRAW

Why should you try to draw a chess game—rather than try to win it?

1. If you are behind in material, with no prospects of regaining it;
2. if you have been outplayed positionally, so that your pieces are badly placed;
3. if you are about to lose material
4. or be mated;

and can do nothing about either of them;

5. if you will be at a disadvantage if you try to avoid a draw—

then by all means, take a draw!

How can you get a draw?

(a) **Stalemate:** see Chapter VIII
(b) **Insufficient material to win:** see Chapter II
(c) **Perpetual check:** see Chapter IX
(d) **Repetition of position:**

The rules say:

1. If a position is repeated three times, with the same Player to move, the Player may claim a draw.

2. If a position has occurred three times, with the same Player to move, the Player may claim a draw.

Two points need to be explained:

(a) The Player *may* claim a draw. He does not have to.
(b) Who is the Player? The person whose move it is *after* the position has occurred three times.

This gives an unfair advantage to one player, who has a choice of claiming a draw when the other player does not. The rules (of the *Federation Internationale des Echecs* (Fide), the body governing all international chess tournaments and matches) were therefore amended, so that the Player who was about to make the move resulting in the three-fold occurrence of position, could call over the tournament director, to tell him he was about to make the move and that he would claim the draw as a result of the three time occurrence.

The rule was amended in this manner for a particular reason. Tournament games are timed by special clocks made so that two clocks are connected by a lever. One clock goes at one time. When a player makes his move, he pushes the lever, stopping his clock, and starting that of his opponent.

Figure 222

When the opponent makes his move, he pushes the lever back, stopping his clock, and restarting that of the first player. The result is that each player is timed only for the number of minutes he is thinking until he makes his move. (Timing in most tournaments ranges from 30 to 40 moves in two hours for *each player;* 15 to 20 moves an hour thereafter. At the end of specified times, usually the first two hours and each hour thereafter *on the chess clock,* the specified number of moves must be made. The player whose clock exceeds the time before he completes the moves, loses the game by forfeit.)

The rules, therefore, are arranged so that a Player makes a claim on his own time. The Tournament Director (and only he) may stop the clocks in order to ascertain the justice of the claim.

To return to the methods of securing a draw.

Figure 223

White is threatened with checkmate by . . . Q x KtP, or loss of the Queen. Luckily, he can draw by:

1. R x P ch — K x R
2. Q – Kt5 ch — K – R1
3. Q – B6 ch — K – Kt1
4. Q – Kt5 ch — K – R1
5. Q – B6 ch and draw by perpetual check.

Figure 224

Here White is not threatened with immediate loss, but he is two Pawns behind. He should be satisfied with:

1. R – B8 ch — K – B2 (not K – Kt2, R – K7 mate)
2. R – B7 ch — K – B1 (not K – Kt1, R – K8 mate)
3. R – B8 ch, with perpetual check.

If White gets ambitious, and tries to win by (1) **R – B7,** threatening (2) R – K8 mate, Black *could* reply (1) **. . . R – R4 ch;** (2) **K – Kt1, R – Kt4 ch.** Now, if (3) K – B1, R – B4 ch, exchanging Rooks, White will play **3 K – R1,** allowing Black to continue (3) . . . R – R4 ch (4) . . . K – Kt4 ch, drawing by three-fold repetition of position. It is not strictly a perpetual check, since White *can* escape.

After **1 R – B7,** Black can reply (1) **. . . R – KB4;** (2) **R – K8 ch,** R – B1. Then (3) R(8) – K7, threatening mate in three moves, by R – Kt7 ch, R x RP ch and R(B) – Kt7 checkmate. Black plays (3) . . . **R(1) x P,** giving the K an escape square at B1. (Fig. 225)

Now White can no longer force a draw by R – B8 ch, R – B1; R – B7, because Black can play R(7) – B2, forcing the exchange of one Rook. White plays:

4. **R – Kt7 ch** — **K – B1**
5. **R(Kt) – Q7,** threatening mate with either Rook. Now Black can force a draw by R – B8 –

Figure 225

B7 — B6 check (not moving the R on B5) because White can not afford to interpose (and exchange) a Rook.

Could White have played (5) R x RP? No, because of . . . R — B2, cutting communication of the WRs. Then (6) R — R8 ch, K — Kt2; (7) R(B) — B8, R — B1! and one Rook must be exchanged. Black plays:

5. . . .	**R — B2**
6. **R — Q8 ch**	**K — Kt2**
7. **R — B6** (not 7 R(B) — B8? R — B1; 8 R — Q7 ch, R(7) — B2).	
7. . . .	**R — KKt7**

Mate is threatened on f1.

8. **R x QKtP**	**R — B8 ch**
9. **R — Kt1**	**R x R ch**
10. **K x R**	**R x P**

and Black will win easily.

Figure 226

A Pawn down, White pins his hopes on a possible King's side attack, playing:

1. **R — Kt3**

Black can not defend the KtP with his R, because of Q — K8 mate. He, therefore, must move the KtP. (1) . . . P — Kt3, the obvious move, would result in (2) **R x P ch, P x R;** (3) **Q x P ch, K — B1;** (4) **Q — Kt7 ch, K — K1;** (5) **Q — Kt8 ch, K — Q2;** (6) **Q — R7 ch.** Here is the point: The Qs are on a diagonal, so that (6) . . . K — B1?? is met by (7) Kt — Q6 ch, R x Kt; (8) Q x Q, winning. If Black does not wish to submit to a repetition of moves by (6) . . . **K — K1;** (7) **Q — Kt8 ch, K — Q2;** (8) **Q — R7 ch, K — K1,** etc., he must play (6) . . . Kt — K2; whereupon (7) Q x Kt ch, K — B1; (8) Kt — Q6 ch (forking K and Q) R x Kt; (9) Q x R—and White is a Pawn ahead!

Black, in the game (Hanauer vs. Donovan, Ventnor City, 1940) played:

1. . . .	**P — Kt4,** whereupon:

2. **R — KB3!** The Kt threatens a repetition at R6 and B7. If Black cuts off the Kt at B5 by (2) . . . Kt — B5, then (3) Kt — R6 ch, K — Kt2; (4) Q — B7 ch, K x Kt; (5) Q x BP ch, K — R4; (6) P — Kt4 ch, K —R5; (7) Q — R6 ch, Kt — R4; (8) Q x Kt mate; or (5) . . . Kt — Kt3, (6) Q x R.

2. . . .	**R — KB1**
3. **Q — R6**	**R — B2**
4. **Q — R5** (threatening Kt — R6 ch)	
4. . . .	**R — B1.** A Rook

move along the second rank is impossible, because of Q — K8 ch.

5. **Q — R6**	**R — B2**
6. **Q — R5**	**R — B1**
7. **Q — R6** Drawn by repetition of moves.	

Another example, with Black to move: (O. ULVESTAD VS. BERNSTEIN, Ventnor City, 1950).

Figure 227

Two Pawns down, Black would be pleased to draw the game. These considerations give him some hope:

The White pieces are precariously placed, the R, attacked by Black's K, protected by the B, which is forkable with the WK by a Kt check on c1.

All White Ps but one are on the third rank—fodder for a Rook.

The Black Pawn at c5 is passed, and supported by K and R. The Black K is centrally located.

Attracted first to the position of the White pieces, Black played:

1. . . .	R – B6
2. R – K5 ch	K – Q5
3. R – K4 ch	K – Q4

To retreat the B is useless: B – Kt1, R – B8

4. R – K5 ch	K – Q5

Drawn by repetition. White could try to win by (2) R – R4, Kt – B8 ch; (3) K – Q2, (Defense to fork by counterfork) R x B ch; (4) K x Kt, R x KtP (operation mop-up) (5) R x P, R x KRP; (6) K – Q2, R – B6; (7) R – R4, P – B5; (8) R – R5 ch, K – K5; (9) P – B5, R x BP; (10) R x R, K x P; (1) P – R4, K – K4; (12) P – R5, K – Q4.

The King, being "in the square" of the WP, can catch it. White takes the Black Pawn, and neither can win: nothing left to win with!

An interesting variation would have arisen after (8) R – R5 ch, if Black had played (8) . . . K – Q5, (9) P – B5, R – B7 ch; (10) K – K1, P – B6!! (11) K x R, P – B7; (12) R – R4 ch. Black can now either lose or win the game:

12. . . .	K – B6, 5 or 4???

13. R – R8, P – B8(Q); R – B8 ch and R x Q. Black loses.

12. . . .	K – K4?? (13) R – QB4. Black loses.
12. . . .	K – Q6! wins, since the Pawn queens.
12. . . .	K – Q4 also wins:

(13) R – R5 ch, K – Q3; (14) R – R6 ch, K – B2; (15) R – R7 ch, K – Kt3 and the Pawn queens.

All of which shows how wise White was to take the draw, by repetition! By trying to avoid it, he might have been at a disadvantage.

Exercise No. 15

I.

Figure 228

II. (Black to play)

Figure 229

III. (Black to play)

Figure 230

IV. (Black to play)

White

Black

Figure 231

There is still another way of obtaining a draw:

(e) By offer and acceptance.

In an informal game, you may do this at any time. In a tournament game, you must abide by the rules governing the offer of a draw. They usually state that such an offer can be made directly at any time after Move 30. Before that move, the offer must be made through the tournament director.

Of course, the second player may accept or

decline the offer. If he accepts, the game is a draw, and each player scores ½ point. If he declines, the game continues.

Many factors enter into an offer and acceptance of a draw. A player may consider a game so even that it is a waste of time to continue. The players may recognize a **"theoretical draw."** One player may be pressed for time (in a clock game) and offer a draw despite a better position. (GEORGE SHAINSWIT, a piece ahead of SAMUEL RESHEVSKY, but with twenty moves to make in a minute, offered a draw—and had it accepted!) A draw might decide a match, or a placement in a tournament, or a qualification in a preliminary round. So long as the draw is not prearranged or in violation of the rights of another player, it is perfectly legitimate to offer and accept a draw. It is part of the game.

Eventually a game ends in **checkmate or stalemate,** or the **fifty-move rule** applies. Many games end before the ultimate conclusion, because a player **resigns,** or a **drawing situation** occurs. Many times a player makes many fine moves, but just at the end, when he should win, he draws, or even loses, because he does not understand how to play when there are only a few pieces left on the board. That is the subject of the next and succeeding chapters.

CHAPTER XI

THE END GAME: GENERAL PRINCIPLES

The End Game comes into being when forces on both sides are greatly reduced, and the primary plan is to gain or increase material advantage by queening a Pawn. Just how greatly the material must be reduced for the game to change from "the middle game" to the "end game" depends upon the position. The simplest ending is one with King and Pawn vs. King; the most complex might involve Queens and one or even more pieces on each side, as well as Pawns. "Queen and Rook endings" are occasionally encountered; endings with four minor pieces on each side are more rare.

One ending may dissolve into another kind: thus, a "Rook and Knight" ending (which means a Rook and Knight on each side, as well as Pawns) may dissolve into a Rook ending or Knight ending; and either, in turn, into a Pawn ending. Each will be treated subsequently—the Pawn ending first, because of its basic character. Here we shall discuss basic principles, and specific terms.

Focus again upon the King—this time not because of his vulnerability, but because of his strength. For, as the major pieces disappear from the board, the King becomes more and more powerful, more and more a fighting piece. His value is close to that of a Knight or Bishop; and he has many qualities which these pieces do not possess.

1. King and Pawns

Offensively, the King is a powerful Pawn raider. The following diagram will help show this:

Figure 232

1. K – Kt6	K – B6
2. K x P	K x P
3. K x BP	K x P
4. P – Kt4	K x P

Five Pawns have been taken.

5. P – R4	P – R4
6. P – Kt5	P x P
7. P x P	P – R5

Each free Pawn will queen, Black with a check. The game should be a draw, but the Pawn ending will change into a Queen and Pawn ending—and you will have to know how to play that!

The King is also a powerful Pawn supporter.

Figure 233

If the WP advances, the Black King goes to Kt2, and captures it: The WK, however, comes to the rescue:

1. K – Q7	K – R2
2. K – K7	K – Kt1
3. P – B7 ch	K – Kt2
4. P – B8 (Q) ch, etc.	

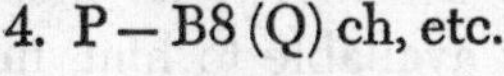

Figure 234

The WK can not catch the Pa5, but he can aid his own Pawns:

1. K – Kt5	**P – R6**
2. P – B6 ch	**K – Kt1** [K – B1

loses because of (3) K – R6, P – R7; (4) K – R7, P – R8(Q); (5) P – Kt7 ch, K – B2; (6) P – Kt8 ch, (Q), K x P; (7) Q – Kt7 ch, K – K3; (8) Q x Q.]

3. K – R6! A Pawn move loses for White!: P – Kt7? K – R2! or P – B7 ch, K – Kt2.

3. . . .	**P – R7**
4. P – B7 ch	**K – B1** (on R1 he is mated)
5. P – Kt7 ch!	

K – R7? loses, for after . . . P – R8 (Q) the Q guards g7.

5. . . .	K x P
6. K – R7	P – R8 (Q)
7. P – Kt8 (Q) ch	K – K2
8. Q – Kt7 ch	Q x Q ch Draw.

Two factors must be noticed:

(1) The King controls the squares left uncovered when the Pawns advance.

(2) Every move must be made at the right **time.**

And a corollary of (2)

(3) If you know two or more moves must be made, the **order** in which you make them may mean the difference between a **win** and a **draw** or a **loss.**

Control of space–order–time. These are the factors in end game play.

How does the King cooperate with his pieces?

2. King and Bishop

The Bishop is limited to his colored square–if he starts on a white square, he must remain on one. The King must, therefore, occupy squares governing the other color; so must the Pawns. In the Bogoljubow–Edward Lasker ending described in Chapter IX (Fig. 212) the continuation (after Black's move in the game (36) . . . K – B2) was:

Figure 235

37. R x R ch	K x R
38. B – Q2	K – K3
39. K – B2	K – Q3
40. K – K3	K – B4 (Intending

. . . K – Kt3 and P – R4, with some counterplay)

41. B – R5	B – B1
42. B – Q8	B – Q2
43. B – R5	P – Kt4

44. B – B3 After some maneuvering, White discovers that he does not have to worry about Black's Q side Ps. He can prevent . . . P – QKt5 by placing his B along the diagonal f8 – a3. The continuation should have been:

44. . . .	P – QR3 (in the

game, Black played . . . P – KR4, and lost the QRP after B – Q4 ch).

45. B – B6	P – Kt5
46. B – K7 ch	K – B3
47. P – Q4	

The Pawns take over the white squares, while WK and B protect the black ones.

47. . . .	K – Q2
48. B – Kt4	K – B3
49. P – Q5 ch	K – Q2
50. K – Q4	B – Kt2
51. P – K5	K – K1
52. P – K6	K – Q1
53. K – K5	K – K1
54. P – Q6	B – B3
55. K – Q4 (P – Q7 ch would win the B)	
55. . . .	P – KR4
56. K – B5	B x P
57. P – Q7 ch	K – K2
58. B – R5 and the QP queens.	

3. King and Knight

Since the Knight guards the color *not* of the square on which it stands, K and Ps should stand on the same colored squares as the Knight's for maximum efficiency. However, the Knight changes his square whenever he moves, so the King, too, will be constantly shifting.

Figure 236

1. P – R5 ch	K – Kt2
2. K – B5	(maximum efficiency for W)
2. . . .	K – B1
3. K – B6	K – Kt1
4. Kt – Q6	K – R2
5. K x P	K – R1
6. K – Kt6	K – Kt1
7. K x P	K – R1
8. K – Kt6	K – Kt1
9. Kt – B7	K – B1
10. Kt – R6	K – K2
11. K – Kt7, and the Pawn marches to R8.	

See also the ending K, B and Kt vs. K (Chapter VIII) for the coordinated use of these pieces.

4. King and Rook

The Rook guards a straight line (rank or file). The King must place himself opposite the opposing King to prevent his escaping or limit his moves. Because of the power of the Rook, mating threats as well as threats to Queen or Pawn will occur.

5. King and Queen

Although the Queen is a very powerful piece, there are some squares which she does not cover. It is the King's job to cover those squares. Because of the King's sensitivity, he must be careful to have shelter available to him, in the form of Pawns or his Queen.

For combined action of King and Queen and King and Rook see the earlier Chapter XIII on elementary checkmates, and the later chapters on specialized endings.

6. General Principles: Pieces

Some general principles apply to all pieces and positions. These affect **centralization, mobility and initiative.** But even these are dependent upon something which every player must have constantly in mind—**a plan.**

There must be a general plan of overall conduct of every game. This is a long-range strategy. When an objective has been gained, particularly when material has been won, another plan must be formulated at once. This is particularly true of an end game. A player with material advantage (say, a Pawn) will want to reduce forces, so that it will be easier to make a Queen of his extra Pawn. If he plays hide and seek with his opponent, he will get nowhere. But if he plans carefully to advance, let us say, on the side where he has material advantage, his opponent willy-nilly must oppose him on those grounds. Then the forces must clash.

Centralization—Mobility—Initiative

Included in every **plan,** there must be consideration of **centralization.** The pieces must be placed as much as possible in the center of the board, where, as we saw in the early chapters, they exert maximum power. This is particularly true of the King in the end game. He must leave his sheltered castled life and go forth to the forefront of battle.

The second principle is that of **mobility.** Your pieces must be able to move freely. The strongest spots for a Rook (open file, 7th rank), a Bishop (open diagonals), a Knight (center square), a Queen (open lines, central location) must be chosen, sometimes, as we have seen, at the sacrifice of material.

The third principle is that of **initiative.** You must press the attack where you have the advantage. Somehow or other, it is harder for a player to make good defensive moves. Place him on the defensive, and you have a psychological advantage, even if not a material one.

Here is a wonderful example: (Bogoljubow vs. Tartakower, New York 1924)

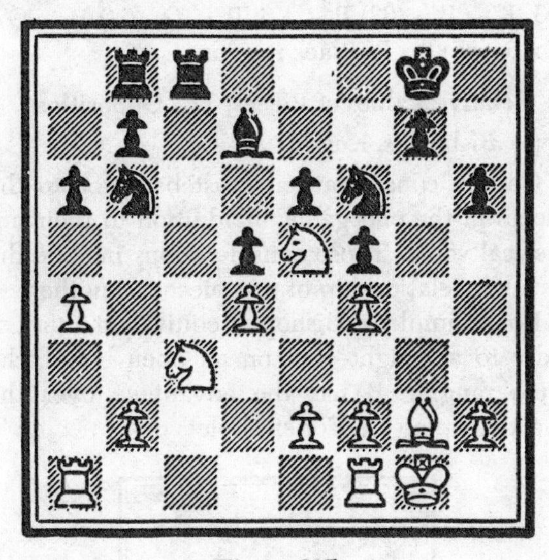

Figure 237

White has had the "jump" on Black since the opening but (we quote Alekhine's notes in the tournament book) "Black has extricated himself nicely, and now threatens by means of (22) . . . Kt – B5 to assume the initiative."

22. KR – B ". . . parries the threat. Kt – B5 will not do at this stage because of (23) Kt x B, Kt x Kt; (24) Kt x QP. (P x Kt, (25) B x P ch and (26) B x Kt)."

But now White offers a Pawn—and just to get his Rook on the seventh rank, its best spot.

22. . . .	B x P
23. Kt x B	R x R ch
24. R x R	Kt x Kt
25. P – Kt3	Kt – Kt3
26. R – B7	

Here it is; and, in combination with the Kt, it dominates the 7th rank. In case of necessity, White can recapture his Pawn by R – K7 and R x P (K6).

White's **plan:** to further restrict the Black forces by B – B3 and P – R4 – R5.

Black's **plan:** to defend the P on QKt7 with a Kt, releasing his Rook for counter attack.

26. . . .	Kt – B1
27. Kt – Q3	Kt – Q3

"threatening Kt – Kt4" (and x QP)

28. P – K3	P – QKt3?

"Hereby the WR gains the square c6 (QB6) and Black's position becomes highly critical. He would have had a simple draw by: (28) . . . R – QB; (29) R x R, Kt x R; (30) Kt – B5, Kt – Q3; (31) Kt x KP, K – B2; (32) Kt – B7, Kt (Q3) – K5, etc."

In other words, Black should gladly have returned his extra Pawn, in order to get rid of the well-placed WR.

29. R – B6	Kt (B3) – K1
30. B – B3	

White threatens (31) B – R5, (32) B x Kt, forcing Kt x B and winning the KP. The Black R would still be tied down to the defense of the QKtP (and QRP).

30. . . .	K – B2
31. B – R5 ch	K – K2

(Not P – Kt3, (32) Kt – K5 ch)

32. P – R4

". . . prevents . . . P – Kt4 and prepares for the crippling of the Black King's side by means of P – R5." (The Plan.)

In the meantime, the Bl K can not chase the WR by . . . K – Q2, because of Kt – K5 ch.

32. . . .	Kt – B3
33. B – K2	

"Threatening (34) Kt – K5, with a winning position; for instance: (33) . . . P – QR4; (34) Kt – K5, R – Kt2; (35) B – R6, etc."

33. . . .	Kt – Q2
34. Kt – K5	Kt x Kt

Forced: Otherwise (35) R – B7, R – Q; (36) Kt – B6 ch.

35. BP x Kt	Kt – Kt 4 (defending the QRP)
36. B x Kt	P x B
37. R – B7 ch	K – B1

Here we are in a R ending, the WR back on the 7th. Black *still* has his extra Pawn, but it is now doubled, and of less worth.

38. P – Kt4

"Necessary, for otherwise Black saves himself by advancing both QKtPs, thereby nullifying a double attack on the Kt and KPs."

38. . . .	R – R

Black gives up two Pawns for some initiative. As a matter of fact, he has practically no moves: . . . P – Kt3?; K – Kt2, P – R4; K – B3, followed by K – B4 – Kt5 – B6, with mate threats.

The Black R must move *now* with the WK at Kt1, in order to allow himself to attack the WQP, the defense of which, the P on K3, will be undermined by . . . P – B5.

39. R – B6	K – B2
40. R x KtP	P – B5
41. R – Kt7 ch	K – B1??

Black misses his last chance! Mobility and initiative he throws away by this cautious move—yes, and centralization, too! He was afraid of (41) . . . K – Kt3; (42) P – R5 ch; but then (42) . . . K – B4! (43) R – B7 ch, K – K5! (44) R x P ch, K – Q6!—and suddenly, the QKtP, hopelessly lost, not only is saved, but becomes a major threat to queen: (45) R – B7, K – B5; (46) R x P, K x P; (47) R – Kt6, R – K1; (48) R x RP, K – B6, with a free ride for the KtP to Kt8.

The remaining moves were:
(42) P x P, R – R8 ch; (43) K – Kt2, R – Q8; (44) R x QKtP, R x P; (45) K – Kt3, P – R4; (46) R – Kt7 (back again!) . . . P – Kt3; (47) P – Kt5, R – Kt5; (48) P – Kt6, R – Kt6 ch; (49) P – B3, R – Kt5; (50) R – Kt8 ch, K – K2. [Black must leave either the KtP or the KP, because if (50) . . . K – B2; (51) P – Kt7, P – Q5; (52) R – KR8, R x P; (53) R – R7 ch.]

(51) P – Kt7, K – Q2; (52) R – Kt8, R x KtP (now the Bl K can defend this R); (53) R – Kt7 ch, K – B3; (54) R x P.

"The KP can not be saved, for instance: . . . K – Q2, (55) P – B5! P x P; (56) P – K6 ch, K – Q3 (B3); (57) P – K7 ch, K – Q2; (58) R – Kt8! P – B5 ch; (59) K – R3 and wins. An instructive variation, which enhances considerably the total merit of this game (it was honored with a special prize)."

Figure 238

(54) . . . K – B4; (55) R x P, P – Q5; (56) P – B5, R – Q2; (57) K – B2, K – Q4; (58) R – K8, R – QR2; (59) P – B6 (White can queen more quickly than Black. He proceeds with his plan). (59) . . . R – KB2 (a momentary blockade); (60) R – K7, R – B1; (61) P – B7, P – Q6; (62) K – Q3, K – B5; (63) P – K6, R – Q; (64) R – Q7, R x R; (65) P x R, Black resigns.

7. Relative Values of Pieces; The Opposition

(a) Bishop vs. Knight

Certain considerations must be given to the pieces in the end game, in addition to their numerical value. Those considerations include the peculiar relationship of one piece to another.

For example, a Bishop is equivalent numerically to a Knight—yet, on an open board, the wide ranging B has the advantage over the short-stepping Kt. For example:

Figure 239

(Hanauer vs. Burdge, Ventnor City, 1939)

White played:

1. K – Q2	Kt – Kt5

2. B – Kt7! and Black resigned, for he can not save his Kt after (3) K – B3, Kt – R7 ch; (4)

K – Kt2, Kt – Kt5; (5) K – Kt3. If (2) . . . Kt – R7, (3) K – B2, followed by (4) K – Kt2, (5) K – Kt3.

The position: WB at Kt7 (b7); Bl Kt at Kt5 (b4) shows the B at its maximum power against a Kt: on the same rank or file, with two squares between.

In a blocked position, however, the Knight has the advantage:

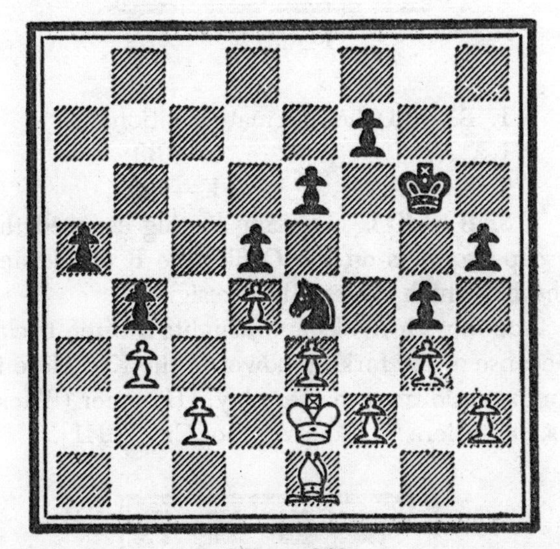

Figure 240

The WB is hemmed in on the K's side by his own Ps, and on the Q's side by Black's. On the other hand, the Bl Kt can hop around, changing the color of his square as the mood fits him:

1. P – B3 (to try for freedom).

1. . . . P x P; (2) 2 K x P, K – B4; (3) P – R3, Kt – Kt4 ch; (4) K – Kt2, K – K5; (5) B – Q2, Kt – B6; (6) B – B1, Kt – K8 ch; (7) K – B2, Kt x P; (8) P – Kt4, P x P; (9) P x P, Kt – R8, and the end is near.

If White stalls, trying to hold the position, Black considers the following:

A plan to play Kt – g5, K – e4 and Kt – f3, to win the Ph2, would be met by White's plan P – c3, x P – b4 and B x P – b4 (or, if Black exchanges on c3, B x P – c3 attacks the P – a5). The Kt must stay on e4 until the King is ready to occupy that spot. Then the Kt can exchange itself for the B, and the K enter e4 on the next move.

1. B – Q2	K – B4
2. B – K1	K – Kt4
3. K – Q3	

Black has waited to see what White would do about his threat of . . . P – R5 (threatening . . . P – R6). The WB remains at K1, for if . . . P – R5 now, P x P ch, K x P; P – B3 dis. ch. wins the Kt.

3. . . .	K – B4
4. K – K2	P – B3
5. B – Q2	Kt x B (the time is ripe)
6. K x Kt	K – K5
7. K – K2	P – K4

Black can hardly afford (7) . . . P – B4? (8) P – R4, P x P e.p??? (9) P – B3 mate.

8. P x P	P x P
9. K – K1	K – B6
10. K – B1	

(b) **The Opposition: King vs. King**

White has the **opposition**—that is, the Kings are on a line with one square between them, and Black has to move. But he has a spare move:

10. . . . P – K5. Now Black has the opposition. White must move his K.

11. K – K1 (best)	K – Kt7
12. K – K2	K x P

Black has won a Pawn. This is enough to win the game—but not easily. Every move must be exactly timed.

13. K – B1 The opposition is in Black's hands, for he can gain it by K – R8 or K – R6. But which one?

Figure 241

Let us say: . . . K – R8. Then (14) K – K, K – Kt8; (15) K – K2, K – Kt7; (16) K – K—and where can Black go? Not . . . K – B6, (17) K – B and he is stuck; lost, even.

Therefore his plan must be . . . K – R6, . . . P – R5, and, after P x P, K x P. Suppose he does it at once: (13) . . . K – R6; (14) K – Kt1, P – R5; (15) P x P, K x P; (16) K – R2! White has the opposition again, and can keep it. (16) . . . K – R4; (17) K – Kt2, K – R5; (18) K – R2! K – Kt4; (19) K – Kt3! The game will be a draw.

But if Black can keep White from R2 after . . . K x P, Black can win the opposition, *and therefore the game.*

His correct move, after all, is, accordingly:

13. . . .	K – R8!
14. K – K1	K – Kt8
15. K – K2	K – Kt7
16. K – K1	K – R6!
17. K – B1	P – R5
18. P x P	K x P
19. K – Kt2	

It doesn't seem to make much difference, but now:

19. . . .	P – Kt6!!
20. P x P ch	K – Kt5

And Black has the opposition. The White King must yield ground.

21. K – B2	K – R6
22. P – Kt4	K x P
23. K – Kt2	It's back again; but

Black now can get a free ("passed") Pawn on the K file.

23. . . .	K – B4
24. K – B2	K – K4
25. K – K2	P – Q5
26. K – Q2	K – Q4 (Why?)
27. K – K2	P x P
28. K x P	K – K4 (You were

right, of course: to get the opposition.)

29. K – K2	K – Q5
30. K – Q2	P – K6 ch
31. K – K2	K – B6
32. K x P	K x P followed by
33. . . .	K x P, and the Pawns will queen.

(c) Rook vs. Knight

As we know, the R is worth two Pawns more than the Knight. In the end game, he might be even more powerful, for two reasons: (1) He can stalemate the Knight. (2) He can mop up Pawns to the right and left, with abandon.

The stalemate position is on a diagonal, with one square between:

Figure 242

1. R – Q4 (the stalemate position)	
1. . . .	K – B3
2. K – K2	K – K4

3. R – Kt4. The King having covered the escape squares on the Q file, the R can attack the Kt, which is lost. Black resigns.

Action with Rooks and Knights is often tricky because of the forking power of the Kts. Here is an example from master play: [Hanauer (Black) vs. Santasiere (White), Ventnor City, 1941].

Figure 243

First examine the position. Black's Knight is slightly better placed than White's, being on the fifth rank to the other's fourth. His Rooks are also better, having more mobility, and attacking, rather than defending. Even the Black King is aggressively placed, ready to participate in an attack on his enemy.

In addition, Black has the initiative, for whenever he attacks the KBP, White must defend it.

There is, finally, a mating attack possible, if the Bl Kt comes to f3 and the Bl R to g1.

The game continued:

42. . . . R – Kt6, threatening Kt x P ch and the aforementioned mate. If (43) Kt x R? P x R ch; (44) K x P, Kt – B4 ch, winning the R on

K3, which can not be defended. (Black wins a Kt for a Pawn.)

43. **Kt – Q2**

Now Black can win a Pawn by (43) . . . Kt – B7; (44) R – K4, Kt – Kt5, but he sees that he has White in an iron grip, and does not want to let him go.

43. . . .	**R – B3**
44. **P – R3**	**P – R4**

White has a few more Pawn moves, but Black can move his Rook along the Bishop file until White runs out of them. Then one of the White pieces has to move, even if White does not want to move it.

This situation is called a **zugzwang.**

45. **R – B1**	**R(3) – Kt3**

Now Black threatens Kt – K3 – B5 and mate on KR6 (h3). If White plays (46) R – B2, Kt – K3, (47) Kt – K4, Kt – B5, he still can't take the R on Kt3 because of . . . P x Kt, forking K and R. Therefore:

46. **Kt – K4**	**R – Kt7 ch**
47. **K – R1**	**Kt – B7**

The WR (e3) is trapped, because of his lack of mobility.

48. **R(3) – K1**	**Kt x R**
49. **R x Kt**	**R x P**

The threat of R (3) – Kt7 forces an exchange of Rooks. The game should then be "easy" for Black to win, since he is the exchange and a Pawn ahead. But the Knight puts up such a tough fight singlehanded that the rest of the moves are included:

50. R – KKt1	R x R ch
51. K x R	R – Kt6
52. Kt x QP	P – Kt3
53. P – R4	R x P
54. Kt – B8	R x P
55. Kt x P	R x P
56. Kt – Q7	R – QB6
57. Kt x KP	K – Kt4
58. K – Kt2	K – B4
59. Kt – B6	R x P
60. Kt x P	R x P

White resigned. His Knight had led the Rook a merry chase.

(d) **Rook vs. Bishop**

The Bishop has so great a range that there is little danger of its being trapped by the Rook. The two Pawns extra value of the Rook is real, however; and only when the Bishop is supported by two extra connected Pawns can he be considered to have equal value. Even then, an active Rook can wreak great havoc:

Figure 244

1. R – K1

White forces the Bl Ps on to White squares, where they will interfere with the action of the B.

1. . . .	P – K5
2. P – B3	P – B4
3. R – Q1 "Restraining" (or holding back) the Pawn.	
3. . . .	K – B2
4. K – B2	K – B3
5. K – K3	K – K4
6. P – B4 ch	K – Q3
7. K – Q4	B – Q2
8. R – QB1	B – B3

The position is blocked. White tries to break through on the King's side:

9. P – R3	B – Q2
10. R – KKt1	P – KR4

Now that is stopped.

11. R – QB1	B – K3
12. R – B5	P – QKt3
13. R – B3	B – Q2
14. R – Kt3	P – QKt4

At last White has created a weakness: The square c5.

15. P – QR4!	More files for the R!
15. . . .	B – B3
16. P x P	B x P
17. R – QB3	B – B3
18. R – B5	B – Kt2
19. P – QKt4	B – B3
20. R – B3	B – Q2

21. R – R3	B – B1 (An eye in each direction)
22. R – R5	B – Kt2
23. P – Kt5	P x P
24. R x P	B – B3
25. R – Kt8	K – K2

White has improved the mobility of his Rook, but his King can not range too far, because those two extra Pawns will start moving.

26. R – Kt8	K – B2
27. R – QB8	B – Q2
28. R – KR8	P – Kt3
29. K x P Finally!	B – K3 ch
30. K – Q4	

(30) K – K5? P – K6! (31) R – R7 ch, K – Kt1; (32) R – QR7, P – K7; (33) R – R1, B – Kt6; (34) R – K1, B – Q8. The WK would have to retreat to Q2, allowing the Bl K to become active.

30. . . .	K – B3
31. P – R4 (P – Kt4 would reduce material too much).	
31. . . .	B – B2
32. R – QKt8	B – K3
33. R – Kt6	K – B2
34. K – K5	B – R7
35. R – Kt7 ch	K – B1
36. K – B6	K – K1
37. R – K7 ch	K – Q1
38. R – K5	K – Q2

39. K x P and, finally, White will gain a passed pawn by K x RP, which he will queen.

End game advantages are seemingly very slight—a square, a blockading Pawn, an open file, an aggressive King—but they are very real; and their sum total is often victory.

(e) **Like Pieces: R vs. R; B vs. B; Kt vs. Kt**

Usually these pieces can balance the power of pieces like them. With no weaknesses the games should be drawn. But the enemy must not be allowed to occupy lines unhampered: R must oppose R on open files, B oppose B on important diagonals, etc. See the following chapters on "R and P Endings," "B and P Endings," etc., for methods of play.

8. The Passed Pawn

(a) **Definition**

A passed pawn is one which has no enemy pawn in front of it on the same or adjoining files. In figure 245

Figure 245

W's Pawn on QB4 is passed, as well as Bl's Ps on Q5 and KR3. W's Pawn on QKt3 can become a passed pawn after the moves P – Kt4, P – R4, P – Kt5, and after . . . P x P, RP x P. Then White will have **connected passed pawns.** The passed pawns in the diagram are all **supported** by other pawns, and therefore immune to capture by the enemy Kings.

It is necessary to establish a passed pawn as a preliminary step on the way to making a queen. But the pawn itself is usually too weak to march alone to the queening square. He must be shepherded carefully by the King (with any available other pieces).

(b) **Value**

At the beginning of the book, we stated the value of a Pawn as 1, in comparison with 3 for the Bishop and Knight, etc. But the potential value of a Pawn is equal to that of a Queen (9 – 10) or even more, since the Pawn can transform himself into any piece (Q, R, B or Kt) on reaching his eighth rank.

(c) **The "Square" of the Passed Pawn**

Sometimes a passed pawn wishes to push on to queen. Can the enemy King catch him? The surest way is to count moves: if both pieces arrive at the queening square in the same number of moves, the Pawn can be caught. In the diagram above, W's QBP reaches QB8 in four moves. So does the Black King. It would be suicide for the Pawn to advance unprotected.

Geometrically, the Pawn can be caught if the enemy King is in a square formed by lines drawn first from Pawn to queening square, then of equal lengths to close the square. The "square" of W's P on QB4 extends to QB8 (five squares) to KKt8 (5 sq.) to KKt4 (5 sq.). If the Black King were on the KR file, he would be outside the square, and could not catch the Pawn.

How about Black's Pawn on Q5 (d4)? His "square" extends to KKt5 (g4) KKt8 (g1) and Q8 (d1). The White King is outside the square; the Pawn can advance safely. Check first by counting moves: 3 for the P; 4 for the WK.

Place the WK at QKt1 (b1). Now he is within the square of the QP, which extends to QR4, QR8 and Q8. But how about the passed pawn on Black's KR3 (h6)? His square extends to KR8 (6 sq.) QB3 (6 sq.) and QB8 (6 sq.); on b1, the WK would be outside the square of the P on h6, and he then could advance.

In the diagram, White, to move, seeing that his passed pawn on QB4 can not safely advance, should move his King to get into the square of the Bl QP. But not blindly: K – Kt3? would be a mistake, because after . . . P – Q6, his two KBPs would form a barrier against his remaining "in the square."

1. K – Kt1

(d) **Distraction Value of the Passed Pawn**

After White's move, neither Black Pawn can advance on its own safely, but one can sacrifice himself for the other:

1. . . .	P – KR4
2. P – Kt4	K – B1 (to get in the square of the KtP, about to become passed).
3. P – R4	K – K1 (now in the square of the RP).
4. P – R5	K – Q1 (staying in the square).
5. P – Kt5	P x P
6. P – R6	K – B2 (again!)
7. P x P	K – Kt3

Now Black is safe: The WPs are stopped, and he can continue with his plan. The KRP advances. When the WK captures it, he is outside the square of the QP, which then marches on to queen.

(e) **Weak Pawns**

When it is recalled that in the diagram, each side started with the same number of Pawns, you may wonder why one side lost the game. If you put your finger on one spot, it would be on the **doubled** KBPs of White. Doubled pawns can not protect each other. They are liable to capture; the spot in front of them is **weak.** We saw above how they interfered with the movement of the WK.

Move the Pawn from KB2 to KKt2 and see the difference: the KRP is not passed, and can not become passed, if the WP remains on Kt2 in this position. The best that Black can do is to establish passed pawns on the K and Q files, to counteract White's pawns to be pawned on the QR and QKt files. The game would be a draw.

Black's Pawn on QR3 (a6) is also weak, being **isolated.** Luckily, in this position nothing can capture it.

(f) **Gaining Material**

In Diagram 238, we saw how the threat of queening a passed pawn might have won a Rook; in Chapter IX (Diagram 210) a passed pawn cost a Bishop, which had to sacrifice itself to prevent the Pawn's queening. In Diagram 214 a Rook was able to sacrifice itself in order to free the passed pawns on their way to queening squares; in Diagram 215 a whole Queen went for the Pawn's freedom. A player should not concern himself if he can not queen a Pawn—let him win a piece, and the brother Pawns will soon queen.

(g) **Blockaders**

Since a passed Pawn is so dangerous, he must certainly be blockaded. By definition, a Pawn is no longer available. Any piece can act as a blockader (even the King) but the lesser value, the better: that is, a Knight is a better blockader than a Rook; a Rook better than a Queen.

A Knight is a particularly good blockader for a special reason: he attacks at the same time the Pawns supporting the passed Pawn.

(Black to move.)

White

Black

Figure 246

The Kt on Q3 is blockading the WP on his Q5. It is also attacking the Ps on K4 and KB4. After:

1. . . .	P x P (fixing the target)
2. P x P	R – Kt5
3. B – B1	R – QR1
4. R – B2	R(1) – R5
5. P – B3	R – R6 one weak-

ness has led to another.

6. K – Kt2	R (Kt) – Kt6
7. B – K2 (If R – B2, R – B6)	
7. . . .	P – R4 (Plan: P –

Kt4 – Kt5, exposing the KKtP to the two Rs.)

8. R – KR1	K – Kt2

The King must enter the battle: support for the P on R4 or a possible . . . P – B4.

9. K – B2	P – B4

This is the time for the dynamite: (a) the Bl P on e5 is no longer attacked as it was on move 7.

(b) the WP on e4 can be defended only with the greatest difficulty.

(c) If (10) P x P, Kt x P, and the threat of . . . Kt – Q5, attacking Rc2, and Pf3 a third time is very powerful.

10. R – R4	P x P
11. P x P	R x P

Now for the still unmoved P on d5, Black has two connected passed pawns.

12. R – Kt2	P – Kt4!
13. R x P	Kt x P ch
14. K – K1	R – R8 ch
15. B – Q1	R – Kt8 ch
16. K – K2	Kt – Kt6 ch
17. K – B2	Kt x R
18. K x R	R x B ch
19. K – B2	P – Kt5

The rest is a matter of time. We leave it to you to work out.

The Bishop is necessarily a defensive blockader, since it is most likely that his Ps will flank the passed pawn, as did the Black Pawns on the last diagram. In the following opening, the Bishop plays an important part as blockader, but he is not the only one in that role:

VIENNA GAME

(1) P – K4, P – K4; (2) Kt – QB3, Kt – KB3; (3) P – B4, P – Q4; (4) BP x P, Kt x P; (5) Q – B3, P – KB4; (6) P – Q3, Kt x Kt; (7) P x Kt, P – Q5; (8) Q – Kt3, Kt – B3; (9) B – K2, B – K3.

Figure 247

The Be6 is a blockader, but he has some range because the QP has been pushed. Black's Pawn on Q5 (d4) blocks the WQP (d3) which would like to go on to Q4. To a certain extent the Kt c6 blockades the WQP, too, defending as it does his P d4.

10. B – B3	Q – Q2

Now the Q is a secondary blockader for K3 (e6). Incidentally it defends the threat (11) B x Kt, Q x B; (12) P x P? because of . . . Q – B6 ch.

11. Kt – K2	B – B4
12. P – B4	O – O
13. O – O?	

Up to now Black's Pawn (d4) has been blockaded by the WP d3. But the WK is now on the diagonal of the B c5.

13. . . .	B x P!

If (14) P x B? P – Q6 ch; (15) K – R1, P x Kt; (16) B x P, B – Q5; (17) R – Kt1, B x P—and the KP does not have to be blockaded any longer—it is off the board!

14. Kt – B4	B – K3

Back to the iron mines, now that he has struck ore!

The game is Spielmann–Romanovsky, Moscow, 1925, in one of the great tournaments of all time.

Examples of Rooks and Queens as defending blockaders will be found in their respective

End Game chapters following. The King was seen to good advantage in figures 244 and 245 and will be met again in future sections.

Exercise No. 16

I. What is White's best move?

Figure 248

II. White's Bishop is attacked. Where should he go?

Figure 249

III. (Black to move)

White

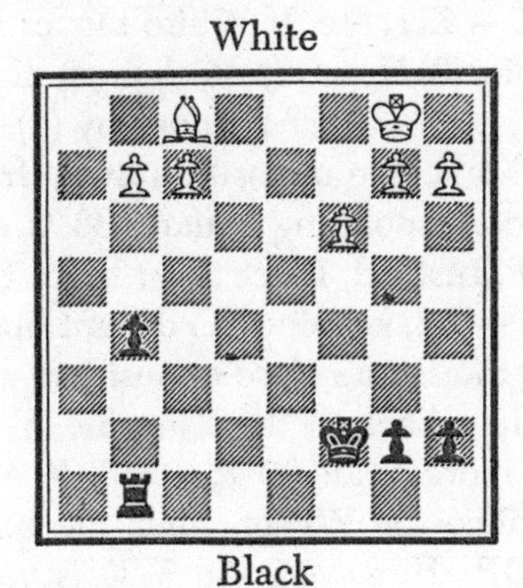

Black

Figure 250

9. Zugzwang Revisited

You will recall that in an earlier chapter, the importance of **zugzwang** was discussed, that is, a situation where a player has to make a move, and whatever he chooses to make will result in loss of some kind. For example, with a WK at g6, WP at f7 and Black K at f8, Black on the move would like to stick, but he has to move his King to e7, allowing the WK to get to g7, and thus support his Pawn to f8. White to move would have to go to f6 (stalemate) or abandon his Pawn, so he, too, would be in a type of *zugzwang.*

Figure 251

In this position, whoever has the move loses, since he must move away from his Pawn, whichever King has to move, therefore, is in zugzwang.

Figure 252

Knowing the above, White will not play K – B5?? since by K – Q5!, Black will place him in zugzwang. Therefore: (1) **K – Kt5.** This, incidentally, gives the WK the **distant opposition.**

Now it is Black's turn to worry. (1) . . . K – Q5 will be met by (2) K – B5, and Black will be in zugzwang. If he plays up: (1) . . . K – B5, White replies (2) K – B6, forcing . . . K – Q5, and then (3) K – B5. Therefore:

1. . . .	**K – B3**
2. K – B5	**K – Q3**

3. **K – B6** Black again is in zugzwang. He must abandon the Pawn.

But knowledge of the elementary ending K and P vs. K will tell him that he can still draw. (See next chapter.) He plays:

3. . . . **K – Q2**
4. **K x P** **K – K2** gaining the opposition. This is a draw.

Another type of zugzwang can be seen in the following diagram:

Figure 253

White, to move, plays:

1. **K – B7** and Black must exchange P for P. After (1) . . . K x P; (2) K x P, K – B5, the WK arrives at QB6, takes the QKtP and queens his before the Bl K can capture the WQRP and queen his. Therefore:

(1) . . . **P – B4**; (2) **P x P, K x P**; (3) **K – K7, K – K4**; (4) **K – Q7, K – Q4**; (5) **K – B7, K – B4**; (6) **K – Kt7 zugzwang!** The Bl K must leave his QKtP. (6) . . . **K – Kt5.**

Now counting moves will show you that it will take White **five** moves to capture the P, move his K and queen his P; whereas it will take Black **six.** Moreover, it is White's move. But there are points about the play which make it interesting:

(7) K x P, K x P; (8) K – R6 (best move; it keeps the Bl K further from his P's queening square); (8) . . . K – Kt5; (9) P – Kt6, P – R5; (10) P – Kt7, P – R6; (11) P – Kt8 (Q) **check** (another setback for Black); (11) . . . K – B6, (12) Q – Kt1, and wins.

Now back to the Diagram: Black to move. If . . . K x P, he is in the same boat as above. But (1) . . . **K – Kt3!** gains the opposition. Now if (2) **K – K7, K – Kt2**; (3) **K – K8, K – Kt1**, always keeping the opposition, and never allowing the zugzwang maneuver shown above.

However, White has a second threat, namely: K x QKtP, and queening the W QKtP. He therefore plays (after (3) K – K8, K – Kt1)

4. **K – Q7!** **K – B2**
5. **K – B7** and wins easily, queening in five moves, while Black takes eight.

One of the reasons for this suddenly great advantage is White's aggressive Pawn position, of which more later.

10. Conjugated Squares

But now let us examine a position where the extra Pawns are equally placed:

Figure 254

With White to move, Black has the opposition, and he can keep it: (1) **K – K7, K – Kt2**; (2) **K – K8, K – Kt1**, etc. If White moves as in the last example, (3) **K – Q7,** Black must not rush to play (3) . . . K – B2?? because by (4) K – Q6! White will take the opposition away from him, since the corresponding square B3 is occupied by the Bl P. Instead, Black must make the move (3) . . . **K – R2,** keeping the **distant opposition,** and ready to assume **close opposition** whenever the WK plays back to the King file. White can make one more trial: (4) **K – Q6, K – R3**; (5) **K – Q5,** since the WP prevents the Bl K from going to RP. However, the WK is rather far afield, and (5) . . . **K – Kt4** forces him back: (6) **K – K6,** whereupon Black regains the opposition by (6) . . . **K – Kt3.**

Study of the position will convince you that certain squares have a relationship to each other: that when the WK is on K6, the Black

King *must* move to Kt3 for Black to draw; when the WK is on K7, the Bl K *must* move to Kt2; if the WK moves to Q7, the Bl K *must* move to R2. These related squares are called **conjugated squares;** they are yoked together like a team of oxen.

Move the right side of the diagram closer to the edge of the board,

Figure 255

thereby depriving Black of an extra file, and White wins:

1. K – K5! Now Black has no corresponding square, and wherever he moves, White gains the opposition.

1. . . . K – R5;	2. K – B6
1. . . . K – R3;	2. K – B6
1. . . . K – Kt3;	2. K – K6, K – Kt2;

(3) K – B5, K – R3; (4) K – B6, K – R4; (5) K – Kt7, etc.

Then, after the exchange of Pawns, the WK captures the QKtP and QRP, thereby defending his own QRP, which he will support to its queening square.

11. Triangulation

The examples above contain a stratagem whereby one side loses a move: that is, the White King does not move directly to B6, but goes to another square first, executing a geometric triangle: (illustration) This process is called **triangulation.** It is vital when a King wants to lose a move, and when no other spare move is available. (Fig. 256)

White has a spare move (P – B3), so that after (1) K – K4, K – Q3 he can switch the zugzwang to Black by (2) P – B3.

But Black has another defense: (1) K – K4, P – B3. Now if (2) P x P ch, K x P; (3) P – B3, Black has a spare move: . . . P – Kt4. If (4) P – Q6, K – K3; (5) P – Q7, K x P; (6) K x P

Figure 256

Black has a miraculous drawing move: (6) . . . P – Kt5!! (7) P x P, K – K2!! (See next chapter.)

When White realizes all this, he will not rush his first move, but play:

(1) K – K3! incidentally, gaining the opposition. Now, if . . . K – Q2, the defense of . . . P – B3 is no longer available to Black, and (2) K – K4, K – Q3; (3) P – B3 forces the win of the KP. Black must play:

1. . . .	P – B3 (or . . . P – B4 (2) P x P, e.p.)
2. P x P ch	K x P
3. K – K4	P – Kt4

4. P – B3 and Black is in zugzwang, losing his KP.

Here White used the principles of triangulation (K – K3 – K4) opposition and zugzwang to work out his win.

12. Aggressive Pawn Position

In connection with Diagram 253 mention of an **aggressive pawn position** was made. In that diagram the Pawns **a4** and **b5** were called aggressive, because they held back the Black Pawns, thereby limiting the space for the Black pieces to maneuver in.

Another type of aggressive pawn position is a **fluid** pawn formation.

Figure 257

The Pawns d5 and c4 are aggressive; so are the Ps a3 and b3 because of their fluidity: in case of necessity, the P a3 can advance, giving White an important spare move; under other circumstances, the P b3 can advance to break up the Black Pawn formation.

Suppose that Black has the opposition. White can gain it by (1) P – R4, but then he, too, can not win: (1) . . . K – Kt3; (2) K – Kt4, K – B3; (3) K – R5, K – B2; (4) K – Kt5, K – Kt2; (5) K – B5, K – B2, etc.

But let him yield ground by (1) **K – Kt4** and if Black is tempted to enter with his King by (1) . . . **K – K4??** (2) **P – R4** (stopping . . . P – R5), . . . K – Q5??? (3) K – B5, K – B6; (4) K – B6, K x P; (5) K x P, K x BP; (6) K – B6, and queens in three moves as against five. The aggressive Pawn e5 won the game.

In the following position, an aggressive pawn position saved the day:

White

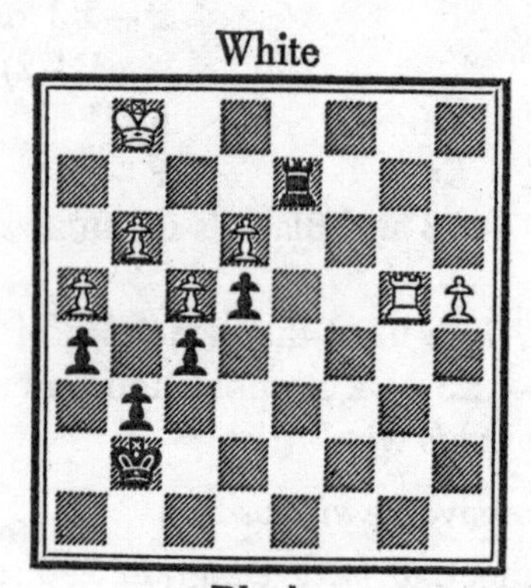

Black

Figure 258

(Kupchik vs. Hanauer, U.S. Championship, 1938)

Black is a Pawn behind, but he has an aggressive Rook as well as his Pawns. The game continued:

41. K – B	R – QR7
42. R – Kt7 ch	K – Kt1?

This move makes matters difficult. . . . K – B3 was much better.

43. R – QR7	R – R8 ch
44. K – K2	R – R7 ch
45. K – K1	

White is willing to give up his KKtP in order to free his King for a march to KB6 or as support for his passed QRP. However,

45. . . .	R – R6
46. K – Q2	R – Q6 ch
47. K – K2	R – Q3!

Black seals off the WK; protects his KtP, and prepares to free his K by a march to QKt1.

48. R – QB7	K – B1
49. R – B3	K – K2
50. P – R5	R – R3
51. R – B5	

White has distracted the Bl R by the advance of his Passed Pawn, and is now ready to bring up his King.

51. . . .	R – Q3

Black will have none of it!

52. R – B7 ch	K – Q1
53. R – B	R – R3
54. R – QR	K – B2

Black's King can now blockade the QRP.

55. K – Q2	R – Q3 ch Again!
56. K – K2	K – Kt2
57. R – QB	R – QB3!

Now Black can even offer the exchange of Rooks. This would be amazing, considering the fact that he has to capture the QRP, but the aggressive pawn position permits it: (58) R x R? K x R; (59) K – Q2, K – Kt4; (60) K – B3, K x P; (61) K – K4, K – Kt5; (62) K – K5, K – B6; (63) K – B6, K – Q6; (64) K x P, K x P; (65) K x BP, K – B6 and queens in three moves, as against five.

58. R – Q1	R – B7 ch

Now Black wouldn't mind taking the KKtP, but White won't give it up.

59. K – B1	R – B6

This move intends a draw by repetition, since White can not interpose his R at Q2. But White has some ideas on the subject:

60. R – Q7 ch	K – R3
61. R – Q6 ch	K x P
62. K – K2	R – B7 ch
63. K – Q1	R – KKt7
64. R x P Got there first!	

But now: Enter the King.

64. . . .	K – Kt5
65. K – K1	K – B6
66. K – B1	R – QR7
67. R – Q6	

It is amusing to see the use White now makes of Black's key square d6, cutting off Black's K in turn.

67. . . .	R – R8 ch

68. K – B2	R – R7 ch
69. K – K1	R – R8 ch
70. K – K2	R – R7 ch
71. K – B1	R – R8 ch
72. K – Kt2	

Draw. White does not dare escape to R3 with his K, because Black could win the KP and queen his. The only other try would be (after 69. K – K1, R – R8 ch) (70) R – Q1, but then (70) . . . R x R ch (71) K x R, K – Q6; (72) P – Kt4, RP x P; (73) P – R5, P – Kt6; (74) K – K1, K x P; (75) K – B1, K – B6; (76) P – R6, P – Kt7 ch; (77) K – Kt1, P – K6; (78) P – R7, P – K7; (79) P – R8 (Q), P – K8 (Q) ch; (80) K – R2, Q – R8 checkmate. The aggressive Pawn!

In subsequent chapters, we shall deal with specific endings, starting with King and Pawn endings, into which others can dissolve.

CHAPTER XII

KING AND PAWN ENDINGS

The primary purpose of an end game, we have seen in the previous chapter, is to increase material by making a Queen out of a Pawn. Before the Pawn can reach his eighth rank, however, he must be a "passed pawn." Once he is "passed," you must decide whether he can march to the queening square by himself, or whether, as is usually the case, he needs the support of your King.

1. To Push or Not to Push

Remember the rule of the square of the Pawn. But remember also that the rule is only for a preliminary survey. After this preliminary glance, exact counting and eye measuring must take place. The following diagrams will show why:

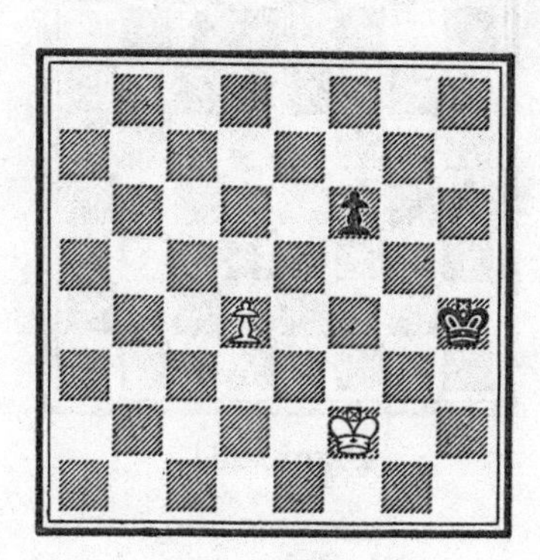

Figure 259

Should White push his P on Q4?

The "square of the Pawn" estimate will show that the Black King can catch the Pawn. But can he keep on catching it? (1) P – Q5, K – Kt4, (2) P – Q6. Now Black finds that his own Pawn is blocking him. He has been "screened off" like a basketball player, but by his own man. The King can not catch the Pawn.

Figure 260

White has a choice of three moves: K x P, P x P and P – R6. In either case, the Black King will be in the square of the Pawn. There is a further danger: if P – R6 or K x P, White is left with a RP, and the ending K and RP vs. K is usually a draw.

The most tempting move is (1) P x P. Then (1) . . . , K – B1; (2) P – Kt7 ch, K – Kt1; (3) K – Kt6. Stalemate!

Now try (1) K x P, K – B1; (2) P – R6, K – Kt1 (3) P – R7 ch, K – R1; (4) K – R6. Stalemate!

Finally, (1) P – R6, K – B1 (in the square); (2) P – R7. The WK prevents K – Kt2, the WP prevents K – Kt1. Black can not stay in the square; White wins.

2. Obtaining a Passed Pawn

A player can obtain a passed pawn in a variety of ways. Usually he has an extra Pawn on one part of the board: two against one, or three against two. The procedure is simple enough:

(a) Advance the Pawn which has no Pawn in front of it up to one square from the adjoining Pawn.

(b) Advance the Pawn next to it until it is abreast.

(c) Obtain contact with the opposing Pawn.

Figure 261

Referring to (a), we see that the P to advance is the KRP: (1) P – R4, then to (b), (2) P – Kt4 and to (c), (3) P – R5. Your RP is now passed.

Suppose (1) P – Kt4?? P – Kt4! and W can not obtain a passed RP except by a sacrifice of his KBP.

In some positions a passed pawn can be obtained even when there is no extra Pawn:

Figure 262

1. P – Kt6	RP x P
2. P – B6	P(Kt2) x P

3. P – R6, a passed pawn on the thruway.

Or:

1. P – Kt6	BP x P
2. P – R6	P (Kt2) x P
3. P – B6	

Figure 263

Sometimes, it is wiser to delay making the pawn passed; or to exchange the right for some other stratagem:

(1) P – R4? would be an error not only because it could be captured after P x P; P x P; but also because the product would be a RP, which could not win except under unusual circumstances.

Correct is (1) K – K4! K – B3. (If . . ., P – Kt5, (2) P – R4) (2) K – Q4, K – Q3; (3) P – Kt4! and Black must yield the opposition: (3) . . . K – B3; (4) K – K5, K – B2; (5) K – Q5, K – Kt3; (6) K – Q6, K – Kt2; (7) K – B5, K – R3; (8) K – B6, winning the KtP.

Each player should be on the alert to prevent the other from obtaining a passed pawn:

Figure 264

White's move. Black has just played . . . P – Kt5. Surely he is not giving up a Pawn for nothing? No, indeed. If P x P, P – B6; P x P, P – R6 and that Pawn queens. If White does nothing on that side of the board, then . . . P – B6 anyhow, and if P x BP, P x RP.

(1) P – B3! Now the Q side Ps stand like the rock of Gibraltar, and it is Black's turn to do some figuring. First, he has to do something about his QKtP—exchange it or push it. Then he must begin to worry about W's KRP, which threatens to become passed after P – Kt5 and P – R6.

If Black can not prevent item (a) (pushing the unopposed Pawn as far as possible before contact) because it has been accomplished, he can stop item (b) (advancing the Pawn next to the unopposed Pawn until it is abreast of the latter). With his King? No, since White can play K – B4, and force P – Kt5 ch. With his Pawn, then. But to get time for this, he must first play:

1. . . .	P x RP
2. P x P	P – B3!

(3) K – B4. White now tries to force the Bl K back with his K. Object: to capture the P on QB4.

3. . . .	K – B2
4. K – B5	It looks good now.
4. . . .	P – Kt3 ch

Going back with the K loses: White plays K – Kt6, then P – R6, capturing the BP. The RP is then easy prey.

5. P x P ch	K – Kt2
6. P – Kt5	P x P
7. K x P	K – Kt1
8. K – B6	K – B1
9. K – K5	K – Kt2

10. K – Q4 White captures the QBP and queens his.

Why did White win? Aggressive pawn position; aggressive King—and, of course, understanding of the principles involved.

Some other points are involved. Suppose on move 2 . . . P – Kt3; (3) P – R6, K – B3 (in the square) (4) P – Kt5 ch! wins. Or, (2) . . . K – B3; (3) K – B4, P – Kt4 ch; (4) K – K4, K – K3; (5) K – Q4, P – B4; (6) P – R6, K – B3; (7) P x P. Black can not approach the RP nor capture the BP.

Finally, (2) . . . K – B3; (3) K – B4, P – Kt3; (4) P – Kt5 ch, K – Kt2; (5) P – R6 ch, K – R2; (6) K – K5, K – Kt1; (7) K – B6, K – B1; (8) P – R7, and the Pawn queens.

3. King and Rook Pawn

We have said several times that King and Rook Pawn could not win against a King except in rare positions. The following will show why:

Figure 265

(1) K – B2, K – R7; (2) K – B1, K – Kt6; (3) K – Kt1, P – R6; (4) K – R1, P – Kt7 stalemate.

If the defending King can reach B1 without being cut off from Kt1 by . . . P – R7, he can draw.

Move the Kings one file to the right, and Black wins:

(WK on d3, Bl K on b3)

(1) K – Q2, K – Kt7, and the Pawn marches in.

4. Outside Passed Pawn

And yet, the Rook Pawn, so weak in itself, is a powerful end game weapon:

Figure 266

(1) K – Q3, K – Q4; (2) P – R5, K – Q3; (3) K – B4, K – B3; (4) P – R6, K – Kt3; (5) P – R7, K x P; (6) K x P—and White is two files nearer the helpless King side Pawns.

This is the theory of the **outside passed pawn:** the side that has a passed pawn farthest away from the main body of Pawns, will generally win!

Exercise No. 17

I.

Figure 267

II.

Figure 268

III.

Figure 269

IV.

Figure 270

5. The Vital Ending: King and Pawn vs. King

With all the excitement and glory and sparkle of the various pieces in chess, the whole game boils down to this ending: **K and P vs. K. Learn to play it perfectly, or you will never know how to play chess.**

Figure 271

(a) White to move; what result?
(b) Black to move; what result?

Answers: (a) Draw. (b) White wins.

In order to win, White must have two things:

1. **His King in front of his Pawn.**
2. **The opposition.**

Let us study each situation in turn: (a) White to move: (1) K – Q4, K – Q3; (2) K – K4, K – K3; (3) K – B4, K – B3. It is obvious that Black will not yield ground. White must try something else.

(4) P – K4, K – K3. We now have another crucial position, which White can not win, if Black plays properly.

Figure 272

Black: (a) must stay in front of Pawn or King, whichever is more advanced;

(b) must, when *forced* to move back, stay in front of the Pawn.

(5) P – K5, K – K2; (6) K – B5, K – B2; (7) P – K6 ch, K – K2; (8) K – K5, K – K1. Now we see why this is necessary: Wherever White moves, Black takes the opposition.

(9) K – Q6, K – Q1; (10) P – K7 ch, K – K1;

(11) K – K6 stalemate! Or (9) K – B6, K – B1; (10) P – K7 ch, K – K1; (11) K – K6 stalemate.

What happens if Black does not move straight back on move 8? (WK on K5, WP on K6; Bl K on K2)

(8) . . . K – Q1? (9) K – Q6! K – K1; (10) P – K7, K – B2; (11) K – Q7 and the Pawn queens.

(8) . . . K – B1? (9) K – B6! K – K1; (10) P – K7, K – Q2; (11) K – B7 and the Pawn queens.

Now back to figure 271. Black to move must yield ground. White advances on the uncovered file:

(1) . . . K – Q3; (2) K – B5, K – K2; (3) K – K5! (3 P – K4?? draws) K – B2; (4) K – Q6, K – B3; (5) P – K4, K – B2; (6) P – K5, K – K1; (7) K – K6! K – Q1; (8) K – B7, and the Pawn is sheltered through to K8.

Figure 273

This position is a draw. If it is White's move, Black has the opposition, and maintains it:

(1) K – K3, K – K4; or, (1) K – B3, K – B4.

If it is Black's move in the diagram, Black can steal the opposition from White by (1) . . . K – K3, since the conjugated square (K2) for White is occupied by his Pawn.

In another type of position it is White who can steal the opposition:

Figure 274

(1) K – K3, K – K2; (2) K – K4, K – K3; (3) P – K3! The spare Pawn move turns the tide. Or (1) K – B3, K – B2; (2) K – B4, K – B3; (3) P – K3! (But not P – K4?? Draw.)

Exercise No. 18

I. WK on KB5; WP on KB4; Bl K on K2, Bl P on K4, White moves.

II. WK on K3, WP on K6; Bl K on Q3, Bl P on K2, White moves.

III. WK on KB6; WPs on KB7, QKt3, QKt4, QB4
Bl K on KB1; Bl Ps on QKt4, QB3, QB4.

IV. WK on QB3; WPs on QKt4, QKt5, QB5
Bl K on QR5; Bl Ps on QKt3, QB2.

6. Stopping a Passed Pawn

The best way to stop a passed pawn is to move your King in front of it; but sometimes the King is far afield, and the pieces must do the work. In the previous chapter we spoke of blockaders, but here we shall notice cases where the pieces, using the strength of their movement, stop the Pawns from afar.

(a) The Rook

The best position for a Rook is behind the Pawn; but sometimes he must defend from the side or front. **Rule 1: Attack the Passed Pawn!**

Figure 275

(1) **R – KKt7** wins. It stops the Pawn, attacks it, and prevents the K from defending it. On the other hand, (1) R – B1 is met by . . . K – B5; (2) K – B2, K – B6; (3) K – Q2, K – B7, and the P queens, winning the R for it.

(1) **R – R3** (attack the Passed Pawn!) . . . **P – R7; (2) R – R3** wins.

If White tried K – Kt3 and R – R1, the Black KKtP would advance to the defense of the RP:

Figure 276

(1) K – Kt3(?), P – KKt4; (2) R – R1, P – Kt5.

Rule 2: In defending against two connected Passed Pawns with a Rook, attack the more advanced Pawn.

(3) R – R1! Now the Pawns are stuck until the King comes up. Otherwise, . . . P – Kt6, and one Pawn queens.

Rule 3: Two connected Passed Pawns on the sixth rank win against a Rook.

(3) . . . K – Kt3; (4) K – B3, K – Kt4; (5) K – Q3, K – R5! This protects the more advanced Pawn. . . . K – B5 only draws. (6) K – K3, K – Kt6; (7) R – Kt1 ch, K – R5 (threatening . . . P – R7 and . . . K – R6); (8) R – R1, K – Kt6; (9) R – Kt1 ch, K – R5; (10) R – R1 drawn by repetition.

Figure 277

Here the Rook has not only to stop the P, but also to worry about the power of the Bishop. He has three files open to him, but if:

(1) R – KR1?? P – Q6; (2) R – R2, B – K7! and White will have to give up his Rook for the Pawn.

(1) R – QB8?? P – Q6; (2) R – B1, P – Q7 and again the Rook must sacrifice himself.

(1) R – QR8! P – Q6; (2) R – R2! (The Pawn must be stopped on a square not governed by the Bishop.)

(2) . . . B – Q8! threatening to cut off the R by . . . B – B7; (3) R – Q2! and holds the Pawn, while his King goes into action.

(b) The Bishop

The Bishop stops a Pawn on a diagonal, controlling a square in front of the Pawn. In the case of two connected Passed Pawns, the B should attack the advanced one.

Figure 278

(1) B – Q5! (Not B – B1? . . . P – B6 and . . . P – Kt7)

(1) . . . K – Kt4; (2) B – B3! K – R5; (3) K – Q3, K – R6; (4) K – K4, P – Kt7; (5) B x P ch, K x B; (6) K x P. The B holds the Ps until the K can take his share in the fighting. He can block out the enemy King, too. In fact if (2) K – Q3, K – Kt5, threatening P – B6; although K – K2 can still stop Black. (K – R6; K – B, K – Kt5; K – K2)

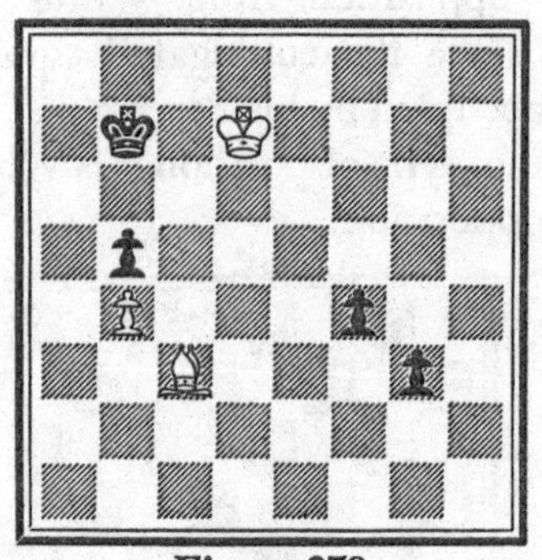

Figure 279

(1) B – K1! (Attack the advanced Pawn!) If (1) . . . P – Kt7; (2) B – B2. But if (1) B – Q2?? P – B6 and . . . P – B7. Or B – Q4?? Again P – B6-7.

(c) **The Knight**

The Knight, because of its limited range, has more difficulty stopping a Passed Pawn. A Rook Pawn especially gives it trouble, since the Kt can stop the P from only one side.

Figure 280

In the diagrammed position, if (1) Kt x BP?? Kt x Kt; (2) P – Kt6, the Bl Kt can play to R3, stopping the P at Kt8. But on (1) **Kt x KtP!** Kt x Kt; (2) P – R6, the RP cannot be stopped.

The following ending was reached in a game at Ventnor City, 1939, between J. W. Collins (White) and the author. Black to move.

White

Black

Figure 281

The Knight will try to sacrifice himself for the two Pawns. For that, the King is needed. But can the Kt hold the Ps in the meantime?

(1) . . . **K – K7,** (2) **P – B6, Kt – Q3** (to allow P – Kt5 would be suicide) (3) **P – B7, K – Q6;** (4) **P – Kt5! Kt – B1!** Now the Ps are stopped, and prey for the King.

The best spot for the Kt is as a blockader: in front of one P and guarding the square in front of the other. He should also be as far as possible from the enemy K.

(d) **The Queen**

The Queen, of course, can stop any Passed Pawn in the same manner as a R or B. Nevertheless, she can often win a game which the others would be lucky to draw.

For example, the Queen can win against King and Pawn on the seventh rank, except as noted below:

Figure 282

(1) Q – KB5 ch, K – Kt7; (2) Q – K4 ch, K – B7; (3) Q – B4 ch, K – Kt7; (4) Q – K3, K – B8; (5) Q – B3 ch, K – K8; (6) K – B3, K –Q8; (7) K – Q3, and the pinned pawn is lost.

(Not 6 K – B2? Stalemate.)

It does not matter how far away the WK is. The Q forces the Bl K in front of the P, and gains a move for the K; then repeats the process for another K move, etc.

If the Pawn is on B7, or R7, however, the King can draw by going to R8, inviting a stalemate.

Figure 283

1. Q – Kt3 ch (or (1) Q – Q4), K – R8!
2. Q x P stalemate.

Place the P on R7, and White has the same trouble: (1) Q – Kt3 ch, K – R8; (2) Q – K1 ch, K – Kt2; (3) Q – K2 ch, K – Kt8 (not K – R8? (4) Q – B1 mate) Q – Kt4 ch, K – R8. The Q can never take breath to allow the K to advance, because of the stalemate.

If, however, the Q can govern the queening square *and* keep the King from Kt7, she can win against a RP:

Figure 284

(1) Q – Q5! (Guards R8 *and* Kt7) . . . K – B7; (2) Q – R1. The same would hold with Bl K at K6 and Bl P at B7: (1) Q – QB4 (Guards B8 and K7) K – Q7 or B6; (2) Q – B1! The ol' demon zugzwang could raise its ugly head:

Figure 285

1) Q – K4! K – Kt8 (forced); (2) Q – K1 mate!

(e) **Counter Threat**

If nothing else can stop a passed pawn, a counter threat might be able to do it. Examine this study by Reti:

Figure 286

(1) **P – R4.** The Black King needs three moves to stop the WP, so the task seems impossible. But there's a Black Pawn ready to queen, also, stopped by the WK, who is in its square. Never say die!

(1) . . . **K – Kt7; (2) P – R5, K – B6.** Now if P – R6, K – Q7, and also queens in two moves thereafter. Therefore: (3) K – Kt3, K – Q5! Again threatens . . . K – K6 and P – B7. (4) K x P, K – B4; (5) P – R6, K – Kt3, and the P is caught.

7. Underpromotion

In Chapter XI, we stated that the potential power of a passed pawn is greater than that of a Queen, because the Pawn can promote itself to a different piece: R, B or Kt. The reasons for a different choice, which is called **underpromotion,** are:

(a) **Immediate mate**
(b) **Avoidance of mate**
(c) **Avoidance of stalemate**
(d) **Gain of material**

Examples will follow.

At one time in the history of Chess, promotion could mean the substitution only of a piece already taken off the board. This is no longer so. If you advance a Pawn to the eighth rank, you may take a second Queen (or a third or fourth one, for subsequent Pawns), or a third Knight, etc.

At one time, also, you could have chosen an enemy piece, or a "dummy Pawn"; and many interesting problems have been composed with those promotions in mind. However, the present rule is:

When a Pawn reaches the eighth rank, a player must substitute for him a Queen, Rook, Bishop or Knight of the same color as the Pawn.

Figure 287

Now, why not always take a Queen? (a) To effect mate.

If White makes a Queen, Black does, too—and with effect. But: (1) **P — Kt8 (Kt)** and it is Black who is mated. This also includes (b). To avoid mate.

Figure 288

(c) to avoid stalemate.

White is material ahead, but if he loses his Pawn on Kt7, he will not be able to win, because B + RP of the wrong color (i.e., the queening square is white; the B's squares black) will not win. Therefore, White must move (and promote) the Pawn.

(1) P — Kt8 (Q) or (R)?? is stalemate

(1) P — Kt8 (B)?? is of no value, since this B has no more power than the other to control the white square a8.

(1) **P — Kt8 (Kt) ch!** is correct. White wins even without the RP. (The Black King can move to QKt2.)

(d) To gain material.

Figure 289

Black has just made a Queen. If White takes it, then . . . K x P, and the game is a draw. But first:

1. P — K8 (Kt) ch K — K3
2. R x Q and White is a Kt ahead.

Following is a beautiful problem which combines many of the themes shown in this and the previous chapter. It is called **"The Lasker Problem,"** because the once World Champion, Dr. Emanuel Lasker was so fond of showing it.

Figure 290

White to play and win:

The first move is obvious: (1) **P — B7.** Black must stop the Q. He can not guard the queening square by . . . R — K1 or R — B4 because he can be captured. (1) . . . **R — K3 ch.** Now White must be careful. If K — Kt7? R — K2 and the P is pinned. If K to the Bishop file, R — K8; P queens, R — B8 ch. If K to the R file, R — B3 immediately. The only move is (2) **K — Kt5.** Then (2) . . . **R — K4 ch;** (3) **K — Kt4, R — K5 ch;** (4) **K — Kt3, R — K6 ch;** (5) **K — B2.** Finally the Rook can no longer attack the King from the rear. All seems over. But Black has one kick left: (5) . . . **R — K5.** Now if P — B8 (Q)?, R — B5 ch; Q x R stalemate! Yet White must promote the P or allow a draw by repetition (K — B3, R — K8; K — B2, R — K5).

(6) **P — B8 (R)!** Underpromotion to avoid the stalemate. White now threatens R — R8 mate. (6) . . . **R — KR5;** (7) **K — Kt3!** The mate threat is now R — B1, and the Bl R is attacked. Both threats can not be avoided. White wins the Rook, with mate soon to follow.

The depth and difficulty of chess, as well as its kaleidoscopic beauty, are inherent in many such "simple" situations.

Exercise No. 19

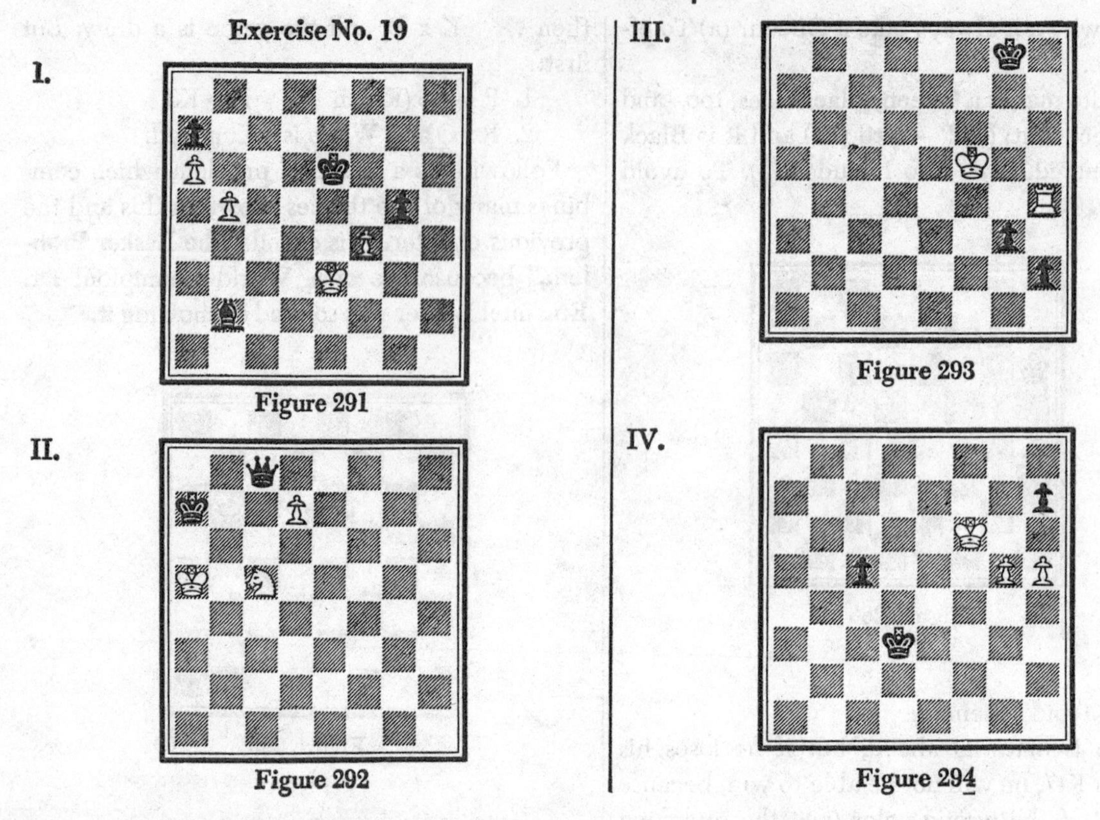

Figure 291

Figure 292

Figure 293

Figure 294

CHAPTER XIII

ENDINGS WITH PAWNS AND PIECES

ROOK AND PAWN ENDINGS

It is in the ending that the Rook comes into his own. Forced at the start of the game to wait until the minor pieces (Kts and Bs) fight over the center of the board and in the middle game to yield precedence to the powerful Queen, the Rooks finds themselves, after the others are removed by exchanges, in possession of the board. Then the strength and subtlety of their play stand out clearly. Let the player who walks into a Rook ending unarmed beware!

First, we must study

1. The Crucial Position

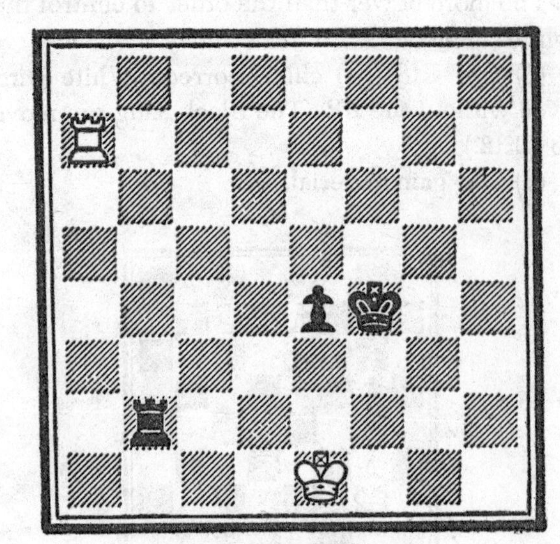

Figure 295

White has his back to the wall. Black threatens to queen a Pawn, with mate of the WK always in mind. But nothing like that need happen:

1. **R – R3.** The Rook stays on the third rank until Black pushes his Pawn: (1) . . . **P – K6.** Then the WR returns to the eighth rank, and checks from the rear:

2. **R – R8**	**K – B6**
3. **R – B8 ch**	**K – K5**
4. **R – K8 ch**	**K – Q6**
5. **R – Q8 ch, etc.**	

The only way for Black to avoid these Rook checks is to play:

2. . . .	R – Kt5. Then after
3. R – B8 ch	K – K5
4. R – K8 ch	K – B6
5. R – B8 ch	R – B5

But now, after (6) R x R ch, K x R; (7) K – K2! and we have the drawn Pawn ending described in the last chapter.

If it were Black's move in the diagram:

1. . . . K – B6 The White King

must now leave the area in front of the Pawn. If (2) R – R3 ch, P – K6; (3) K – Q1 (or (3) R – R1, to stop the mate, R – KR7! and wins the WR) K – B7, and wins.

2. **R – B8 ch.** This allows White to choose the side his King will escape to; after R – R8, R – Kt8 ch, he must go to the Q side.

2. . . .	**K – K6**
3. **K – B1**	

Rule: If your King *has* to move from in front of the Pawn go to the short side. This gives your Rook more room to maneuver.

3. . . .	**R – Kt8 ch**
4. **K – Kt2**	**K – K7**
5. **R – QR8**	**R – Kt7**
6. **R – R1**	**P – K6**
7. **K – Kt3**	**R – Q7**
8. **K – Kt2**	**K – Q6 ch**
9. **K – B1**	**R – KR7**
10. **R – R3 ch**	**K – K5**
11. **R – R8 and draws.**	

This ending is so difficult that it is best to prevent it by remembering the "crucial position" given at the start of the chapter. As a matter of fact, if the files of the Rooks were changed in the diagram, so that the WR stood on **b7** and the Bl R on **a2**, Black would win.

What can we learn from the position?

2. General Principles

1. Keep your Rook mobile. Give it plenty of room to move in. If you have a choice of moves, select the one which gives the **Rook** the most space.

2. Watch for the "crucial position" K, R and P vs. K and R above.

3. Be alert to an exchange which will give you the K and P vs. K ending discussed in the previous chapter.

4. Remember to keep your Pawns **aggressive.**

5. Centralize your King.

How these principles can be applied to an ending in actual play will be seen from the following position:

(W. Shipman vs. M. Hanauer
Manhattan C.C. vs. Marshall C.C., 1954)

White

Black
(White to Move)
Figure 296

Black is a Pawn behind, but has some compensation in his well centralized King. He must avoid the exchange of Rooks in most positions, although at the moment (1) R – Kt3? would not be good for White, because Black's King can capture the resultant P at QKt3, and queen one move before White. He should exchange as many Pawns as possible, keeping in mind the R plus P vs. R ending described above.

The game continued:

40. **K – K3,** **K – Q4**

41. **R – Kt3.** A difference: The Bl K can not approach the P at QKt3 in time to capture it. But Black is prepared:

41. . . .	**R – K5 ch**
42. **K – Q3**	**R – Q5 ch**
43. **K – B2**	**K – B3.** R – B5 ch

would be useless: R – B3 or K – Kt2 or K – Q2 would stop all checks.

44. **R – KKt3** **P – KKt4**

Aggressive Pawns; mobile Rook. . . . R – K2? R – Kt6 ch, and White would have the initiative.

45. **R – Kt4.** Black must yield the fourth

rank, but he sets up a balloon barrage on the fifth:

45. . . . R – Q4
46. P – KR4 R – B4

47. P x P. The sealed move. (At the end of a session of tournament play (in this case four hours) the player whose turn it is writes his move on his score sheet and seals it in an envelope, not making it on the board, nor disclosing it.) Better is (47) P – B3 which would exchange one P less.

47. . . . **R x P ch**
48. **K – Kt3** **P x P**
49. **R x P** **R – K7!!** Mobile Rook! Black threatens continual checks along this file. If the WK strays from the QRP, say to the Q file, the Bl R goes to the QR file and wins the QRP. White could even walk into a mate, if he goes to QR5 after R – K5 ch, for then . . . P – Kt3 ch and R – R5 mate.

White

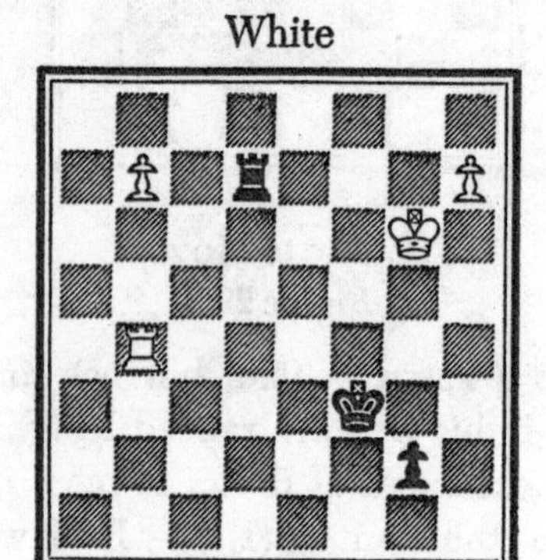

Black

Figure 297

50. **R – Kt3** **P – Kt4!** Aggressive Pawn! If Black permits P – R4, his King will be driven back to defend his P.

51. **P – R3** **K – B4**
52. **R – Kt5 ch** **K – B3.** Centralized King! The importance of this will appear later.

53. **R – Kt4.** The only move to stop the Rook checks on the K file and to make progress at the same time.

53. . . . **K – B4**

54. **R – Kt3.** Threat: R – B3 ch, K – Kt3; R – B2, R – K6 ch; R – B3. The Black King is cut off from the King side, where the decisive action will be.

54. . . . **R – K5.** Preparing for the exchange of the Q side Ps.

55. **K – B3** **R – QR5**
56. **K – Q2** **K – Q4.** The Bl K stays with his White counterpart.
57. **K – K2** **P – Kt5**
58. **P x P** **R x P.** Now for the "crucial position."
59. **R – B3** **K – K4.** White has been aiming for K – B2, but then R – B5!! K – Kt3, R x R ch; K x R, K – B4, with the opposition and a draw.
60. **P – Kt3** **R – Kt7 ch**

61. K – B1. The WK is cut off. White must either allow the Bl K to get in front of the P or offer an exchange of Rs—leading to a drawn P ending. The remaining moves were: (61) . . . K – K3; (62) R – B8, K – K2; (63) R – B4, K – K3; (64) P – Kt4, K – K4; (65) R – B5 ch, K – K3; (66) R – B3, R – Kt5; (67) R – Kt3, K – B3; (68) K – Kt2, K – Kt4; (69) K – R3, R – Kt8. Still active! Draw agreed.

3. The Lucena Position

When the defending King is cut off from a passed pawn by the attacking Rook, and the attacking King is near the Pawn, the position is won. A Spanish author named LUCENA discovered this almost five hundred years ago:

Figure 298

1. **R – K4** This is the first step in "building a bridge."

1. . . . **R – Kt7**
2. **R – Q4 ch** **K – B2**
3. **K – K7** **R – K7 ch**
4. **K – B6** **R – B7 ch**
5. **K – K6** **R – K7 ch**
6. **K – B5** **R – B7ch**

7. R – B4 and the Pawn queens

4. **Reaching the Lucena Position**

Obviously, if White can reach the Lucena position, he can win; if Black can prevent it by confronting the Pawn with his King, he can draw.

Reuben Fine (*Basic Chess Endings*) devotes twenty-six pages and hundreds of examples in order to give the player specific cases of wins and draws. We refer you to that book for a detailed study. Generally, the following rules will hold:

(a) The further the Black King can be cut off, the better the winning chances.

(b) Rook and Knight Pawns are special examples.

(c) The Black Rook for its best defensive powers must occupy the first rank and the Rook file.

(d) The Black King should be on a rank in front of the rank of the Pawn.

For our purposes the following examples will suffice:

Figure 299

White to play, will, of course, move (1) R – K1, and cut off the Black King even further. Then he will win rather easily: (1) . . . K – B4; (2) K – B4, R – B1 ch; (3) K – Q5, R – QKt1; (4) R – QKt1, K – B3; (5) P – Kt5, K – K2; (6) K – B6, K – Q1; (7) P – Kt6, R– B1; (8) R – KR1, and wins.

The feature of the play is the cut-off switch: when the WR has to defend the P, the WK is centrally placed in order to prevent the Bl K from returning to confront the Pawn.

Black, to move, can draw—by moving the King, of course, closer to the Pawn—but only by going to the *one* square which will prevent W's K from dominating the center; namely, (1) . . . **K – K3**; (2) **R – Q4, K – K4!** (3) **R – Q7, K – K3.** If the WR leaves the Q file, the Bl K edges closer. (4) **R – Q4, K – K4;** (5) **K – B3, R – KR1** (the ideal defensive square) (6) **P – Kt5, R – QKt1.** The King can not defend the P; he would be **overloaded,** and Black could take it anyhow. (7) **R – KR4** trap: if Bl takes the P, a hurdle check. (7) . . . **K – Q3** (in front of the Pawn!) (8) **K – Kt4, K – B2.**

The Rook Pawn is always a special case. The Black King must be cut off at least five files away (B file) if the Pawn has reached the seventh rank:

Figure 300

(1) **R – KR1, K – K2;** (2) **R – R8, K – Q3;** (3) **R – QKt8, R – QR7.** The first step has been completed—winning the QKt file. Now the King marches out.

(4) **K – Kt7, R – Kt7 ch;** (5) **K – B8, R – B7 ch;** (6) **K – Q8, R – KR7.** Is the WK out or in? (7) **R – Kt6 ch, K – B4.**

Now where would you go? The logical move seems R – QR6; but then the Bl R, using its maximum power, would check on the KR file. The WK could not go to the 6th rank because of . . . R – R3 ch and . . . R x R. He would have to approach the R via the 8th and 7th rank. When he got to the KB file, Bl would play . . . R – QR1, K – Kt4 and K – Kt3, winning the Pawn.

(8) **R – B6 ch!** Besides the immediate threat (K x R, P – R8 (Q) check!) this gives the WK a **bridge** on the B file.

(8) . . . **K – Kt4;** (9) **R – B8, R – R1 ch;** (10) **K – B7, R – R2 ch;** (11) **K – Kt8** and wins.

On move 8, if . . . **K – Q4,** (9) **R – R6!** and the WK has a shelter on QKt5 from the Rook checks.

Exercises

(A) WK on QR8, WR on Q1, WP on QR7, Bl K on K2, Bl K on QKt7. Prove that this is a draw.

(B) WK on QR3, WR on Q1, WP on QR4, Bl K on K4, Bl R on QR1. Prove: White to play wins. Black to play draws.

5. Rook and Two Pawns vs. Rook

(a) The player with two Pawns ahead should win if the Pawns are connected unless:

1. A blockade occurs before one Pawn reaches the 6th rank.
2. The WR is badly placed; or
3. Stalemate is possible.

(b) If the Pawns are disconnected, there is a win, unless the Ps are the RP and BP on the same side of the board.

Figure 301

Black, to move, keeps the WK cut off from the Ps by (1) . . . **R – K8.**

(2) **R – Kt8** threat: R – Q8 ch; if (2) . . . K x P; (3) P – B7. (2) . . . **R – B8 ch; (3) K – Kt5, R – Kt8 ch;** (4) **K – B5, R – B8 ch; (5) K – Kt6, R – Kt8 ch;** (6) **K – B7, R – B8 ch;** (7) **K – K8, R – K8 ch;** (8) **K – Q8, R – KR8;** (9) **K – B8.** A long journey to defend the BP! Now if, . . . K x P, not (10) P – B7?? K – B3! (11) K – Q8, R – R1 ch; (12) K – K7, R – R2 ch Draw! But White plays (10) **R – Kt6,** cutting the Bl K off the 3rd rank: (10) . . . **K – B4;** (11) **K – Kt7, R – R3;** (12) **R – Kt1 wins.**

(9) . . . **R – R2;** (10) **R – Kt5, R – KKt2;** (11) **K – Kt8, R – KR2;** (12) **K – R8** completes the grand tour! White now threatens R – Kt8 or 7 and then–Q8 or 7. Black can not check. (12) . . . **R – R8;** (13) **R – Kt8, R – R8 ch;** (14) **K – Kt7, R – Kt8 ch;** (15) **K – B8, R – QB8;** (16) **R – Kt7, K x P;** (17) **P – B7, K – B3;** (18) **K – Kt8** and wins R for P. The King's back and forth maneuvers often feature R endings.

The following positions would be draws:

(1) **Blockade:** WK at K5, WR at KR3, WPs at QKt4, QB3; Bl K at his QB5, Bl R at Q8.

(2) **Badly Placed Rook:** WK at KKt3; WR at KR6; WPs at KR5, KKt5.

Bl K at KKt2, Bl R at QR4.

(3) **Stalemate Possible:** WK at K3; WR at QB7; WPs at Q6, K5; Bl K at K3, Bl R at QKt5.

(R – K5 ch)

In the endings R, BP and RP vs. R, one position must be avoided:

Figure 302

This is a win for White, as follows:
(1) R – K8, R – QR8; (2) K – B8, K – Kt3; (3) P – B7, K – B3; (4) R – QKt8, R – R3; (5) K – Kt8.

White, in order to win the ending, will give up his RP, and try to get a position with K and BP where the Bl K is cut off as above. We give one example of the type of play possible, with the warning that the starting position was in a match between the then second and third best players in the world, and that the game, which should have been drawn, was won by Carl Schlechter from Dr. S. Tarrasch.

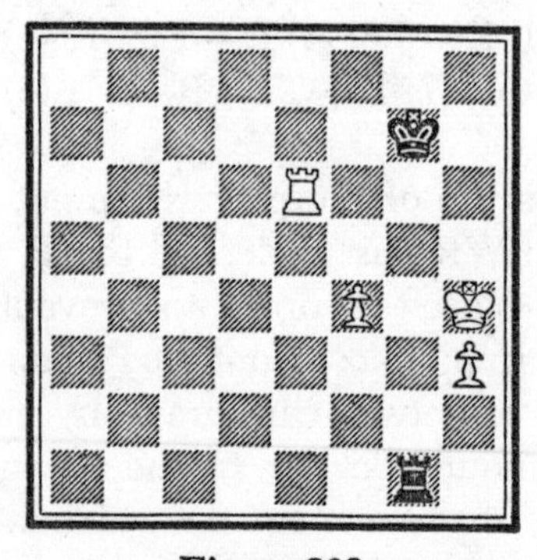

Figure 303

(1) **R – K3** (threat R – Kt3 ch) **K – B3; (2) R – KKt3, R – QR8; (3) K – Kt4, R – R1** (maximum power); **(4) R – Kt3, R – Kt1 ch; (5) K – B3, R – Kt8; (6) R – Kt8, R – B8 ch; (7) K – Kt4, R – Kt8 ch; (8) K – R5.**

In the game, Black now played (8) . . . R – Kt2, and after (9) R – B8 ch, K – K2; (10) R – B5, K – K3; (11) R – KKt5, R – R2 ch?? (another error); (12) K – Kt6, R x P; (13) R – K5 ch, White reached a Lucena position and won.

The reason for the loss? Black did not realize that the function of the King was to stay in front of the BP, which is the only P White can win with; to win with the RP, White should have had to cut off the Bl K on the QB file, as we saw above.

(8) . . . **K – B2! (9) R – Kt6, K – Kt2; (10) P – R4, K – B2; (11) R – Kt5, K – B3; (12) R – Kt5, R – KB8; (13) R – Kt6 ch, K – B2!** (Not K – B4; R – Kt8, and the Bl K will be driven off as in the S.–T. game) **(14) R – Kt4, R – QR8; (15) K – Kt5** (If K – R6, R – R3 ch; K – R7? R – B3, and the WK is trapped in R7 and R8. The Bl K just oscillates between B1 and B2, and White can do nothing) **(15) . . . R – R1; (16) P – R5, K – Kt2; (17) R – Kt1, R – R4 ch; (18) K – Kt4, R – R7; (19) R – Kt1, R – Kt7 ch; (20) K – B5, R – KR7; (21) R – Kt7 ch, K – R3.** This is the "right side" of the BP: The Rook must maneuver in the wide open spaces of the Q side. **(22) K – B6, R x P; (23) P – B5, R – R8; (24) R – Kt2.** The crucial position in the ending. If now . . . K – R2, K – B7; or . . . K – R4, R –Kt8– in either case, White wins. (24) . . . **R – R6! (25) K – B7, R – QR6; (26) R – Kt7, R – R1.**

We now have a drawn position. If the WR leaves the 7th rank, the Bl R checks on it. Otherwise, the Bl K defends along the Kt file until the P goes to B7. Then . . . K – Kt2, . . . R – KB1, and a blockade.

6. Other Rook and Pawn Endings

Generally, the more Pawns on the board, the better the chances for a win for the player who is ahead. The following more specific generalizations may help.

(a) **R and 2 Ps vs. R and 1 P:**

1. A win if the two Ps are passed.
2. Possible win if one P is passed.
3. Draw if no passed pawns.

(b) **R and 3 Ps vs. R and 2 Ps**

1. Probable draw if all Ps on one side of the board.
2. Chances for win better if Ps on both sides.
3. A passed Pawn increases winning chances.

(c) **R and n Pawns vs. R and (n-1) Pawns:**

The rules above apply, with better chances for a win as n increases.

Better than memorizing the above statements, which merely show what you might expect to accomplish, is an application to a specific position:

(M. Hanauer vs. H. Sussman, Marshall Chess Club Championship, 1937)

Figure 304

Black to move, played (18) . . . **R(B) – B1.** White sums up his chances as follows:

1. He is a Pawn ahead.

2. If all Rooks are exchanged, he has a won P ending because of the extra P and the fact that there are Ps on both sides of the board.

3. Black has no weaknesses. His P position is solid. Weaknesses must be created.

4. White has weakness—two isolated Ps on the Q side.

5. One weak White P is on a "half-open" file, where the Bl Rs can attack it.

6. The WK must come to the aid of the weak Ps.

7. The WRs are well placed, one on an open file; both able to defend the QBP. The WR on

d5 can act "as a bridge" for the centralization of the WK.

19. R – Kt3 R – B2 defending the KtP and the second rank, while preparing to double Rooks on the QB file.

20. K – B1 QR – B1
21. R – Q3 P – QKt3

Black frees his Rs by this move, but:

(a) it creates a weakness–holes on QR3 and QB3;
(b) it is defensive, not aggressive;
(c) it does not tend toward the exchange of Ps that Black should try for.

Better would be . . . P – QR4, threatening . . . P – R5. If P – R4 in answer, then . . . R – K2, followed by . . . R – B5. W's Rs would then have to continue their defensive positions.

22. K – K1 K – B1

23. K – Q2. Part one accomplished. One Rook is now free. (23) . . . K – K2; (24) R – Kt4. On an open rank, the Rook intends, by R – K4 ch, to seize another file, and to drive back the Bl K.

24. . . . R – B5

The fruits of correct play: the exchange of one Rook.

25. R x R R x R

26. R – Q4 On an open rank! Black can not exchange again and give W a passed QP.

26. . . . R – B4
27. R – QR4 R – B2

The Bl R is now in a defensive position.

28. K – Q3 K – Q3

29. P – K4 Having centralized his K, White advances on the side where he has the majority of Ps.

29. . . . K – K3
30. P – KB4 K – Q3
31. R – Q4 ch K – K2
32. R – Q5 on the open rank! K – K3
33. K – Q4 K – K2

White's pieces are as centrally located as they can be. Now for the continuation of the K side advance.

34. P – KR4 K – K3
35. P – Kt4 K – K2
36. P – B4 K – K1
37. P – K5 K – K2
38. P – KB5 R – B1!

Black sees that the KR file will be opened. He wants to be the first to enjoy it. White could proceed by moving his K to QKt4, and then play P – B5 (ridding himself of his weakness) followed by an attack on the QRP by K and R. This is feasible because the WR on Q5 cuts off the Bl K. However, White has another idea:

39. P – Kt5 P x P
40. P x P R – KR1
41. P – B6 ch P x P
42. KtP x P ch K – K1
43. P – QR4 R – R5 ch
44. K – B3 R – R6 ch
45. K – Kt4!

The King takes advantage of the hole on B6 to go to B7, threatening R – Q8 mate!

45. . . . P – R4 ch
46. K – Kt5 R – Kt6 ch
47. K – B6 R – Kt5

48. P – B5?? White wants the Black BP to act as a protection on the B file while he plays K – B7. But the WQBP is just as good, and R – Q4! was the move.

48. . . . P x P
49. K – B7 R – Q5! stopping the mate threat. If R x P, R x RP.

50. R – Q6!! Zugzwang!

If . . . R x R; P x R, and the Pawn queens. The BR and QBP can not move. Therefore:

50. . . . K – B1
51. R – R6 K – Kt1

Black has avoided mate, but the aggressive WPs carry the day:

52. R – R8 ch K – R2
53. P – K6! P x P

54. P – B7 This wins the Rook and the game: (54) . . . R – B5; (55) P – B8 (Q); R x Q; (56) R x R, K – Kt2; (57) R – B1, P – B5; (58) K – Q6, Resigns.

Exercise No. 20

Following is an ending from actual play. White is Sidney Bernstein, U. S. Finalist and winner of Marshall and Manhattan C.C. Championships in 1939 and 1941. This is a game from the 1939 Marshall C.C. Tournament.

You are Black; it is your 35th move.

White

Black

Figure 305

(a) Which is White's weakest Pawn?
(b) How can Black plan to capture it?
(c) What counterplay must Black prevent?
(d) How must he prevent it?
(e) How does the move in answer to (d) further Black's plan?
(f) Which move must Black make first?
(g) Why?

35. . . . **R – R4**
36. **P – QR3**

(h) Is K – Kt3 better?

36. . . . **P – B5**
37. **P – R3**

(i) White move next—K – Q4 or R – R5?

37. . . . **K – Q4**
38. **R – Q2** **R – R5**

(j) How does White save his QP?

39. **P – QKt3!** **R x RP**
40. **R – K2**

(k) How does Black save his KKtP?

40. . . . **K – Q3**
41. **K – B4**

(l) Two reasons for this move?

41. . . . **R – R4**
42. **P – QKt4** **R – Q4**
43. **R – R2** **R – KB4**
44. **R – KB2** **P – Kt4 ch**
45. **K – Q3** **K – Q4**

(m) What is Black's current threat?
(n) How can White stop it?

46. **R – B2**

(o) What other plan does White stop by this move?
(p) How can Black proceed?

46. . . . **P – B6**
47. **R – B5 ch** **K – Q3**

(q) Can White now play R x R?

48. **P x P** **R x P ch**
49. **K – K4**

(r) Can Black play . . . R x P profitably?

49. . . . **R – B5 ch**
50. **K – K3** **R – B4**
51. **R – B8** **P – K4**

(s) Do you approve of (52) P x P ch?

52. **R – KKt8!** **P x P ch**
53. **K x P** **R – B5 ch**
54. **K – B3** **R – B6 ch**
55. **K – Q4**

(t) Can Black win?

55. . . . **R – B5 ch**
56. **K – B3** **R – B4**
57. **K – Q4** **K – K3**
58. **K – K3** **K – B3**
59. **R – Kt8**

(u) Can Black win here?

59. . . . **K – Kt3**
60. **K – K2** **R – Q4**
61. **K – B3** **R – Q6 ch**
62. **K – Kt2**

(v) Not K –Kt4?

62. . . . **R – Q7 ch**
63. **K – Kt1**

(w) Why not K – B3?

63. . . . **K – B4**

(x) Would . . . R – Q4 be better?

64. **R x P ch** **K – B5**
65. **R – B5**

(y) Is R – Kt8 as good?

65. . . . **R – Q8 ch**
66. **K – B2** **R – Q7 ch**
67. **K – Kt1** Draw

And well earned by White!

BISHOP AND PAWN ENDINGS

1. General Principles

In endings where there are a Bishop and several Pawns on each side, a great deal depends upon the squares the Bishops stand on.

If the Bishops stand on different colored squares (i.e., WB on white, Bl B on black, or vice versa) the game is probably a draw, even when one side has the advantage of a Pawn. Even two Pawns will not win, if the other side establishes a blockade. (See the ending Bogoljubow vs. Edward Lasker, later in this chapter.)

If the Bishops are on the same colored squares, the side which has an extra Pawn should win, all other things being equal. A positional advantage, such as the Pawn position (the other side having a doubled Pawn or isolated Pawns) may equally result in a win.

In planning the method of playing a Bishop ending, attention must be given to:

(a) **Centralization** of K and B.

(b) **Mobility** of K, B and Ps.

(c) **Attention to Pawn structure.**

(d) **Control** by K of squares not covered by the B. The Ps assist now one, now the other.

(e) **The Ps should be on the color** *not* **that of the B's square, so that the B has free movement.**

(f) K and B **alone** *draw* vs. K.

(Roy T. Black vs. M. Hanauer, N. Y. State Championship, 1953)

White

Black

Figure 306

Black has the advantage, because the WPs are all on white, requiring the defense of them by K and B, and limiting the WB's squares. In addition, the two WK side Ps are isolated, the KBP **pinned.** The game continued:

37. . . .	P – Kt3

The last P off white! Now if (38) B – K4, the Bl B can move off the diagonal temporarily.

38. B – Q3	K – B3
39. K – B2	K – K4
40. K – K3	

For the moment, Black's plan of playing his K to KB5 is stopped.

40. . . .	B – Q2
41. B – B1	B – K3!

Attack the advanced Pawn!

42. B – Kt2	P – Kt4

White is in complete zugzwang:

If B – B, P – QKt5, followed by B – B4 – QKt8 and B x QRP. If the K moves to Q3, K – B5, – K6 – B7. If P – R4, P – Kt5, followed by . . . B x KtP.

43. P – Kt4	B x QRP
44. B – B1	B – B5
45. B – Kt2	P – R3

Another zugzwang, like a progressive squeeze at contract bridge.

46. B – R1	B – B8

White resigned.

2. The Basic Ending: B and P vs. B

(a) Bishops of opposite color; draw.

(b) Bs of the same color;

(1) if the defending King is in front of the P, draw. Exception: P on 7th, K on 8th square of the color of the B.

(2) if the defending King is behind the Pawn, he can draw only with:

the opposition

mobility of his B on fairly long diagonals.

Examples will clarify:

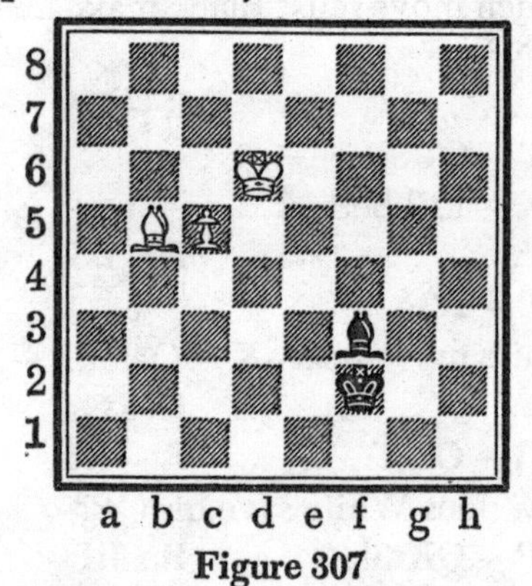

Figure 307

(For the rest of this chapter, we shall return to the algebraic notation.)

1. Bb5 – c6	Bf3 – e2
2. Bc6 – d5	Be2 – b5
3. Bd5 – e6	Kf2 – e3
4. Be6 – d7	Bb5 – f1
5. Pc5 – c6	Ke3 – d4
6. Pc6 – c7	Bf1 – a6
7. Kd6 – c6	Kd4 – e5
8. Kc6 – b6	Ke5 – d6

9. Bd7 – g4 zugzwang! If the B moves off the diagonal a6 – c8, the P queens. If the K moves, K x B. White wins. Compare Fig. 308.

The Bl K is closer; the Bl B has two good diagonals crossing at f7: a2 – g8 and e8 – h5.

(1) Bb3 – f7, Bh5 – e2; (2) Bf7 – g6, Be2 – c4; (3) Bg6 – h7, Bc4 – b3; (4) Bh7 – g8, B x Bg8! and (5) . . . K x P. Draw. (Fig. 308)

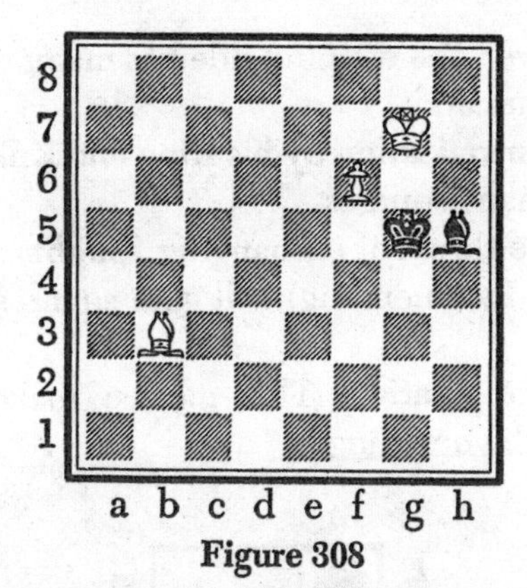

Figure 308

The **close opposition** is essential in the above example: the Bl K must prevent B – g6 with the B.

3. Two Bishops and Pawns vs. Two Bs and Ps

This is a very complicated ending, where planning and strategy on both sides are essential. The general principles involved can best be gained from the following exercise:

Exercise No. 21

Two Bishops and Pawns Ending

Here is an ending where the only pieces besides the Kings are Bishops and Pawns. It was the crucial game in the Marshall Chess Club Championship of 1951, played when the author (White) was one point ahead of his opponent (Black).

(M. Hanauer–White. Bernard Hill–Black.)

Figure 309

The following had to be considered:

(1) King and Bishop alone can not win against a King.

(2) King and two Bishops can win against a lone King.

(3) King, Bishop and Rook Pawn (Pawn on the **a** or **h** files) can win only if the queening square (a8 or h8 for White; a1 or h1 for Black) is of the same color as the squares on which the Bishop travels. Thus, with only the **a** Pawn left, White must also have the Bishop now on e2; with the **h** Pawn, he must have the Bishop now on e3.

(4) King and Rook Pawn alone can not win against a King.

(5) The White King must be centralized, yet may have to defend the Pawn on b2.

(6) White should advance on the side where he has more Pawns than his opponent (the King's side, files **e** to **h**). Black should advance his Pawns on the **a** and **b** files in order to obtain a Passed Pawn.

(7) White should try to slow up the Black advance, in order to gain time for his own advance.

(8) The side trying to **draw** the game will exchange as many Pawns as possible, **even giving up one Bishop** for the **last** Pawn of his adversary.

(9) Endings with Bishops on opposite colored squares ("Bishops of opposite color") are very hard to win, even when one side is a Pawn ahead.

(10) However, if one side has two connected Passed Pawns, he will usually win, even if the Bishops are "of opposite color."

The game continued:

30. Be2 – f3

(a) What is the threat?

30. . . .	Bd6 – e7
31. Pg2 – g4	Pa6 – a5

(b) Are these good moves?

32. Pe4 – e5 ch	Bb3 – d5

(c) Should White exchange Bishops?

33. P x Pf6	Be7 x Pf6

(d) Should Black play Bd5 x Bf3, and hope for a draw because of Bishops of opposite color?

34. Bf3 – e2	Ph7 – h6

(e) Why not Bd5 – g2?

(f) Is Black's move a good one?

35. Pg4 – g5	Ph6 x Pg5
36. Pf4 x Pg5	Bf6 – e5
37. Ph3 – h4	Pa5 – a4
38. Be3 – d2	

(g) What are the reasons for this move?

38. . . .	Bd5 – e4
39. Ph4 – h5	Kc6 – c5
40. Be2 – d1	

(h) And for this one?

40. . . .	Kc5 – c4

41. Ph5 – h6	Pg7 x Ph6
42. Pg5 x Ph6	Be4 – d3

(i) Which Bishop must White not exchange?

43. Bd1 – c2	Bd3 x Bc2
44. K x Bc2	Pb5 – b4
45. Bd2 – c1	Be5 – d4

(j) White now has two ways to try to win. Find them. Each plan involves opposing the Black Bishop on the diagonal a1 – h8.

46. Bc1 – g5

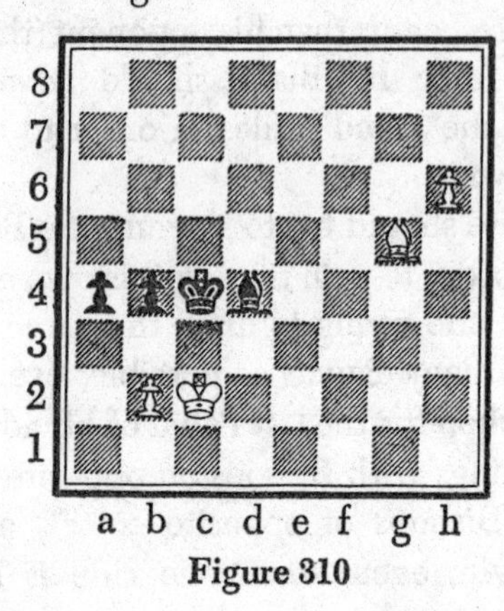

Figure 310

46. . . .	Bd4 – e5

(k) Can Black do anything else?

47. Bg5 – e7

(l) Now how can Black spoil White's plan?

47. . . .	Be5 – f4
48. Ph6 – h7	Bf4 – e5
49. Be7 – g5	Be5 – d4
50. Bg5 – c1	

(m) What should Black do now?

51. . . .	Bd4 – f6??
52. Pb2 – b3 check!	Pa4 x Pb3 check
53. Kc2 – b1!	Black resigns.

(n) Why does Black resign?

(o) Why couldn't White have made the same moves (52 – 3) on moves 46 – 7?

KNIGHT AND PAWN ENDINGS

These endings are very tricky. A locked Pawn position will often result in the loss by each side of his Pawn to the opposing Knight. The Knights, because of their peculiar move, in which they hop from one color to another, are very annoying to the opposing Kings. Then, too, the side which is ahead in material, must remember that Knight and King can not win against a King.

However, the winning side has many weapons at his command:

(1) **Centralization by his King and Knight** will control many squares.

(2) The threat of **exchanging Knights** (leading to a won Pawn ending) will gain squares for his Knight.

(3) **Triangulation.** This means: make a triangle with your King.

Figure 311

The White King is attacked by the Black Knight. He wants to go to e8, but if he does, the Knight checks at d6. First, therefore, the King goes to d7. The Knight can not go to d6, because the King will take him. He must move away (to a7 or b6—a Black square), whereupon the King goes to e8, and the Knight can not check him on the next move. White gains a move for his plans, and repeats the process as often as he likes.

Following is a position from the 1953 Candidates' Tournament (Taimanov vs. Stahlberg).

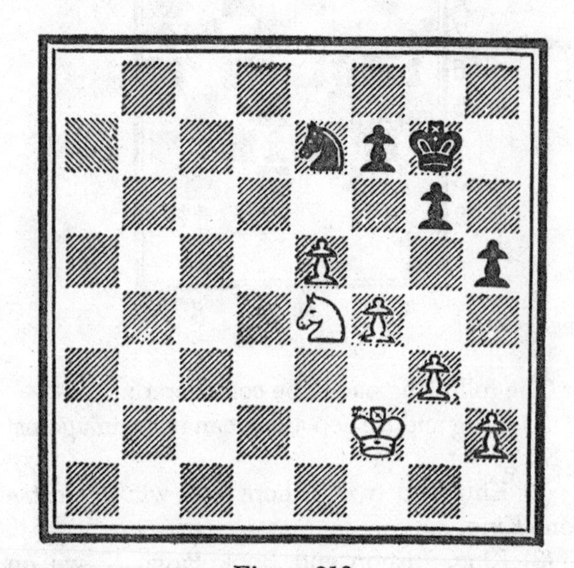
Figure 312

Let's look it over:

1. The Pawns are on one side of the board. This makes it hard to win.

2. White is a Pawn ahead. He should try to make it a Passed Pawn, and then a Queen.

3. White has more space to move in. The Black King may have trouble getting out into the open.

4. White controls f6 and g5 with Knight and Pawns. Black can not easily exchange Pawns.

5. The Black Pawn at h5 is weak, being advanced. The Pawn at g6 must stay there, in order to protect the P on h5.

(a) What are White's first two objectives?

The game continued:

44. Kf2 – f3	Kg7 – f8
45. Kte4 – d6	Kte7 – c6
46. Kf3 – e4	Kf8 – e7

(b) Now how is White to prevent . . . Ke7 – e6?

47. Pf4 – f5!

(c) Why can Black not capture this Pawn?

47. . . .	Ktc6 – b4
48. Pf5 – f6 ch	Ke7 – f8

Mission #1 accomplished. The Black King is driven away from the center.

(d) Can the **e** Pawn become passed?

(e) Which Pawn can become passed?

(f) What is White's next plan?

(g) How can he accomplish it?

49. Ktd6 – b7

(h) Why this move?

49. . . .	Ktb4–a6
50. Ke4 – d5	Kta6 – c7 ch
51. Kd5 – d6	Ktc7 – b5 ch
52. Kd6 – d7	Ktb5 – d4
53. Kt b7 – c5	

(i) Why not Kd7 – d8?

53. . . .	Ktd4 – f5

(j) Why must Black move the Knight?

54. Kd7 – d8	Ktf5 – d4
55. Ktc5 – d7 ch	Kf8 – g8

Mission #2 accomplished!

(k) Next plan?

56. Kd8 – e8	Ktd4 – e6
57. Ke8 – e7	Pg6 – g5

(l) Why not a Knight move?

58. Ke7 – e8

(m) Is White stalling?

58. . . .	Kte6 – c7 ch

(n) Now what does White do?

59. Ke8 – d8!	Ktc7 – e6 ch
60. Kd8 – e7	Kte6 – d4
61. Ktd7 – c5	

Next mission accomplished! Now to get away from the troublesome Knight!

61. . . .	Ktd4 – c6 ch
62. Ke7 – d6	

(o) Why not to e8?

62. . . .	Ktc6 – a5

(p) Now how does White progress?

63. Pe5 – e6	Pf7 x Pe6
64. Kd6 – e7!	Kta5 – c6 ch
65. Ke7 – e8	

(q) What can Black do?

65. . . .	Ktc6 – e5
66. Ktc5 x Pe6	Kte5 – f7!

(r) Next plan? Yes, still a plan!

67. Ke8 – e7	Pg5 – g4
68. Kte6 – g7	Ktf7 – h6
69. Ktg7 x Ph5	

White presses Black.

(s) Could he win more according to plan?

69. . . .	Kth6 – f5 ch
70. Ke7 – e8	Ktf5 – d6 ch

(t) Now what?

71. Ke8 – d7	Ktd6 – f5
72. Kth5 – g7	

Two Pawns ahead, White can give up one for a won Pawn ending. If Black captures, he is soon forced away from his last Pawn.

72. . . .	Ktf5 – h6
73. Kd7 – e7	Kth6 – f7
74. Ktg7 – f5!	

The Black Knight must move; the White Knight checks at h6, and the f Pawn goes through. Black resigns.

To sum up: **Plan, centralize, plan, plan, plan!**

Answers to the preceding questions (a) through (t):

(a) To centralize his King and to prevent Black from centralizing *his*.

(b) *Not* by Ph3, g4, etc., because White would have to exchange Pawns right down the line.

(c) He will lose his **h** Pawn: (47) . . . Pg6 x Pf5 ch (?) (48) Ktd6 x Pf5 ch, Ke7 – e6; (49) Ktf5 – g7 ch, Ke6 – e7; (50) Kt x Ph5.

(d) Not if Black doesn't let it: when it goes to e6, it can be captured.

(e) The f Pawn, after P – e6, Pf7 x Pe6.

(f) To drive the Black King from the f file to the g file.

(g) By getting his King to d8 and his Knight to d7.

(h) White wants the square d6 for his King. If he moves Ke4 – d4 instead, Black plays Kt – c6 ch, and then Kt – b4 ch – c6 or d3, attacking the King and Pawn e5.

(i) Because of Ktd4 – c6 ch and Kt x Pe5.

(j) Otherwise, (54) P – e6, Pf7 x Pe6; (55) Kt x Pe6 ch and Black is forced to exchange Knights.

(k) K – e7, P – e6, P – f7 ch and P – f8 (Q).

(l) On a Knight move, White would play Ktd7 – c5, followed by P e6.

(m) No. He is trying to exhaust the Black Pawn moves, to force a Knight move. Obviously, the Black King can not move away from the f Pawn.

(n) He makes a triangle to gain a move.

(o) The Pawn e5 is *en prise* (can be taken).

(p) The e Pawn is ready to make the f Pawn passed.

(q) Stop the Pawn temporarily.

(r) 1. Exhaust the Black Pawn moves.
2. Force a Knight move.
3. Play Kt – d8.
But not Kt – d8 at once, because of . . . Kt x Kt and . . . K – f7, winning the f Pawn.

(s) Yes—by K – e8 and Kt – f5.

(t) Make a triangle? It can be done only via d8—whereupon the Black King goes to f7.

First White must centralize his Knight!

ROOK VS. MINOR PIECE ENDINGS

In Chapter XI several of these endings were discussed under "Relative Value of the Pieces: R vs. B and R vs. Kt." In this section we shall discuss:

1. R vs. B alone.
2. R vs. B with Pawns.
3. R vs. Kt alone.
4. R vs. Kt with Pawns and 2 Rs vs. R and Kt with Pawns.

In the exercise, we shall meet R, Kt, Ps vs. R and Ps.

1. Rook vs. Bishop Alone

The Bishop's side can draw if his King can get into the "right" corner (the corner *not* of the B's square) and if the B has access to the square next to it.

Figure 313

The King is in the "right" corner. All the B has to do is to remain on the diagonal a2 – g8, then interpose on a Rook check:

1. R – QKt7	B – B5
2. R – Kt8 ch	B – Kt1
3. R – B8	Stalemate!

The Rook can win if the enemy King is in the "wrong" corner, or can not get to the "right" corner.

(Black to move)

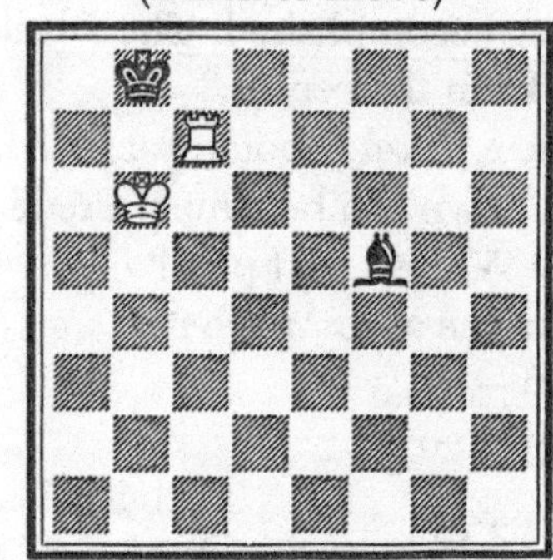

Figure 314

The Bl K is cut off from the "right" corner, which would be KR1 (or QR8) (h8 or a1). White's threat is R – KB7, attacking the B, and threatening mate at KB8.

If the B interposes on its QB1 (c8) the Rook makes a **tempo** along the 8th rank (e.g., R – KR8). Then the Bl K must move, and R x B mate.

In the "wrong corner" there is always a square between it and the B. Therefore, no stalemate.

Understanding White's threats, Black moves his B to squares where it can not be attacked simultaneously with mate threats:

1.	**B – Kt8** (b1)
2. **R – B1**	**B – R7** (a2)
3. **R – B2**	**B – Kt6** (b3)

4. **R – QKt2** Now the R has taken away the three hideaway squares (a2, b1, b3). The B must go out in the open.

4. . . .	**B – B5** (c4)
5. **R – KR2**	

The Black King, which has been waiting to escape to B1, now is unable to move there, because of R – QB2 pinning the B.

5. . . .	**B – K3**
6. **R – R8 ch**	**B – B1**
7. **R – B8**	**K – R1**
8. **R x B mate.**	

2. Rook vs. Bishop and Pawns

One Pawn will not help the Bishop much, unless it is well advanced and threatening to queen. Otherwise, the Rook forces the Pawn to advance, captures it, and then renews his threats. Here is a study by Sackmann:

Figure 315

1. **R – B5**	**B – R6** (If P – B5; R – QKt5)
2. **R – B1**	**B – Kt5**

3. **R – B3** (Now the B has no moves: . . . B – R4; R – R3 or B – Q7, R – Q3 or B – K8; R – K3)

3. . . .	**P – B5**

4. **R – B5** This is the point: not to take the P (by R – B4) and allow the K to escape; but to continue to threaten the B until it is demobilized.

4. . . . **B – B6** (If 4. . . . P – B6; (5) R – QKt5, P – B7; (6) R x B, P – B8 (Q); (7) R – Kt8 ch, Q – B1; (8) R x Q mate)

5. **R – B7** (Not R – QB5? K – B1!)

5. . . . **B – Q5** (other B moves are equally hopeless.)

6. **R – Q7**	**B – B4**
7. **R – Q8 ch**	**B – B1**

8. **R – QB8** Now is the time . . . **P – B6**

9. **R x P** Now the B blocks the K from going to B1

9. . . .	**K – R1**
10. **R – B8**	**K – Kt1**
11. **R – R8**	**K – R1**
12. **R x B mate.**	

Two Pawns with the Bishop should draw easily; may even win, if they are connected and on the 5th rank or further. As usual, a RP forms an exception, because the R can sacrifice itself for B and P; and K + RP can not win. Of course, the R can draw if he can sacrifice himself for 2 Ps.

The Ps must be careful not to advance without King support, but even with it may not win.

(Black to move)

Figure 316

1. . . .	**K – B5** (Not . . . P – K6ch; R x P)
2. **R – R4 ch**	**K – B6**
3. **R – R3 ch**	**K – B7**

Fine now claims that Black wins, giving the line (4) R – R4, P – K6 ch; (5) K – B2, P – K7; "and White has no time to take the P." However, Black's K need not be allowed to remain on its best square, where it is now, and from which it can support the KP to its 8th.

4. **R – R2 ch!**	**K – Kt6**
5. **R – R7**	**P – K6 ch**

6. **K – K1** Now if . . . P – Q6; (7) R – Q7, K – B6; (8) R – Q4, B – Kt4; (9) R – Q5! and the R continues to attack the B from the Q file, keeping an eye on the Q Pawn, which will be captured if it goes to Q7. The game would be a draw by repetition.

The K must, therefore, support the Ps.

6. . . .	**K – B6**
7. **R – Q7**	**K – K5** (Again, if P – Q6; R – Q4.)
8. **R – QB7**	**K – Q6**

9. **K – Q1**	**K – B6**

10. **R – K7!** Preventing P – Q6; R x P. Even a sacrifice of the B will not help Black:

10. . . .	**K – Q6**
11. **R – QB7**	**P – K7 ch??** This loses
12. **K – K1**	**K – K6**
13. **R x B**	**P – Q6**
14. **R – B3!**	**K – Q5**

15. **R – R3** (Not K – Q2?? P – K8 (Q) ch wins.)

15. . . .	**K – K6**
16. **R – Kt3**	**K – Q5**
17. **K – Q2**	**K – B5**

18. **R – B3** ch–and White wins. Black must, therefore, agree to a draw on move 10.

An example from actual play (Hanauer vs. H. Morris, Ventnor City, 1940).

Figure 317

Black has two Ps for the "exchange," but it is White's move, and he can get possession of an "absolute seventh" rank, at the same time chasing the B off his powerful long diagonal. The game continued:

(35) R – B7, B – R3; (36) R x P, B – B5; (37) R – QB1, P – QKt4; (38) P – QR4, R – Kt4; (39) P x P?? This blunder is due to time trouble. Of course, White should have played P – R5, winning in a few moves.

(39) . . . B x P; (40) R – R5, B – K1; (41) R x R, P x R

The lines are tightly drawn; all the Ps on one side, the Bl K with a haven on h6. How can White win? First, centralize the K; then, at the right moment, give up the R for B and P. But the initial move forces the KtP to move, thereby weakening the B. (Fig. 318)

(42) R – B5! P – Kt5; (43) K – B2, K – Kt2; (44) K – K3, K – R3; (45) K – B4, B – Q2; (46)

Figure 318

K – K5, K – Kt4; Part I completed. But how to proceed? Most tempting is P – Kt3, but it leads to only a draw!!

Visualize this position: WK on KB6, WR on QB5, WPs on KKt3 and R2; Bl K on KR2, Bl B on B4; Bl Ps as now.

Then R x B, P x R; K x P, P – R5!!

If K x P, P x P; P x P, K – Kt3 draws; if P x P, White has only RPs, and can not win.

Luckily, White saw this (as you should, after your study of P endings) and played:

(47) **K – K4 ch, B – B4 ch;** (48) **K – K3, P – R5;** (49) **R – R5, K – B3;** (50) **K – B4, P – Kt4 ch;** (51) **K – K3, K – Kt3;** (52) **R – R6 ch, K – B2;** (53) **K – Q4, B – K3;** (54) **K – K5, B – B5;** (55) **R – QB6, B – Q6;** (56) **P – Kt3.** Now that the B has no haven on B4, this is possible. (56) **. . . P x P;** (57) **P x P, K – Kt2;** (58) **R – Q6.** One of the KtPs is now lost. (58) **. . . B – K7;** (59) **K – B5, B – B6;** (60) **K x P, K – B2.**

The next step is R x P. But Black must not be allowed to take the opposition thereafter.

(The position now is: WK g5, Re6, Pg3; Bl Kf7, Bf3, Pg4)

(61) **R – B6 ch, K – Kt2!** (62) **R – B4, B – Q8;** (63) **R – Q4, B – B6;** (64) **R – Q7 ch, K – Kt1;** (65) **K – R6, K – B1;** (66) **K – Kt6.**

Now, Black is embarrassed: . . . B – K5 ch? K – B6! and W threatens mate on Q8. If the K moves to K1, R – K7 ch wins the B; if to Kt1, R – Kt7 ch wins the P.

Best is . . . B – Kt7. Then R – Q8 ch, K – K2; R – QKt8, B – B6; K – Kt7, K – K3; R – KB8, as in the game.

(66) **. . . K – K1;** (67) **R – KB7!! B – K5 ch;** (68) **K – Kt7, B – B6;** (69) **R – B4!**

Now, after R x KtP, B x R; K x B, the best square the Bl K can find would be on the B file, and White, by K – R5, would gain the opposition and win. Black resigned.

3. Rook vs. Knight

This should be a draw, if King and Knight stay together in the center of the board. All the wins for the Rook (when K and Kt are together) occur when the K is in the corner.

Figure 319

(a) White to play wins.
(b) Black to play draws.

(a) (1) K – Kt6, K – Kt1; (2) R – Kt1, Kt – B1 ch; (3) K – B6 ch, K – R1; (4) K – B7, Kt – R2; (5) R – Kt8 mate.

(b) (1) . . . Kt – B1; (2) R – Kt1, Kt – K2! (The only move. If (2) . . . Kt – R2, K – Kt6; or (2) . . . Kt – Q3, (3) K – Kt6, K – Kt1; (4) K – B6 ch) (3) K – Kt6, K – Kt1; (4) R – K1, Kt – B1 ch; (5) K – B6, Kt – R2 ch; (6) K – Kt6, Kt – B1 ch; (7) K – R6, K – B2.

The last three moves show why the R can not win (except as above). The WK can not maintain the opposition, because the Kt checks him when it interposes, forcing him to yield a square to the Bl K.

4. Rs vs. Kts with Ps

A most remarkable ending occurred in Ventnor City, 1941, in the following position:

Figure 320

(Dr. A. Mengarini vs. W. W. Adams)

From the point count, White should win easily, being at least the value of two Pawns ahead. But the two Passed Pawns on c5 and d4 have tremendous value.

(1) . . . K – Q2; (2) P – QR4, Kt – K4. A sacrifice to free the terrors. (3) R x P, P – Q6; (4) R – Kt7 ch, K – K3; (5) P – R5, P – Q7; (6) R – B1, P – B5; (7) P – R6, Kt (2) – B3; (8) P – R7, Kt x P; (9) R x Kt.

Black, of course, would win against one Rook —but against two!! plus a Pawn!!!

(9) . . . K– Q4; (10) R – QB7 White intends to capture each P with a R. (10) . . . K – Q5; (11) K – Kt3 (a winning glint in his eye. Otherwise 11. R – Q drew.) (11) . . . P – B6; (12) P – R4, Kt – B5; (13) R – B4 ch, K – K4; (14) R – QB5 ch, K – K3. And now the miracle: (15) R(B5) x Kt?? (It was the other R that should have taken, followed (after P – Q8(Q) by R x P.) (15) . . . P – Q8(Q). Now if R x P, Q – K8 ch. (16) R(KB4) – K4 ch, K – Q4; (17) R(K4) – Q4 ch, Q x R and White resigned.

Exercise No. 22

(from a game J. Levin vs. H. Hahlbohm, U. S. Championship, 1942)

Figure 321

White, to move, has three Pawns for his piece —a numerical equivalent, but he has to get them moving. One needs immediate protection.

(a) How should he defend the QBP?
(b) What compensation can he get, if he loses it?

1. P – B4

(c) How can Black coordinate his pieces?

(1) . . . R – QB3; (2) R – B1, Kt – Q7

(d) What should White do now?

(3) P – QB5, K – B3; (4) K – B2, P x P

(e) Why does Black feel he can do this now?

(5) **R – B2, Kt – K5 ch; (6) K – B3, K – B4**

(f) What is Black's threat?

(g) How does White stop it?

(7) **P – Kt4 ch, P x P e.p.; (8) P x KtP**

(h) What is White's threat?

(8) . . . **R – KKt3; (9) R – KKt2**

(i) How does Black stop P – Kt4 ch?

(j) Will . . . Kt – Q3 do?

(9) . . . **R – Kt5; (10) P x P, P – B3**

(k) Why not . . . Kt x P?

(11) **R – Kt1, Kt – Q7 ch; (12) K –K2, Kt – K5** Drawn.

(l) Should Black be content with a draw?

(m) Should White?

To summarize:

In endings with Rs vs. Kts or Bs, the side with the

(a) **Rook should (1) centralize R and K; (2) create and attack weaknesses; (3) exhaust enemy Pawn moves by "tempo" moves; (4) keep the R mobile; (5) force the enemy King into a corner—with a B, the "wrong" corner.**

The side with the

(b) **Bishop or Knight** should (1) centralize **piece and King; (2) keep P position fluid; (3) supplement power of piece with Ps by control of different squares; (4) advance where it has the majority of Ps.**

Each side must plan.

Each side should try to direct the play toward the portion of the board where he has the majority of Ps or the strength of position.

ENDINGS WITH SEVERAL MINOR PIECES

With several minor pieces on the board, endings become increasingly difficult. The following general principles should be kept in mind constantly.

(1) **Plan.** Have a long-range plan, and several short-range plans which will carry it out.

(2) **Study your opponent's plan.** Try to make moves forwarding your plan which at the same time will hold up his.

(3) **Save time.** Sometimes one move is the difference between a win and a draw or loss.

(4) **Centralize.** Your pieces are stronger in the center.

(5) **Keep your pieces mobile.** We have seen how a Rook on the 7th is worth more than a Pawn on occasion. **Seize open lines.**

(6) **Use Pawns intelligently.** With a Bishop, keep your Pawns on the opposite squares; if your **opponent has a B, put your Pawns offensively on the B's squares, defensively on the opposite squares.**

(7) **Make use of the tactics you know:** blockade, restraint, control. Look for favorable opportunities to use them in your plan.

(8) **Watch for combinations.** Pins can occur frequently; forks and hurdles less so.

(9) **Simplify to favorable endings.** Use your knowledge. The best means of simplifying is to put your plan into execution. Don't go piece chasing *just* to simplify.

The study of two endings will show how these principles are applied by masters.

(Santasiere vs. Burdge, Ventnor City, 1940)

Figure 322

This is a rare ending—four minor pieces on each side. Black already has a passed QRP, but his pieces are more confined, the "Bl" B being defensively placed. White will try to create a passed Pawn or two in the center, but to make two Ps passed will give Black the chances for a second passed Pawn on the other side. The game continued:

22. **B – R3.** Seize the open diagonal! Black can not dispute this, for if . . . B – Q3? B x Kt! B x B; B x BP.

22. . . . **B – Q1.** Threatening P – Kt4, furthering the plan to secure another passed P.

23. **Kt – Kt1.** It is hard to believe that this is an "attacking" move; but the plan is to play (24) Kt – K1, (25) P – B3, (26) Kt – B3 and (27) (or after further preparation) P – K4. The French motto is: "**Reculer pour mieux avancer.**"

23. . . . **K – B2**

24. **Kt – K1** **B – K2.** Another reason for . . . B – Q1.

25. **B x B** **K x B.** Another reason for (23) Kt – Kt1 now is apparent: blockade of the QRP.

26. **P – B3** **Kt – Q3**

27. **Kt – B3.** Blockade on QR4; attack on Q5 and "overprotection" of the P on QKt5—that and support for P – K4 make a great deal out of one move.

27. . . . **P – Kt3.** Black decides to "hold" the position, but his move is "bad" for the B, and creates holes on his Black squares.

28. **P – Kt4!** Not only the BP, but the KKtP and KRP are thereby attacked.

28. . . . **K – B3**

29. **Kt – Kt2** **P – Kt4** Directed vs. Kt – B4 (xQP)

30. **K – B2** **P – R3**

31. **Kt – K1.** There is no future on Kt2, so the Kt goes to QB2, to support the P on Q4.

A moment of survey: Bl's passed Pawn is still on R4, immobile. White's plan of advancing his center Ps is developing. White clearly has the initiative.

31. . . . **B – R1**

32. **Kt – B2** **B – Kt2**

33. **P x P** **Kt x BP**

34. **P – K4.** With his pieces most advantageously placed, White makes the "big push."

34. . . . **Kt – K2** Blockade!

35. **Kt – K3** **K – K3**

36. **Kt – R4** **K – Q3**

37. **K – Kt3** **K – B2**

38. **Kt – B3.** White threatens P – K5, with the entry of the WK. If the Bl K returns to the King side, arriving at Kt2 just after the WK reaches R5, White can win in two ways: (a) B – B2 – Kt3, winning the QP, (b) B – B5, winning the QKtP. Black's next move is more or less forced:

38. . . . **P x P**

39. **P x P.** Thus White has achieved his first strategic aim.

Figure 323

39. . . . **Kt – KB3**

40. **Kt – B4** **Kt – Kt3**

41. **P – Q5.** Attacking, White places his Ps on the color of the enemy Bishop. On the other hand, the tempting move P – K5 is met by Kt – Q4! taking advantage of the square **d5.** (If Kt x Kt, B x Kt, B x Kt, Bx Kt)

41. . . . **Kt – Q2**

42. **B – B2** **Kt(Kt3) – K4**

43. **Kt – K3**

A temporary retreat. "When you have the advantage in space, avoid exchanges," advises Santasiere in his notes to the game in the tournament book.

43. . . . **P – R4.** Defensive: to keep out the K, and attacking: to get a passed Pawn.

44. **P – R4!** White allows the PP to become a protected PP, in order to get the square KB4 for his King. Black should decline, play P x P, and try to activate his own K.

44. . . . **P – Kt5**

45. **K – B4** **Kt – B6**

46. **Kt – B5** **B – B1**

47. **Kt – Kt7** **Kt x P**

"White sacrifices an important Pawn to gain an inch in the center."

48. **P – K5!** **Kt – Kt7 ch**

49. **K – K4**

"Necessary: On K – Kt3, Kt – K8 wins the KP. Now W's long-term strategy will be put to a clear and severe test."

49. . . . **Kt – B4 ch**

50. **K – Q4** **P – KR5**

51. **P – K6** **K – Q1**

52. **Kt – K2** **P – R5** "The dead resurrected."
53. K – K5 Kt – K6
54. B – Kt1 P – KR6 (on . . . P – Kt6; Kt – Kt1)
55. **Kt – Kt3** **P – R6**

"Looking rapidly from extreme right to extreme left, with an eye to the center, is no pastime for anyone with a stiff neck!" says Santasiere.

56. **B – R2** "To prevent the check at B5"
56. . . . B – Kt2
57. P – Q6 Threat: P – K7 ch – K8 (Q)
57. . . . Kt x P One PP has won a piece.
58. **Kt x Kt ch** K – K1 (else K – B6 – K7)
59. **Kt – B7 ch** K – Q1
60. **Kt – K6 ch** Better is Kt – Q4 – B6 ch
60. . . . K – K1
61. Kt(6) – Q4 B – B1
62. B – K6 B x B
63. **K x B.** Now the QP queens before either RP—and with check. **Black resigns.** An exciting ending—and a well-earned victory for a strategic plan.

(M. Hanauer vs. Larry Evans, Marshall C. C. Championship 1946-7)

Figure 324

White is a Pawn ahead, but the Bishops of opposite colors make the win difficult. His plan is to advance on the King's side, where he has the Pawn majority. The presence of the Bl K in the center makes it hard for Black to coordinate his Rs. The game continued:

17. P – B3 B – Q4
18. **B – Kt5.** This prevents O – O – O, and makes it difficult for Black to contest the Q file. If . . . O – O, White can sink his B in at KB6, protect it with P – K4 – 5, and start a mating attack with a R on the 4th rank.
18. . . . P – KB4
19. P – K4 P x P
20. P x P B – B5 (Not . . . B x P? R – K1)

White has his passed Pawn, and Black still can't castle. How to turn this to account?

21. R – B5! K – Q2
22. R – B5! B – K3
23. R – Q1 ch K – B1

The Bl QR is locked in. White now turns his attention to the K's side, where he is a Rook ahead for the moment.

24. R – K5 B – Kt5
25. R – Q4

White now has several alternate plans:

(a) to double on the 7th;

(b) to attack the square **c7** with B and both Rs;

(c) to advance the KP.

25. . . . P – Kt3
26. R – K7 R – QKt1 (defending the BP via QKt2)
27. P – K5 P – KR4
28. **P – K6.** The Bl B is cut off from its Q2, and the Rooks threaten to double.
28. . . . R – Kt2 so that if R(4) – Q7, B x P!
29. **R(7) – Q7!** threatening mate on Q8. If . . . R – Kt1; (30) R – Q8 ch, K – Kt2; (31) P – K7! and the Pawn queens. **Black resigned.**

Here the strategic idea (make and queen a Passed Pawn) was combined with mating threats and with harassing checks against the King, which prevented a coordinated defense. We now turn to one of the most difficult end games: Queen endings.

QUEEN AND PAWN ENDINGS

These are among the most difficult endings to win. The side which has the advantage must always watch for a series of checks by the other side's Queen, which will lead to a draw. Following are the points which must be kept in mind:

(1) **Keep pawns on both sides of the board.**

(2) **Centralize your Queen.**

(3) **Advance on the side where you have an extra pawn.**

(4) **Use your King (a) to help advance the Pawn and (b) to threaten mate.**

(5) **Watch your opponent's Queen.** Here is a game between two great players, A. Gilg and E. Colle, from the Carlsbad tournament of 1929:

(COLLE)

Figure 325

Let's look at the position: **White** is a pawn ahead. His Queen is in the center; his King is safe. There is only one Pawn on the Queen's side of the Board, next to Black's Pawn; and there is danger that these Pawns will be exchanged—in which case, the game will be a draw.

White's extra Pawn is a doubled Pawn. He must get rid of it (by exchange) to straighten out his Pawns before he can make a Passed Pawn on the King's side.

White has control of the White squares, because of the position of his Queen. This helps him control the fourth and fifth ranks, because he can check the Black King at a8, d5 and e4.

The game continued:

43. Qd5 – f3. This gives White another check at f8, and prevents the tempting move (43) . . . Pb5 – b4, since White can check at f8 and then take the Pawn b4 with his Queen.

Black can not exchange Queens because he will have a lost Pawn ending. He plays:

43. . . .	Qc3 – c5
44. Pg3 – g4	Qc5 – d6 ch

Why not Pb5 – b4? Because White can win the Pawn when it goes to b4 by Q – a8 ch, K – h7; Q – e4 ch. Even though Black gets the P on f2 in exchange, he would soon lose because of the Passed Pawn.

45. Kh2 – h3	Qd6 – b8
46. Qf3 – e3	Qb8 – f8

Again Pb5 – b4 fails, because of Qf3 – b3, pinning it and winning it.

47. Pf2 – f3	Qf8 – b8

Now we have another reason for not playing Pb5 – b4: After (48) Pa3 x Pb4, Qf8 x Pb4; (49) Qe3 – e8 ch, Kh8 – h7; (50) Qe8 – e4 ch, Qb4 x Qe4; (51) Pf3 x Qe4, White has a won Pawn ending.

The winning side should always watch for an opportunity to exchange Queens, in order to get a winning Pawn ending. However, he should not try to do *only* this. If his plan is sound, he will find opportunities for doing it often enough.

48. Pg4 – g5. Continuing his plan. But now a new threat is added: If the Black Queen leaves the 8th rank, White can play Q – e8 ch and P – g6 checkmate!

48. . . .	Qb8 – c8 ch
49. Pg2 – g4	Ph6 x Pg5
50. Qe3 x Pg5	Qc8 – c3
51. Qg5 – h5 ch	Kh8 – g8
52. Qh5 – d5 ch	Kg8 – f8

If the Black King went to h8, he would walk into the mating threat mentioned above: (52 . . . Kg8 – h8); (53) Pg4 – g5, Q x Pa3; (54) Pg5 – g6. The only ways to stop mate on the 8th rank are: a. (54) . . . Q – f8; (55) Q – h5 ch, Kh8 – g8; (56) Q – h7 mate! or b. (54) . . . Q – a5; (55) Q – c5, Q – d8; (56) Q – h5 ch, K – g8; (57) Q – h7 ch, K – f8; (58) Q – h8 ch, K – e7; (59) Q x Pg7 ch, K – e6; (60) Q – f7 ch, (61) P – g7 and (62) P – g8 (Q).

53. Qd5 – d6 ch	Kf8 – f7
54. Kh3 – g3	

Figure 326

The first phase is over. White has got rid of his doubled Pawn. His Queen is centralized; the threat of Pb5 – b4 is permanently stopped, and the threat of Pg4 – g5 – g6 forces a weakening Pawn move by Black.

The invasion of the Black Queen via the first rank (Qc3 – c1) is prevented by Q – f4 ch.

54. . . .	Pg7 – g6
55. Qd6 – b4	Qc3 – a1
56. Qb4 – f4 ch	Kf7 – g7
57. Qf4 – e3	Kg7 – f7
58. Pg4 – g5	Qa1 – b1
59. Qe3 – f4 ch	Kf7 – g8
60. Qf4 – b8 ch	Kg8 – h7
61. Qb8 – c7 ch	Kh8 – g8
62. Qc7 – c3	Kg8 – f7
63. Pf3 – f4	

Next phase: The march of the White King to attack the Black Pawn on b5. The Black King goes over to defend it.

63. . . .	Kf7 – e6
64. Qc3 – e5 ch	Ke6 – d7
65. Qe5 – e3	Kd7 – c6
66. Kg3 – f3	Qb1 – f1 ch
67. Kf3 – e4	Qf1 – b1 ch
68. Qe3 – d3	Qb1 – e1 ch
69. Ke4 – d4	

White threatens to exchange Queens by Q – c3 ch or Q – e4 ch. Black must therefore allow the White King to attack the undefended Black Pawn at g6.

69. . . .	Qe1 – g1 ch
70. Kd4 – e5	Qg1 – c5 ch
71. Ke5 – f6	Qc5 – f8 ch
72. Kf6 x Pg6	Qf8 x Pf4
73. Qd3 – c3 ch	Qf4 – c4

Leave the Black Queen alone! If you exchange, you give Black a Passed Pawn, which he will make into a Queen the move before you queen your g Pawn. The ending will then be a draw.

74. Qc3 – f3 ch	Kc6 – b6
75. Qf3 – e3 ch (Centralize!)	Kb6–a6 Not . . . Kb6–a5, Q–a7 mate!
76. Kg6 – f6	Qc4 – f1 ch
77. Kf6 – e7	Qf1 – a1
78. Ke7 – f7	Qa1 – f1 ch
79. Kf7 – e8	Qf1 – c4
80. Qe3 – e7	Qc4 – d3

Now the last phase: advancing the Passed Pawn to queen it. Of course, shepherd dogs WK and WQ guard their WP sheep.

81. Qe7 – f6 ch	Ka6 – b7
82. g5 – g6	Kb7 – b8
83. Qf6 – d8 ch	Black resigns

In the above ending, the Qs remained on the board until the end. Nevertheless, to the "points" enumerated above, we should add:

(6) Try to reduce the game to a simple Pawn ending. And for the defender:

(7) Avoid exchange of Qs when behind.

(8) Watch for opportunities for perpetual check.

In the following position, White was about to make a Queen. Black said: "Go ahead and make it!"—and White agreed to a draw!

Figure 327

1. P – Kt8(Q)	**Q – K4 ch**
2. Q(Kt8) – Kt7	**Q – K1 ch**
3. Q(R7) – Kt8	**Q – R4 ch**
4. Q(Kt7) – R7	**Q – K4 ch, and**

drawn by perpetual check.

(Janowski vs. Tartakower, N. Y., 1924)

Figure 328

Black is the exchange ahead, but White has

a Pawn for it. That is not enough for an end game, so it would be foolish for White to exchange Queens. Black's King is entirely exposed, devoid of protecting Ps; his Rook is out of play. Both parties would be happy to draw, although White has some attacking chances.

30. B – Kt6	Q – B8 ch
31. K – B2	K – B1

32. B – B5 Threat: B – Q6; Q – R7 – Kt8 ch. Nothing can stop it except a counter threat.

32. . . .	P – Kt5
33. B – Q6	P x P
34. Q – R7	P x B
35. Q – Kt8 ch	K – Q2
36. Q x B ch	K – Q1
37. Q – Kt8 ch	K – Q2
38. Q – R7 ch	K – Q1
39. Q – R5 ch	K – B1
40. Q – R6 ch	K – Q2
41. Q – Kt7 ch	K – Q1 and drawn

by perpetual check. The attempt to escape, if made on move 35—after Q – Kt8 ch—Q – B1; Q – Kt6 ch, K – K1; Q – Kt5 ch, Q – Q2; Q – Kt8 ch, Q – Q1; Q – Kt5 ch would have been unsuccessful.

Exercise No. 23

This ending is from a game in the same tournament (Carlsbad, 1929) as the Gilg–Colle game.

(Sämisch)

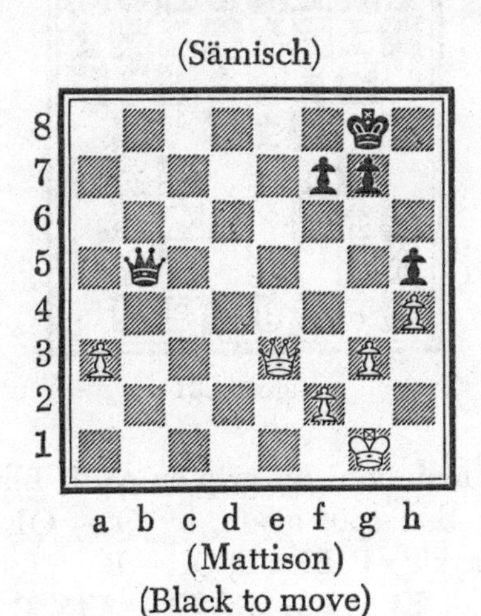

(Mattison)
(Black to move)

Figure 329

1. White is a Pawn ahead. What is his primary aim?

2. If Black checks the White King, where should he go to avoid more checks?

3. Should White give up his Pawn on a3 in exchange for the Black Pawn on h5?

4. On what line should the White Queen stay, in order to (a) help the a Pawn to queen; (b) protect the King?

5. What is Black's best delaying action?

The game continued:

45. . . .	Qb5 – a4
46. Qe3 – c5	Pg7 – g6
47. Qc5 – b4	

6. If Black exchanges Queens, can his King catch the White Pawn?

7. Should he exchange?

47. . . .	Qa4 – d1 ch
48. Kg1 – g2	

8. Why not Kg1 – h2 right away?

48. . . .	Qd1 – d5 ch
49. Kg2 – h2	Qd5 – f3
50. Qb4 – b8 ch	Kg8 – h7

9. Now how can the White Queen defend f2 and help the a Pawn?

51. Qb8 – a7	Qf3 – d5
52. Pa3 – a4	Kh7 – g7
53. Pa4 – a5	Pg6 – g5

10. Why does Black do this?

54. Ph4 x Pg5	Ph5 – h4

11. Why not 54 . . . Q x Pg5?

55. Pg3 x Ph4	Qd5 – e4
56. Kh2 – g3	Qe4 – e5 ch

12. How can White stop the checks?

13. Can he now afford to give up the a Pawn?

57. Pf2 – f4	Qe5 – e1 ch
58. Qa7 – f2	Qe1 x Pa5

14. What now is White's plan?

59. Qf2 – e3	Qa5 – a2
60. Ph4 – h5	Kg7 – h7
61. Qe3 – d3 ch	Kh7 – h8
62. Ph5 – h6	

15. The immediate threat is ________?

62. . . .	Qa2 – a1
63. Qd3 – e3	

16. This stops ________?

17. And threatens ________?

63. . . .	Kh8 – h7
64. Qe3 – e4 ch	Kh7 – g8
65. Qe4 – e8 ch	Resigns

18. Why?

CHAPTER XIV

THE MIDDLE GAME

The **Middle Game** is that part of the chess game that comes between the opening and the end game. But where does the Middle Game start? And when does it finish? That all depends upon the structure of the position developing from the opening moves: Pawn structure and piece alignment. The armies rush to the front; after preliminary skirmishes and probing for weaknesses, they clash on a wide front. That is the Middle Game.

In the early chapter on openings it was stressed that control of the center squares was vital. The player who has control of the center splits his opponent's forces and limits their field of action. But what is important for the middle game strategy is the fact that:

Rule One: A player who has control of the center can attack on the wings.

Its corollary is just as important:

Rule Two: A player can not attack on the wing unless he has control of the center.

1. King's Side Attacks

The following games will illustrate the two rules.

Game #1: Reti opening. M. Hanauer vs. A. Schoenberg (Brilliancy Prize, Metropolitan Chess League, New York, 1938).

(1) **P – QB4, Kt – KB3**; (2) **Kt –KB3, P – K3**; (3) **P – KKt3, P – Q4**; (4) **P – Kt3, Kt(1) – Q2**; (5) **B – Kt2, P – B3**; (6) **B – Kt2, B – Q3**; (7) **P – Q4.** Black was threatening . . . P – K4, arguing possession of the square **d4.** White stops it, but temporarily gives up the square **e4,** which Black immediately occupies.

(7) . . . **Kt – K5**; (8) **O – O, P – KB4**

Black's Pawn position is the type known as the "Stonewall." It gives up **e5** permanently (since no Bl P can guard that square) in exchange for a strong **e4.** White, however, can still argue about **e4** with his Pf2 (–f3).

(9) **Kt – K5, O – O**; (10) **Kt – Q2, Q – K1**; (11) **P – K3, Kt(2) – B3**

In this game, the **middle game** seems to start

Figure 330

at this point. The pieces are not all developed, but White, feeling that he has control of the center, begins to attack on the King's wing.

(12) **P – B3, Kt – Kt4**; (13) **P – KR4, Kt – B2**; (14) **P – KKt4! P x KtP**; (15) **P x KtP, B x Kt**; (16) **P x B, Kt – Q2**; (17) **Kt – B3.**

Figure 331

White maintains his grip on **e5.** If Black tries to attack that spot again, by Q – Q1 (– B2), White plays P x P, BP x P; QR – B

(17) . . . **Kt – R3**; (18) **Kt – Kt5, R x R ch**; (19) **B x R, Kt – B1**; (20) **B – Q3, Q – K2**; (21) **Q – B2.**

The sacrifices begin: if (21) . . . Kt x P, (22) B x P ch, K – R1; (23) B – Kt6, Kt x P (e3); (24)

Q – K2! Kt x B; (25) Q – R5 ch, K – Kt1; (26) Q x Kt. The Bl Q must vacate K2 for the K, and still keep an eye on K1. . . . Q – Q2 is forced, but then B – R3 cuts off the K's escape, and Black is mated.

21. . . . **P – KKt3.** This stops the check at his R2, but (a) creates a weakness on his B3 and (b) sticks his chin out into the right cross of P – R5.

(22) R – KB1, B – Q2 Finally! **(23) Q – Kt2, B – K1; (24) R – B6, B – Q2; (25) P – R5, Q – Kt2.**

Figure 332

White's pieces are at their maximum powers; Black's are still cramped and uncoordinated. There ought to be a way of ripping open Black's position.

(26) Kt x RP! K x Kt (If . . . Kt x Kt; R x KtP); **(27) P x P ch, K – Kt1; (28) P – Kt5, Kt – B4.** The only square, but it opens the long diagonal. **(29) B x Kt, P x B; (30) P – K6, B – K1.**

Figure 333

(31) R x Kt ch! K x R.

If Q x R; Q – R2! and mate is forced at R8 or, after . . . Q – Kt2; B x Q, K x B; Q – R7 ch, K – B1; P – K7 mate.

(32) B x Q ch, K x B; (33) Q – R2, Resigns.

From the above game, we learned that if one has control of the center, he can advance on the wing. But there are other things we can learn:

Rule Three: Avoid a rigid Pawn position.

Rule Four: Do not play defensively only. Your defensive play must include a counter attack.

Rule Five: When you have the advantage in space and position, put your pieces in the places where they exert maximum power.

Rule Six: When your pieces have achieved maximum power, look for a sacrifice which may break open your opponent's position.

Game #2 Queen's Gambit Declined; Tarrasch Defense

White: Arthur W. Dake

Black: I. A. Horowitz

(1) P – Q4, P – Q4; (2) P – QB4, P – K3 (Black *declines* to accept the offer of the gambit Pawn) **(3) Kt – QB3, P – QB4. The Tarrasch Defense,** named after DR. SIEGBERT TARRASCH, a world master and one of the best tournament players in the world during the years 1895-1910. Dr. Tarrasch preached the virtues of Black's third move, and proved it by game after game of tournament play and victory—until the methods of playing against it were discovered and standardized. It is still a powerful gambit weapon, as the present game shows.

(4) BP x P, KP x P; (5) Kt – B3, Kt – QB3; (6) P – KKt3. This is the **Rubinstein Variation,** the idea of which is to put pressure on the square d5 via a fianchetto of the KB, while d4 is controlled and blockaded by the Q, QB and the Kts. **(6) . . . Kt – B3; (7) B – Kt2, B – K2; (8) O – O, O – O; (9) P x P.** (Fig. 334)

Now, if B x P, White occupies Q4 with a Kt (after (10) Kt – R4, B – K2; (11) B – K3 or (10) Kt – QKt5). Black, therefore, sacrifices the QBP in order to occupy d4 with his QP, thereby gaining at least a temporary control of the center. He chases the WKt from QB3 (and from control of e4) occupying the White squares, with B, Kt and R.

(9) . . . P – Q5! (10) Kt – QR4, B – B4; (11) Kt – K1, Kt – K5; (12) Kt – Q3, R – K1; (13) B – B4, B – B3; (14) R – B1, Q – Q2.

Figure 334

Figure 335

Black's control of the center is admirable: His' pieces are well coordinated, whereas White's are split, and in unnatural places.

But White has a Pawn—and he should start the wheels moving where he is a Pawn ahead: namely, by P – QKt4, Kt – Kt2, P – QR4 and P – Kt5 (with the support of his R and Q). Instead, however, he advances on the King's side, opening up thereby the squares around his own King. This is a strategic mistake, because he **does not have control of the center.** Let us see what happens:

(15) **P – KKt4? B – Kt3** (Of course not . . . B x P; P – B3) (16) **P – B3, Kt – Kt4;** (17) **B – Kt3** (threatening P – B4 – B5) **P – KR4;** (18) **P – R4, Kt – K3;** (19) **P – Kt5, B – Q1;** (20) **B – R3.**

This move must be considered carefully. It is not merely a pin, but the beginning of the fight for the square **f5.** If White can play P – B4 – B5, he might work up something. The next

Figure 336

moves are made with **f5** the primary consideration.

(20) . . . **Q – Q4;** (21) **P – Kt3, B – B4;** (22) **B – Kt2.** It would not do to exchange this B, which is plugging up the drafty K's position. (22) . . . **B – B2;** (23) **P – B4.** Same for the other B! (23) . . . **B – K5;** (24) **B – R3, P – KKt3;** (25) **Kt(4) – Kt2, Kt – Kt2;** (26) **Kt – B4, Kt – B4;** (27) **K – R2.** Better is B – K1, but White offers his B (for the Kt) to remove a piece from **f5.** (27) . . . **Kt x B;** (28) **K x Kt, R – K2!**

Figure 337

Black develops his last piece, the QR, always cementing his hold on the center. White, to get some freedom, now gives back his Pawn. (29) **Kt – Q6, B x Kt(d6);** (30) **P x B, Q x P(d6);** (31) **K – R2, QR – K1;** (32) **R – KB2, B – Q4.**

"Reculer pour mieux avancer"—with the Rooks on the open file.

(33) **Q – Q2, R – K6;** (34) **R – KKt1, Q – K2;** (35) **B – B1, Q – K3!** (Hitting **f5** again. White can not blockade the spot with a P, for if P – B5; Q – Q3 ch; Kt – B4, R(1) – K5); (36) **Kt – Kt4, Kt x Kt;** (37) **Q x Kt, R – K5;** (38) **Q – Q2, B – B3.** The threat is now . . . B – Kt4, which White can not prevent by Q – Kt4 because of

. . . P — Q6, nor P — QR4, because of . . . Q x P.

(39) B — R3, Q — Q3; (40) R — Q1, B — Kt4; (41) P — K3

Figure 338

White hopes to get the QP for his KP, but Black's control of the K file extends all the way down, and after the next move P x P would be met by R — K7.

(41) . . . Q — Kt3! (42) R — B3, P x P; (43) Q — K1, P — K7 ("The Passed Pawn's lust to expand," Nimzovitch used to call this); (44) R — QB1, Q — Q3; (45) K — Kt3, R x P (the King is a poor defender); (46) R x R, R — K6 ch; (47) K — Kt2, Q x R; (48) R — B8 ch, K — R2, White resigns.

Since White did *not* have control of the center, his wing attack, opening up his King's position was doomed to failure. The Black pieces infiltrated, and finally won.

A word of caution: Black could still have *lost* the game on move 48 if he had played . . . K — Kt2; (49) Q — R1 ch, K — R2; (50) R — R8 mate! Respect every move of your opponent!

2. Queen's Side Attacks:

(a) The Minority Attack

A King's side attack is easy to see because it is natural to attack the King; but an attack on the Queen's side, when there is no apparent weakness and no outstanding object like the King, is more difficult to imagine. One such attack is the famous "minority attack," illustrated in the following game:

White: V. Smyslov U.S.S.R.—Black: A. Bisguier, U.S.A.

(U.S.A.—U.S.S.R. Match—Moscow, 1955)

(1) P — QB4, KKt — B3; (2) KKt — B3, P — K3; (3) P — KKt3, P — Q4; (4) B — Kt2, Kt — B3; (5) P x P, P x P; (6) O — O, P — KKt3; (7) P — Q4, B — Kt2; (8) Kt — B3, O — O; (9) B — B4, Kt — K2; (10) R — B1, P — B3.

The opening is not a usual one, but resembles the so called "Exchange Variation" of the Queen's Gambit Declined. White controls e5; Black can put pressure on e4. But the WBs point toward the B1 Q's side. Black's Pawns seem strong on that side, and there are four of them to White's three.

White, however, starts an attack with his QRP and QKtP against that seeming stronghold. This is the famous "minority attack."

Figure 339

(11) P — QKt4! P — QR3; (12) P — QR4, Kt — K5; (13) Kt — K5, Kt — Q3; (14) P — Kt5.

Figure 340

Now we see the reason for the minority attack: to undermine the support of the Pd5, thereby weakening the Black center.

(14) . . . RP x P? Black would do better to move . . . B — K3, supporting his QP and not vacating a4 for the WKt. He hopes, however, to get counterplay on the Q's side.

(15) P x P, Kt x P? (16) Kt x Kt, P x Kt; (17) R — B5, Q — Kt3. Protecting the Pb5 directly and the Pd5 indirectly: B x Pd5? Kt x B; R x Kt,

B – R6; R – K1, QR – Q1; R x R, R x R; P – K3? B x Kt! B x B, P – B3; B – B4, P – Kt4.

(18) **Q – Q3! Kt – B3; (19) R x QP, R – R5; (20) R x P, Q x P; (21) Kt x Kt, P x Kt; (22) Q x Q, R x Q; (23) R – QB5** (Not B x P? B – R3; R – Kt2, R x B!) (23) . . . **B – Q2; (24) P – K3, R – Q7; (25) B x P.**

Figure 341

As a result of the minority attack, all the Q side Ps have disappeared, and White remains with a solid KP plus. With all the Ps on one side of the board, Black has hopes for a draw, but his next move allows the exchange of one Rook, and yields a dominating square (d5) to the WB. Black should play . . . B – R6 and . . . R(1) – Q.

(25) . . . **R – B1?? (26) R – Q5! R x R; (27) B x R, R – B4; (28) R – Kt1!** This gains an open file with a **tempo**, for if . . . R x B? R – Kt8 ch, B – B1; B – R6.

(28) . . . **B – KB1; (29) P – K4.** First use: support of the "outpost" B on Q5. (29) . . . **B – B1; (30) R – R1, R – Kt4; (31) R – R8, B – KR6,** a threat similar to White's. **(32) B – R2.** The Bs cut the Bl R off from White's first rank. (32) . . . **K – Kt2; (33) R – R7.** Black's KBP is lost. (33) . . . **P – Kt4; (34) B – K3, B – QB4; (35) B x B, R x B; (36) P – B4!** Loophole for the King–and attack. (36) . . . **R – B7; (37) B x P, K – B3; (38) P x P ch, K x P; (39) B – Q5, P – R4; (40) R – R2,** Black overstepped the time limit; but now that the WK can escape, his game is won.

(b) Attacks on Opposite Wings

On occasions when the Kings castle on opposite sides, the motto is: **Speed!** Who gets there *firstest* with the *mostest* wins.

An example from tournament play:
White: John Foster
Black: M. Hanauer
(Marshall C.C. Championship 1950-1)

(1) P – Q4, Kt – KB3; (2) P – QB4, P – K3; (3) Kt – QB3, B – Kt5 (The Nimzo-Indian defense, named after Aron Nimzovitch) **(4) Q – B2, Kt – B3 (Zurich Variation). (5) P – K3, O – O; (6) Kt – B3, R – K1; (7) B – K2, P – Q3; (8) B – Q2, P – K4; (9) P – Q5, Kt – K2; (10) P – K4, Kt – Kt3.**

Figure 342

White is slightly embarrassed here, despite the innocent look of the position. If (11) P – QR3, for example, B x Kt! Then (12) B x B, Kt – B5; (13) B – B1, B – Kt5! He decides to keep the Kt from B5:

(11) P – KKt3, B – R6! (12) O – O – O, P – KR3.

Ordinarily, the rule, when Kings are castled on opposite sides of the board is:

Rule Seven: Avoid Pawn moves in front of the castled King.

Reasons: (a) Pawn moves lose control of squares.
(b) An advanced Pawn is an object of attack.

But here it is more important to keep the B from KKt5, because of the pin, and the Kt from KKt5, because it will chase the B on h3, and release the KRP for the King's side attack.

(13) B – B1, Q – Q2; (14) Kt – KKt1, B x B; (15) R x B.

White has wasted time undeveloping his pieces in order to chase the Bl B. Now Black opens up the files in front of the WK.

(15) . . . **P – B3; (16) Kt(1) – K2, P x P; (17) KP x P, QR – B; (18) P – Kt3.**

Another weakening **P** move; but if Q – Kt3, B x Kt; Kt x B, P – QR3 and . . . P – QKt4.

(18) . . . **P – QR3; (19) Kt – R4, B – R6 ch.**

Rule Eight: Do not exchange when you are at-

tacking—unless you see an immediate advantage. Exchanges relieve the defending side by giving him more room for fewer pieces.

Figure 343

(20) **K – Kt1.** The game now enters the combination stage (see Fig. 343). W threatens Kt – Kt6. (20) . . . **Kt x P!** (21) **Q – Q3, P – Kt4!** (22) **Q x Kt(5), Q – B4 ch!**

When you attack, make use of every open line. If . . . P x Kt; Kt – B3, Q – B4 ch; Q – K4. Speed is of the essence!

(23) **K – R1, P x Kt.** Black threatens Q – B7.

Figure 344

If (24) B – B1, Black will not exchange but play B – Kt5 (preventing Q – Q2). Then (25) P – QR3, P x P!! (26) P x B, Q – B7; (27) Q – Q2, P – Kt7 ch; (28) B x P, Q x Q.

White defends his B2 with his Kt, which then goes on to defend the spot **b8.** But his King is too greatly exposed.

(24) **Kt – Q4, Q – Q6;** (25) **Kt – B6, Q – B7;** (26) **B – B1** (26. R – QKt1 is no better: . . . R x Kt! 27. Q x R, Q x B!! 28. Q x R ch, Kt – B1, and the threats of Q – B6 or Q5 ch force mate).

(26) . . . **P x P;** (27) **P x P, Q x KtP;** (28) **R – K1, R – Kt1!** White resigns.

After Kt x R, R x Kt; Q – K4, B x B; R – K2, Q – B6 ch; K – R2, Q – R6 mate.

In the above game, White lost so much time that he was never able to start his own attack.

(c) Attacks on Pawn Chains

Some openings result in two chains of Pawns stretching across the center files. These chains have characteristics with which you must become familiar. For instance, after the Moves: **(King's Indian Defense,** QP Opening)

(1) P – Q4, Kt – KB3; (2) P – QB4, P – KKt3; (3) Kt – QB3, B – Kt2; (4) P – KKt3, P – Q3; (5) B – Kt2, O – O; (6) P – K4, P – K4; (7) P – Q5, two chains of Pawns have been formed.

Figure 345

For each player, the idea of allowing the other's Pawn chain to remain unchallenged is contrary to the ideas of attack, initiative, mobility, etc. Therefore, he must attack. But where?

Rule Nine: Attack the base of the pawn chain.

The base of Black's pawn chain is **c7,** and a very solid base it is, too. White must, therefore, transfer the base to d6, by a series of moves such as Kt – B3, O – O, B – K3, Kt – K1, Kt – Q3, P – QR3 and P – QKt4, followed by P – B5.

In the meantime, Black will be busy on White's pawn chain, with its spear point on **d5.** Black can choose to hit **e4** via Kt – K1 (or R4) and P – KB4; or hit **c4** by means of P – QB4 (fixing the Pawn on **c4**) P – QR3 and P – QKt4, with support of the Kt now on QKt1 (via QR3 and QB2) the QB (to Q2) and the QR (to QKt1).

Understanding this, it is easy to follow the plans of two of the leading world players in the following game:

White: S. Gligoric (Yugoslavia)

Black: T. Petrosian (U.S.S.R.)

(Belgrade, 1954) QP Game: Benoni Counter.

(1) P – Q4, Kt – KB3; (2) P – QB4, P – QB4; (3) P – Q5, P – K4; (4) Kt – QB3, P – Q3; (5) P – K4, Kt(1) – Q2; (6) Kt – B3, P – QR3; (7) B – K2, B – K2; (8) O – O, O – O; (9) Kt – K1, Kt – K1; (10) Kt – Q3, Kt – B2 (see Fig. 346);

Figure 346

(11) P –QR4, R – Kt1; (12) B – K3, B – Kt4.

Black is all set for . . . P – QKt4, but he sees that if he plays it now, White answers RP x P, P x P; P x P, Kt x P; Kt x Kt, R x Kt; Kt x KP! uncovering the Be2 on the Rb5. He, therefore, wishes to exchange Bs, to relieve his cramped position.

(13) Q – Q2, B x B; (14) Q x B, P – KR3

He now tries to exchange Qs on the same square. **(15) P – R5.** Now there is no time for . . . Q – Kt4, because of Q x Q, P x Q; P – QKt4, P x P; Kt x P, P – Kt4; Kt – B6!

However, pressure on **b5** has been released, so:

(15) . . . P – QKt4! (16) P x Pe. p. (Pa5 x Pb6), **Kt x P (Kt3); (17) P – QKt3, R – R1.**

The base of the W pawn chain is now at Q Kt3. The QBP would be *en prise* if the KtP were

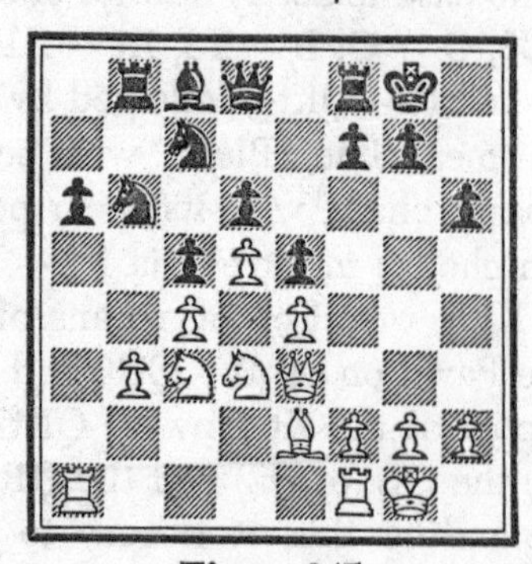

Figure 347

pushed, and using moves to protect the QBP would give Black time for . . . P – QR4. White, therefore, attacks the pawn chain from the other wing:

(18) P – KB4, P x P; (19) Q x KBP, P – B3

This holds back P – K5 temporarily.

(20) Kt – Q1, Q – K2. Black wants to protect his QP while he maneuvers the Kt **b6** via **d7** to **e5.**

(21) Kt – K3, P – KKt4?! A weakening move that neither of us would make, in order to induce the WQ to block his B from KKt4, where the B would exchange for the **Bc8** and then allow the Kt to enter **f5.** The WKP must be protected, so Black expects Q – B3, but:

(22) Kt – B5! B x Kt; (23) Q x B, Q – R2; (24) Q – Kt4, R(R) – K1; (25) R – B5, Kt – Q2; (26) R(R) – KB1, R – K2.

If . . . Kt – K4; Kt x Kt, BP x Kt; R x R ch, R x R; R x R ch, K x R; Q – B8 ch, Kt – K1; B – R5, Q – K2; P – KKt4! and Black, in zugzwang, must lose the pinned Kt.

White threatens Kt – B4, for if R x P? B – Q3, R – Q5; R x KtP ch! and B x Q ch! Black moved . . . R – K2 in order to defend his KBP by R (K2) – KB2.

Figure 348

(27) P – QKt4! Hitting the pawn chain. **(27) . . . P x P; (28) P – B5! P – KR4; (29) Q – Kt3, R x P; (30) P – B6.** It is important to remove this Kt, because he defends the base of the P chain in front of the King (Pf6). **(30) . . . R x B; (31) Q x QP, Kt – Kt4; (32) Q x KtP.** Self-restraint! But there is a combinative reason: **(32) . . . Kt – Kt1; (33) R x KtP ch!! K – B2.** (If P x R; Q x R mate.) **(34) R x P ch!! K x R; (35) Q x R ch, K x R; (36) P – R4 ch;** and **Black** faced with . . . K x P; Q – B4 mate or . . . K – Kt3; Kt – B4 mate **resigned.**

The destroyed pawn chain unleashed a pawn roller, which drove away the defending Kts. Result: A mating attack.

(d) **Doubled Pawns: Blockade; then Destroy.** The weaknesses of doubled Pawns lie in (a) their inability to defend each other, (b) their lack of mobility. When your opponent has doubled Pawns, you must, therefore, blockade them first, and attack them later. In doing so, however, you must not neglect play in the center, for then your opponent can work up a strong attack. Let us see how our grandmaster Reshevsky solved the problem against World Champion Botvinnik in the Match Tournament for the World Championship in 1948:

White: M. Botvinnik
Black: Samuel J. Reshevsky

Nimzo-Indian Defense

(1) P – Q4, Kt – KB3; (2) P – QB4, P – K3; (3) Kt – QB3, B – Kt5; (4) P – QR3 (the Saemisch Variation) **(4) . . . B x Kt ch; (5) P x B, P – B4!** The doubled Pawns are immediately blockaded.

Figure 349

Black's plan of destruction aims at the Pc4, and includes the moves Kt – QB3 – QR4; P – QKt3 and B – R3; and Q – Q2 – QR5 (if the WQ leaves the diagonal). It may also include R – QB1, and, at the right time, P x P, uncovering the R on the WP on QB4.

In the meantime, however, White will not be sleeping. He will be attacking by B – Q3; Kt – K2 – Kt3 (– B5 or R5); P – K3 and P – KB4 – 5 – 6.

Black must, therefore, remember that his plan is a long-range plan, and must watch the always crucial center:

(6) P – K3, O – O; (7) B – Q3, Kt – B3; (8) Kt – K2, P – QKt3; (9) P – K4, Kt – K1; (10) B – K3, P – Q3; (11) O – O, Kt – R4; (12) Kt – Kt3, B – R3; (13) Q – K2, Q – Q2; (14) P – B4, P – B4!

Figure 350

White's attack is held back, and Black is ready to proceed against the Pc4.

(See below for the conclusion of this game.)

Now let us see what happens when Black stubbornly proceeds on his course. Make the first nine moves as above, then continue:

(White: D. Bronstein Black: M. Najdorf)
(Budapest, 1950)

(10) O – O, P – Q3; (11) P – B4, B – R3?? (Black should play . . . P – B4, as above) **(12) P – B5! P – K4; (13) P – B6!** and ripping a hole in the Black King's position (13 . . . Kt x P; 14. B – Kt5 and 15. B x Kt) White won quickly.

Back to the Botvinnik-Reshevsky game:

(15) QR – K1, P – Kt3; the Black Kt can now defend the Ps e6 and f5 from g7. White sees no future in P – Q5, so moves his R to threaten P – K5.

(16) R – Q1, Q – KB2; the Queen moves away from the line of the WR, always eyeing the center. Again Black resists playing . . . Q – R5, because of (17) P – Q5, B x P; (18) P x KP, B x P; (19) P x P, P x P; (20) B x QBP, B – Kt6; (21) B – Kt5, B x R; (22) Q – K6 ch.

(17) P – K5 aiming at the Q side P chain, which Black immediately supports.

(17) . . . R – B1; (18) KR – K1, P x KP; (19) QP x KP.

The center is now completely blocked. Black has only to worry about an invasion on the Q file while he sets out for the weak White Queen's side Pawns.

Figure 351

(19) . . . **Kt – KKt2;** (20) **Kt – B1, KR – Q1;** (21) **B – KB2, Kt – R4.** White intended B – R4, securing the Q file for himself. Black spoils the plan, for only the B can defend the WP on f4, the Q being needed to defend the Pc4.

(22) **B – Kt3, Q – K1;** (23) **Kt – K3, Q – R5;** (24) **Q – R2.** For the moment, White can defend; but now Black contests the Q file.

(24) . . . **Kt x B;** (25) **P x Kt, P – KR4.**

The Pawn chain must be preserved. This stops P – KKt4, which would attack it.

(26) **B – K2.** Otherwise, Black doubles Rooks on the Q file, and captures the QBP, the B(Q3) being pinned on the R (Q1). If 26. B – B2, B x P; 27. B x Q, B x Q; 28. B – Q7, R – Kt1 (not R – B2? B x P ch!) 29. R – Q6, K – B2; (30) P – B4, K – K2; 31. R(1) – Q1, Kt x P; 32. R x P ch, K – B2; 33. R – B6 ch, K – Kt2; 34. Kt x Kt, B x Kt; 35. R(1) – Q6, B – B2 and 36. P – K6 is impossible, because of . . . K x R. Of such depth are World Champions made!

(26) . . . **K – B2;** (27) **K – B2, Q – Kt6;** (28) **Q x Q, Kt x Q.**

Figure 352

Black threatens Kt – Q7 – **K5 ch x** QBP. If (29) **Kt – B1, K – K2;** (30) **K – K3, Kt – R4!** (31) Kt – Q2, R – Q2, doubling the Rs on the Q file.

(29) **B – Q3, K – K2;** (30) **K – K2, Kt – R4**

The WK now blocks his B, which screens the Q file, whereon Black can now double his Rooks. White sees a forthcoming zugzwang, and makes a violent attempt to change the course of the game:

(31) **R – Q2, R – B2;** (32) **P – Kt4**

A Pawn sacrifice for Black's KKtP or the KR file—which will White get?

32. . . . **R(B2) – Q2!** Neither!

33. **P x BP, KtP x P;** (34) **R(K) – Q1, P – R5;**

Figure 353

This is as fine a zugzwang as you are likely to see. The White pieces *must* remain where they are for if:

—either Rook moves, . . . Kt x P wins.
—the K moves, . . . Kt – Kt6 wins.
—the Kt moves, . . . Kt x P wins.
—the B moves, . . . Kt x P wins.

(35) **K – K1, Kt – Kt6;** (36) **Kt – Q5 ch, P x Kt;** (37) **B x P, Kt x R;** (38) **R x Kt, P x P!**

Not . . . R – B2; P x P, and trouble (39) **B x R, R x B;** (40) **R – KB2, K – K3;** (41) **R – B3, R – Q6;** (42) **K – K2** and White resigned.

Black carried out his plan perfectly: blockade, then attack. But he did not neglect play in the center. Eventually White, to counter Black's threats, had to give him control of the center, and then he won quickly.

Knowing these openings, we can see how a variation is born. This is the reasoning:

(1) If White can gain in any way from the opening, it is because of his attack on the Black King who is castled, on the King's side.

(2) The Queen's side is blocked, and the Bl K should be safer there.

(3) The Q's side pieces must be developed for the plan of attack on W's QBP. Therefore:

White: E. Geller Black: B. Spassky
(U.S.S.R. Championship 1955)

(1) P – Q4, Kt – KB3; (2) P – QB4, P – K3; (3) Kt – QB3, B – Kt5; (4) P – QR3, B x Kt ch; (5) P x B, P – B4; (6) P – K3, Kt – B3; (7) B – Q3, P – Q3; (8) Kt – K2, P – QKt3; (9) O – O, **Q – Q2**; (10) P – K4, **B – R3**; (11) B – Kt5, **O – O – O!**

Black now says: "Take me, and open a file against your King." White believed he was committed to the King's side attack, took the dare—and lost.

Figure 354

By now, it must be clear that a Middle Game does not just "happen." It stems from the opening, from understanding of many openings, and from knowledge of variations of one opening and similar variations of other openings. In the next chapter, we shall try to add to your knowledge of the opening.

CHAPTER XV

THE OPENINGS OF CHAMPIONS

1. What Opening Shall I Play?

This is the question every chess player asks himself before he sits down to the board. The more important the game, the more searching the question. Here are some answers to it:

In off-hand games, play a variety of openings. No amount of reading or studying can give you the knowledge you gain when you play a game over the board. *Then* you have to make a move, a choice of one move, each time you play; and that choice, which eliminates other moves, develops your judgment and power to "think chess."

TWO POPULAR OPENINGS: KING'S INDIAN AND SICILIAN DEFENSE

There are only six first moves that White would make in a tournament game: P – K4, P – Q4, P – QB4, P – KB4, Kt – KB3 and Kt – QB3. Other moves are considered by good players to be inferior or even downright bad. Four of the other possible moves might be tolerable, because they can lead into variations where thev might be useful: namely, P – K3, P – QB3, P – Q3 or P – KKt3. However, they are not so good as the others, because they allow Black to seize the center squares and they also, in the first three cases, interfere with lines of development for Kts or Bs.

Of the approved moves, two are made far more than the others: namely, P – Q4 and P – K4. Games starting with P – QB4 or Kt – KB3 often change ("transpose") into P – Q4 games on the second or third move. We shall, therefore, first consider 1. P – Q4. Remember the general rules for development set forth in Chapter IV:

—Develop your pieces toward the center.

—Control lines and squares in the center.

—Castle to connect and make use of your Rooks.

—Make Pawn moves only when they are necessary for center control or piece development.

—Move first the pieces whose moves are most limited.

And now for 1. P – Q4

White occupies a center square and attacks QB5 and K5. What should Black do?

1. . . . Kt – KB3

This is the 1. **King's Indian Defense.** It is shown first because it is the most popular defense nowadays, for several reasons. One reason is that it leads to a tough game, with many pieces on each side, and plenty of room to maneuver them. Another reason is that Black can reach his setup (the first eight or nine moves) almost unhindered: if White makes strenuous efforts to stop Black, he will only weaken his position.

1. . . . Kt – KB3 attacks the squares e4 and d5, thereby controlling them without occupying them. If White plays 2. P – Q5? then . . . P – B3; 3. P – QB4, P x P; 4. P x P, Q – R4 ch 5. Kt – B3, P –K3–and White will have to exchange his center Pawn, since 6. P – K4? is met by . . . Kt x P.

2. P – QB4 P – Q3
3. Kt – QB3 P – K4

In QP openings, the QBP is usually advanced to QB4 before the QKt goes to B3. The QBP attacks **d5**, as does the Kt. White can now exchange Ps and Qs, making the Bl K move, and preventing him from castling. Black can avoid this by moving 3. . . . QKt – Q2 before 4. . . . P – K4, but experience has shown that his K can find a safe haven at c7, and that he can develop harmoniously, while the WP on c4 prevents the WB now on f1 from attacking the Pf7. Therefore, Black does not worry about the double exchange.

4. Kt – B3 QKt – Q2
5. P – KKt3 P – KKt3
6. B – Kt2 B – Kt2

It is this type of development that gives the name "Indian" to the opening–from games played in India many years ago. The Black Bishop attacks the center from afar. White has **fianchettoed** his KB, to attack the White center squares.

7. O – O O – O
8. P – K4 P – B3

Black wants to use his Queen to continue the attack on the Black squares. One way of doing this is . . . P – QR4 – R5; . . . Q – R4 – Kt5; another is . . . Q – Kt3. White wishes to support his QP with B – K3, but if he does it at once, Black will play . . . Kt – Kt5, and capture the B on K3. Therefore:

9. P – KR3 stopping . . . Kt – Kt5.

Black now makes a move with a plan typical of this kind of game in mind:

9. . . . Kt – KR4

Plan:. . . P – KB4, opening up the B file for the R, and attacking White's solid phalanx of Ps.

10. B – K3 Q – K8

These were the opening moves of the 21st game of the 1951 World Championship match between M. Botvinnik (White) and D. Bronstein.

Following is another variation, with the first eight moves made in the more usual order:

KING'S INDIAN DEFENSE: VARIATION 2

(1) P – Q4, Kt – KB3; (2) Kt – KB3, P – KKt3; (3) P – KKt3, B – Kt2; (4) B – Kt2, O – O; (5) P – B4, P – Q3; (6) O – O, QKt – Q2; (7) Kt – B3, P – K4; (8) P – K4.

Figure 355

This might be called the typical King's Indian setup.

(8) . . . **P x P; (9) Kt x P, R – K1; (10) R – K1, Kt – B4; (11) P – KR3, P – QR4.**

Black's last move supports the position of his Kt on **c5.** It also will lead to a Q's side attack by . . . P – R5, . . . Q – R4, etc. With his next move, White sets a trap:

12. Q – B2

Black is tempted to play . . . Kt(3) x P; (13) Kt x Kt, B x Kt winning a Pawn; but (14) B – Kt5! Q – Q2 (P – KB3? (15) B x P! B x B; (16) Kt x B ch); (15) QR – Q1, Kt x Kt; (16) R x Kt,

Figure 356

P – QB4; (17) QR – K1, R x R; (18) Q x R soon wins for White: e.g., . . . Q – K3; (19) Q – Kt1! Q – B4; (20) R – K8 ch, K – Kt2; (21) Q x Q, P x Q; (22) B – K7, B x P; (23) B – Q5. The pin can never be relieved, and White gets a mating attack.

12. . . . P – R5! Continuing his plan.

A game between two leading Yugoslav masters B. Ivkov (White) and S. Gligoric (Black) continued:

(13) B – Kt5, P – B3; (14) B – B4, KKt – Q2; (15) R(R) – Q1, Kt – K4; (16) Kt – Kt1, Q – R4; (17) R – K2, Q – Kt5 (attacking the QBP); (18) Kt – R3 (threatening to win the Q by B – Q2) (18) . . . Q – R4; (19) B – K3, Q – B2; (20) P – B4, Kt(K4) – Q2; (21) B – B2, Q – R4; (22) K – R2, Kt – B3; (23) B – K1, Q –Kt3; (24) B – QB3, R – K2; (25) R(Q) – K1, B – Q2.

Finally all White's pieces are developed!

Figure 357

White's KP often proves harder to defend than Black's QP in this opening.

KING'S INDIAN DEFENSE: VARIATION 3, THE YUGOSLAV VARIATION

(1) P – Q4, Kt – KB3; (2) P – QB4, P – KKt3; (3) Kt – QB3, B – Kt2; (4) P – K4, P – Q3; (5) P – KKt3, O – O; (6) B – Kt2, P – B4; (7) P – Q5, Kt – R3; (8) Kt – B3, Kt – B2; (9) O – O, P – QR3; (10) P – QR4, R – Kt1.

Figure 358

Black will play . . . P – QKt4 whether or not White plays P – R5. The open QKt file and the center Pawn formation strengthen the power of the B on KKt2.

KING'S INDIAN DEFENSE: VARIATION 4

(Botvinnik vs. Borisenko, U.S.S.R. Championship, 1955)

(1) P – QB4, Kt – KB3; (2) P – Q4, P – KKt3; (3) P – KKt3, B – Kt2; (4) B – Kt2, O – O; (5) Kt – B3, P – Q3; (6) Kt – B3, Kt – B3; (7) P – Q5, Kt – QR4.

Figure 359

White must be very careful how he meets this unusual move, which seeks to increase the Bishop's power. For instance P – Kt3? Kt x QP; or Q – R4, P – B4; followed by . . . B – Q2. The best move is:

(8) Kt – Q2, P – B4; (9) Q – B2, P – K3.

Black does not neglect play in the center. White threatens a "Pawn roller" attack by P – K4, P – B4 and P – K5.

(10) O – O, P x P; (11) P x P, R – K1; (12) P – Kt3 (now safe), . . . **P – QKt4; (13) B – Kt2, R – Kt1; (14) P – QR3, B – Q2; (15) R – K1, Kt – Kt2; (16) Kt(3) – K4.**

White's center development has taken advantage of the Bl Kt's excursion. If . . . Kt x QP; (17) B x B, K x B; (18) Kt x QP! Kt x Kt; (19) Q x BP, and White will regain his piece, with a Pawn ahead.

Notice that the World Champion was in no rush to move his Pawns, making use of a square (e4), usually occupied by a P, for his pieces.

KING'S INDIAN DEFENSE: VARIATION 5

(1) P – Q4, Kt – KB3; (2) P – QB4, P – KKt3; (3) Kt – QB3, B – Kt2; (4) P – K4, P – Q3; (5) Kt – B3, O – O; (6) **B – K2.**

White's sixth move avoids the . . . Kt – QR4 variation, since the QBP is protected.

(6) . . . **P – K4.** This is not a Pawn sacrifice, since P x P, P x P; Kt x P is met by . . . Kt x P, uncovering the B on W's Kt.

(7) O – O, Kt – B3; (8) P – Q5, Kt – K2.

When the King's Indian was first played (1922-5) this Knight went back to QKt1, and after . . . P – QR4, to QB4. The move . . . Kt – K2 is the beginning of a different idea: the start of a King's side attack. White, in turn, attacks the Q's side with his Pawns and pieces.

(9) Kt – K1, Kt – Q2; (10) B – K3, P – KB4; (11) P – B3; P – B5; (12) B – B2, P – KKt4.

The center being firm, Black feels free to attack on the wing. His last move opens **g6** for the Kt, and makes ready to attack the base of W's Pawn chain on f3.

Figure 360

(13) Kt – Q3, Kt – B3; (14) P – B5, Kt – Kt3; (15) R – B1 (preparing to occupy the file soon to be opened) . . . **R – B2.** Defending the second rank, and preparing to occupy the KKt file before the push . . . P – Kt5.

(16) P x P, P x P; (17) Kt – Kt5, P – Kt5; (18) Q – Q2, B – B1 (defending the QP, the base of his P chain); **(19) R – B2, P – QR3.**

Figure 361

The moves above are from a game between two grandmasters, M. Najdorf (Argentina) and P. Trifunovic (Yugoslavia). After (20) **Kt – R3,** Black could have pressed his attack by . . . P – Kt6! a Pawn sacrifice opening Black squares f4 and g3 for the Black Kts.

The synchronization of the Black pieces must be admired: as each piece leaves a square, another enters it, and for a different purpose. Notice, too, that the first exchange, and of just one Pawn each, was made on move 16. Good players build their positions slowly, hoarding their squares as a miser does his gold.

The number of different types of positions arising from Black's opening moves has made the King's Indian Defense very popular. Play it, and see why.

2. Sicilian Defense (P – K4, P – QB4)

Just as popular as the King's Indian is the Sicilian Defense, when White's first move is P – K4. The reasons are the same: White has to play Black's opening, instead of calling the turn himself; the game is a bitter struggle, with many pieces on the board, and a great deal of room for maneuvering. Frequently, the players castle on opposite sides of the board, and there is opportunity for each one to attack the opponent's King.

SICILIAN DEFENSE: VARIATION 1, RICHTER ATTACK

Kurt Richter, a German master, invented this attack to avoid the Dragon Variation. See Variation 5.

(1) **P – K4, P – QB4;** (2) **Kt – KB3, P – Q3;** (3) **P – Q4, P x P;** (4) **Kt x P, Kt – KB3.**

This move is essential in all Sicilian Defenses, to prevent White from playing P – QB4, which would give him a strong hold on the center.

(5) **Kt – QB3, Kt – B3;** (6) **B – KKt5.** This is the Richter move, preventing . . . P – KKt3 and . . . B – Kt2, since after . . . P – KKt3, B x Kt would ruin Black's Pawn position.

White

Black

Figure 362

(6) . . . **P – K3;** (7) **Q – Q2, P – QR3.**

It is necessary to keep a WKt from his QKt5, for if . . . B – K2; O – O – O, O – O; Kt(4) – Kt5, and the move B x Kt would force P x B or win the QP.

(8) **O – O – O, B – Q2;** Black must not move . . . B – K2, because of Kt x Kt and B x Kt. The Q must be free to recapture on **f6** while the B guards **d6.**

(9) **P – B4, P – R3.** Black forces the retreat of the B to R4, where it is unprotected, in order to make the ensuing combination.

(10) **B – R4, Kt x KP** unpinning by counterattack. This, however, is a sacrifice by White.

(11) **Q – K1** protecting the B, attacking the Kt, and pinning the KP.

(11) . . . **Kt – B3**

(12) **Kt – B5** White regains his Pawn, for if . . . P – Q4; Kt x QP, the Bl KP being pinned.

WHITE

BLACK

Figure 363

(12) . . . **Q – R4;** (13) **Kt x QP ch, B x Kt;** (14) **R x B; O – O – O;** (15) **R – Q2.**

SICILIAN DEFENSE: RICHTER VARIATION 2

When Variation 1 was played in the 1955 Soviet Championship, the Lithuanian player, Mikenas (Black) played on move 12:

(12) . . . **Q – B2.** This looks bad, because White can attack the Q immediately by Kt – Q5 —but that was exactly what Black intended: the Kt move covered his QP. The game continued: (13) **B x Kt, P x B;** (14) **Kt – Q5, Q – Q1;** (15) **B – Q3;** and now Black took advantage of the forked Kts by blocking the King file: (15) . . . **Kt – K4!**

After (16) **P x Kt, BP x P;** (17) **Q – Kt4, P x Kt(Q4);** (18) **Kt x P ch, B x Kt;** (19) **Q x B, Q – K2;** (20) **Q x QP, B – B3** Black had a free, open position, with a passed King's Pawn, and actually won the game.

SICILIAN DEFENSE: VARIATION 3

(1) **P – K4, P – QB4;** (2) **Kt – KB3, P – Q3;** (3) **P – Q4, P x P;** (4) **Kt x P, Kt – KB3;** (5) **Kt – QB3, P – QR3;** (6) **B – K2, P – K4.**

Black's fifth move is explained by his sixth: he does not want a WKt or B on QKt5.

Usually a "deterrent" move like P – R3 is not good, since it weakens the square Kt3; but in the Sicilian Defense it fits into the whole scheme of defense: attack on the Q's side; occupy the QB file with Q and R; occupy the square c4 with a Kt or B; drive the WKt from c3 by P – Kt4 – 5 (b4). P – R3 supports P – Kt4, which is an important move in the scheme.

White has tried a number of different sixth moves: e.g., B – KKt5, B – Q3, P – B4 and P – KKt3. (6) B – K2 is the latest attempt to defeat this variation.

Figure 364

(7) Kt – Kt3, B – K2; (8) O – O, Kt(1) – Q2; (9) P – QR4. A two-edged move. It stops . . . P – QKt4, but leaves a hole at Kt5 (b4). Here, however, the Bl Kt, being at Q2 and not on B3, is not in position to occupy the hole.

(9) . . . P – QKt3; (10) B – K3, B – Kt2; (11) P – B3, O – O; (12) Q – Q2, Q – B2; (13) R(B) – Q1; R(B) – Q1.

Black overprotects his weak spot, the QP.

(14) B – B1, B – B3; (15) Q – B2, Q – Kt2; (16) B – QB4. White must prevent the push . . . P – Q4, which would free all Black's pieces. He makes his last move even though he realizes Black intends to occupy the QB file. Black also would like to play . . . P – QKt4-5, but White has the move Kt – R5 waiting for him.

(16) . . . Kt – B4? (17) Kt x Kt, QP x Kt.

The backward QP has disappeared, and the open Q file becomes the base of operations. Each player has a square (d5, d4) for his pieces; but whereas White is ready to occupy his square (d5) Black is not. We must conclude, therefore, that . . . Kt – B4 was not a good move, and that Black should have continued (16) . . . R(R) – B1, or even better, have developed his Kt to QB3 earlier in the game.

Thus, we find a later game in the same tournament continuing (from the diagram) (7) Kt – Kt3, B – K2; (8) O – O, O – O; (9) B – K3, P – QKt3; (10) P – B3, B – Kt2; (11) Q – Q2, Q – B2; (12) R(B) – Q1, R – Q1—and White felt he had to play (13) Kt – Q5 to prevent Black's . . . P – Q4. After (13) . . . Kt x Kt, (14) P x Kt, Black's weak spot was covered by a WP. The game ended in a draw.

SICILIAN DEFENSE: VARIATION 4, SCHEVENINGEN VARIATION: . . . P – Q3 AND . . . P – K3

(1) P – K4, P – QB4; (2) Kt – KB3, P – Q3; (3) P – Q4, P x P; (4) Kt x P, Kt – KB3; (5) Kt – QB3, P – QR3; (6) B – K2, **P – K3**; (7) **O – O, Q – B2**; (8) **P – B4, Kt – B3**; (9) **B – K3, B – K2.**

Figure 365

When this opening was first played, White usually tried a storming of Black's position by P – KKt4-5, while Black moved . . . Kt – R4 – B5 and . . . P – Kt4-5, attacking on the Q's side.

In order to meet Black's Kt maneuver, which attacks the Be3 and Pb2, White retreats his Be3 to c1; but to avoid blocking his QR, has to move his Q and R, as follows:

(10) **Q – Kt1! O – O; (11) Q – Kt3, B – Q2; (12) R(R) – Q1.** The WQ is now well placed for (a) control of K5 and Q6; (b) a King's side attack.

(12) . . . **K – R1; (13) K – R1, P – QKt4; (14) P – QR3** (otherwise . . . P – Kt5 and . . . Kt x KP) (14) . . . **R(B) – Q1; (15) B – Q3, B – K1; (16) Kt – B3!** This move stops . . . P – K4, and prepares P – K5, opening up the WBs for a King's side attack, and driving away the defending Kt.

White

Black

Figure 366

You may wonder why Black did not execute the maneuver Kt – QR4 – B5. The reason is that he had the move . . . P – K4 constantly in mind. In a recent game (Tscherbakov–Kotov) White did not play (16) Kt – B3, but (16) Q – R3, with the idea of P – KKt4-5. But he neglected the rule:

Do not attack on the wings unless the center is secure.

Black played (16) . . . Kt x Kt; (17) B x Kt, P – K4! and even after the brilliant moves (18) Kt – Q5! Kt x Kt; (19) P x Kt (threatening mate on h7) . . . P – Kt3; (20) Q – R6! (If . . . P x B; (21) P – B5) . . . K – Kt1; (21) B – B3, B – B1, Black held fast and started a winning counterattack in the center.

SICILIAN DEFENSE: VARIATION 5, DRAGON VARIATION

(1) P – K4, P – QB4; (2) Kt – KB3, P – Q3; (3) P – Q4, P x P; (4) Kt x P, Kt – KB3; (5) Kt – QB3, **P – KKt3; (6) B – K2, B – Kt2; (7) O – O, Kt – QB3;** (8) **B – K3, O – O;** (9) **Q – Q2, B – Q2.**

The opening gets its name from the Black formation, which certainly looks like a dragon:

White

Black

Figure 367

Following is an interesting game between Horowitz (White) and Reshevsky, played in New York, 1951:

(10) P– B4, R – B1; (11) P – KR3

Former World Champion Max Euwe, who annotated the tournament book, says that (11) B – B3 would have saved time; White did not have to worry about Kt – QR4 (– B5) because he could play P – QKt3; (if then . . . Q – B2; Kt – QKt5).

(11) . . . **Kt x Kt; (12) B x Kt, B – B3; (13) Q – K3, Kt – Q2; (14) P – K5, P x P; (15) P x P, P – K3.**

This stops P – K6, but weakens his KB3. **(16) B – B3, B x B; (17) R x B, R – B5.**

Do you see the threat? . . . R x B, . . . Kt x P, and Kt x R (or – B6) ch, winning the Q. **(18) R – Q1, Q – R4; (19) Kt – K4.**

The sacrifice is not good now, because of (. . . R x B; R x R, Kt x P;) Kt – B6 ch.

(19) . . . **B x P; (20) B x B, Kt x B; (21) Kt – B6 ch, K – Kt2.** Not . . . K – R1? Q – R6 forces mate.

(22) Kt – R5 ch, P x Kt; (23) Q – Kt5 ch, K – R1. The Kt cannot interpose, because the Bl Q would be *en prise.*

(24) Q – B6 ch, K – Kt1; (25) Q – Kt5 ch. Not R – Kt3 ch?? for the Kt, no longer pinned, can interpose on Kt3. **Drawn by perpetual check.**

SICILIAN DEFENSE: VARIATION 6

(1) P – K4, P – QB4; (2) Kt – QB3

White gives up P – Q4, treating the opening like Black playing a King's Indian.

(2) . . . **Kt – QB3; (3) P – KKt3, P – KKt3;**

(4) B – Kt2, B – Kt2; (5) P – Q3, P – Q3; (6) B – K3, R – Kt1; (7) Q – Q2, P – QKt4; (8) Kt(1) – K2, Kt – Q5; (9) O – O, P – Kt5; (10) Kt – Q1, P – K3; (11) Kt – B1, White is now ready to advance in the center by P – QB3 and P – Q4, or on the wing by P – KB4-5.

White

Black

Figure 368

The variety of positions arising from the Sicilian Defense, with chances for both sides, has made it, too, justly popular. We now turn to other openings.

FURTHER OPENINGS OF CHAMPIONS: QUEEN'S PAWN OPENINGS

3. The Queen's Gambit

(1) P – Q4, P – Q4; (2) P – QB4, P x P. This is the Queen's Gambit accepted.

White hopes to regain his Pawn and then have a stronger center position, because Black has one center Pawn less; Black hopes to be able to develop his pieces while White occupies himself regaining the Pawn. Black also has the maneuver . . . P – QB4–x QP to equalize the Center Pawn situation.

Black can not hold on to the Pawn if White tries to regain it: (3) P – K3, P – QKt4?? (4) P – QR4, P – QR3??; (5) P x P or . . . (4) P – QB3?? (5) P x P, P x P; (6) Q – B3, winning the Rook on a8.

Black can, however, counterattack fiercely against (3) P – K3 by . . . P – K4! If then (4) P x P? Q x Q ch; (5) K x Q, B – K3. If White plays, instead (4) B x P, then Kt – KB3 and, again, if (6) P x P? Q x Q ch; (7) K x Q, Kt – Kt5! White must prevent . . . P – K4 by:

(3) Kt – KB3! Kt – KB3! (to control e4 and d5) **(4) P – K3.** Now if . . . P – QKt4, (5) P – QR4, P – QB3; (6) P x P, P x P, (7) P – QKt3! P x P; (8) B x P ch and (9) Q x P.

(4) . . . **P – K3; (5) B x P, P – B4; (6) O – O, Kt – B3; (7) Kt – B3, B – K2; (8) P x P!** White makes the Bishop move twice, thereby "gaining a move." (8) . . . **Q x Q; (9) R x Q, B x P; (10) P – QR3, P – QR3; (11) P – QKt4, B – R2; (12) B – Kt2.**

Figure 369

White has an advantage in development which makes it hard for Black to continue with normal moves. For example, if . . . P – QKt4?? (13) Kt x P! P x Kt; (14) B x P, B – Q2, (15) R x B! K x R; (16) Kt – K5 ch, K – K2; (17) Kt x Kt ch, K – B1; (18) B – K5, and White wins by advancing his Passed Pawns.

QUEEN'S GAMBIT: VARIATION 2

(1) P – Q4, P – Q4; (2) P – QB4, P x P; (3) Kt – KB3, P – QR3. This variation was made popular during the World Championship match between Alexander Alekhine (then champion) and Ewfim D. Bogoljubow in 1931. It is still considered strong, being played in a recent World Championship between Botvinnik and Smyslov (Black). The idea is for Black to feint a defense of the QBP, forcing P – K3. Then he pins the Kt, weakening White's hold on e5. This is how the Botvinnik-Smyslov game continued:

(4) P – K3, B – Kt5; (5) B x P, P – K3 Essential! The threat was (6) B x P ch, K x B; (7) Kt – K5 ch, when the Bg4 would be twice attacked; therefore, . . . Kt – KB3 was no defense.

(6) Q – Kt3 unpinning the Kt, and hitting the weak spot QKt7, which the Bl B can no longer defend.

(6) . . . **B x Kt; (7) P x B, P – QKt4; (8) B –**

K2, Kt – Q2; (9) P – QR4, P – Kt5; (10) Kt – Q2, KKt – B3; (11) Kt – K4, P – B4; (12) Kt x Kt ch, Q x Kt; (13) P – Q5, P – K4; (14) P – R5, B – Q3; (15) P – K4, O – O; (16) B – K3.

Figure 370

Black now should attack White's Pawn chain by . . . Q – K2 and P – B4. Instead, he opened the QB file by the sacrifice . . . P – B5. White captured the P, held it, and won.

White, in spite of the fact that he won, was not satisfied with his opening. Being the World Champion, he was critical of his own play and, in a later game of the match (the 10th) he varied as follows:

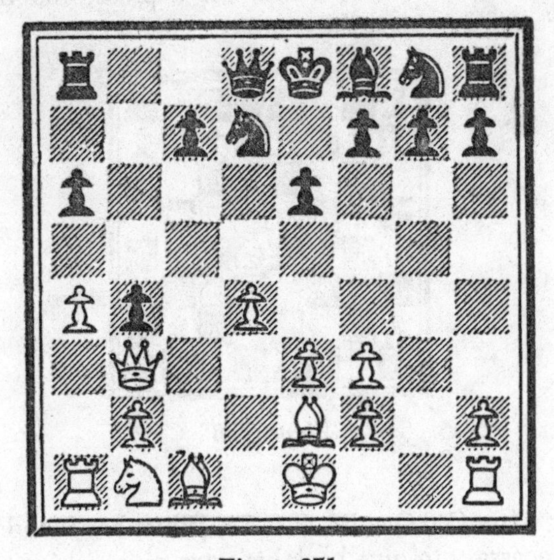

Figure 371

(After move 9 . . . P – Kt5), (10) P – B4, Kt(1) – B3; (11) B – B3, R – R2; (12) B – B6, B – K2; (13) Kt – Q2, O – O; (14) Kt – B4, P – QR4. The White Kt must not be allowed on a5.

(15) Kt – K5, White has a strong grip on the center, from which Black can extricate himself, if at all, with great exertion.

(15) . . . Kt – Kt1; (16) B – Q2, Kt – Q4.

At last Black threatens something (P – B3).

(17) P – K4, Kt – Kt3; (18) B – K3, B – Q3 and again (B x Kt). (19) B – Kt5, Q – R5; (20) R – QB1, K – R1.

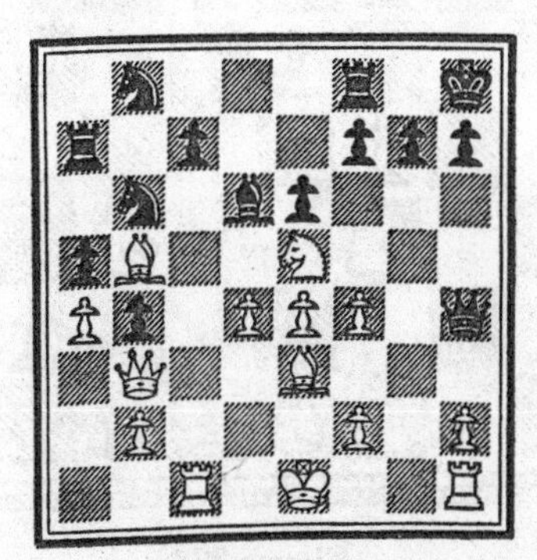

Figure 372

Now White should have cleared the third rank for his Queen by B – Q2, with his grip on the center still potent. But even World Champions are fallible! He vacillated—and lost!

(21) B – K2? B x Kt; (22) QP x B, Kt(1) – Q2; (23) B – Kt5? R – Q1; (24) B – Q2? Kt x P! (25) Q – K3—if P x Kt, Q x KP ch and . . . Q x R ch—(25) . . . Kt – Kt5; (26) Q – KKt3, Q x Q; (27) BP x Q, Kt – B7! (28) K x Kt, R x B ch; (29) K – K3, R x KtP—and the two Passed Pawns won easily: (30) R – QKt1, R x R; (31) R x R, P – QB4; (32) R – Q1, R – R1, (33) R – Q6, R – QKt1; (34) K – Q2, P – B5; (35) K – B2, P – Kt3; (36) R – B6, P – B6; (37) K – Kt3, R – QB1. White resigned, for he must exchange Rooks to avoid, e.g., R x Kt, P – B7; R – B6, R x R; B x R, P – B8(Q).

4. **Queen's Gambit Declined**

If Black does not want to accept the Pawn, he may defend it by (2) . . . P – K3 (the Orthodox Defense) or (2) . . . P – QB3 (the Slav Defense). Each of these has many variations, of which we will discuss the main ones in the following pages:

VARIATION 1: THE ORTHODOX DEFENSE

(1) P – Q4, P – Q4; (2) P – QB4, P – K3; (3) Kt – QB3, Kt – KB3; (4) B – Kt5, B – K2; (5) P – K3, QKt – Q2; (6) Kt – B3, O – O; (7) R – B1, P – B3.

Figure 373

The play now branches into two lines, the most popular being: (8) B – Q3, P x P; (9) B x P, Kt – Q4; (10) B x B, Q x B; (11) O – O, Kt x Kt; (12) R x Kt, P – K4; (13) Kt x P, Kt x Kt; (14) P x Kt, Q x P; (15) P – B4, Q – B3; (16) P – B5, P – QKt4; (17) B – Q3, P – Kt5.

Figure 374

Q.G.D.: VARIATION #2: THE ORTHODOX DEFENSE

(8) Q – B2. This variation may be called "the battle of the tempo." White wishes to recapture the Pc4 without first moving his Bf1; Black wants to force White to move the Bf1 before he makes the P exchange.

(8) . . . P – KR3; (9) B – R4, P – QR3; (10) P – QR3, P – QKt4; (11) P – B5, P – K4; (12) P x P, Kt – K1; (13) B x B, Q x B; (14) P – QKt4, Kt x KP; (15) Kt x Kt, Q x Kt; (16) Kt – K2, P – B4; (17) Q – B3.

Figure 375

Q.G.D.: ORTHODOX DEFENSE: #3 VIENNA VARIATION

(1) P – Q4, Kt – KB3; (2) Kt – KB3. (This move, in place of (2) P – QB4 and (3) Kt – QB3, is the big difference.) 2. . . . P – Q4; (3) P – QB4, P – K3; (4) B – Kt5, B – Kt5 ch; (5) Kt – B3, P x P. This is one of the few times where it is safe to take *and hold on* to the gambit Pawn.

(6) P – K4, P – B4; (7) P – K5, P x P; (8) Q – R4 ch, Kt – B3; (9) O – O – O, B – Q2; (10) Kt – K4, B – K2; (11) P x Kt, P x P; (12) B – R4, Kt – R4.

Black has three Pawns for a piece, and the Pawns dominate the center.

Figure 376

After (13) Q – B2, P – K4, White has found it necessary to give back his extra piece: (14) Kt x QP, P x Kt; (15) R x P, Kt – B3.

Now, if (16) R x B, Q x R; (17) B x KBP, Kt – Kt5! or (17) Kt x P ch, B x Kt; (18) B x B, O – O! (19) B x P, QR – B1; (20) K – Kt1, Kt – Kt5! (21) Q – K4, R x B! (22) Q x R, Q – B4 ch, and Black wins, for if (23) K – B1, R – B1 or if (23) K – R1, Kt – B7 ch; (24) K – Kt1, Kt – R6 dis. ch., wins the WQ.

Q.G.D.: ORTHODOX DEFENSE: #4 LASKER VARIATION

(1) P – Q4, P – Q4; (2) P – QB4, P – K3; (3) Kt – QB3, Kt – KB3; (4) B – Kt5, B – K2; (5) P – K3, O – O; (6) Kt – B3, P– KR3; (7) **B – R4, Kt – K5.** The former World Champion (1894-1921), Dr. Emanuel Lasker, invented this variation, the purpose of which is to relieve the Black position by the exchange of two minor pieces. (8) **B x B, Q x B;** (9) **P x P, Kt x Kt;** (10) **P x Kt, P x P;** (11) **Q – Kt3, Q – Q3;** (12) **P – B4, P x P;** (13) **B x P, Kt – B3** (threatening . . . Kt – R4) (14) **Q – B3, B – Kt5;** (15) **O – O, B x Kt;** (16) **P x B, R(R) – Q1.**

(Dr. Euwe vs. E. Eliskases, Noordwijk, 1938)

Figure 377

The position looks deceptively simple, but the open King Knight file leads to exciting play. The following game will give an example:
(M. Hanauer vs. Dr. Bruno Schmidt, New York, 1952.)

Make the first ten moves as above. Then, after (11) **Q – Kt3, R – Q1.** This is the alternative to . . . Q – Q3. (12) **P – B4, P x P;** (13) **B x P, Kt – B3;** (14) **Q – B3.**

(The recommended move is (14) Q – Kt2).
(14) . . . **B – Kt5;** (15) **O – O, B x Kt;** (16) **P x B, Q – B3;** (17) **B – K2, R – Q2;** (18) **K – R, Kt – K2;** (19) **R – KKt1, P – QKt3;** (20) **QR – B1.** Directed against . . . P – B4, but Black forces the move anyhow. (20) . . . **R – QB1!** (21) **P – B4, P – B4;** (22) **B – Kt4.** (Now Black can win White's Q for his two Rs by . . . P x P; Q x R ch, Kt x Q; B x R (not R x Kt ch, R – Q1) Kt – Q3; KR – Q1, etc. He sees, however, that he can check with his Q, play . . . P – B4, shutting out the B, and then continue hitting the White center. Therefore:)

22. . . . Q – B3 ch

Figure 378

23. P – Q5!!

This opens the diagonal a1 – h8 for the WQ. If . . . Kt x P; B x R, threatening Q x P (g7) mate. If . . . R x P; B – B3. Why not:

23. . . . Q x P ch? (24) **P – K4!! Q x P ch;** (25) **P – B3! Q – Q5;** (26) **B x R,** and Black can not capture the B because of the same mate on g7. White won in a few more moves.

5. QUEEN'S GAMBIT DECLINED SLAV DEFENSE

(1) P – Q4, P – Q4; (2) P – QB4, P – QB3; (3) **Kt – KB3, Kt – KB3;** (4) **Kt – B3, P – K3;** (5) **P – K3.**

This is the triumph of the Slav Defense: it forces White under threat of capturing (and holding) the gambit Pawn, to shut in his QB.

5. . . . **QKt – Q2;** (6) **B – Q3**

Figure 379

The critical position. Black has five consequent moves: . . . P x P (**Meran Defense**); . . . B – Kt5 (**Romih Defense**). . . . B – Q3, . . . B – K2 and . . . P – QR3 (**Semi-Slav**).

White often attempts to avoid the Meran Defense by (instead of (6) B – Q3) (6) Q – B2, or (6) Kt – K5. There is no reason to go to such lengths, provided that you learn the following variation:

VARIATION #1: MERAN DEFENSE

(6) . . . **P x P,** (7) **B x BP, P – QKt4;** (8) **B – Q3, P – QR3;** (9) **P – K4, P – B4;** (10) **P – K5, P x P;** (11) **Kt x KtP.**

(This position was explained under "Desperadoes."

(11) . . . **Kt x KP;** (12) **Kt x Kt, P x Kt;** (13) **Q – B3, B – Kt5 ch;** (14) **K – K2, QR – Kt1**

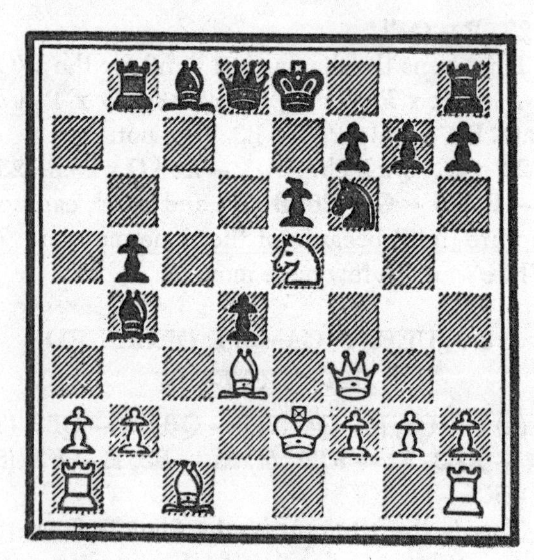

Figure 380

Black's life hangs by a hair—but it's a tough hair! The 8th game of the 1951 World Championship match continued: (D. Bronstein, White, vs. M. Botvinnik.)

(15) **Kt – B6, B – Kt2;** (16) **B – KB4, B – Q3;** (17) **Kt x Q, B x Q ch;** (18) **K x B, R x Kt;** (19) **B x P ch, K – K2;** (20) **B – Q2, R – QKt1;** (21) **P – QR4, Kt – Q4;** (22) **P – QKt3, P – B4;** (23) **KR – QB1, P – K4;** (24) **K – K2, P – K5;** (25) **R – B6, KR – QB1**—and the game ended in a draw.

SLAV DEFENSE: VARIATION #2, ROMIH VARIATION

(1) P – Q4, P – Q4; (2) P – QB4, P – QB3; (3) Kt – KB3, Kt – KB3; (4) Kt – B3, P – K3; (5) P – K3, QKt – Q2; (6) B – Q3, **B – Kt5.** This move has had its ups and downs: **down** after the 1948 Match Tourney and **up** after the following game played by Larry Evans (Black) vs. David Brønstein (U.S.A. vs. U.S.S.R., Moscow, 1955.)

(7) **P – QR3, B – R4!** If this B is chased again, he goes back to B2 to guard his K4. (8) **Q – B2, O – O;** (9) **O – O, B – B2;** (10) **B – Q2, P x P;** (11) **B x P, P – K4;** (12) **B – R2, P – KR3;** (13) **QR – K1, R – K1;** (14) **P x P, Kt x P;** (15) **Kt x Kt, R x Kt!!**

Figure 381

Black's last move is a brilliant developing move, threatening a King's side attack (. . . R – KR4, Kt – Kt5, Q – R5, etc.) and forcing White to play sharply. But Black has seen through the complications now to come, and emerges from them a Pawn plus.

(16) **P – B4, B – B4;** (17) **P – K4, B – Kt3 ch;** (18) **K – R1** (if (18) B – K3, B x KP!) (18) . . . **R x P!!** (19) **Kt x R, Kt x Kt.** Two threats: Kt x B and Kt – Kt6 or B7 ch, winning the Q, force: (20) **R x Kt, B x R;** (21) **Q x B, Q x B;** (22) **B – Kt1, R – Q1.** White can regain his P by Q – R7 – R8 ch x KtP; but then . . . Q – K7 sets him a tough problem, since after Q – K5 ch, Q x Q; P x Q, B – Q5. Black has the better end game.

The game continued: (23) **B – B2, K – B1;** (24) **R – K1, B – B4;** (25) **P – R3, P – KKt3;** (26) **R – Q1, Q – R4;** (27) **R – KB1, R – K1;** (28) **Q – B4, Q – Kt4;** (28) **Q x Q, P x Q.**

Black is still his Pawn ahead, and even though it is doubled, he should win, since the WQ side Ps are on black squares and his K and R are more active than White's. We must report, however, that the game was drawn. The strength of Black's opening, nevertheless, was proved.

SLAV DEFENSE: VARIATION #3

(1) **P – Q4, P – Q4;** (2) **P – QB4, P – QB3;** (3) **Kt – KB3, Kt – KB3;** (4) **Kt – B3, P x P;** (5) **P – K3, P – QKt4;** (6) **P – QR4, P – Kt5.**

Black sells back the Pawn for a gain in de-

Figure 382

velopment. The W Kt must retreat, and Black gains temporary control of **d5** and **e4**. If Kt – Kt1, Black plays . . . B – R3, exchanging the B for the strong WB or for a Kt. The usual move is:

(7) **Kt – R2, P – K3; (8) B x P, B – K2.**

At Hastings, in 1937, S. Reshevsky (Black) found that an attempt to control **d5** and **e4** quickly by: (8) . . . **QKt – Q2**; (9) O – O, **B – Kt2**; (10) Q – K2, **P – B4**; (11) R – Q1, **Q – Kt3** was doomed to failure when his opponent W. Fairhurst (White) played (12) P – K4!! taking advantage of the position of the Bl K in the center: if (12) . . . Kt x KP; (13) P – Q5!! or if (12) . . . B x KP, Kt – K5! Reshevsky had to play (12) . . . P x QP, and after (13) Kt x P, B – B4; (14) Kt – Kt3, O – O; (15) Kt x B, Kt x Kt; (16) B – K3, White had the advantage.

(9) **O – O, O – O**; (10) **Q – K2, B – Kt2**; (11) **R – Q1, P – QR4**; (12) **B – Q2, Kt(1) – Q2**; (13) **Kt – B1, P – B4**; (14) **Kt – Kt3, Q – Kt3**; (15) **B – K1, R(B) – Q1.**

Figure 383

SLAV DEFENSE: VARIATION #4

(1) P – Q4, P – Q4; (2) P – QB4, P – QB3; (3) Kt – KB3, Kt – KB3; (4) Kt – B3, P x P; (5) P – QR4.

White makes sure of regaining his P, but this yields **b4** to a Black Kt or B, the B being able to pin the WKt covering **e4**.

(5) . . . **B – B4**; (6) **P – K3, P – K3**; (7) **B x P, B – QKt5**; (8) **O – O, Kt(1) – Q2**; (9) **P – KR3.**

White prevents the pin of his Kt on f3. A number of games have continued (9) Q – K2, O – O; (10) P – K4, B – Kt5 or . . . B – Kt3.

(9) . . . **O – O**; (10) **Kt – R4, B – K5**; (11) **Kt x B, Kt x Kt**; (12) **Kt – B3, Q – K2**; (13) **Q – B2, KKt – B3**; (14) **P – R5, P – QR3**; (15) **P – K4, P – K4**; (16) **R – R4, P – B4**; (17) **P – Q5, Q – Q1**; (18) **B – Q2, B x B**; (19) **Kt x B, Kt – K1**; (20) **B – K2, Kt – Q3.**

Figure 384

These are the opening moves of the match Smyslov (White) vs. Geller, for the U.S.S.R. Championship, 1955. Black held firm and drew this game, although in the diagrammed position White has the advantages of a B for a Kt, and more space. Notice how Black, as soon as the WQP was passed, made his Kt a blockader, and how he is now ready to attack the WP chain by . . . P – B4.

SLAV DEFENSE: #5, ANTI-MERAN GAMBIT

(1) P – Q4, P – Q4; (2) P – QB4, P – QB3; (3) Kt – KB3, Kt – KB3; (4) Kt – B3, P – K3; (5) **B – Kt5, P x P**; (6) **P – K4** (Fig. 385), **P – Kt4**; (7) **P – K5**, (7) . . . **P – KR3** (attack the pinning piece!) (8) **B – R4, P – Kt4.**

There are now two branches:

(a) (9) P x Kt, P x B; (10) Kt – K5, Q x BP; (11) B – K2, Kt – Q2! (12) Kt x P(c6), B – Kt2; (13)

Figure 385

B – B3, P – QR3; (14) O – O, B – Kt2; (15) P – QR4, P – Kt5; (16) Kt – K4, Q – B5; (17) P – KKt3, P x P; (18) RP x P, Q – B2; (19) Kt x P, R – Q1. The forces are equal, but the White center is under heavy bombardment. On the other hand, the Black position is full of holes.

(b) The main line is:

(9) Kt x KKtP, P x Kt; (10) B x KtP, Kt(1) – Q2; (11) P x Kt, B – QKt2; (12) B – K2, Q – Kt3; (13) P – QR4, P – Kt5; (14) P – R5, Q – R3; (15) Kt – K4, O – O – O; (16) Q – B2, P – B4; (17) B x P, Q – B3; (18) B – Q3, P – Kt6.

Figure 386

White can not take the Pawn, for after . . . P – B5, his Kt on K4 will be loose; but after (19) Q – B4, P x P; (20) Q x Q ch, B x Q; (21) R – QB1, B – Kt5 ch or

(19) Q – K2, P x P; (20) R – QB1, B – Kt5 ch; (21) K – B1, Kt – B4, the position is considered even.

For players who like mix-ups, this is one of the finest; but each move must be exactly timed: for instance, in the U.S.A. vs. U.S.S.R. Radio Match, 1945, Arnold Denker (White) played (13) O – O, and lost quickly to M. Botvinnik, who continued . . . (13) O – O – O; (14) P – QR4, P – Kt5; (15) Kt – K4, P – B4; (16) Q – Kt1, Q – B2. In the main variation above, it can be seen that castling is not necessary for White—on the twentieth move, he is still not castled—but is essential for Black in his attack on the White center. The loss of this one (unnecessary) move cost White the game.

6. QUEEN'S GAMBIT DECLINED: CAMBRIDGE SPRINGS DEFENSE

This defense combines the moves . . . P – K3 and . . . P – B3 with an attack by B and Q on the Ktc3, and a veiled attack on the WBg5. It was introduced at a great tournament in Cambridge Springs, Pa., in 1904, won by Frank J. Marshall, and was made popular by its use in the World Championship match of 1927 between Capablanca and Alekhine.

(1) P – Q4, P – Q4; (2) P – QB4, P – K3; (3) Kt – QB3, Kt – KB3; (4) B – Kt5, QKt – Q2; (5) P – K3, P – B3; (6) Kt – B3, Q – R4.

Figure 387

The trap to be avoided is (7) B – Q3, Kt – K5; (8) B x Kt, P x B, and Ktf3 and Bg5 are attacked.

(7) Kt – Q2, B – Kt5; (8) Q – B2, P x P; (9) B x Kt

Forced, if White wants to regain his P. Black has the two Bs; White more space after the ensuing moves.

(9) . . . Kt x B; (10) Kt x P, Q – B2; (11) P – QR3, B – K2; (12) P – KKt3, O – O; (13) B – Kt2, B – Q2; (14) P – QKt4, P – QKt3; (15) O – O.

This position was reached in the 29th game of

Figure 388

the Alekhine-Capablanca match. Black tries to force . . . P – QB4, White to prevent it. White also has a target in the weak Bl QBP.

7. Q.G.D.: EXCHANGE VARIATION

To avoid the complications of the Slav or Cambridge Springs Defenses, some players exchange the WQBP:

(1) P – Q4, P – Q4; (2) P – QB4, P – K3; (3) Kt – QB3, Kt – KB3; (4) B – Kt5, QKt – Q2; (5) **P x P, P x P**; (6) **P – K3, B – K2**; (7) **B – Q3, O – O**; (8) **Q – B2, P – B3**; (9) **Kt – B3, R – K1**; (10) **O – O, Kt – B1.**

Figure 389

Now comes the famous "**minority attack**":

(11) **R(R) – Kt1! Kt – K5**; (12) **B x B, Q x B**; (12) **P – QKt4!**—to be followed by **P – Kt5** with or without P – QR4, as circumstances dictate.

We refer you to the games Capablanca vs. Alekhine: 23rd, 25th and 27th match games, Buenos Aires, 1927; Spielmann vs. Thomas, Carlsbad, 1929 and Reshevsky vs. Capablanca, Margate, 1935, as interesting examples of the "**Exchange Variation.**"

8. Q.G.: COLLE SYSTEM

The Belgian master EDGARD COLLE conceived the idea of supporting his QP by P – QB3 and forcing an early advance of the WKP, as follows:

(1) P – Q4, P – Q4; (2) **Kt – KB3**, Kt – KB3; (3) **P – K3**, P – K3; (4) **B – Q3**, P – B4; (5) **P – B3**, Kt – B3; (6) **QKt – Q2**, B – Q3; (7) O – O, O – O; (8) **P x P, B x P**; (9) **P – K4.**

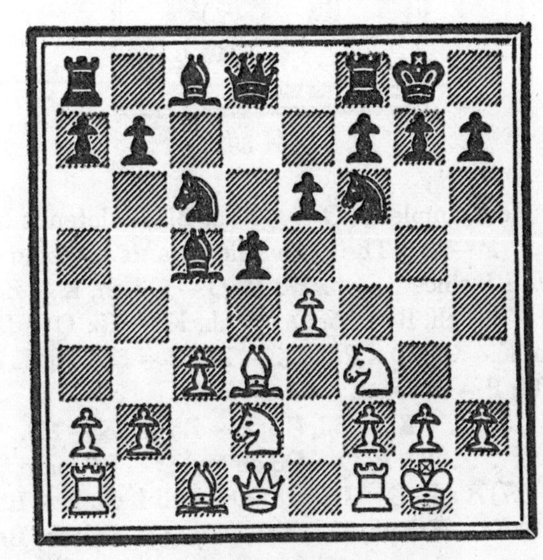

Figure 390

Like all modest openings, this, too, seems deceptively simple, but if Black tries to rush matters by, let us say, (9) . . . P – Q5(?) he will find out its latent power; (10) Kt – Kt3, B – Kt3; (11) P – K5, Kt – K1; (12) P x P, Kt x P?? (13) Kt x Kt, B x Kt; (14) Kt x B, Q x Kt?? (15) B x P ch, winning the Queen.

Best methods of defense consist of a King's Indian type of setup for Black. . . . QKt – Q2 (instead of Kt – QB3) is often played, in order to prevent the exchange of the WQP for Bl's QBP, but it is most important to weaken the power of the B on d3.

Following is a brilliancy prize won by Colle (see Fred Reinfeld's **Colle's Chess Masterpieces**) at Nice, 1930, from the Irish master J. J. O'Hanlon:

(1) P – Q4, P – Q4; (2) Kt – KB3, Kt – KB3; (3) P – K3, P – B4; (4) P – B3, P – K3; (5) B – Q3, B – Q3; (6) QKt – Q2, QKt – Q2; (7) O – O, O – O; (8) R – K1, R – K1; (9) **P – K4, QP x P**; (10) **Kt x P, Kt x Kt**; (11) **B x Kt, P x P** (trusting, but careless). (12) **B x P ch!** (Fig. 391)

(12) . . . **K x B**; (13) **Kt – Kt5 ch, K – Kt3**; (14) **P – KR4!!** (threatening P – R5 ch) . . . **R – R1**; (15) **R x P ch!!**

Figure 391

How simple! If Q – Q3 ch, Black defends by . . . P – B4. The R sacrifice wants to remove the BP since if . . . P x R; Q – Q3 ch, K – B3; Q – B3 ch, B – B5; Q x B ch, K – K2; Q – B7 ch, K – Q3; Q x P ch, K – B4; P – Kt4 ch, K – Kt4; P – R4 mate.

(15) . . . Kt – B3; (16) P – R5 ch! K – R3. If . . . R x P, Q – Q3 ch and Q – R7 mate.

(17) R x B, Q – R4; (18) Kt x P dbl. ch, K – R2; (19) Kt – Kt5 ch, K – Kt1; (20) Q – Kt3 ch, Resigns.

9. GRUNFELD DEFENSE

(1) P – Q4, Kt – KB3; (2) P – QB4, P – KKt3; (3) Kt – QB3, P – Q4.

Introduced in 1922 by the Austrian master Ernst Grunfeld, this has been one of the hardiest defenses to P – Q4. It is a good alternative to the King's Indian, leading to games of great complexity. The leading proponent of the day is V. Smyslov. Here is the way he played it (as Black) vs. Dr. M. Euwe, in the 24th round of the Match Tournament, in 1948:

(4) Kt – B3, B – Kt2; (5) Q – Kt3. Unusual, a Q move so early in the opening; but this is the "sharpest" line.

(5) . . . P x P; (6) Q x BP, O – O; (7) P – K4, B – Kt5; (8) B – K3, KKt – Q2. This is Smyslov's line. The Kt hits the squares c4 and d5 and blocks the WQ from the Pb7.

(9) Q – Kt3, Kt – Kt3; (10) P – QR4, P – QR4; (11) P – Q5. With this variation, Euwe won his game vs. Smyslov in Round 14, but the latter has a new idea based on the weakness of the square b4.

(11) . . . B x Kt; (12) P x B, Q – Q3; (13) Kt – Kt5, Q – Kt5 ch; (14) Q x Q, P x Q; (15) Kt x P, R x P.

Figure 392

Black has the better game.

GRUNFELD DEFENSE: VARIATION 2

(1) P – Q4, Kt – KB3; (2) P – QB4, P – KKt3; (3) Kt – QB3, P – Q4; (4) P x P, Kt x P; (5) P – K4, Kt x Kt; (6) P x Kt, B – Kt2; (7) B – B4, P – QB4; (8) Kt – K2, P x P; (9) P x P, O – O; (10) O – O, Kt – B3; (11) B – K3, B – Kt5; (12) P – B3, Kt – R4.

Figure 393

Black wishes to force B – Q3; then play . . . B – K3. In the match Bronstein-Boleslavsky, to determine the world challenger in 1951, White played B – Q3, and after . . . B – K3, P – Q5 anyhow, sacrificing the exchange to . . . B x R. The misplaced Kt and resultant weakened King position (. . . P – B3 forced to prevent B – R6) were enough compensation: White won.

Recently White has tried (13) B – Q5, whereupon . . . B – B1; (14) B – Kt5, P – KR3; (15) B – R4, P – QR3; (16) P – QR4, B – Q2; (17)

Q – Q2, R – B1; (18) KR – B1 (to prevent . . . Kt – B5), R x R ch; (19) R x R, B x QRP! (20) Q – Kt4 (forking B and KP) P – KKt4! (21) B x KKtP (if B – K1, B – Kt4) P x B; (22) Q x B, P – K3; (23) B – R2, Kt – B3, with advantage to Black. (Ilivitsky-Korchnoi, U.S.S.R., 1955.)

Another possibility: (13) B x P ch, followed by (14) P x B was found to be better for Black.

10. DUTCH DEFENSE

(1) P – Q4, P – K3; (2) P – QB4, P – KB4.

Black draws the lines clear; he wants to control the White squares, and start an early K side attack against an expected castling. (3) **P – KKt3.** White says: "Me, first." (3) . . . **Kt – KB3;** (4) **B – Kt2, B – K2;** (5) **Kt – QB3, O – O;** (6) **P – K3, P – Q4.** A "stonewall" formation—complete with hole at e5. (7) **KKt – K2, P – B3;** (8) **P – Kt3.**

It is surprising that White does not play (7) Kt – KB3, aiming for K5. But he prefers to be free to drive away the Bl Kt from e4 by P – KB3.

(8) . . . **Kt – K5;** (9) **O – O, Kt – Q2;** (10) **B – Kt2, Kt(2) – B3.**

Figure 394

This seems the likely time for (11) P – B3, but after . . . Kt x Kt; (12) Kt x Kt, P – Kt4! (13) P – K4, P – Kt5, White's formation is undermined.

DUTCH DEFENSE: VARIATION #2

(1) P – Q4, P – K3; (2) P – QB4, P – KB4; (3) P – KKt3, Kt – KB3; (4) B – Kt2, B – K2; (5) Kt – QB3, O – O; (6) P – K3, **P – Q3.** The idea is to play . . . P – K4. (7) **KKt – K2, P – B3;** (8) **O – O, P – K4;** (9) **P – Q5, Q – K1;** (10) **P – K4, Q – R4;** (11) **KP x P, B x P.**

Figure 395

White here played (12) **P – B3,** to prevent . . . B – R6 and . . . Kt – Kt5. A suggestion of (12) P – B5 was made, but after . . . B – R6, (13) P – B3 (forced) Kt – R3! (14) P x BP, Kt x P —or (14) P x QP, B x P; (15) P x P, B – B4 ch Black has a tenable position.

Both the "Dutch" variations are from the Botvinnik-Bronstein 1951 match.

11. NIMZO-INDIAN DEFENSE

This defense was explained in detail in the Botvinnik-Reshevsky game in the chapter on "The Middle Game." Here, however, is another important variation:

(1) P – Q4, Kt – KB3; (2) P – QB4, **P – K3;** (3) Kt – QB3, **B – Kt5;** (4) **P – K3, P – B4;** (5) **B – Q3, Kt – B3;** (6) **Kt – B3, P – Q4;** (7) **O – O, O – O;** (8) **P – QR3, B x Kt;** (9) **P x B, QP x P;** (10) **B x BP, Q – B2;** (11) **B – Q3, P – K4;** (12) **Q – B2, B – Kt5;** (13) **Kt x P, Kt x Kt;** (14) **P x Kt, Q x P;** (15) **P – B3.**

Figure 396

Black has the happy choice between . . . B – Q2 and . . . B – K3, both good moves. In the latter case, he will play . . . P – B5 and Kt – Q2 – B4.

12. CATALAN OPENING

(1) P – Q4, P – Q4; (2) P – QB4, P – K3; (3) P – KKt3.

White induces Black to capture his QBP, thereby opening the diagonal of the fianchettoed KB. Black hopes to profit from the fact that White must recapture the P with his Queen, developing his pieces by attacking her, and being able thereby to oppose Bs on the diagonal a8 – h1.

(3) . . . P x P; (4) B – Kt2, Kt – KB3; (5) Q – R4 ch, B – Q2; (6) Q x BP, B – B3; (7) Kt – KB3, QKt – Q2; (8) Kt – B3, Kt – Kt3; (9) Q – Q3, B – Kt5.

Figure 397

(10) O – O, O – O; (11) R – Q1, P – KR3.

13. QUEEN'S INDIAN DEFENSE

This is possible only after the moves: **(1) P – Q4, Kt – KB3; (2) P – QB4, P – K3; Kt – KB3** (not (3) Kt – QB3).

(3) . . . P – QKt3; (4) P – K3, (the alternative line is (4) P – KKt3) **. . . B – Kt2; (5) B – Q3, B – K2; (6) O – O, O – O; (7) P – QKt3, P – Q4; (8) B – Kt2, QKt – Q2; (9) Kt – B3, P – B4; (10) Q – K2.**

Figure 398

QUEEN'S INDIAN DEFENSE: VARIATION #2

(1) P – Q4, Kt – KB3; (2) P – QB4, P – K3; (3) Kt – KB3, P – QKt3; (4) P – Kt3, B – Kt2; (5) B – Kt2, B – K2; (6) O – O, O – O; (7) Kt – B3, Kt – K5.

Black *must* occupy this square before White: It is the basis of his defense. If now Q – B2, Kt x Kt; Q x Kt, B – K5!

(8) Kt x Kt, B x Kt; (9) B – B4, P – Q3; (10) Q – Q2, Kt – Q2; (11) QR – Q1.

Figure 399

White's plan of development has prevented the freeing moves . . . P – K4 or . . . P – QB4.

(11) . . . P – KB4; (12) Kt – K1, B x B; (13) Kt x B, B – B3; (14) Q – B2. White has an edge.

QUEEN'S INDIAN DEFENSE: VARIATION #3

(1) P – Q4, Kt – KB3; (2) P – QB4, P – K3; (3) Kt – KB3, P – QKt3; (4) P – KKt3, B – Kt2; **(5) B – Kt2, B – Kt5 ch; (6) B – Q2, B x B ch; (7) Q x B! O – O; (8) Kt – B3, Kt – K5! (9) Q – B2, Kt x Kt; (10) Kt – Kt5!** (Fig. 400)

This variation is possible only when White has not castled; for then Black could spoil matters by . . . Kt x KP ch.

(10) . . . Kt – K5! (11) B x Kt, B x B; (12) Q x B, Q x Kt; (13) Q x R, Kt – B3; (14) Q – Kt7, Kt x P.

(Euwe–Capablanca, Match, 1931)

Figure 400

14. ALBIN COUNTER GAMBIT

This is a good gambit to save for a "surprise," but it is not entirely sound. The following game was played (as Black) by its greatest present proponent, Weaver W. Adams. His opponent, Martin Stark, won the best-played game prize as White at Ventnor City, 1943:

(1) P – Q4, P – Q4; (2) P – QB4, **P – K4**; (3) **P x KP, P – Q5.**

White must not play (4) P – K3??, for then . . . B – Kt5 ch; (5) B – Q2, P x P! (6) B x B? P x P ch! (7) K – K2, Q x Q ch and (8) . . . P x Kt.

(4) **Kt – KB3, Kt – QB3**; (5) **P – KKt3, B – QB4**; (6) **B – B4, KKt – K2**; (7) **B – Kt2, Kt – Kt3**; (8) **QKt – Q2, P – B3?** (Too soon!) (9) **P x P, Kt x B**; (10) **P – B7 ch! K x P**; (11) **P x Kt, P – KR3.**

Figure 401

(12) **Kt – Kt3, Q – Q3**; (13) **Kt – K5 ch, Kt x Kt**; (14) **P x Kt, Q – QKt3** (. . . Q x P? (15) B – Q5 ch, winning the Bc5); (15) **B – Q5 ch, K – K2**; (16) **Q – Q3, R – B**; (17) **R – KKt1, B – B4**; (18) **R x P ch, K – K1**; (19) **B – K4, B x B**; (20) **Q x B, P – Q6**; (21) **O – O – O! B x P**; (22) **K – Kt1, R – Q1**; (23) **P – K6** and Black, faced with Q – Kt6 ch and P – K7 **resigned.**

15. OTHER DEFENSES TO P – Q4

(a) Tarrasch Defense: See Dake vs. Horowitz game.

(b) Chigorin Defense: (1) P – Q4, P – Q4; (2) P – QB4, **Kt – QB3.**

(c) Marshall Defense: (1) P – Q4, P – Q4; (2) P – QB4, **Kt – KB3**; (3) **P x P, Kt x P.**

(d) Symmetrical Defense: (1) P – Q4, P – Q4; (2) P – QB4, **P – QB4.**

(e) QB Defense: (1) P – Q4, P – Q4; (2) P – QB4, **B – B4**; (3) Kt – KB3, P – K3; (4) Q – Kt3.

THE RUY LOPEZ

Suppose White does play (1) **P – K4, can't I** do the same? (1) . . . **P – K4.** Then if he moves his Kt, (2) **Kt – KB3** what about (2) . . . **Kt – QB3?** What's the best White can play next? (3) **B – Kt5: the Ruy Lopez Opening.**

The strength of this opening is latent. The "obvious" threat of (4) B x Kt, QP x B; (5) Kt x P is not real, because of countermoves (5) . . . Q – Q5 or (5) . . . Q – Kt4. But the threat of these moves, once the WKP is protected, is always present. Then, too, Black, to develop, must eventually move his QP, whereupon his QKt will be pinned. Black's best procedure is to drive the B once, by (3) . . . **P – QR3**, (4) **B – R4**; then counterattack by (4) . . . **Kt – B3**; (5) **O – O** and then play either (5) . . . Kt x KP, an open but difficult defense, or (5) . . . B – K2, blocking the King file. In the latter case, Black must remember that after (6) R – K1, (6) Q – K2 or (6) Kt – B3, (6) . . . P – QKt4 is necessary, the WKP now being protected. The main variations follow:

RUY LOPEZ: VARIATION 1, HOWELL VARIATION

(1) P – K4, P – K4; (2) Kt – KB3, Kt – QB3;

Figure 402

(3) B – Kt5, P – QR3; (4) **B – R4, Kt – B3**; (5) **O – O, Kt x P.** (Fig. 402)

(6) **P – Q4** White tries to open the King file quickly. (6) . . . **P – QKt4**; (7) **B – Kt3, P – Q4**; (8) **P x P, B – K3.** The Bl QP must be defended. (8) . . . B – K3, which develops a piece, is better than . . . Kt – K2, which blocks the Bl B on f8. (9) **Q – K2, Kt – B4**; (10) **R – Q1.**

Figure 403

This powerful variation was reintroduced by Keres and Smyslov in the World Championship of 1948. Its main threat is P – QB4, attacking both the QP and the QKtP.

(10) . . . **P – Kt5.** If now P – B4, P – Q5

(11) **B – K3**—threatening B x Kt, B x B; B – R4!

(11) . . . **Kt x B**; (12) **RP x Kt, Q – B1.** Out of the pin, but White still can play: (13) **P – B4!** The key move! (13) . . . **QP x P** (better than P x P, e.p.; Kt x P); (14) **P x P, P – R3**; (15) **QKt – Q2, B – K2**; (16) **Kt – Kt3, O – O**; (17) **B – B5!** and White had a slight advantage. Since Black (Reshevsky) played the considered best moves, the variation was considered so good for White that, with only rare exceptions, it disappeared from tournament play. One exception was:

RUY LOPEZ: VARIATION 2

(1) P – K4, P – K4; (2) Kt – KB3, Kt – QB3; (3) B – Kt5, P – QR3; (4) B – R4, Kt – B3; (5) O – O, Kt x P; (6) P – Q4, P – QKt4; (7) B – Kt3, P – Q4; (8) P x P, B – K3; (9) Q – K2, **B – K2**; (10) **R – Q1, Kt – B4**; (11) **P – B4, P – Q5.**

So played Tolush (Black) in the 18th Championship of the U.S.S.R. (1950). Idea: if (12) P x P, P – Q6; (13) Q – B1, Kt x B; (14) P x Kt, Kt – Kt5 or (14) R x QP, Kt x R; (15) R x Q ch, Kt x R.

Figure 404

This variation seems to make the defense (5) . . . Kt x P playable.

RUY LOPEZ: VARIATION 3

(1) **P – K4, P – K4**; (2) **Kt – KB3, Kt – QB3**; (3) **B – Kt5, P – QR3**; (4) **B – R4, Kt – B3**; (5) **O – O, B – K2**; (6) **R – K1, P – QKt4**; (7) **B – Kt3, P – Q3**; (8) **P – B3, O – O**; (9) **P – KR3.**

Figure 405

White wants to play P – Q4. His ninth move prevents a pin by the Black Bishop on g4, and prepares for a Pawn storm on the King's side, after long preparation.

(9) . . . **Kt – QR4**; (10) **B – B2, P – B4**; (11) **P – Q4, Q – B2**; (12) **QKt – Q2.**

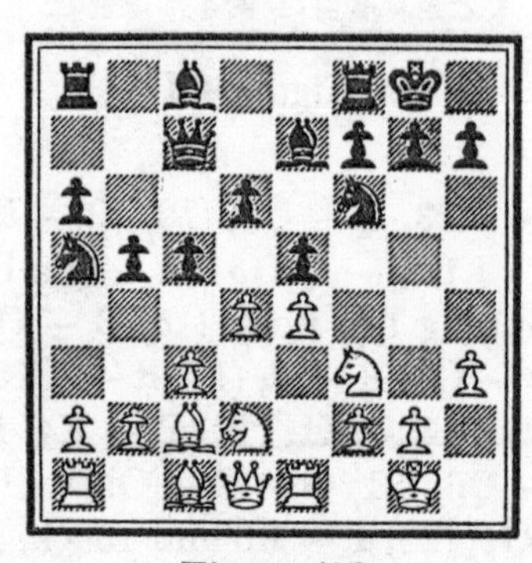

Figure 406

This is the "close defense." In a game at Zagreb (Yugoslavia), 1955, Ivkov (Black) continued:

(12) . . . **B – Q2,** to which Smyslov (White) answered: (13) **Kt – B1, Kt – B5;** (14) **Q – K2, KR – K1;** (15) **P – QKt3, Kt – Kt3;** (16) **P x KP, P x P;** (17) **P – B4,** securing d5 for the WKts. The game, however, was drawn.

An earlier form of this defense was even "closer," (from Diagram 406).

RUY LOPEZ: VARIATION 4

(12) . . . **Kt – B3;** (13) **P – Q5, Kt – Q1;** (14) **Kt – B1, Kt – K1;** (15) **P – KKt4, P – Kt3;** (16) **B – R6, Kt – KKt2;** (17) **Kt – Kt3, P – B3;** (18) **K – R2, Kt – B2;** (19) **B – K3.**

White prepares to occupy the KKt file, while Black combines the counterthreat of . . . P – B4 with defense on the KKt file.

Black's game is so cramped that many attempts to open it up have been made. The latest is a variation by Paul Keres:

RUY LOPEZ: VARIATION 5, KERES VARIATION

(1) P – K4, P – K4; (2) Kt – KB3, Kt – QB3; (3) B – Kt5, P – QR3; (4) B – R4, Kt – B3; (5) O – O, B – K2; (6) R – K1, P – Kt4; (7) B – Kt3, P – Q3; (8) P – B3, O – O; (9) P – KR3, Kt – QR4; (10) B – B2, P – B4; (11) P – Q4, Q – B2; (12) QKt – Q2.

(12) . . . **R – Q1;** (13) **Kt – B1, BP x P;** (14) **P x P, P – Q4.**

Black opens the center, in order to take advantage of the fact that his Rook is on the same file as the WQ.

Figure 407

Obviously (15) QP x P? would be met by P x P, and (15) KP x P by P x P. For a while, Black had a great deal of success with the Keres variation, but a game from the 1955 British Championship (at Aberystwyth, Wales) continued as follows:

White: Phillips Black: Moore

(15) **Kt x P, P x P;** (16) **B – B4, Q – Kt3;** (17) **B – K3, B – Kt2;** (18) **Kt – Kt3, B – Q4;** (19) **Kt – B5, B – B1;** (20) **B – Kt5!**

This B has moved three times, each time with a discovery threat or a pin. The last move undermines the Bl KP with the threat of B x Kt and Q – Kt4 (. . . P – Kt3; Kt – K3).

(20) . . . **B – K3;** (21) **Kt – R6 ch! P x Kt;** (22) **B x Kt, R x P.**

Black has won the center Pawn, but his King is fatally exposed.

(23) **Q – R5, B – Kt2.** If . . . R – Q7; R – K3 and R – Kt3 check.

(24) **B x B, K x B;** (25) **B x P, R – K1.** The Black King wants to escape under the protection of his Rooks.

(26) **R – K3, Q – B2;** (27) **P – B4.** The best that Black can do now is . . . K – B1, whereupon Q x RP ch, K – K2; Q – R4 ch! P – B3; Q x RP ch, etc.

(27) . . . **Kt – B5?** (28) **R – Kt3 ch, K – B1;** (29) **Q x RP ch, K – K2;** (30) **Kt – B6 ch,** winning a Rook. Black resigned.

RUY LOPEZ: VARIATION 6, MARSHALL DEFENSE

(1) P – K4, P – K4; (2) Kt – KB3, Kt – QB3; (3) B – Kt5, P – QR3; (4) B – R4, Kt – B3; (5) O – O, B – K2; (6) R – K1, P – QKt4; (7) B – Kt3, **O – O;** (8) **P – B3, P – Q4.**

Figure 408

F. J. Marshall, the American champion from 1909-36, introduced his defense in a spectacular game against Capablanca in 1918. "Capa" won with White, but new lines have since been discovered, and the latest variation is:

(9) **P x P, Kt x P;** (10) **Kt x P, Kt x Kt;** (11) **R x Kt, P — B3!** Previously, Black had played . . . Kt — B3 or . . . B — Kt2.

After (12) **P — Q4, B — Q3;** (13) **R — K1, Q — R5;** (14) **P — KKt3, Q — R6;** (15) **Q — Q3** White can defend himself: if (15) . . . **B — KB4;** (16) **Q — B1; Q — R4;** (17) **B — Q1.** W's extra Pawn, on the Q side, is momentarily of no great value, since it is difficult to make its weight felt. On the other hand, Black has much greater development and center control. This is a good "surprise" variation to hold in stock. Remember the key moves: (7) . . . **O — O** (instead of . . . **P — Q3**) (8) . . . **P — Q4** and (11) . . . **P — B3.**

The Ruy Lopez is so popular an opening, and has been played so many times, that many defenses against it have been tried, and are still being tried and revived. Some of the other important defenses follow:

RUY LOPEZ: VARIATION 7, BERLIN DEFENSE

(1) **P — K4, P — K4;** (2) **Kt — KB3, Kt — QB3;** (3) **B — Kt5, Kt — B3;** (4) **O — O, Kt x P;** (5) **P — Q4, B — K2;** (6) **Q — K2, Kt — Q3;** (7) **B x Kt, KtP x B;** (8) **P x P, Kt — B4.**

RUY LOPEZ: VARIATION 8, STEINITZ DEFENSE

(1) **P — K4, P — K4;** (2) **Kt — KB3, Kt — QB3;** (3) **B — Kt5, P — Q3;** (4) **P — Q4, B — Q2;** (5) **Kt — B3, Kt — B3;** (6) **O — O, B — K2;** (7) **R — K1, P x P** (forced); (8) **Kt x P, O — O;** (9) **B x Kt, P x B;** (10) **B — Kt5, P — KR3;** (11) **B — R4, R — K1;** (12) **Q — Q3.**

Figure 409

Now Black can play (13) . . . **Kt — R2** or (13) . . . **Q — Kt1** (a Capablanca maneuver); (14) **P — QKt3, Q — Kt3.**

RUY LOPEZ: VARIATION 9, EXCHANGE VARIATION

(1) **P — K4, P — K4;** (2) **Kt — KB3, Kt — QB3;** (3) **B — Kt5, P — QR3;** (4) **B x Kt, QP x B;** (5) **P — Q4, P x P;** (6) **Q x P, Q x Q;** (7) **Kt x Q, B — Q3;** (8) **Kt — B3, Kt — K2;** (9) **O — O.**

Figure 410

With Queens exchanged, there does not seem to be much play for White to try to win; nevertheless, this is exactly the variation and these are exactly the moves chosen by Dr. Emanuel Lasker against J. R. Capablanca in the crucial game of the (St. Petersburg) 1914 Grandmaster Tournament, where White had to play for a win. In the diagrammed position, Black's best move is . . . **P — B4** followed by . . . **B — Q2** and . . . **O — O — O.**

RUY LOPEZ: VARIATION 10, STEINITZ DEFENSE DEFERRED, DURAS VARIATION

(1) **P — K4, P — K4;** (2) **Kt — KB3, Kt — QB3;** (3) **B — Kt5, P — QR3;** (4) **B — R4, P — Q3;** (5) **P — QB4.**

White's fifth move, the invention of Duras, takes advantage of Bl's self-pinning of his Kt by . . . P — Q3. It gains firm control of d5 and retains the possibility of P — Q4. It also prevents . . . P — QKt4. A modern (1950) game shows how the players fight for the square d4:

(5) . . . **B — Kt5;** (6) **P — Q3, P — KKt3;** (7) **Kt — B3, B — Kt2;** (8) **Kt — Q5, P — KR3** (to prevent a pin of his KKt); (9) **P — QKt4!** (threatening P — Kt5 — Kt6 ch and Kt x QBP or — QB7) (9)

. . . K – B1. Black refuses to release d4 (e.g., by B – Q2) **(10) B – Kt2, Kt(1) – K2; (11) P – KR3, B x Kt; (12) Q x B, Kt – Q5; (13) B x Kt, P x B.**

The square is occupied—but by a Pawn. The game (Konstantinopolsky-Petrosian, XVIIIth Russian Championship) was drawn.

RUY LOPEZ: VARIATION 11, SCHLIEMANN DEFENSE

(1) P – K4, P – K4; (2) Kt – KB3, Kt – QB3; (3) B – Kt5, **P – B4.** A risky defense, but another good surprise; this was carried through to a successful conclusion by Arthur Bisguier in the Interzonal Tournament at Goteborg, 1955, vs. Boris Spassky (U.S.S.R.) White:

(4) Kt – B3, Kt – B3; (5) Q – K2 (Better is P x P) **(5) . . . Kt – Q5; (6) Kt x Kt, P x Kt; (7) P – K5, Kt – Kt5; (8) P – KR3, Kt – R3; (9) Kt – Q1, Q – K2; (10) P – QB3, P – B3; (11) B – Q3, P x P; (12) QP x P, Kt – B2; (13) B x P, Q x P; (14) Kt – K3, B – B4; (15) O – O, P – Q4; (16) Q – Q3, B x B; (17) Kt x B, O – O; (18) B – K3, B x B; (19) Kt x B, QR – K.**

Black has an edge in development and center control, and won a well-played end-game.

One last variation, showing the consequences of going "all-out" for the WKB:

RUY LOPEZ: VARIATION 12

(1) P – K4, P – K4; (2) Kt – KB3, Kt – QB3; (3) B – Kt5, P – QR3; (4) B – R4, **P – QKt4?! (5) B – Kt3, Kt – R4; (6) O – O! P – Q3; (7) P – Q4, Kt x B; (8) RP x Kt, P – KB3; (9) Kt – B3, B – Kt2; (10) Kt – KR4, Kt – K2; (11) Q – B3, Q – Q2; (12) R – Q, Q – K3; (13) P x P, QP x P; (14) B – K3, P – Kt4?**

As we know, Black's 14th move can not be good. White is perfectly developed; whereas Black's KB is still shut in, and Black is not yet castled. For him to advance on the wing, *must* be fatal; and yet it was a grandmaster (Taimanov) who was tempted, by what he thought would be an exchange of Q's and Kt's, into the move (XXII U.S.S.R. Championship, 1954). Spassky (White) now played:

(15) Kt x QKtP!! RP x Kt; (16) R x R ch, B x R; (17) Q – R5 ch, Q – B2; (18) R – Q8 ch, winning the Black Q. After **(18) . . . K x R; (19) Q x Q, P x Kt; (20) Q x BP, R – Kt; (21) P – B3, P – R6; (22) P – Kt3, K – K; (23) Q x P, R – Kt3; (24) Q x P ch, B – B3; (25) Q – Kt8 ch, K – B2; (26) Q x P** White won easily by advancing his passed Q-side Ps.

If we have spent many pages on the Ruy Lopez, it is because it is the most important P – K4 opening. One book (by Levenfish on KP openings) devotes 1,310 columns, with notes and subvariations, to the Ruy Lopez!

OPENING MAGIC

What good does it do to know about all the variations in this book (and in other books)?

The good chess player is a magician. By sleight of hand, he can shift from one opening to another before his opponent is aware of what he is doing. Knowing the proper timing of moves, he can induce his adversary to play a variation where a piece is misplaced or takes an extra move to reach a square.

For example: **(1) P – K4, P – QB4; (2) Kt – KB3, P – Q3.** That's a Sicilian Defense, of course, as we learned some time ago. **(3) B – Kt5 ch, Kt – B3; (4) O – O, B – Q2; (5) P – B3, Kt – B3; (6) R – K1, P – K4; (7) P – Q4, B – K2; (8) P x KP, P x P; (9) QKt – Q2, Q – B2.**

Now let's look at the position carefully.

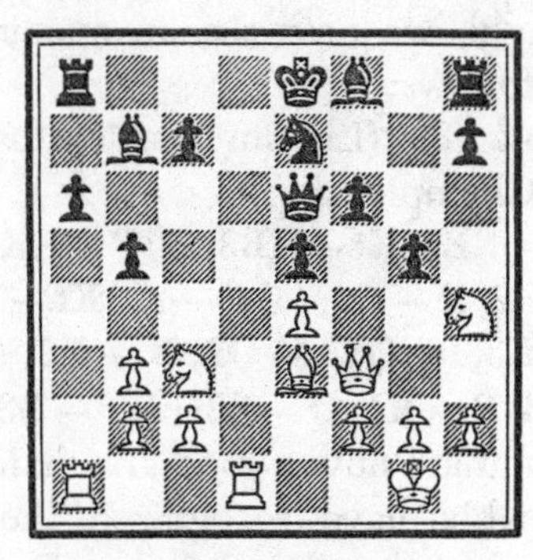

Figure 411

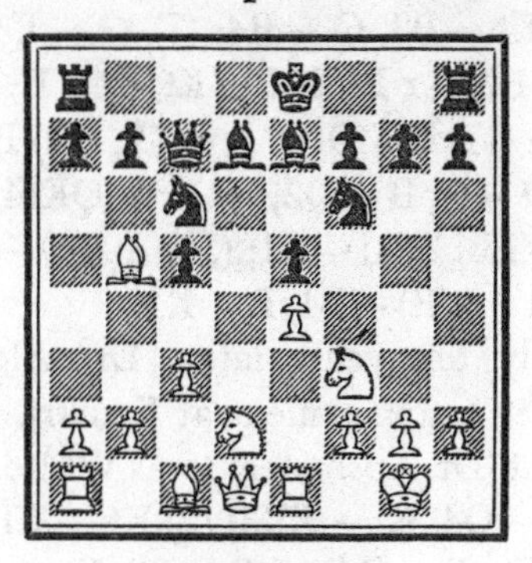

Figure 412

It has a strangely familiar look—not a Sicilian, at all, but a Ruy Lopez, after the moves (1) P – K4, P – K4; (2) Kt – KB3, Kt – QB3; (3) B – Kt5, P – QR3; (4) B – R4, Kt – B3; (5) O – O, B – K2; (6) R – K1, P – QKt4; (7) B – Kt3, P – Q3; (8) P – B3, Kt – QR4; (9) B – B2, P – B4; (10) P – Q4, Q – B2; (11) P x KP, P x P; (12) QKt – Q2, Kt – B3.

Where is the difference? The Black Pawns are on QR2 and QKt3—not QR3 and QKt4. In addition, the Black Bishop is on Q2 and not QB1. The usual square for the WB would be QB2, but he is still on QKt5, from where he can capture the Kt on QB3.

How can White gain from the differences in the positions? (1) The square QB4 is free—in the regular Ruy Lopez opening, it would be attacked by the Bl P on his QKt4. (2) The WB, as we have said, can capture the Bl Kt. (3) The Bl B on Q2 is misplaced, blocking the Kt on KB3 from coming to the defense of the KP.

White played (10) **Kt – B4!** and soon gained a considerable advantage, since he was able to double up Black's Pawns when Black struggled to stay even in material.

(10) . . . **O – O;** (11) **B x Kt, B x B;** (12) **B – Kt5, QR – K1;** (13) **Kt(B3) x P, Kt x P;** (14) **B x B, R x B;** (15) **Kt x B, P x Kt,** and now White must play (16) P – B3, exchange Rs after the Kt retreats, and have the better end game.

Example 2: In 1927, a great World Championship match was played between José Raul Capablanca, the Champion, and Dr. Alexander Alekhine, challenger and winner of the match. Game #11 went as follows: **Queen's Gambit Declined: Cambridge Springs Defense:** (1) P – Q4, P – Q4; (2) P – QB4, P – K3; (3) Kt – QB3, Kt – KB3; (4) B – Kt5, QKt – Q2; (5) P – K3, P – B3; (6) Kt – B3, Q – R4; (7) Kt – Q2, B – Kt5; (8) Q – B2, P x P; (9) B x Kt, Kt x B; (10) Kt x P, Q – B2; (11) P – QR3, B – K2; (12) B – K2, O – O; 13) O – O, B – Q2; (14) P – QKt4, P – QKt3; (15) B – B3, R(R) – B1; (16) R(KB) – Q1, R(KB) – Q1; (17) R(R) – B1, B – K1.

Exactly ten years later, Dr. Alekhine was playing in a tournament at Kemeri, Latvia. His opponent, Dr. Apsheneek, was White:

(1) **P – Q4, Kt – KB3;** (2) **Kt – KB3, P – B4;** (3) **P – K3, P – Q4;** (4) **P – B3, Kt – B3;** (5) **B – Q3, B – Kt5;** (6) **QKt – Q2, P – K3;** (7) **Q – R4, Kt – Q2;** (8) **B – Kt5.**

Figure 413

Let's see now: what do we have? It's easy to see—just stand on your head! **White** is playing a Cambridge Springs Defense! He has not gained a move, because the WB has taken two moves to go to QKt5. The game continued:

(8) . . . **Q – B2;** (9) **P x P, B x Kt;** (10) **Kt x B, Kt x P;** (11) **Q – B2, P – KKt3.**

Dr. Alekhine remembered the improvement Capablanca found in a later (the 29th) game of the match. In the 11th game, White played B – K2–KB3, then found he had to play P – KKt3 to keep the Bl Q from KB5. In the 29th game, he fianchettoed the B immediately, saving a move.

(12) **O – O, B – Kt2;** (13) **R – Q1, O – O;** (14) **B – Q2, P – QR3;** (15) **B – KB1, P – QKt4;** (16) **B – K1, KR – B1;** (17) **QR – B1, QR – Kt1.**

Compare this position with the diagram—colors reversed! Impressed by the caliber of White's (his own previous) moves, Dr. Alekhine could only draw the game.

These games are no accidents. Not too many years ago, players began to realize the importance of the fact that a good defense ought to make a good opening, especially since when White played the moves, he was a move ahead. Accordingly, we now see an opening like the one that follows:

Example 3: (Lisitsin vs. Antoshin, 22nd U.S.S.R. Championship)

(1) **Kt – KB3, Kt – KB3;** (2) **P – KKt3, P – Q4;** (3) **B – Kt2, P – B4;** (4) **O – O, Kt – B3;** (5) **P – Q3, P – K3;** (6) **QKt – Q2, B – K2;** (7) **P – K4, O – O;** (8) **R – K1, Q – B2;** (9) **P – B3.** (Fig. 414)

Since you are now a good armchair detective, you probably have recognized the fact that **White** is playing a King's Indian Defense, with

Figure 414

colors reversed. However, since you are a good detective, you will want to dig further into the facts:

(9) . . . **P – QKt4;** (10) **Kt – B1, P x P;** (11) **P x P, B – Kt2;** (12) **B – B4, P – K4;** (13) **B – Kt5, R(B) – Q1;** (14) **Q – B2, Kt – QR4.**

Figure 415

Now look again. Suddenly the position has the aspects of a Ruy Lopez, Morphy Defense, with center Pawns exchanged and the WB at KKt2 instead of QB2.

Example 4:

Another game from the same tourney (Smyslov-Kan):

(1) **P – K4, P – QB4;** (2) **Kt – KB3, P – K3;** (3) **P – Q3,** White omits P – Q4, thus changing what started out to be a Sicilian Defense: (3) . . . **Kt – QB3;** (4) **P – KKt3, P – Q4;** (5) **Q – K2, Kt – B3;** (6) **B – Kt2, B – K2;** (7) **O – O, O – O;** (8) **P – B3, P – Kt3** into what looks like a King's Indian, colors reversed; (9) **P – K5, Kt – Q2;** (10) **P – KR4, R – K1;** (11) **Kt – R3, P – B3;** (12) **P – Q4,** but which turns out to be a type of French Defense! (Fig. 416)

Further examples of related openings are:

Example 5: The English Opening

(1) **P – QB4, P – K4;** (2) **Kt – QB3, Kt – KB3;**

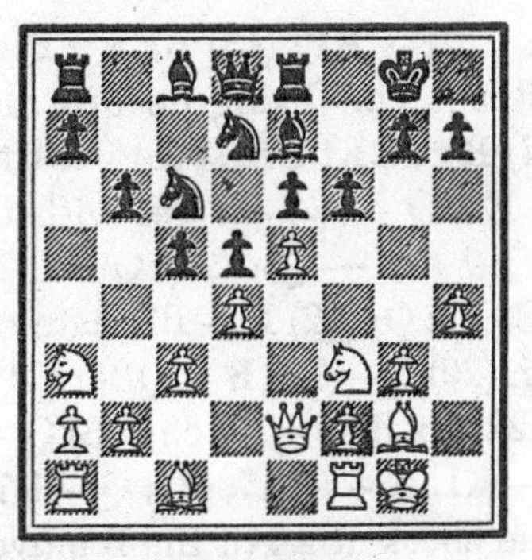

Figure 416

(3) **P – KKt3, P – Q4;** (4) **P x P, Kt x P;** (5) **B – Kt2, Kt – Kt3;** (6) **Kt – B3, Kt – B3;** (7) **O – O, B – K2;** (8) **P – Q3.**

Figure 417

This is a Sicilian Defense, in reverse, with White playing the "defense." He can continue (9) **B – K3,** (10) **R – B,** (11) **Kt – QR4** and (12) **Kt – B5;** or (9) **P – QR3,** (10) **P – QKt4,** (11) **B – Kt2.**

One interesting attempt to wrest a greater advantage from the "extra move" White has in such an opening, occurred in a game M. Hanauer vs. Matthew Green, Marshall Chess Club Championship, 1940, which continued: (from the diagram)

(8) . . . **O – O;** (9) **B – K3, P – B4;** (10) **P – QR4! P – QR4;** (11) **B x Kt!** This exchange of a B for a Kt is unusual, but Black is saddled with doubled QKtPs, and White's extra P on the other side (the QP) starts moving:

(11) . . . **P x B;** (12) **Q – Kt3 ch, K – R1;** (13) **P – K3!!** The point. . . . Q x P; KR – Q, Q – R3; Kt – QKt5, and even though Black can defend against Kt – B7, his Q is shut out of the game.

(13) . . . **P – B5!** The correct countermove. If now KR – Q, B – KKt5. However:

(14) **P – Q4!** An amazing P sacrifice.

(14) . . . **BP x KP; (15) BP x KP, P x P; (16) Kt x P, R x R ch.** Giving up this file loses the game; (17) **R x R, Kt x Kt;** (18) **P x Kt, Q x P ch;** (19) **K – R1, Q – Q3** (moves with the QB are hopeless: . . . B – Q2; (20) Q – B7, R – K1; (21) Q x B, R x Q; (22) R – B8 mate or (19) . . . B – KKt5; (20) Q – B7! B – QB4; (21) P – KR3! Q – K6; (22) P x B, Q – R3 ch; (23) Q – R5).

(20) **R – K1! B – KKt5; (21) Q – B7! Black resigned:** the check at K8 (if the B moves from e7) is fatal, and if . . . B – KB1, B – Q5 threatens mate at KKt8.

What a whale of a difference one move makes!

Example 6:

If you will remember the Tarrasch Defense to the Queen's Gambit: (1) P – Q4, P – Q4; (2) P – QB4, P – K3; (3) Kt – QB3, P – QB4; (4) BP x P, KP x P; (5) Kt – B3; Kt – QB3; (6) P – KKt3, Kt – B3; (7) B – Kt2, B – K3; (8) O – O.

Figure 418

At this point, Black has to come to a crucial decision: on . . . B – K2, (9) P x P, and he must play . . . B x P, with an inferior position or the gambit line . . . P – Q5 (as in the game Dake-Horowitz, in the chapter on the Middle Game). If he does not like gambits, he must avoid the Tarrasch Defense.

A game played by the author (White) in Philadelphia 1936, against David Polland, Black, proceeded as follows:

(1) **P – QB4, P – QB4;** (2) **Kt – QB3, Kt – KB3;** (3) **P – KKt3, Kt – B3;** (4) **B – Kt2, P – K3;** (5) **Kt – B3.** Now Black realizes that if he plays . . . P – Q4, then P x P, P x P; P – Q4 leads into a QGD, Tarrasch Defense, which he does not like. He therefore plays:

(5) . . . **P – QKt3,** which is met by (6) **P – Q4!** and after . . . **P x P;** (7) **Kt x P, B – Kt2,** (8) **Kt(4) – Kt5!**

Figure 419

White threatens Kt – Q6 ch. . . . P – Q4, which looks logical, is impossible, because four White pieces attack that square. Black, therefore, plans on defending his Q3:

(8) . . . **Kt – QR4;** (9) **B x B, Kt x B;** (10) **B – B4, P – Q3;** (11) **Q – R4!** Threatening two double checks, the more dangerous one being (after, e.g., . . . Kt – B4;) Kt – B7 ch, K – K2; Q – B6, R – B1; Kt(3) – Kt5, and if . . . Kt – K1 (. . . P – K4; B – Kt5!) Q x Kt ch, Q x Q; B x P ch, K – Q2; Kt x Q, K x Kt; O – O – O.

(11) . . . Q – Q2 is met by Kt – B7 ch, the Q being pinned.

(11) . . . **Kt – Q2;** (12) **R – Q1.**

Black can not maintain a Kt on QB4; Kt (Kt) – B4; Q – R3, P – QR4; P – QKt4; and if . . . P x P; Q x R.

(12) . . . **P – K4?** The hole at d5 is too weak: (13) **Kt – Q5! R – B1;** (14) **Q x P,** Black resigns.

A case where the cure (avoiding the Tarrasch Defense) is worse than the disease.

A similar position can arise from a Caro-Kann Defense: (1) **P – K4, P – QB3;** (2) **P – Q4, P – Q4;** (3) **P x P, P x P;** (4) **P – B4.**

However, if Black tries to set up the usual White position: (4) . . . **Kt – KB3;** (5) **Kt – QB3, P – KKt3?** (6) **B – Kt5!** and the attack on the QP forces . . . **P x P.**

Example 7:

Now for a final example of related openings: (1) **P – Q4, P – KB4.** The **Dutch Defense.** For years, this opening did not have a good reputation, but constant use of it by Botvinnik in the AVRO tournament, 1938, and by both players in the 1951 match vs. Bronstein has effected a revival.

(2) **P – KKt3, P – K3;** (3) **B – Kt2, Kt – KB3;** (4) **Kt – KB3, B – K2;** (5) **O – O, O – O;** (6) **P – B4, P – Q4;** (7) **P – Kt3, P – B3;** (8) **B – QR3.**

White exchanges Black's "good" Bishop (the one not on the same colored square as his Ps). (8) . . . QKt – Q2. It is better not to exchange, and develop W's Kt. **(9) Q – B1, Kt – K5; (10) QKt – Q2, Kt – Q3;** (11) **P – K3, Kt – B2; (12) KR – Q1, R – K1.**

Figure 420

Black is all set for . . . P – K4, but he hesitates to play it before developing his QB. The position is Flohr-Ragozin, Saltsjöbaden, 1948.

The related opening is **Bird's Opening:**

(1) **P – KB4, P – Q4;** (2) **P – K3, Kt – KB3;** (3) **Kt – KB3, B – Kt5.** A chess paradox: White, having the move, permits his Kt to be pinned; in a similar position, the Bl Kt would not yet be developed!

(4) **B – K2, B x Kt?!** This is part of the fight for e5, but a player can rarely give up a B for Kt with no additional compensation so early in the game.

(5) **B x B, QKt – Q2;** (6) **P – B4, P – K3;** (7) **P x P, P x P;** (8) **Kt – B3, P – B3;** (9) **O – O, B – K2;** (10) **P – Q3, Kt – Kt3.**

Figure 421

White (Dr. S. Tartakover) has prevented . . . P – K4 by exchanging Ps, but Black (E. Grunfeld) equalized the game (Vienna, 1917).

White can not play **Bird's Opening** without knowing about **From's Gambit:**

(1) **P – KB4, P – K4!** (2) **P x P, P – Q3;** (3) **P x P, B x P;** (4) **Kt – KB3, P – KKt4;** (5) **P – Q4, P – Kt5;** (6) **Kt – Kt5.** (The older line was (6) **Kt – K5.**) (6) . . . **P – KB4;** (7) **P – K4, P – KR3;** (8) **P – K5, B – K2;** (9) **Kt – KR3, P x Kt;** (10) **Q – R5 ch, K – B1;** (11) **B – QB4, Q – K1;** (12) **Q x P (R3), Kt – QB3.**

Figure 422

The gambit changed into one for White, who has compensation for his lesser material in the exposed Black King.

On the other hand, Black can not blithely play a From's Gambit unless he is prepared to play a King's Gambit:

(1) **P – KB4, P – K4;** (2) **P – K4!**

There is a related gambit for White after:

(1) **P – Q4, P – KB4;** (2) **P – K4, P x P.**

This is called the **Staunton Gambit.** It was played most recently in a crucial game at Hastings, 1953-4, between David Bronstein (U.S.S.R.) White, and C. H. O'D. Alexander (England) Black.

(3) **Kt – QB3, Kt – KB3;** (4) **P – KB3** an all-out gambit. If (4) B – Kt5, P – Q3; (5) B x Kt, KP x B; (6) Kt x P White regains his Pawn; but Black by . . . Q – K2; (7) Q – K2, P – Q4 gets the better position.

(4) . . . **P x P;** (5) **Kt x P, P – KKt3;** (6) **B – KB4, B – Kt2;** (7) **Q – Q2, O – O;** (8) **B – R6, P – Q4;** (9) **B x B, K x B;** (10) **O – O – O, B – B4;** (11) **B – Q3, B x B;** (12) **Q x B, Kt – B3;** (13) **QR – K1, Q – Q3;** (14) **K – Kt1, P – QR3;** (15) **R – K2, QR – K1;** (16) **KR – K1, P – K3;** (17) **Kt – K5, Kt – Q2.** (Fig. 423)

Black forced White to retreat his Kt, soon was able to play . . . P – K4, and, retaining the gambit pawn, eventually won the game.

Figure 423

Enough of openings. If you want more, or are looking for a specific one, search the "chess bibles," the tomes by Reuben Fine (*Practical Chess Openings* and *Modern Chess Openings*, 6th Edition); by W. Korn, (*Modern Chess Openings*, 8th Edition); by Paul Keres in Russian; by Max Euwe in Dutch, or in translations (only a few translated into English) or in his *Chess Archives*, which discuss the openings, as they are played in the most recent tournaments and matches. Best of all, play them yourself and find out by experience which moves are better than others. You now have enough range and vision to set out by yourself.

CHAPTER XVI

THE LAWS OF CHESS

SUGGESTIONS TO THE PLAYER

Every game must be played according to an official set of rules or laws. Following is the official Code of the Laws of Chess adopted by the General Assembly of the World Chess Federation (Federation Internationale des Echecs) at the 23rd Congress of the Federation, Stockholm, 1952, and amended at the 24th Congress, Schaffhausen, Switzerland, 1953.

LAWS OF CHESS

1. Introduction.

The game of chess is played between two opponents by moving men on a square board called a "chessboard."

2. The Chessboard and its Arrangement.

i. The chessboard is composed of 64 equal squares alternately light (the "white" squares) and dark (the "black" squares).

ii. The chessboard is placed between the players in such a way that the corner square to the right of each player is white.

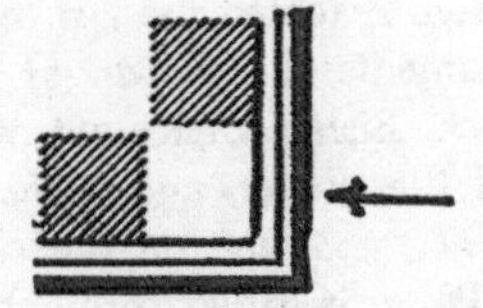

Figure 424

iii. The eight rows of squares running from the edge of the chessboard nearest one of the players to that nearest the other player are called "files."

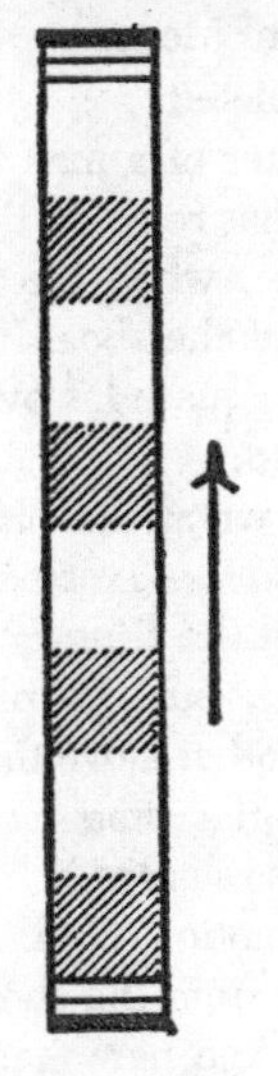

Figure 425

iv. The eight rows of squares running from one edge of the chessboard to the other at right angles to the files are called "ranks."

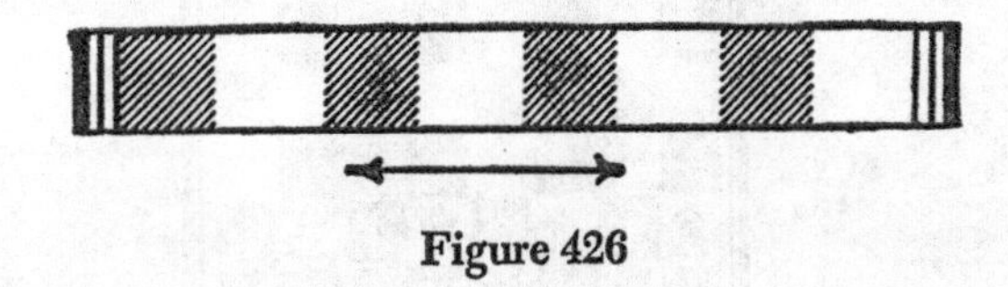

Figure 426

v. The straight rows of squares of one color, touching corner to corner, are called "diagonals."

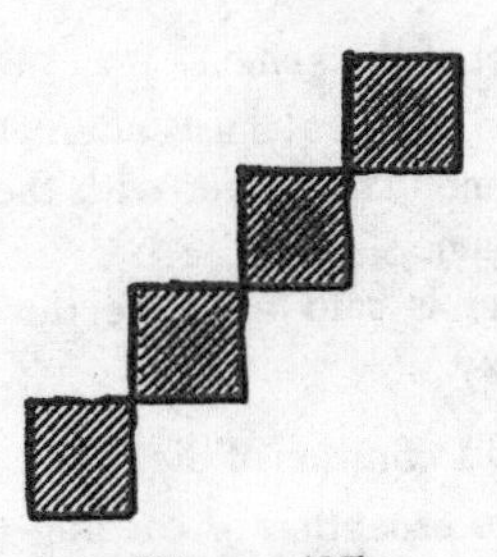

Figure 427

3. The Chessmen and their Arrangement.

At the beginning of the game, one player commands 16 light-colored men (the "white" men), the other, 16 dark-colored men (the "black" men).

These men are as follows:

One white King with the usual symbol in print of ♔

One white Queen with the usual symbol in print of ♕

Two white Bishops with the usual symbol in print of ♗

Two white Knights with the usual symbol in print of ♘

Two white Rooks with the usual symbol in print of ♖

Eight white Pawns with the usual symbol in print of ♙

One black King with the usual symbol in print of ♚

One black Queen with the usual symbol in print of ♛

Two black Bishops with the usual symbol in print of ♝

Two black Knights with the usual symbol in print of ♞

Two black Rooks with the usual symbol in print of ♜

Eight black Pawns with the usual symbol in print of ♟

The initial position of the men on the chessboard is as follows:

Figure 428

4. Conduct of the game.

i. The two players must alternate in making one move at a time. The player with the White men commences the game.

ii. A player is said to "have the move" when it is his turn to play.

5. General Definition of the Move.

i. With the exception of castling (article 6), a move is the transfer of a man from one square to another square which is either vacant or occupied by an enemy man (a man of the opposite color).

ii. No man, except the Rook in castling, or the Knight (Article 6) may cross a square occupied by another man.

iii. A man played to a square occupied by an enemy man captures, in the same move, this enemy man, which must be immediately removed from the chessboard by the player making the capture. See Article 6 for capturing *"en passant."*

6. Moves of the Individual Men.

The King. Except in castling, the King moves to any adjacent square that is not attacked by an enemy man. **Castling** is a move of the King and either Rook, counting as a single move (of the King) executed as follows: The King is transferred from his original square to either of the nearest squares of the same color in the same rank; then that Rook toward which the King has been moved is transferred over the King to the square which the King has just crossed. Castling is permanently impossible (illegal) if the King or castling Rook has previously moved. Castling is momentarily prevented: (a) if the King's original square, or the square which the King must cross, or that which it will occupy, is attacked by an enemy man; (b) if there are any men between the King and the Rook toward which the King must move.

(Author's note: If one castling Rook has moved, the player can still castle on the other side, there being no other reason to prevent him.)

The Queen. The Queen moves to any square (except as limited by Article 5, No. 2) on the file, rank, or diagonals on which it stands.

The Rook. The Rook moves to any square (except as limited by Article 5, No. 2) on the file or rank on which it stands.

The Bishop. The Bishop moves to any square (except as limited by Article 5, No. 2) on the diagonals on which it stands.

The Knight. The Knight's move is composed of two different steps: first, to a contiguous square along the rank or file, and then, still moving away from its square of departure, to a contiguous square on a diagonal.

The Pawn. The Pawn moves forward only.

(a) Except when capturing, it advances from its *original* square one or two vacant squares along the file on which it is placed, and on subsequent moves only one vacant square along the file. When capturing, it advances to either square, contiguous to its own, on the diagonal.

(b) A Pawn attacking a square crossed by an enemy **Pawn, which has been advanced two squares,** may capture, but only in the move immediately following, this enemy Pawn, as if the latter had been advanced only one square. This capture is called taking *"en passant"* (or **"in passing"**).

(c) Any Pawn reaching the last (eighth) rank must be exchanged immediately, *as part of the same move,* for a Queen, Rook, Bishop or Knight of the same color, at the choice of the player, and *without reference to the other men still remaining on the chessboard.* This exchange of a Pawn is called **"promotion"** and *the action of the promoted man is immediate.*

(The italics are the author's. The last clause means that a promoted Pawn, becoming a piece, gives check on its rank, file (R, Q) or diagonal (B, Q) or within its range (Kt) as soon as the exchange is made.)

7. Completion of Move.

A move is completed:

(a) in the transfer of a man to a vacant square when the player's hand has released the man;

(b) in a capture, when the captured man has been removed from the chessboard and the player, having placed on its new square his own man, has released the latter from his hand;

(c) in castling, when the player's hand has released the Rook on the square crossed by the King; when the player has released the King from his hand, the move is not yet completed, but the player no longer has the right to make any other move than castling;

(This means the time clock can not be pushed until the Rook is released.)

(d) in the promotion of a Pawn, when the Pawn has been removed from the chessboard and the player's hand has released the new man after placing it on the promotion square; if the player has released from his hand the Pawn that has reached the promotion square, the move is not yet completed, but the player no longer has the right to play the Pawn to another square.

(He can not, for example, make a capture; or, having made one, retract it for a straight move or a different capture.)

8. **The Touched Man.**

Provided that he first warns his opponent, the player having the move may adjust one or more men on their squares.

Except for the above case, if the player having the move touches one or more men, he must make his move by moving or capturing the first man touched which can be moved or captured.

No penalty is entailed if the opponent does not claim a violation of the rule before himself touching a man, or if none of the moves indicated above can be made legally.

(This is an important change from the old rule, which forced a player making an illegal move to move his King.)

9. **Illegal Positions.**

i. If, *during a game*, it is found that an illegal move has been made, the position shall be reinstated to what it was before the illegal move was made.

ii. If, during a game, one or more men have been accidentally displaced and incorrectly replaced, the position shall be reinstated to what it was before the displacement took place, and the game shall be continued. If the position cannot be reinstated, the game shall be annulled and a new game played.

iii. If, after an adjournment, the position has been reinstated incorrectly, it shall be re-established to what it was at the adjournment and the game shall be continued.

iv. If, during a game, it is found that the initial position of the men was incorrect, the game shall be annulled, and a new game played.

(This, too, is a change. The old rule stated that the incorrect position held after five moves.)

v. If, during a game, it is found that the board has been wrongly placed, the position reached shall be transferred to a board correctly placed, and the game shall be continued.

10. **Check.**

i. The King is in check when the square on which it stands is attacked by an enemy man; the latter is then said to give check to the King.

ii. Check must be parried by the move immediately following. If check cannot be parried, it is said to be "mate." (See Article II, No. 1.)

iii. A man intercepting a check to the King of its own color can itself give check to the enemy King.

11. **Won Game.**

i. The game is won by the player who has mated the enemy King. (See Article 10, No. 2.)

ii. The game is won by the player whose opponent resigns the game.

12. **Drawn Game.**

The game is drawn:

i. When the King of the player who has the move is not in check, but such player cannot make any legal move. The King is then said to be "stalemated."

ii. By agreement between the two players.

iii. Upon demand by one of the players when the same position appears three times, the same player having the move each time. The position is considered the same if men of the same kind and color occupy the same squares. The right to claim the draw belongs exclusively to the player:

(a) who is in a position to play a move leading to such repetition of the position, if he declares his intention of making such move;

(b) who is in a position to reply to a move which has produced the repeated position.

If a player makes a move without claiming a draw in the manner prescribed in (a) and (b), he loses the right to claim the draw; this right is restored to him, however, if the same position appears again, the same player having to move.

iv. When a player having the move demonstrates that at least 50 moves have been made by each side without the capture of any man, or the movement of any Pawns. This number of fifty moves may be increased for certain specific positions, provided that this increase in number and these positions have been clearly established prior to the commencement of the game.

SUPPLEMENTARY REGULATIONS FOR TOURNAMENTS AND MATCHES

13. **Recording of Games.**

In the course of play, each player is required to record the moves of his game in a clear and legible manner on a prescribed score sheet. (See Supplement No. 1)

14. **Use of the Chess Clock.**

i. Each player must make a certain number of moves in a given period of time, these two factors being specified in advance.

ii. Control of each player's time is effected by means of a clock equipped with special apparatus for this purpose.

iii. At the time determined for the start of the game, the clock of the player who has the White men is set in motion. In the continuation of the game, each of the players, having made his move, stops his own clock and starts his opponent's clock.

iv. Upon the execution of the prescribed number of moves, the last move is not considered as being completed until after the player has stopped his clock.

v. Every indication given by a clock or its apparatus (the flag attached to some chess clocks) is considered as conclusive in the absence of evident defects. The player who wishes to claim any such defect, is required to do so as soon as he himself has become aware of it.

vi. If the game must be interrupted because of some

situation for which neither player is responsible, the clocks shall be stopped until the situation has been adjusted. This should be done, for example, in the case of a defective clock to be exchanged, an illegal position to be corrected, or when the man which a player has announced he wishes to exchange for one of his Pawns that has reached the last rank, is not immediately available.

vii. When, in the case of Article 9, Nos. i and ii, it is not possible to establish the time used by each player up to the moment of irregularity, each player shall be allotted up to that moment an amount of time proportional to that indicated by the clocks when the irregularity is observed.

Example: After Black's 30th move, it is found that an irregularity took place at the 20th move. If for these 30 moves, the clocks indicate 90 minutes for White and 60 minutes for Black, it shall be assumed that the times used by the two players for the first 20 moves were in proportion, thus:

White $\frac{90 \times 20}{30} = 60$ minutes

Black $\frac{60 \times 20}{30} = 40$ minutes

15. Adjournment of the Game.

1. If a game is not finished upon conclusion of the time prescribed for play, the player having the move shall write his next move in unambiguous notation on his score sheet, place his and his opponent's score sheets in an envelope, seal the envelope, and then stop the clocks. If the player has made the said move on the chessboard, he must seal this same move on his score sheet.

ii. Upon the envelope shall be indicated:

(a) the names of the players;

(b) the position immediately before the sealed moves;

(c) the time used by each player;

(d) the name of the player who has sealed the number of that move.

iii. Custody of the envelope must be assured.

16. Resumption of an Adjourned Game.

i. When the game is resumed, the position immediately before the sealed move shall be set up on a chessboard, and the time used by each player at the time of adjournment shall be indicated on the clocks.

ii. The envelope shall be opened only when the player having the move (the player who must reply to the sealed move) is present. That player's clock shall be started after the sealed move has been made on the chessboard.

iii. If the player having the move is absent, his clock shall be started, but the envelope shall be opened only at the time of his arrival.

iv. If the player who has sealed the move is absent, the player having the move is not obliged to reply to the sealed move on the chessboard. He has the right to record his move in reply upon the score sheet, to place the latter in an envelope, to stop his clock, and to start his opponent's clock. The envelope should be placed in security and opened at the time of his opponent's arrival.

v. If the envelope containing the sealed move at the time of adjournment has disappeared, and it is not possible to re-establish, by agreement of the two players, the position and the times used for the adjourned game, or if, for any other reason, the said position and said times cannot be re-established, the game is annulled, and a new game must be played in place of the adjourned game. If the envelope containing the move recorded with Section 4 hereof has disappeared, the game must be resumed from the position at the time of adjournment, and with the clock times recorded at the time of adjournment.

vi. If, upon resumption of the game, the time used has been incorrectly indicated on either clock, and if such mistake has been established by either player before making his first move, the error must be corrected. If the error is not then established, the game continues without correction.

17. Loss of the Game.

A game is lost by a player:

i. Who has not completed the prescribed number of moves in the time specified.

ii. Who arrives at the chessboard more than one hour late.

iii. Who has sealed an illegal move, or one so inaccurately or vaguely defined as to render impossible the establishment of its true meaning.

iv. Who, during the game, refuses to comply with these laws of chess. If both players arrive at the chessboard more than one hour late, or refuse to comply with these laws of chess, the game shall be declared lost by both players.

18. Conduct of the Players.

i. (a) During play the players are forbidden to make use of notes, manuscripts or printed matter, or to analyze the game on another chessboard; they are likewise forbidden to receive the advice or opinion of a third party, whether solicited or not. (b) No analysis is permitted in the playing room during play or during adjournment. (c) Players are forbidden to distract or annoy their opponents in any manner whatsoever.

19. Tournament Director or Match Referee.

To manage the competition, a tournament director or match referee must be designated. His duties are:

(a) to see that these laws of chess are strictly observed;

(b) to supervise the progress of the competition, to establish that the prescribed time limit has not been exceeded by the players; to arrange the order of resumption of play in adjourned games, to supervise the arrangements set forth in Article 15, above all to see that the information is correct; to assume custody of the sealed envelopes until such time as adjourned games are resumed; etc. . . .

(c) to enforce the decisions he has reached in disputes that have arisen during the course of the competition;

(d) to impose penalties on the players for all infractions of these laws of chess.

20. **Interpretation of the Laws of Chess.**

In case of doubt as to the application or interpretation of these laws, the F.I.D.E. shall examine the evidence submitted, and render official decision.

Decisions published in the *Revue de la F.I.D.E.* are binding on all affiliated federations.

SUPPLEMENT NO. 1

CHESS NOTATION

F.I.D.E. Laws at present recognize only the two most generally known systems of notation: the algebraic system and the descriptive system.

Each affiliated unit is free to employ whichever of these two notations it prefers. (The U.S.C.F. accepts both.)

ABBREVIATIONS*

(* Descriptions of Algebraic (a — h, 1 — 8) and Descriptive systems are omitted by us.)

O – O Castles with the Rook h1 or h8 (short castling); with the KR.

O – O – O Castles with the Rook a1 or a8 (long castling); with the QR.

: or x Captures.

† (a dagger) or Ch—Check

‡ (double dagger)—Mate

! Well played

? Poorly played

[?! Risky, but gives some chances]

SUPPLEMENT NO. 2

EXPRESSIONS IN GENERAL USE

i. **Piece.** A general term comprising all chessmen except the Pawn.

(In American usage, a Queen or Rook is a **"major piece,"** a Bishop or Knight is a **"minor piece"**; the term **"man"** is used to designate both pieces and Pawns.)

ii. **To interpose.** To place a man between one's own King and the enemy piece giving check. A check by a Knight cannot be parried by interposing.

iii. **Pinned Man.** The man interposed to parry a check, whose freedom of movement is thereby destroyed, is said to be **"pinned."**

(This refers to an **"absolute pin."** In common parlance a piece or Pawn is called "pinned" when its movement would expose a player to loss of material through capture of the piece it uncovers when it moves.)

iv. **Discovered Check.** Check by a piece whose action has been unmasked by the moving of another man.

v. **Double Check.** Check simultaneously obtained by moving a man which itself gives check, and which at the same time uncovers the action of a piece which also gives check.

vi. **Long Castling (or Queen Castling).** Castling with the Rook at a1 or a8 (Queen-Rook).

vii. **Short Castling (or King Castling).** Castling with the Rook at h1 or h8 (King-Rook).

viii. **Winning the Exchange.** To exchange a Kt or B for a Rook.

(The "Exchange" is sometimes called the "Quality.")

ix. **Losing the Exchange.** To exchange a Rook for Kt or B.

x. **"I adjust" (or "*J' adoube*").** Expression used when the player adjusts a man on its square, (in order to forewarn his opponent—see Article 8).

(This completes the official rules.)

SUGGESTIONS TO THE PLAYER

You have read the official rules above, and doubtless understand them. But, you may ask, do you have to abide by all the rules when you play a game "for fun?" The answer is: Yes. Play strictly according to the moves at all times. Above all, abide by Article 8 of the rules, which says, in effect:

1. **Touch—move.** If you touch one of your men you must move it.

If you touch one of your opponent's men, you must capture it.

—Unless you have first said "J' adoube," or "I adjust."

Then, if you have moved one of your men onto a square, don't try to take the move back.

Article 7 says that the move is completed when you have released your man on its new square. Play "touch—move," and expect your opponent to do the same.

2. **Think—decide—move.** When it is your move, you must come to some decision. You take into account your plan, your opponent's plan, and his immediate threat. Decide which move is most urgent; then having made up your mind, make the move on the board.

3. **Have no regrets.** Once your move is made, don't start worrying about what you could have done. A new position is in front of you. Study it. Forget the past one. Only on rare occasions can you get it back again.

4. **Respect your opponent's rights.** When it is your opponent's turn to move, he is entitled to quiet—at least, from you. Do not talk to him or to someone else while it is his turn. If someone wants to talk to you, go away from the table and from your opponent's hearing.

Never discuss a game in progress. If you have a question, copy down the position and discuss it after the game. You are liable to lose the game (Article 17, IV) if you receive the opinion of a third party, whether solicited or not (Article 18). Consider your team!

5. **Respect your opponent's play!** No matter what you are planning, always consider your opponent's move

carefully. Many the player who has fallen into a trap because he "didn't look" at the move the other fellow had made.

6. **Respect your opponent.** Don't play inferior moves just because your opponent does not have a strong reputation. You can never recover from a bad opening if your opponent plays even reasonably well.

In the 1935 World Championship match, many observers reported that the champion, Alexander Alekhine, after building up a lead in games (4-1; then 7-5) came into the playing room under the influence of alcohol. When he saw his lead in games vanish, he grew more serious—but too late! He lost the match.

In the return match, 1937, Alekhine again drank—but this time milk! He won the match.

Some years ago, the author used to play with an old-time player, A. C. Clapp, at the Marshall Chess Club. Before each game, he would extract from his pocket two twisted Italian cigars one of which he would offer his opponent, making it a condition to playing a game, and stating that that was his handicap. The author could do nothing but accept the challenge, out of respect for his opponent. The resultant games offered abundant opportunities for original play.

7. **Win and Lose gracefully.** If you win a game, you can afford to be generous. Find some part of your opponent's game to praise. On the other hand, if you lose a game, turn down your King pleasantly, and tell your opponent how well he played. Be a good loser and winner.

8. **Play with stronger players.** The best way to improve your game is to play with stronger players. The fondest memories the author has are of games played with Dr. Emanuel Lasker, Capablanca, Alekhine and Nimzovitch—when he was a young and inexperienced player.

A very strong player, or master, may not be willing to play with you on a man-to-man basis. However, they often give exhibitions, where they play 20 or 30 players at one time. Try to get one of those 30 boards!

Some clubs have lightning or rapid-transit tournaments once a week, in which each player must make each move within ten seconds. The good players give handicaps to the novices. When you have played enough so that you have a fairly good idea of what is going on in a game, try to enter one of those tournaments.

9. **Join a group or club.** A group may be active in your neighborhood—join it!

If you go to a school, ask whether the school has a chess club. There you will find players of all kinds and at all levels.

Many parks have meeting places for chess players. In Central Park, New York City, there is a special pavilion for chess players; in Washington Square Park, concreted tables for outdoor play. Any park with a bench has a ready-made table and chairs. Look for the chess bench; bring your set. Your opponent will materialize.

Best of all, join a chess club. The clubs attract the best players. Merely to have the privilege of watching their games is to improve your chess learning.

10. **Read books.** Books are records—usually of the best games played in the world. A good tournament book will have an analysis of the openings played in the tournament. Every game you play over will add to your knowledge of all facets of the game.

Your public library has many books you can borrow—free. Some can be found in central reference rooms. The largest collection in the United States (if not in the world) is in the Cleveland Public Library, the J. G. White collection. A recent gift to the New York Public Library (by Gustavus A. Pfeiffer) has acted as a spur to the improvement of its collection. Other great libraries of chess books in the U.S.A. are at Harvard University (Silas W. Howland collection) and at Princeton University.

11. **Build your own library.** The finest items in your own library would be a record of all your games. Make a habit of writing down your games as you play them—then save them.

A second series of items can be culled from clippings from the newspapers. Some papers print columns once a week; others print news, with games, of tournaments in progress. They make a valuable source of good games.

Support your chess papers, magazines and writers. The latest news and games are presented to you by experts in three forms. *Chess Life*, the newspaper of the U. S. Chess Federation, is a bi-monthly paper. The leading U. S. magazines are *Chess Review* and *The American Chess Bulletin*. Various states issue annual bulletins.

Other English language magazines are *Chess* and *British Chess Magazine* (England), *Chess World* (Australia), *Canadian Chess Reporter* (Canada), and the *South African Chess Review*.

Your own magazine will be able to obtain books and magazines in foreign languages for you.

Specialists in all kinds of chess books (new and old) in the United States are the University Place Book Shop (Walter Goldwater) and Dr. A. Buschke, both in New York City.

12. **Go to Tournaments.** Watch the masters at work! Hear analyses made by leading players during the course of the games—but out of earshot of the players. Predict moves to come—and let the players prove you are right or wrong.

13. **When you play an off-hand game:** Try all the openings. Only by playing an opening will you really be able to understand it. When you have to make a single choice each move, the reason for preferring one move to another, or for making moves in a certain order, will become clear to you. Then, too, different openings lead to different situations, giving you a chance to practice the ideas you have learned, and to try out new ones of your own.

14. **When you play a match or tournament game:**

(a) **Play an opening you know well.** You will feel more relaxed if the moves you make are familiar to you.

(b) **Consider each move carefully.** Think over each move, even if you think you "know a line by heart." Your opponent may have changed the order of his moves. If so, the position is completely different, and you may be able to make a move entirely different from that you (and he) expected.

(c) **Know the latest analyses.** Lines change continually: a variation discarded for years because of the result of one game may be revived when some player discovers the error the original loser made. The best players constantly try out new lines which they have prepared and studied before each tournament. Play over the published games—then try the new lines yourself, first in off-hand games, then in a tournament.

(d) **Play an opening you think is unfamiliar to your opponent.** But make sure you know what you're doing!

At Ventnor City, 1941, before the author was to play Robert Durkin, he tried to guess what opening might be unfamiliar to this young player, who had shown great knowledge of the then popular lines. He decided that the Queen's Gambit accepted, as played in the 1931 World Championship, would be just outmoded enough at the time he, as a newcomer, might have been attracted to serious chess.

When the tournament was over, a book of the games was published. Mr. Durkin wrote the notes hundreds of miles away in Milwaukee. This is what he wrote about the first two moves:

(1) P – Q4, P – Q4

"!When I beheld this move, my first impulse was to summon the tournament director, the referee and anyone else in authority that was handy, to protest Hanauer's unfair tactics. You see, I had prepared for a Queen's Indian defense."

(2) P – QB4, P x P

"!!This was entirely too much! It has a touch of the diabolic! How on earth did Hanauer guess I knew nothing about the Q.G. Accepted without resorting to voodoo? In Milwaukee, my opponents always declined the P like gentlemen, but—oh, well—I can't be happy all the time."

This surprise did not prevent Mr. Durkin from playing very well, however. It was only with great difficulty that the game was drawn by the author (and him, he says further in the notes).

(e) **Avoid your opponent's favorite opening—unless,** of course, you have studied his games carefully, and have spotted a weakness. Even then, he may have spotted it, too, and be waiting to correct it. The great American player Harry Nelson Pillsbury saved a variation for *eight years* to play against Dr. Emanuel Lasker at Cambridge Springs, 1904. At Avro, 1938, Paul Keres was waiting with a prepared opening against Samuel Reshevsky. So was every one else, but Keres got there first, and won a crucial game.

(f) **Vary your openings.** In one Marshall C. C. Championship, the author played . . . P – K3 (French Defence) in answer to P – K4 in Round One. Thereafter, every one played (1) P – K4 against the author. Three French Defenses resulted, but in the fourth game with Black, the author played (1) P – K4, Kt – KB3 (Alekhine's Defense) having been blessed with a very recent analysis found in a foreign magazine. The analysis plus the surprise scored a point.

(g) **Play the board.** Your opponent may be hiding something, but the position, as you see it, is open to inspection. Play the best move you can discover, in accordance with your plans, and with consideration of your opponent's plan. Don't play a move you know to be bad, hoping to "get away" with something. The board is open to him, too.

Play your best, and the game will repay you in many ways.

CHAPTER XVII

CHESS EVENTS—PAST AND PRESENT

The history of the chess champions of the world and of the U.S.A. has been obscured in the lack of organization which makes for uncertainty. Chess still depends, to a great extent, upon patrons who are willing to contribute the money necessary for the players' expenses, for the renting of the playing hall, and for compensation to the players for their efforts in producing masterpieces of science and skill. More recently, various governments have found it fitting to contribute sums from their educational or cultural budgets to the staging of international chess matches.

The Netherlands, spurred on by its world champion, Dr. Max Euwe (1935-7) and the fact that the home of the International Chess Federation (F.I.D.E.) is within its borders, was the first country to recognize chess in its budget. It has continued to be one of the foremost. Others, such as the U.S.S.R., Argentina and Yugoslavia, have followed suit. The U.S.A. has not, until recently, recognized a contribution to a chess event as an item deductible on an income tax report. Fortunately, now a contribution to a specific fund for the furthering of chess events is being recognized. We await the time when the government itself will sponsor an international team match.

One of the saddest commentaries upon chess events of the past thirty years is the fact that many "natural" matches have never taken place. Most notable is the "return" match between Alekhine and Capablanca, which stumbled upon the inability of the sponsors to raise $10,000 for eight years—until the U.S.A. went off the gold standard in 1935, and Alekhine demanded his guarantee in "gold dollars." Even then, less than $18,000 would have been required. But the match has been lost to the chess world forever.

Other "naturals" were Kashdan vs. Marshall in the late 20's; Reuben Fine vs. Samuel Reshevsky in the 30's or 40's; and now, in 1956, Reshevsky vs. Botvinnik.

If Botvinnik could bring himself to the point where he would accept challenges from players 2, 3 and 4 in that order, we might have the last-mentioned match. But national pride and the F.I.D.E. rules preclude such a possibility. Reshevsky was not even entered in the 1956 "Candidates' Tournament," the winner of which would become the official (and only) challenger to a world title match in 1957.

Under the present set-up, "zonal" tournaments are held in various sections of the earth, the winners of which qualify for a large "interzonal" tournament. The first seven places in the interzonal meet the challenger (or winner of the previous interzonal) in a double-round "Candidates' Tournament." The winner of the Candidates' Tournament is the official challenger.

In the history of chess, many famous names have dominated the game. Foremost of these are:

THE WORLD CHAMPIONS

An "official" world's championship has been in existence only since 1886. However, certain men were recognized in their day as the best players in the world. These were:

RUY LOPEZ, Spain	1570–1575
LEONARDO DA COUTRY, Italy	1575–1587
GRECO, Italy	1622–1634
PHILIDOR, France	1745–1795
LABOURDONNAIS, France	1834–1840
ANDERSSEN, Germany	1851–1858
MORPHY, U.S.A.	1858–1863
STEINITZ, Austria	1866–1894
DR. EMANUEL LASKER, Germany	1894–1921
J. R. CAPABLANCA, Cuba	1921–1927
A. A. ALEKHINE, Russia, naturalized	1927–1935
French	1937–1945
MAX EUWE, Holland	1935–1937
M. BOTVINNIK, U.S.S.R.	1948–date

The most important matches for the world title (official only since 1886) are the following:

Year	*Winner-Loser*	*W*	*L*	*D*
1834	L. C. de la Bourdonnais—Alexander MacDonnell	45	27	13
1843	Howard Staunton—P. C. F. St. Amant	11	6	4

1858	Paul Morphy–Adolf Anderssen	7	2	2
1866	Wilhelm Steinitz–A. Anderssen	8	6	0
1870	Wilhelm Steinitz–J. H. Blackburne	5	0	1
1872	Wilhelm Steinitz–J. H. Zukertort	7	1	4
1876	Wilhelm Steinitz–J. H. Blackburne	7	0	0
1886	Wilhelm Steinitz–J. H. Zukertort	10	5	5
1889	Wilhelm Steinitz–Chigorin	10	6	1
1890	Wilhelm Steinitz–Gunsberg	6	4	9
1892	Wilhelm Steinitz–Chigorin	10	8	5
1894	Emanuel Lasker–W. Steinitz	10	5	4
1896-7	Emanuel Lasker–Steinitz	10	2	5
1907	Emanuel Lasker–F. J. Marshall	8	0	7
1908	Emanuel Lasker–Tarrasch	8	3	5
1909	Emanuel Lasker–D. Janowski	7	1	2
1910	Emanuel Lasker–Carl Schlechter	1	1	8
1910	Emanuel Lasker–Janowski	8	0	3
1921	Jose Raul Capablanca–Em. Lasker	4	0	10
1927	Alexander A. Alekhine–J. R. Capablanca	6	3	25
1929	A. Alekhine–Ewfim D. Bogoljubow	11	5	9
1934	A. Alekhine–E. D. Bogoljubow	8	3	15
1935	Dr. Machgelis Euwe–A. Alekhine	9	8	13
1937	A. Alekhine–M. Euwe	11	6	13
1951	M. Botvinnik–D. Bronstein	5	5	14
1954	M. Botvinnik–V. Smyslov	7	7	10
1957	V. Smyslov–M. Botvinnik	5	3	16

The World Champion retains his title in case of a drawn match.

In 1948 a Match Tournament was held to determine the World Champion. This was won by Mikhail Botvinnik with 14 points of a possible 20, followed by Smyslov 11, Reshevsky and Keres 10½ and Euwe 4. Botvinnik thereby became World Champion. According to World Federation (F.I.D.E.) rules, he could lose it only by losing a match to a single challenger in a match of 24 games. Thus, the fact that he lost to Reshevsky in the U.S.A.–U.S.S.R. match of 1955 (1½-2½, one loss; three draws) did not affect his title; nor did his finishing third in the XXII Soviet Championship, 1955.

U.S.A. CHAMPIONS

First American Chess Tournament: New York, 1857

1. Paul Morphy
2. Louis Paulsen

Second American: Cleveland, 1871

1. G. H. Mackenzie
2. Henry Hosmer

Third American: Chicago, 1874

1. G. H. Mackenzie
2. H. Hosmer

Fourth American: Philadelphia, 1876

1. James Mason
2. Max Judd

Fifth American: New York, 1880

1. G. H. Mackenzie
2. James Grundy

Sixth American: New York, 1889

1. and 2. Mikhail Chigorin and Max Weiss

The irregular quality of the times during the years of the above tournaments now disappeared with the tourneys themselves: No more were held until 1936!

In the meantime, Frank James Marshall won the U.S. title after a series of international successes and a match with Jackson W. Showalter of St. Louis, Mo. No further matches were forthcoming. Finally Marshall resigned his title, and the U. S. Championships were started on a biennial basis. Winners were:

1936 New York:

1. Samuel Reshevsky
2. Albert C. Simonson

1938 New York:

1. Samuel Reshevsky
2. Reuben Fine

1940 New York:

1. Samuel Reshevsky
2. Reuben Fine

1942 New York: 1 and 2, Isaac Kashdan and Samuel Reshevsky. Reshevsky won the play-off match 7½-3½ (won 6, lost 2, drew 3). Reshevsky also defeated Israel A. Horowitz in a match (won 3, drew 13).

1944 New York:

1. Arnold S. Denker
2. Reuben Fine

1946 New York:

1. S. Reshevsky
2. I. Kashdan

1948 South Fallsburg, N. Y.

1. Herman Steiner
2. I. Kashdan

There was now a lapse of *three* years before the next tournament and, again, the next. Whether this is a new U.S.A. policy remains to be seen. In 1951, the tournament was notable for the fact that Samuel Reshevsky finished *second* –the first time in any U. S. Championship he had entered.

1951 New York:

1. Larry Evans

2. Samuel Reshevsky

1954 New York:

1. Arthur Bisguier
2. L. Evans

In 1954, a "U. S. Candidates Tournament" was held to determine five places in the finals, along with the "seeded" players. This also may be a new policy, although it was the first time it had been done: in previous years, there were elimination tournaments, or preliminaries, from which winning players qualified to play with the "seeded" masters. In 1951, 24 masters were invited to the U. S. Championship Finals. Twelve qualified for the final round.

In addition to the championship tournament, the U. S. Chess Federation holds an "open" tournament each year, usually in some midwestern city. This was started in Chicago, 1934, continued in Milwaukee, in 1935, and has been played in Philadelphia, 1936, Chicago, 1937, Boston, 1938 and 1944, New York, 1939, Dallas, 1940 and 1942, St. Louis, 1941, Syracuse, 1943, Peoria, 1945, Pittsburgh, 1946, etc.

In 1955, it was held in Los Angeles; in 1956, Oklahoma City.

The U. S. Chess Federation has held Women's Championship Tournaments, usually at about the same time as the Men's. In 1955, Gisela K. Gresser and Nanny Roos tied for first place, and are sharing the title. Previous winners have been Adele Belcher, Mary Bain and May Karff, as well as Mrs. Gresser.

An "Open" Women's Tourney is held annually in conjunction with the men's. This has led to the development of strong women players all over the country. The quality of play has steadily improved.

An annual "lightning" tournament (10 seconds a move) is held, usually in conjunction with the "open." On some occasions a "national lightning" has been held. Reuben Fine has invariably won this tournament.

Most states hold their "State Tournaments" annually. In New York, this is held in an up-state city. Rome, Utica, Binghamton, Syracuse, Buffalo and (most frequently of late) Cazenovia are the usual sites. They also hold "state lightning" tournaments at the same time.

Various clubs hold annual championships. These are probably the seat of the greatest player development. The lists of players in a Marshall Chess Club or Manhattan Chess Club Championship, in the Washington Chess Divan, the Mechanics Institute of Philadelphia, the Chess and Checker Club of Chicago or the Los Angeles Chess Club read like a roll-call of the chess masters of the U.S.A.

There are also "invitation tournaments" to which U.S.A. masters and, often, foreign masters and grandmasters are invited. The latest was the Rosenwald Invitation Tournament of 1955-6 (at the Manhattan and Marshall Chess Clubs) won by Arthur Bisguier and Larry Evans, ahead of Samuel Reshevsky. Other great tournaments were held in Cambridge Springs, 1904 (won by Frank Marshall, ahead of Dr. Lasker); the Rice Memorial, 1916 (won by Capablanca); New York, 1924 (1. Dr. E. Lasker, 2. Capablanca); New York, 1927 (1. Capablanca, 2. Dr. Alekhine); New York, 1931 (1. Capablanca, 2. Kashdan); New York, 1948-9 (1. R. Fine, 2. M. Najdorf); and New York, 1951 (1. S. Reshevsky, 2. M. Euwe and M. Najdorf).

A series of invitation masters' tournaments were held at Ventnor City, N. J., beginning in 1939. The purpose was to encourage the younger masters and some strong but "unknown" players. Following were the winners of these tournaments:

1939 M. Hanauer; 1940 Sidney Bernstein and M. Hanauer; 1941 Jacob Levin; 1942 Abie Yanofsky; 1943 George Shainswit and Anthony E. Santasiere; 1944 Weaver W. Adams.

In 1945, the tournaments were unfortunately discontinued. One "open" tournament was held there subsequently.

College tournaments have been held annually. At one time there was a Harvard-Yale-Princeton-Columbia League, with a cup provided for permanent possession of any team winning it ten (!) years in succession. When Columbia proceeded to accomplish this unbelievable feat, the league disintegrated, Columbia and the other teams joining the Intercollegiate Chess League. This group holds an annual individual and team tournament at Columbia University. Its leading directors have been Milton Finkelstein and Elliot Hearst.

The New York Interscholastic Chess League has been flourishing for some forty years. The author has been associated with it as player, teacher-coach and director (1938-56). Among the players recently developed by the Interscholastic Chess League are Edmar Mednis, William Lombardy, Larry Evans, Robert and Donald Byrne; earlier Elliot Hearst, Carl Pilnick, Sol Rubinow and Dan Mayers; still earlier, Fred Reinfeld, Nat Grossman, Reuben Fine, Sidney Bernstein, A. E. Santasiere, Nat Halper and the author.

If we have omitted *your* club, it is for want of space. Join the U. S. Chess Federation, and have your results recognized in its official organ, the bi-weekly paper *Chess Life*. You can find early results (1935-1946) in a series of marvelous yearbooks published with many games of our masters, experts and junior players. Who knows? Your first published game may be as rare some day as an early Leonardo da Vinci—or should we say Emanuel Lasker or Reuben Fine?

ANSWERS

EXERCISE NO. 1

1. 2nd rank
2. 8th rank
3. 1 – a3, b4, c5, d6, e7, f8
   2 – a3, b2, c1
4. e4, e5, d4, d5
5. White Rooks – a1, h1
   Black Rooks – a8, h8
6. White Knights – b1, g1
   Black Bishops – c8, f8
7. White King – e1; Queen – d1
   Black King – e8; Queen – d8
8. The long diagonals (a1 – h8 and h1 – a8)
9. White: King: g1
   Queen: e3
   Rooks: d2, e1
   Bishop: f1
   Knights: c3, f3
   Pawns: a3, b2, d4, e4, f2, g3, h3
   Black: King: h8
   Queen: e7
   Rooks: b8, f8
   Bishop: c4
   Knights: b6, d7
   Pawns: b5, c6, d6, e5, f7, g6, h7

EXERCISE NO. 2

(a) R d5 x R d7; R d5 x B g5; R d5 x Kt d2
(b) R d7 x Q a7; R d7 x R d5; R d7 x Kt g7
(c) R a1 – h1 ch
(d) R f8 – f3 ch

EXERCISE NO. 3

1. R f5 – f7 *check*, winning the Bishop.
2. B c4 – d5 *check*, winning the Knight.

The Pawn, of course, cannot capture the Knight, because a Pawn captures diagonally.

3. K d3 – e4, getting out of check, and forking Rook and Knight.
4. Q h2 – d6 *check*, winning the Rook.

Q – f2 ch would attack King and Rook also but Black could move R c5 – f5, getting out of check and defending the Rook at the same time.

5. B d2 – f4 *check*, winning the Rook.

White could also win the Kt on a3 by B – b4 *ch*, but the Rook is worth 5; the Kt only 3. Then, too, when the Bishop lands on a3, the Black Rook can check the White King (by R h2 – h3 *ch*) and win the Bishop.

6. R f5 – c5 check, winning the Bishop on *c*2.

The Black King cannot take the Rook, because he will come within range of the White King ("go into check") which is illegal. The White Rook could also check on f6, winning the Knight–*but* he would then lose his Rook, because the B c2 can capture it on g6.

7. Kt c4 – d6 *check*, winning the R on e4.

The Knight would then be protected by the White King, and would protect the P g3. **A mistake would be Kt c4 — e5 *check*, because of R e4 x Kt e5.**

8. There is a good reason for this diagram, to remind you that **no piece is worth as much as a checkmate.** B x Q a1 is tempting; so might B x R g1 be–but the correct move is B d4 – c5 *checkmate!*

EXERCISE NO. 4

1. (1) R h3 – h8, pinning the Queen.
2. (1) B g2 – d5, pinning the Rook.

(1) P f4 – f5, forking R + Kt, is met by R e6 – f6, pinning the Pawn (and, incidentally, getting the Rook out of danger). However, once the Rook is pinned (by B – d5) P – f5 is the move to win the Rook for nothing. Try it.

3. (1) R a1 – e1, pinning the Knight.

Black can defend the Knight with his King in three ways, but:

1. . . . K – d7   2. B – g4 pinning and winning the Kt, now twice attacked.
1. . . . K – f7   2. B – d5
1. . . . K – e7   2. B – g4 or d5 – the Rook still pins the Knight.

The hurdle attempt R a1 – a8 ch (x B h8) fails, because the Knight plays back to d8.

4. R g2 – e2 check, winning the B e8. It would be better to win the Rook, but he happens to be protected by the B.
5. Q g1 – a1, pinning the R e5. By now you realize what a powerful weapon the pin is! On the other hand the attempts to win either Rook by Q – h1 ch or h2 ch are spoiled by B – h5 ch – when the R's gain time to move away.
6. Some fun with the Queen:

1. Q d1 – a1 Pin!	B h6 – g7 Defense!
2. Q a1 – h1 Pin!	R e5 – h5 Defense!
3. Q h1 – a8 Pin!	No defense.

EXERCISE NO. 5

Game #8

a. Q h5 x P f7 checkmate.

b. (1) Q d8 – e7, (2) Q d8 – f6, (3) P g7 – g6, (4) Kt g8 – h6.

c. After 3 . . . Kt g8 – h6, 4 P d2 – d4, the B c1 threatens to capture the Knight.

Kt g8 – e7? Allows mate on f7.

Game #9

d. Kt x P f7 or B x P f7 ch.

e. O – O (Castles).

f. It meets the threat by a developing move.

g. P d7 – d5.

h. Same as (f).

i. Black must Castle quickly. He should, therefore, do it first. Compare Rule 4.

j. (1) It moves a piece twice before development is completed. (2) It forces Black to make a move he wants to make in his development.

k. Only temporarily. See what happens when he tries to keep it!

l. B c5 – d4. This prevents P d3 – d4, which might allow White's King to escape.

m. (1) 12 Kt x P d5. This threatens 13. . . . Kt d5 – e3 ch, and 14 . . . Kt x B c4. Black can make these moves even if white plays 13 P d3 – d4, because the Knight, after capturing the Bishop on c4, attacks the W Queen.

(2) Black can also try 12 P b7 – b5! If 13 B x P b5, P c7 – c6! 14 B x P c6 (not P x P because the B would be loose) Kt x B c6 15 P x Kt c6. White has lost his good B; Black has developed his Knight by exchanging it. He is now ready for 15 . . . Q – e7, 16 . . . R a8 – e8, etc.

n. To trade for time. If he can distract the Black pieces by luring them away from his King, he might get his pieces out.

o. 14 . . . P c7 – c5; 15 . . . Kt b8 – c6, etc.

p. No. He should continue his attack against the White King.

q. The Queen may want to go to h4. The Knight, having less choice, should be moved first. Also, the Kt move clears the way for the R a8.

r. The R d5 has many choices. Out with the undeveloped pieces!

s. 1. 17 . . . R e8 – e1 ch wins the Queen after 17 Q d2 – f2.

2. The same move wins the Rook h1 after 17 P h3 x B g4.

t. He should rip open the pawns around the White King. This can **not** be done by 17 . . . R e8 – e2, 18 Q d2 – f4, B g4 – f3 simply because of 19 Q x B f3 (not Q x Q h4, R x P g2 mate). We need that Knight! It can come to e5 because the P d4 is pinned.

u. After 19 P x Kt f3, B x P h3! 20 Q d2 – f2? R e8 – e2! 21 Q f2 x R e2, B h3 x R f1 discovered check, 22 K – g1, B x Q e2 or - - - - - - - - - - 20 Q d2 – f4, Q x Q f4, 21 B x Q f4, B x R f1.

v. Doesn't virtue always triumph? Well, it does this time.

w. Not so long as you keep checking.

x. g3 and h1 are both good. But make sure you win more than just the Queen.

y. Not Q x Q ch, of course.

EXERCISE NO. 6

I. 1.	**Kt e4 – f6 double check**	**K h7 – h8**
2.	Q c2 – h7 checkmate	

(After 1 Kt– g5 dbl check, the Black K can escape via g8 and f8.)

II. **R c3** – c8 double check–and mate. **(Don't be led astray by mere material.)**

III. **B e3** – g5 dis. ch.! White pins the Queen, which he can now win for his Bishop, leaving him with enough material to win the game (K and R is K). If B – d4 dis. ch., Q f6 – e6, and white must give up R for Q, with a draw, since K and B can not win v.K.

IV. 1. R d4 – d8 check. This is not really a discovered check; rather, it is a check with a discovered pin. The King, however, must move – since the Rook which is checking him can not be captured by the pinned Q. After 1 . . . K h8 – g7; 2. B x Q f6 ch., R x Q f6, the game is even, and should end in a draw. Any other first move by white would lose: 1. R d4 – d3? Q x B c3 or 1. R d4 – f4? Q x B c3.

V. 1.	B h7 x Kt f5 dis. ch.	Kh 8 – g8
2.	B f5 – h7 ch.	K g8 – h8
3.	B h7 – g6 dis. ch.	K h8 – g8
4.	R h3 – h8 ch.	K g8 x R h8
5.	Q f1 – h3 ch.	K h8 – g8
6.	Q h3 – h7 checkmate.	

White continued to force Black to walk into a discovery. First, he captures the Kt, which could interpose at h6; then he blocks the line of the Queen, to prevent her from interposing on the same square. The R e4 is only incidental.

VI. 1.	R g5 x P g7 ch.	K g8 – h8
2.	R g7 x P f7 dis. ch.	K h8 – g8
3.	R f7 – g7 ch.	K g8 – h8
4.	R g7 x Kt e7 dis. ch.	K h8 – g8
5.	R e7 – g 7 ch.	K g8 – h8
6.	R g7 x B g4 dis. ch.	K h8 – h7
7.	R g4 x Q g1 an amusing seesaw!	

EXERCISE NO. 6A

I. 1.	Q e4 x R a8 (desperado!)	Q d8 x R d1 (desperado!)
2.	Q a8 x R e8 ch (desperado!)	Kt c7 x Q e1
3.	R f1 x Q d1	

(Not, however: 1 Q x R e8 ch because Kt x Q e8 defends the Q d6.)

II. 1. R a2 x Kt a7. In this situation, White loses less by giving up R for Kt than by giving up a whole Knight (2 B. 3).

If the K were on e1, he could play 1 P c3 – c4. If then . . . B x Kt f3, 2 P c4 – c5; of 1 . . . P b5 x P c4, the Rook is no longer attacked, and White can move his Kt and then his R.

But in the position above, Black can capture this pawn with **check.**

III. 1.	B c4 x P d5	R c8 x R c3
2.	B d5 x P e6 ch	K g8 – f8
3.	B e6 x Kt d7.	

The desperado Bishop mops up!

IV. 1. Q f4 x R c7! Overloaded! Both the Q d7 and

R c8 must guard the 8th rank, so neither can capture the WQ:

1. . . .	Q d7 x Q c7
2. R e2 – e8 ch	R c8 x R e8
3. R e1 x R e8 checkmate *or*	
1. . . .	R c8 x Q c7
2. R e2 – e8 ch	Q d7 x R e8
3. R e1 x Q e8 checkmate.	

EXERCISE NO. 7

1. White: K on KKt1; Q on Q1; Rs on QR1, K1; Bs on QB1, QB2; Kts on QKt1, KB3; Ps on QR2, QKt 2, QB3, Q4, K4, KB2, KKt2 and KR3.

Black: K on KKt1; Q on QB2; Rs on QR1, KB1; Bs on QB1, K2; Kts on QR4, KB3; Ps on QR3, QKt4, QB4, Q3, K4, KB2, KKt2, KR2.

2. Black K on KKt8; Q on QB7; Rs on QR8, KB8; Bs on QB8, K7; Kts on QR5, KB6.

EXERCISE NO. 8

I. *B – KKt4* (g4)

If 1. – P – K3, 2. R x B R x R 3. B x Pch and 4. B x R.

If 1. – R – Q1 or Q 3 2. R x B, R x R 3. B – K6 check and 4B x R.

The following moves are not correct:

1. B – B4?	P – K3
1. B – B3?	B – K3
1. P – B4?	B – K3 or B3

1. R x B? R x R 2. B – B4 P – K3, 3. B x R, P x B —no gain.

II. 1. R x Kt, Kt x R, 2. R x Kt, R x R, 3. Kt – K7ch and 4. Kt x R. Not 1. P – B4 or B – B4 because of – Kt – Kt3.

EXERCISE NO. 9

I. 1. R x R (capture the pinning piece.) It would make White only momentarily happy to play 1. R x Q?? when after–R x B ch 2. K – R, R x BP dis. ch. 3. K – Kt, R – Kt7ch 4. K – R, R – Kt6ch 5. R – Q5, B x Rch 6. Q – K4, B x Qch 7. R – B3, B x R check he found he was mated!

II. 1. Q – Q4ch, P – K + 3
2. Q x R, Kt x Q
3. B x R

III. 1. R – Q5 B x R
2. B – K4 White saves his Queen.

1 B – Kt3??? with the intention of B – Q5 fails because of B x Q check.

IV. 1. Kt – B7 (attack the pinning piece!)

1. . . .	R – Q3 (must go off the K file.)
2. B – Q5	B – Kt6

3. Kt – Kt4 (avoiding – R x Kt and – B x Kt).

As a first move, Kt – B4 would not do, because Black could retain the pin by R – K1. White could also not succeed with 1. Kt – B6ch, because of – R x Kt 2. P x R P x B 3. P x P B x P (although this would limit his loss).

Also 1. Kt – Q4 is met by – R – Q3 2. Kt – B6ch R x Kt.

V. 1. R – R7 (Defense to Pin by Counterpin.)

Black can play either 1. . . . Q x Bch 2. R x Q R x R (R2) or 1. . . . R x R 2. B x Qch, K x B coming out with even material. He can not move his Rook except along the second rank, since it is pinned on his King.

VI. 1. K – Kt3 (or R3) R x Kt
2. K – Kt4 – White regains his piece, by moving away with a counterthreat.

EXERCISE NO. 10

I. 1. R(Kt3) – K3	Counterthreat: Pin
1. . . .	R – B2 (Pin.)
2. B – Q4	R x R (The Kt is still pinned.)
3. B x R	

Moving the other Rook loses:

1. R(B3) – K3?	P – B4 (Threat: P – B5)

2. R(Kt3) – B3, R – QB1; 3. B – Q4 Kt – Q7!! with an attack on one Rook, and a forking threat (on f1) against the other.

II. Black's move. Disregarding all the pins, hurdles, etc., he played:

1. . . .	Q x Kt

Now if 2. R x R, Q x Q 3. R x Q, B x B check 4. R x B, R x R, and forces are even.

Or after 2. R x R, Q x Q 3. R x R?? B x Bch 4. K – Kt Q – Kt3ch – and Black wins.

Of course, if 2 B x Qch, B x Bch 3. Q x Bch R x Q forces are even.

White played:

2. R — B8 check!! in order to lure the B away from from the crucial diagonal— R – Q1 is not possible, since after R x Rch the pinned Q can not recapture.

2. . . .	K — R2

If 2. – K – B2; 3. R x R Q x Q 4. R x R check K – K3 5. P x Q B x Bch 6. K – Kt K x R 7. R – KKt8 and White wins.

3. Q – B2 check—escaping from the B fork.

3. . . .	P – B4

3. . . . Q – K5 does no good because of 4. B x Qch, B x Bch; 5. Q x Bch, R x Q; 6. R x R.

4. B x Q	R x Rch
5. Q – Q	R x B

Now, if White is greedy, and tries to escape with his Queen; e.g., Q – Kt3 or Q – R5, Black plays R – Q8 double check and mate!!

6. Q x R!!	B x Rch
7. K – Kt	B x P

8. R – QR8, winning the RP and eventually the game.

A study of the above diagram is worth several chapters on tactics.

EXERCISE NO. 11

I. 1. P – Kt8 (Rook) wins; but *not* 1. P – Kt8 (Queen)

– stalemate! *nor* 1. P – Kt8 (Bishop) – White can not win because the Bishop can not command the Queening square (R8): (see XI 1 – a)

Both these would result in a draw.

1. P – Kt8 (Knight) check would *win*, altho more slowly. Work it out, making the RP into a Queen, and avoiding stalemate.

II. White is having his troubles, for if 1. R – B4 B x Kt 2. R x B P – Q7 3. R – Q4 P – Kt7 and Queens.

Training his eyes on Black's King, however, he plays:

1. **Kt — B6 ch**	**K — R1**
2. **R — Kt8 checkmate!**	

III. Again White is having his troubles, what with both minor pieces attacked, and the Knight pinned, in addition. He sees that if he can get to Kt7 with his Q, he can effect a checkmate. But for that he needs two moves, and his Bishop will disappear in one. In addition, Black can protect by – P – B3.

White sees also that he can mate on KR7 by Kt – B6 ch and Q x RP. The trouble is: Black can capture the Kt on B6!

What about 1. B x P? Then, if K x B 2. Q – Kt4 ch K – R1 3. Q – Q4ch P – B3 (not – K – Kt 4 Kt – K7 mate!) 4. Kt x BP doesn't look bad! But if 1. B x P Q x Kt! 2. Q – Kt4 Q – B4, threatening the Q and two mates (on B1 and f1).

How about 1. Kt – K7ch K – R1 2. B x Pch K x B 3. Q – Kt4ch K – R1 4. Q – Q4ch – spoiled by – P – B3.

Yet there *must* be something, with so many mate threats. How can we combine the moves Q – Kt4, Kt – B6 and the B on the diagonal to our best advantage?

Speed is essential. Check, check, check – that's what we need. And forced moves by Black.

Thus arises the solution:

1. **Kt — B6 check**	**P x Kt** (forced: otherwise, mate by Q x RP)
2. Q – Kt4 check	K – R1 (forced)
3. B x P check mate!	

IV. This is obviously a stalemate situation. White must continue to give moves to Black:

1. P – K3	P x Pch
2. K – K1!	P – K7 ("Take me. I dare you.")
3. P – Q4 ("All in good time.")	P x P
4. K x P	P – Q6ch ("How about this one?")
5. K – Q1 ("No, thanks.")	P – Q7
6. P – B5	P x P
7. P – Kt6	P – B5
8. P – Kt7	P – B6
9. P – Kt8 (R) mate!	

EXERCISE NO. 13

I.

1. **P x B** (threatening R – R8 mate!)

1. . . .	**B — Q3**
2. **Q — B8 ch**	**K — K2**
3. **Q — K6 ch**	**K — Q1**
4. **Q x B ch**	**K — B1**
5. **R — R8 ch**	**K — Kt2**
6. **R — Kt8 ch**	**K — R2**
7. **Kt — B6 ch**	**K — R3**
8. **Q — R3 mate!**	

The Black Q is pinned! The final mate, showing the "absolute seventh," which, in this case, is the Q Kt file, is prettier than Q x Q, which would also be mate.

The whole solution was given to show further how Q and R cooperate.

II.

1. Q x Kt	P x Q
2. R – Kt 7 ch	K – R1
3. R x P ch	K – Kt1
4. R(Kt7) – Kt7 checkmate.	

III.

1. Q x P ch	R x Q
2. R – B8 ch	R – B1
3. R x R mate	

This might be called the "absolute 8th" rank.

IV.

1. Q – R8 ch	R – K1

The K may not move (to Kt2) because of Q – K R8 mate. If Q – K1, the same move follows:

2. Q – KR1	Q – Kt2

If (2) . . . K – B1 (3) R – R8 ch, K – K2, (4) R – R7

3. Q – Q5 ch	K – B1

If . . . Q – B2 (4) R – R8 ch K – Kt 2, (5) R – R7 ch!

4. R – B4 ch	K – K2
5. Q – Kt 7 ch winning the Q.	

This is an interesting example of the shuttle powers of Q and R.

EXERCISE NO. 14

I. The sacrifice is *not* correct. As the tournament book points out ("1941 The Ventnor City Invitation Chess Tournament," published by R. Dessauer, Ventnor, N. J.):

The pressure of normal development moves would soon resolve the game in White's favor: (from the diagram)

19. **P — K5!**	**B — K2** (forced: if . . . B x P; (20) B – B3, Kt – Q4; (21) Q x R).
20. **QR — B**	**B — Q2**
21. **B — B3**	**Kt — Q4**
22. **B x Kt**	**P x B** (if . . . Q x B, (23) Kt – B6)
23. **R — B7**	**Q — Kt1** (if B – Q Kt5 (24) R x B!)
24. **Kt — B6**	**B x Kt**
25. **R x B (K7)**	threatening (26) P – K6 and R(1) – B1

The sacrifice was worth only a draw at best: from where we left off when presenting the problem: 5 . . . P — B5; (6) Q – Kt4, Kt – Q2; (7) Q – K7, Kt – K4; (8) Q – B8 ch, K – Kt3; (9) Q – Kt8 ch, K – R3, (10)

Q – B8 ch, K – Kt3; (11) Q – Kt8 ch, etc.

In the game, after (5) . . . P – B5, White played (6) P – K5? and Black answered . . . B – R6?? an unnecessary brilliancy of his own: B – B4 was better.

The play continued: (7) P x P ch, K – Kt3; (8) Q x B! R x R (9) Q – R5 ch, K x P (10) Q – R4 ch, K – Kt2; (11) Q – Kt5 ch, K – B1; (12) Q x R ch, K – Kt2. White has won all his material back, and a Pawn additional–yet the game wound up a draw.

II. The sacrifice is not correct: After (1) R x B (?) R x Q; (2) R x R ch K – B; (3) R x Kt P, the Black Queen is free: (3) . . . **Q — B4**; (4) R (1) – K7, Q – Kt8 ch; (5) K – R2, Q – B4! (6) R – B7 ch, K – Kt1; (7) R – Kt7 ch, K – B1; (8) Kt – Q7 ch, R x Kt; (9) R x R, **Q — B5 ch** and if K – Kt1, the Q checks at c1 and f4; whereas, if P – Kt3, the Q checks at f2 and f1: perpetual check, and a draw.

This time White saw the counterthreat and did not sacrifice! Instead, he squeezed his opponent to death by: (31) Q – Kt6! R(1) – K1; (32) P – KR4 P – KR4; (33) Q – Q6 R – Q; (34) Q – B4 R(1) – K1; (35) Q – Q6 R – Q; (36) Q – Kt6 R(1) – K1; (37) P – B3 P – B4; (38) Q – Q6 R – Q1; (39) Q – B4 R(1) – K1; (40) Q – R6 P – Kt3; (41) Kt – Q3 P – B5; (42) Kt x P B – B4; (43) R x R ch R x R; (44) Q – R7 ch Resigns.

III. This ought to be a breather.

1. **O — O!**	(King in the Center!)
1. . . .	**B — K3**
2. **R — K1**	**Kt — K2**
3. **B — Kt5**	**Q — Kt3**
4. **Q — R4 ch**	**Q — B3**
5. **Kt — Kt5**	(threatening Kt – B7 ch)
5. . . .	**B — Q2**
6. **Kt (3) — Q4**	**Q — K Kt3**
7. **Q — Kt4** (stopping 0-0-0- because of Kt – Q6 ch)	
7. . . .	**Q x B**
8. **Kt — Q6 ch**	**K — Q**
9. **Kt x BP ch**	**Resigns:** The Q is lost.

EXERCISE NO. 15

I. (1) Kt — B6, P — B4; (2) R — Q7! B — B3; (3) Kt — R7 ch, K — Kt1 (or K1) (4) Kt — B6 ch, K — B1; (5) Kt — R7 ch, and draws by perpetual check.

Not (4) . . . K – R1?? (5) R – R7 mate.

If the Kt checks at Q7 on move 2, the Black K escapes to QB1.

A tricky defense is (1) . . . **R — R6 ch.** The WK must not go to Q4, for he will allow . . . P – B4 ch with tempo, followed by . . . B – B3 **(2) K — B2!** This tempo is needed to prevent . . . R – R6 and . . . R – R3. If now . . . R – R6? K x B. **(2) . . . R — R7 ch; (3) K — K3!** If the K goes on the Kt file, the BPR can check at Kt7 and return to Kt3, preventing the Kt check at B6. **(3) . . . B — Q4** (attempting to interpose at B2) **(4) Kt x B, P x Kt.** The Black Pawns are doubled, and weak. (5) R – R5, R – R6 ch; (6) K – Q4, R – R5 ch; (7) K x P, R x P; (8) K x P, K – B2; (9) K – K5, K – Kt3; (10) K x R, K x R; (11) K x P. This is a draw by exhaustion.

II. A famous ending: Marshall vs. Dr. Emanuel Lasker, New York, 1924: **(1) . . . Q — K3 ch! (2) Q x Q stalemate!**

If (2) K – B4, Q x Q ch, (3) K x Q, White has insufficient material to win (K + Kt vs. K = Draw).

III. From a Yugoslavian Tournament, Vospernik-Janosevic, Novi Sad, 1955:

1. . . . R x B ch; (2) K x R, B x P ch; (3) K — K3, P — R5; (4) K — B4, B — K3; (5) R — Kt7 Draw.

Not (5) K – Kt5? P – R6; (6) R – R1, B – Q4, followed by . . . P – R7 – R8 (Q).

In the main variation, the WK can hold the hP from g3.

IV. Marshall vs. Alekhine, New York, 1924:

Black to make his 23rd move, traps the WR, only to meet a sacrifice:

23. . . .	P – Kt3
24. Kt x Kt	P x R
25. Kt – B7	P x QP! Black finds a

counter combination to draw:

26. Kt x R	P x P!
27. Kt x R	P x P ch
28. K x P	Q – Q7 ch
29. K – Kt1	Q – K6 ch (Q x R ch? Q – B1)
30. K – Kt2	Q – B6 ch
31. K – Kt1	Q – K6 ch
32. K – Kt2	Q – B6 ch

and drawn by perpetual check.

EXERCISE NO. 16

I. This is a Greco Counter-Gambit, the opening moves of which are: (1) P – K4, P – K4; (2) Kt – KB3, *P – KB4;* (3) Kt x P, Q – B3; (4) P – Q4, P – Q3; (5) Kt – B4, P x P; (6) Kt – B3, Q – Kt3; (7) B – B4, Kt – KB3.

The answer is: (8) Kt – K3! This blockader stops the KP, defends KKt2 and blocks the QP, which can not move forward without being captured.

Grandmaster Aron Nimzovich, in his book *My System,* stated that even on move 6, the correct move was Kt – K3.

II. (1) B – Kt1! Maximum power against the Kt. (B – K4), same idea, would allow . . . P – Q4, forcing an exchange of Ps, and giving Black the square *d5* for his Kts. After (1) B – Kt1, White will chase the Kt (2 B – Q2) develop the other B (B – Q3) and start a Q side offensive (P – QKt4, P – QR4, P – Kt5).

III. 1. . . . R – KB1 forcing the WKBP onto a white square.

2. P – B3	P – Kt5

Attack the pinned Pawn!

3. B – K2	R – K1
4. B – Q1	R – K8 (pin)
5. K – B2	P – Kt6 (queening threat)
6. P – B4	R – B8 (threatening R – B7)
7. B – B3	R x B! and the KKt Pawn queens.

EXERCISE NO. 17

I. Main line:

(1) P – B6, P x P; (2) P – Kt6, P x P; (3) P – R6 and queens.

Secondary Defense:

(1) P – B6, K – Q3; (2) P x P, K – B2; (3) P – R6, K – Kt1; (4) K – Kt3, K – B2; (5) K – B4, K – Kt1; (6) K – B5, K – B2, (7) P – Kt6 ch, P x P ch; (8) K – Kt5, K – Kt1; (9) K – B6 (no stalemates today!) P – Kt4; (10) K – Kt6, P – Kt5; (11) P – R7 mate.

II. (1) **BP x P!** This assures White of the outside passed pawn. After (1) RP x P?? P – R5! Black would have it. (1) . . . **P x P;** (2) **P x P, K – Kt4;** (3) **K – K4, K x P;** (4) K x P, K – B6; (5) K – Q5, P – B5; (6) P – R4, P x P; (7) K x P, P – R6! (8) P x P, K – K5; (9) K – B5, K – Q6. (If . . . K – K4; P – B4, K – K3; K – Kt6!) (10) P – B4, K – B6; (11) K – Q5, and the BP queens.

III. (1) P – R4! K – Kt1; (2) K – Kt6, P – Kt4; (3) P x P, P – B5; (4) P – Kt6, P – B6; (5) P – Kt7, P – B7; (6) P – Kt8 ch mate. Or:

(1) . . . P – Kt4; (2) P x P, P – B5; (3) P – Kt6, P – B6; (4) P – Kt7, P – B7; (5) P – Kt8 (Q), P – B8 (Q); (6) Q – Kt7 ch, K – Kt1; (7) Q – Kt7 checkmate.

IV. There's more than meets the eye:

(1) **P — R5!!** Strangely enough, the logical move P – Kt5 does not win, as we shall see later.

1. . . .	K — K3
2. **P — Kt5**	K — Q2. This is the only way Black can get "in the square" of the Rook Pawn.
3. **P x P**	**K — B1**
4. **K — B2**	**P — Kt5!** The Pawns take measures to defend themselves. If P x P? White can only draw.
5. **K — K2**	**K — Kt1**
6. **K — Q3**	**P — R5** (After . . . P x P, (7) P x P, P – R5, the WK can get back "in the square" by K – K2. He can then capture both K side Ps before Black can return to the KB file to confront him.)
7. **P x P**	**P — B6**
8. **K — K3!!**	**P x P**
9. **K — B2**	**P — R6**
10. **P — Kt5** and wins.	

Now why won't (1) P – Kt5 win? Black can get "into the square" of the KtP by . . . K – K5 after he captures: (1) . . . **P x P.** What about (2) **P — R5,** instead of recapturing? Black now has a passed QKtP, and he can push that. (2) . . . **P — Kt5** White queens first, but Black queens immediately thereafter, and **with a check,** after which he will at least draw.

EXERCISE NO. 18

I. 1. **K x P**

II. 1. **K — Q4**

III. 1. **P x KtP, P(B3) x P;** (2) **P x P, P — Kt5;** (3) **K — K6.**

If (1) . . . P(B4) x P; (2) P – Kt6, P – B4; (3) P – Kt7, P – B5; (4) P – Kt8 (Q) mate.

(1) P x BP does not win: (1) . . . P x P, and if (2) P x P stalemate.

IV. (1) **K — B4, P x P;** (2) **P x P, K — R4;** (3) **P — B6, K — Kt3;** (4) **K — Kt4, K — R2;** (5) **K — B5, K — Kt1;** (6) **P — Kt6, K — B1** (6) . . . P x P? (7) K x P, K – B1; (8) P – B7); (7) **P — Kt7 ch, K — Kt1;** (8) **K — Q5, K — R2;** (9) **K — K6; K — Kt1;** (10) **K — Q7.**

(3) P – Kt6? draws: . . . K – R3; (4) K – Q5, K – Kt2; (5) P x P, K x P, and the K is in front of the Pawn.

(5) . . . K – R1; (6) P – Kt6, P x P; (7) K – Q6, K – Kt1; (8) K – Q7.

EXERCISE NO. 19

I. (1) **P — Kt6** **K — Q4!**

If (1) . . . P x P; (2) P – R7 wins. The King gets into the square of the RP by the counter threat . . . B – Q5 ch. If (2) P – Kt7, B – B8 ch; (3) K moves, B x P. (2) **P x RP, B — Q5 ch;** (3) **K — B3, B x P;** (4) **P x P, K — K3** and draws. The King holds one P; the B the other.

A hasty move like (1) . . . **P x P ch** would lose for Black. The WK would go to a white square, and nothing could catch the RP. But which white square? Not B3 because of . . . B – Q5 (P – K7, B – K4); nor Q4 because of . . . P – B6 (K x P, B – Q5). The correct square is Q3: (2) **K — Q3.** This stays "in the square" of the Pawn, and hangs on to the square d4 (Bl Q5). Black would not be able to catch the WP.

II. (1) **P x Q (B)**

Making a Queen or Rook equals stalemate.

If you make a Kt, you can not win the game (K + 2Kts vs. K is a draw, unless the Bl K goes voluntarily into a corner.) The only winning promotion is to a Bishop.

III. (Keres vs. Eliskases, Noordwijk, 1939) Problem: How to stop the two passed pawns? Answer: By counter threat.

(1) **K — B6, P — Kt7;** (2) **R — Kt4 ch, K — B1.** (If . . . K – R2, R – R4 ch) (3) **R — QR4,** threatening mate on R8. (3) . . . **K — K1** (4) **K — K6, K — Q1;** (5) **K — Q6, K — B1;** (6) **K — B6, K — Kt1.** No more mate threats, but: (7) **R — Kt4 ch, K — R2;** (8) **R — R4 ch, K — Kt1,** (9) **R — Kt4 ch, K — B1;** (10) **R — QR4,** etc.

IV. (1) **P — Kt6, P x P;** (forced; if Black allows P x P, White will have an extra Pawn to queen after capturing Bl's QBP. (2) **P x P, P — B5;** (3) **P — Kt7, P — B6;** (4) **P — Kt8 (Q), P — B7;** (5) **Q — Kt5!** (The only move to win.) (5) . . . **K — K7;** (6) **Q — QB1.**

EXERCISE NO. 20

(a) The QP. It is isolated, and can be attacked by K and R.

(b) R – R4 – R5; K – Q4 and R – B5 ch.

(c) W can play R – K3 – K5 ch, driving the Bl K back from Q4.

(d) P – B5.

(e) It is an advance on the K side, where Black has the majority of Ps.

(f) R – R4.

(g) Otherwise P – QKt4; the plan is spoiled, and White can get a passed pawn on the Q side.

(h) No. Black can advance his K to Q4 and K5, going to the assistance of his K side Ps, if necessary.

(i) K – K4, because it keeps the possibility of two plans.

(j) By sacrificing the QRP. The loss of the QP would mean the loss of the game because of the then passed Bl KP.

(k) The R can defend it from R4.

(l) 1. Keep the Bl K from Q4; 2. Threatens P – QKt4 and K – Kt5.

(m) . . . P – K4; P x P, R x P; and . . . R – K6 ch.

(n) Threat of R – QB5 ch and K – K4.

(o) . . . P – Kt5 and . . . R – Kt4.

(p) . . . P – B6.

(q) No. After . . . P x R; P x P, P – Kt5; BP x P, P x P, White would have to play K – K3 to get into the square of the RP. Black would play . . . P x P and win by distant passed P.

(r) No. R x KKtP would draw easily.

(s) No. . . . R x P ch would force K – Q3 to avoid the loss of the QKtP, whereupon . . . R – K8 – KKt8 – KKt6.

(t) Yes, by . . . R – KKt6 and K – K3 – B2, forcing the WR away from the RP. The two passed Pawns should then win against the one White will get when he takes the QKtP. (After the WR is chased from the KKt file, Bl can play R x RP.)

(u) No longer: (59) . . . R – B8; (60) R – Kt6 ch!! K – Kt2; (61) R x P, R – KKt8; (62) R – KB5, R – Kt6 ch; (63) R – B3!

(v) Because of . . . R – Kt6 mate.

(w) If K – B3, R – KR7; K – Kt4, R – Kt7 ch; K – B3, R – Kt6 ch.

(x) It still would not win: K – B2, K – B4; K – B3, R – Q6 ch; K – Kt2.

(y) It would lose after . . . K – Kt6. The R stays on the B file to check the WK, and stays on the 5th rank to keep an eye on the KKtP.

EXERCISE NO. 21

(a) Pe4 – e5, **discovered check.** The check must be defended by B – d5 or a King move; and then White plays Pe5 x Bd6.

(b) Yes, in accordance with (6) above: each side advances where he has more Pawns.

(c) No, for then the Black King could walk in and capture the White Pawns. Incidentally, White played Pg2 – g4 before Pe4 – e5 check in order to avoid the Bishop exchange. If the Pawn were still on g2, it would be lost if the Bf3 moved away.

(d) No; for he would have lost a Pawn by (33. . . . Bd5 x Bf3), (34) P x Be7, Kc6 – d7; (35) Be3 – c5. The Bishop on c5 holds the Black a and b Pawns, while the White King forces a second white Passed Pawn on the King's side.

Besides, why should Black expect to lose? Material is still even; he has no weaknesses in his position; his King is better placed than White's.

(e) Against (34) . . . Bd5 – g2, White plays first Pg4 – g5 (a zwischenzug, or in-between move) and then Ph3 – h4.

(f) To exchange Pawns and draw, yes—but strategically no! Black should play Pa5 – a4, advancing where *he* has the majority of Pawns.

(g) 1. To slow up the Black Pawns. 2. To oppose the Black Be5 on the long diagonal.

(h) Same as g1 – if Pb5 – b4, the a Pawn is not protected (*en prise*).

(i) The one on Black squares, since the h Pawn queens on a Black square.

(j) 1 . . . B to g5, e7, f8 and g7; followed by P – h7 – h8. Black spoils this in the game.

2. . . . P – b3 ch, P x P ch; K – b1, followed by B – b2, P – h7, B x B and P – h8.

This will not work on the next move, as will be explained later.

(k) Yes! He could – and must – play Kc5 – d4.

(l) (47) . . . Be5 – f4 (as in the game) spoils the plan, for if (48) Be7 – f8, B x Ph6! (49) Bf8 x Bh6, Pb4 – b3 ch; (50) Kc2 – c1, Pa4 – a3!! (51) Pb2 x Pa3, Kc4 – b5.

White is left with a Rook Pawn and a Bishop of the wrong color, since the queening square a8 is White, and his Bishop is on a Black square.

When the P on h6 is attacked, White must, therefore, push it to h7 – whereupon Plan #1 is spoiled.

(m) Black should move his King, to b5 preferably, in order to meet Pb2 – b3 with Pa4 – a3, keeping the White Bishop away from the squares on the diagonal a1 – h8. By allowing the King to remain on c4, he lets him be checked. White then can clear b2 for his Bishop.

(n) Black can not stop B – b2, B x B and P – h8, becoming a queen.

(o) The difference is: the Pawn on h7 instead of h6. With the Pawn still on h6, the following moves could now be made:

(53) . . . Bf6 – c3; (54) Bc1 – b2, Kc4 – d3; (55) Ph6 – h7, Kd3 – d2; (56) B x Bc3, P x Bc3; (57) Ph7 – h8 (Queen), Pc3 – c2 check; (58) Kb1 – b2, Pc2 – c1 (Q) check, and draws!

The extra tempo (gain of time) in pushing the Ph6 – h7 was needed in order to win the game. White played a plan (#1) he knew would not succeed (with correct play by Black) in order to lull Black into thinking that he (Black) had forced the Pawn to h7, and to assume that White had not wanted to push it there. In reality, the Pawn had to be on h7, for Plan #2 to succeed!

It is true that Chess is a science; but above all it is a struggle between the minds of two players. Nothing must ever be taken for granted: the only moves you can not make are those which would move a piece incorrectly or would expose a King to check.

EXERCISE NO. 22

(a) R – QB1. However, he really can not defend it in the long run.

(b) Time to centralize his King and get his Ps rolling.

(c) Black should take advantage of the immediate position of the pieces to play (1) . . . **P — R6.** Then if (2) **P — Kt3, Kt — Q7;** (3) **R — QB1, Kt — B6 ch!** If (4) K – R1, R – K3! (5) R – B3, Kt x QP! and wins. White must play (4) **K — B2, Kt x RP;** (5) **P — KB5,** but Black has obtained a passed RP for distractive purposes.

(d) (3) **P — QB5.** If . . . P x P? P – Q5!

(e) Because after (5) P – Q5? R – QR3 (6) R x P?? Kt – K5 ch.

(f) . . . P – B5.

(g) By threats on the King side.

(h) P – Kt4 ch, forcing Black to abandon the Kt.

(i) By blockading it.

(j) No, for then: (9) P – K4 ch, K – B3; (10) P – K5 ch or (9) . . . K – K3; (10) P – B5 ch!

(k) Then (10) R – KR2 and (11) R – R5 ch.

(l) Yes, for if (12) K – B3, Kt – B3? (13) R – R1, and the Rook retreat is forced, whereupon the Ps start rolling.

(m) He has no choice, unless he gives up the KtP – then he has losing chances.

This was the end of a very exciting game.

EXERCISE NO. 23

1. To queen the Pawn on the a file.
2. To the square h2.
3. No. It is almost impossible to win when all the Pawns are on one side of the board.
4. On the diagonal a7 to f2.
5. To blockade the a Pawn with his Queen.
6. Yes. After K – f8, he is "in the square" with the Pawn on b4.
7. No. While the Black King captures the P on the b file, the White King will be gobbling up the Black Pawns.
8. After (48) Kg1 – h2, Qd1 – c2, (49) Qb4 – c5, Qc2 – a4 –and White has not advanced.
9. From a7.
10. He can't just watch the a Pawn queen. By opening up the position, he hopes for a perpetual check.
11. Because of (55) Q – d4 ch (stopping Ph5 – h4) and (56) Pa5 – a6.
12. By using his f Pawn and his Queen.
13. Yes. He has two extra Pawns on the King side, and the advance of the Pawn to f4 gives an extra protection to e5 and a chance to exchange Queens.
14. (a) To centralize his Queen.

    (b) To advance the h Pawn, in order to queen it or in order to threaten mate.

    (c) To exchange Queens, even at the cost of a Pawn, for he will still have a won Pawn ending.
15. Q – d4 ch and Q – g7 mate.
16. It stops the checks on the first rank.
17. It threatens to exchange Queens by a check on e5.
18. The f Pawn is lost, and the exchange of Queens forced. White then wins the Pawn ending.